AN APACHE ODYSSEY
Indeh

Daklugie, son of Juh.

AN APACHE ODYSSEY

Indeh

UNIVERSITY OF OKLAHOMA PRESS : NORMAN

EVE BALL

WITH NORA HENN
AND LYNDA A. SÁNCHEZ

Foreword by Dan L. Thrapp

Library of Congress Cataloging-in-Publication Data

Ball, Eve.
  Indeh, an Apache odyssey.
  Bibliography: p.
  Includes index.
  1. Apache Indians—History. 2. Apache Indians—Biography. 3. Indians of North America—Southwest, New—History. 4. Indians of North America—Southwest, New—Biography. 5. Daklugie, Asa, d. 1955. I. Henn, Nora. II. Sánchez, Lynda. III. Title.
  E99.A6B16 1988   979'.00497   88-40212
  ISBN 0-8061-2165-3

     4   5   6   7   8   9   10   11   12   13   14   15   16   17   18   19   20   21   22   23

This book is dedicated to the Apaches with profound admiration for their unparalleled courage and with gratitude for their generous aid.

CONTENTS

ILLUSTRATIONS

PREFACE

After the publication of *Indeh* in 1980, many of Eve Ball's Apache friends would come by her home in Ruidoso, New Mexico, and leaf through the book, pointing with pride to a grandfather's or aunt's photograph or name. The book was as well received by the Apaches as it was by others who were knowledgeable about southwest history. It was considered another remarkable achievement by the woman whom many referred to as "Grandmother" or "The Old White Lady with Many Stories."

When most people face retirement, Eve had embarked on a new career. Undoubtedly, her years as an English teacher had refined her writing skills and prepared her for the writing and research that she began at about the age of sixty. During the ten years of my personal association with Eve as her assistant, I accompanied her on many research trips and speaking engagements where audience reaction was overwhelming. There was no generation gap with Eve! She continued to dispel many myths about aging and women's roles as she set out in her determined manner to write and interpret history and to record oral tradition.

In 1980, Eve was nominated, with her coauthors, for the Zia Award of the New Mexico Press Women. In 1982 the Western Writers of America conferred on her their highest honor, the Saddleman Award. In 1983 she was nominated for the United States Medal of Freedom and was the recipient of a joint congressional resolution acclaiming her work to preserve the heritage of the West. Also in 1983 she was inducted into the Western Heritage Division of the Cowgirl Hall of Fame.

All of us who knew this gracious woman over the years will remember her kindness and willingness to help young writers and students of history. Both Nora Henn and I were among the lucky ones in that we worked intimately with this great woman. Eve was responsible for encouraging me to continue her work as well as my own research projects.

Over the years there were many awards and special praises. And when Eve died in 1984, she received one last honor. In a memorial service at Saint Joseph's, the magnificent stone mission in the heart of Mescalero Apache country, old friends presented music and eulogies in Apache and English.

Although Eve Ball's adobe home, once surrounded by wild Castilian roses and many native flowers, will no longer be a meeting place where people gather to tell their legends or speak of history and "the way of things," a lone stately spruce remains as a symbol of this talented and dedicated woman. Like that magnificent tree, Eve Ball often stood alone through her ninety-four years. The tree was planted more than thirty years before her death by Ace Daklugie, the primary narrator of this book. He had brought it to her as a surprise for one of the few white women he ever respected.

—LYNDA A. SÁNCHEZ

Lincoln, New Mexico

FOREWORD

BY DAN L. THRAPP

A goodly share of this important book concerns Juh, the ablest of the militant Apaches after Victorio, although his fame was mainly among his own people, while for his enemies it lay submerged beneath the flood of reports, and ballyhoo, surrounding his subordinate, Geronimo, in every way a lesser man. Glimpses of the Juh saga flare out of the memory and understandings of his surviving son, Asa (Ace) Daklugie, who himself reincarnated many of the qualities of his great progenitor: his arrogance, his vision and supreme ability, self-assurance sometimes bordering on blindness, and an implacable hatred of all White Eyes—except for one, the remarkable author of this remarkable volume.

It was in the war year of 1942 that an attractive, wide-eyed young educator arrived in the Ruidoso highlands of New Mexico, little aware that in the years ahead she would become as much a part of the legends of this historically intriguing region as the red and the white people whose lives she would research and about whom she would write.

Eve Ball was born in the Cumberland country on the Kentucky side of her grandfather's plantation. It sprawled to the south, spilling over the border of Tennessee; but despite its expansiveness, its southern beauty, and grace, Eve would not long remain there. Thus she experienced a varied life in Texas and Kansas before finally reaching New Mexico. Here, on the very rim of the Mescalero Apache reservation, the wanderings ceased. She commenced her life's real work, though some might call it an avocation since in our perplexing culture it is difficult to make a living at anything so creative and productive as the task she set about.

White characters abounded in her new homeland—and *characters* many of them were, indeed. These interested her initially as evidenced by magazine pieces she penned in those early days. But soon she became conscious of the darker-hued men and women who lived beyond the white folks' towns. They were Apaches, most of them Mescaleros, of course, for it was their reserve in the beginning, but about 1913 they had freely shared it with the remnants of the Chiricahua and the Warm Springs, and the Nednhis and the Bedonkohes, allied bands with whom they had fought heroically for their homeland and lost out only to irresistible white pressure, being all but destroyed in the process. After nearly three decades of eastern exile the remnants of these peoples had been permitted to return as far west as Mescalero. Here they dwelt—many of them bitterly seasoned by their experiences and the injustices inflicted upon them—aloof, hurt, withdrawn.

Eve Ball was intrigued. About thirty years ago she began interviewing those she could persuade to talk with her, having no idea at that early date of writing books from their memories. She spoke no Apache in the beginning, and concedes that she does not speak that difficult language even today, so the interviews must be in English. She took down their words in shorthand and later typed them up. The papers gradually accumulated until today, with related materials, they occupy several filing cabinets in her home. It was a process of accretion. She might hold brief conversations with an Apache woman who, becoming convinced of the questioner's sincerity and genuine interest, on a subsequent visit would bring a friend to contribute. The two might introduce Eve Ball to others. And so it went over the years until she had accumulated records in depth from at least sixty-seven individuals of these bands.

Many with whom she talked in the early years had personal knowledge of the great figures of their wild free days. A few had even accompanied the People on the campaigns and had survived the sanguinary affrays—and bore the scars to prove it. And much time was involved in all this work, in bringing them out and recording what they had to relate.

"There is a vast difference in knowing *about* the Apache and in *knowing him,*" she confessed in a letter written in 1966.

Much that she learned from these Indians came not from their personal experiences, however, but from the archives of their memories, the memories of unlettered people who employ that tool, sharpened by culture-training to be as reliable for their purposes as the written record is for whites. No Apache, Daklugie once told her, "had to repeat anything more than twice to know it."

"And they do have remarkable memories, trained memories," she wrote in a 1968 letter. "The safety of the entire group might depend upon the exact transmission of a message from one chief to another, or to some other group." In addition, it was through trained memories that the culture history of the People most frequently was passed from generation to generation.

"Occasionally they amaze me by telling what I said, perhaps ten years ago, when I've forgotten any of the conversation we had had, although I might recall the essential fact discussed," she went on. "I can't do that. I take every word they say in shorthand. Often I am surprised when I type it to find something I missed completely while writing shorthand. When it is typed, then sometimes it takes an Apache to interpret the English. Often I ask the one who dictated it for an explanation, and if I don't see him, just call to the one working in the garden to come in and tell me what it means. No white person could get all of it, nor even a small percentage of it, unless he'd dealt with the Apaches a long time. They have their own ways of telling things."

One day about two decades ago, Eve Ball received a visitor who was to provide her with the most revealing narrative she had received to that time. He was James Kaywaykla, who had come from Oklahoma to Mescalero for a ceremonial event, although it was not his first visit to New Mexico. Kaywaykla had been of the committee that selected Mescalero as the home for those of the Chiricahuas and Mimbres who wished to remove there from Oklahoma in 1913. Now he had returned. He would relate to Eve his recollections of his career, commencing with the savage massacre at Tres Castillos in Chihuahua where Victorio had been killed and, except for himself and a few others, his people all but wiped out. From his memories, drawn out in many interview sessions, Mrs. Ball assembled *In the Days of Victorio* (1970), the first book to appear from her growing wealth of transcribed discussions. The present three-part volume is much more ambitious. Rather than relying on one primary oral source, Mrs. Ball has brought all the vast array of interview material under one cover.

Among the close friends she had made was Ramona, daughter of the famous chief Chihuahua and wife of Daklugie. Ramona was as open and friendly as her husband was aloof and hostile. Yet he, as the son of the great Juh, was the most important non-Mescalero Apache on the reservation; and the more Mrs. Ball worked with the Indians, the more determined she became to persuade Daklugie to be interviewed. Through Ramona she set about trying to crack the reserve of this taciturn man.

"It took four years to get him to talk," she recalled. Although Ace had spent a dozen years at Carlisle, and he had served as interpreter for Stephen M. Barrett to whom Geronimo had dictated his life's story in Oklahoma, "he pretended for long that he couldn't speak English!"

Gradually she and Ramona chipped away at Daklugie's reserve and at long last he consented to reply, grumpily at first, to her questions. Before long he was speaking freely, although peppering his remarks with outbursts of impatience, of disdain for even this white woman who he seemed to agree was the one White Eye with a serious interest in his people. Obviously she sought from them only their knowledge, their history, their points of view—not befriending them in order to steal something from them, or to cheat them—to give them an opportunity to tell the world their side of a heroic story.

The result then is Daklugie's book that you now hold in your hands—not his alone, of course, but largely Daklugie's. His comments frequently are short tempered, explosive, prideful, belligerent, ironic, curt at times and again loquacious, impatient of white understandings or the lack of them, and yet always honest, often frank, and with nothing whatever subservient about them.

An odd charm warms this account. There are hints that, before the long series of interviews was terminated in 1955 by the death of Ace, this forthright leader of his people had come to more than tolerate this member of an alien and hated race, a folk which had deprived his people of all that made life good.

By then Ace had long since learned to work with these people he could not beat.

"He was so determined to become an effective leader of his people, and for their benefit, that he accepted, at least on the surface, the strange and to him detestable practices of the white race in order to deal with them on their own level," Eve Ball once wrote. "But he never ceased hating them. I strongly suspect that he decided to give his accounts to me . . . just as he went to Carlisle—he did want his knowledge of occurrences preserved and I happened to be available." But it came to be more than that. Much more.

One singular aspect of this book that may raise an eyebrow here and there is the evident reliance Ace and others of his people placed on religion, on *their* religion.

Eve Ball recalled the "long years of patient effort" she spent in order to "really get to know the Apache religion." It is a subject upon which they are very reticent—as are not all peoples?

"They'll tell you that they believe the doctrines taught by their [Christian] churches, but how many of them know what those doctrines are? Then the Apache says that his religion is the only thing the white man hasn't stolen from him, and that he wants to keep it. He has no desire to share it with any other race. And he fully believes that the white man feels compelled to cram his own religion down the throat of all he encounters. It is only in times of tragedy or great stress that the Apache reveals his ideas. And he does that unintentionally. So, is it a breach of confidence to write of it? Sometimes I think so. But without a knowledge of how he thinks along those lines, nobody can hope to understand him."

Mrs. Ball conceded, in a summary opinion, that "I never truly liked Ace," but she adds in the same breath, "I had great respect and admiration for him, particularly for his integrity and for what he was trying to do for his people." Much of that I think comes through in this work.

Something else surfaces in this book: a hint of how Eve Ball became so much a part of the Apache saga in the Ruidoso country, and an integral element of its legend.

A score of years ago I wrote to the superintendent of the Mescalero Reservation asking some questions about the Chiricahua-Warm Springs people living there. He referred me with some finality to Mrs. Ball as the *only* white person in whom they had complete trust and to whom they had confided such information as I desired to know. Today should you ask serious questions about those people of any white in the region (or probably of any Apache) the reply would be identical: see Mrs. Ball.

Her expertise and her fame extend beyond her Indian brothers and sisters, of course.

Most serious historians who have worked in or written about that enchanting region have come to depend upon her knowledge and her generosity with it in pursuing their studies. Among these have been Maurice Fulton, Harwood Hinton, Leland Sonnichsen, Leon Metz, Robert Mullin, Angie Debo, and countless others. For all of them she is more than a repository of its history and legends; she is a part of them, as she has come to share with the Apaches in their own saga. This you will understand long before you finish this book. It will bring to you, as it has brought to all of us, a gladness that she came this way, and in our time.

INTRODUCTION

"My father was a good man; he killed lots of White Eyes."

With this auspicious beginning the book was launched. It had required four years for me to obtain this first interview with Ace Daklugie, the dominant patriarch of the Mescalero Apache Reservation. The aged Indian was the son of Juh (pronounced Hō), Chief of the Nednhi Apaches, the fiercest and most implacable band of that indomitable people. Though I had known Daklugie's wife, Ramona, well, the aloof Daklugie, formally courteous, would not condescend to talk with White Eyes. Ramona, her brother Eugene Chihuahua, and Daklugie's daughter Maude Geronimo had long been my friends but had been unable to secure an audience for me with him. Knowing him to be the key to the past history of this band, I feared I could expect little information from any of the Chiricahua or Nednhi Apaches until he decided to give me his confidence.

Ramona had assured me that, if I could find her husband in the right mood, he could recall much interesting knowledge of his father, his uncle Geronimo, and his tribe—but he had consistently refused to talk with inquiring White Eyes, even though both she and Eugene had repeatedly urged him to help preserve the history and traditions of the Nednhi. Daklugie was the only member of the tribe left who had experienced the tribulations of military expeditions against the Apaches.

One day, while on my way to see Eugene and his wife, I had to pass Daklugie's home en route, and I saw Eugene sitting on a bench in front of Daklugie's house, crying. I knew that his sister Ramona was dying of a malignancy, so I stopped and went to him. When he could speak, he said, "The white medicine man has told me he can do nothing for Ramona. I want to make medicine for her—it is her only chance to live—but our preacher says it is a pagan rite and has forbidden it."

"I know your minister," I told him, "and think he is a very good man. But he is just a man. Why don't you do what your heart tells you is right? Is there any conflict between your Apache beliefs and the teachings of the church?"

"Not that I can see," replied Eugene.

Ramona died, and Ace Daklugie never entered their house again; immediately after her death, everything in the house was destroyed, including the iron cookstove and a Lenox dinner service Ramona had won in a statewide garden contest. When her possessions had been destroyed, her home stood vacant for over two years. Had the family obeyed tribal custom, it would have been burned; but the government forbade that. Daklugie moved to the home of his granddaughter, Evangeline Kazhe, thirteen miles or so away.

I waited more, I thought, than the conventional time before attempting to see Daklugie. When I did, his granddaughter Evangeline would come to the door and say, "I'm sorry, but my grandfather is not at home" (his out-stretched, booted legs would be plainly visible across the doorway behind her), or she would say, "My grandfather is sleeping," or, "He is sick."

I had become well acquainted with Eugene Chihuahua and his wife Jennie, and occasionally they asked of my progress with Daklugie. I had given up hope of ever getting the information and said so. "He's always been so," said Eugene. "And you are right about his knowing what happened. But whether or not he will ever give it to anyone, I don't know."

Four years later, in August, Gertrude Ogilvie came to ask if I was attending the ceremonials at Gallup due to begin in two days. "It's too late for reserva-tions," I told her. "There are no motels within driving distance. One has to make arrangements weeks ahead to get a room in Gallup."

"Why don't we get a tarp and some bedrolls and go?"

We arranged for the trip and, while we were talking, in walked Daklugie's daughter, Maude Geronimo. Her hearing was very poor, and it was an effort to make her understand. I told her that we were leaving early the following morning for Gallup.

"Take me," she said. "I'll wear my beaded buckskin robe and moccasins and march in the parade. I'll get a room at the performer's village where they will give me my meals."

Why not? Maude wanted to go. She would meet old friends and enjoy visits with them. I told her that we'd planned to get into Gallup in time to see the parade and that we would pick her up at her home in Carisso Canyon at three the next morning.

She left about eleven. At three that afternoon she returned with her father. He refused to come into the house and seated himself in a chair on the lawn. Mrs. Ogilvie and I joined him and Maude. It was a warm day; the windows and doors of adjoining apartments were open, and people began coming and seating themselves until we ran out of chairs. Then they sat on the grass. Dak-lugie was telling stories about Jim Thorpe, with whom he was in school, and of Lewis Tewanema, a Hopi runner who held a record in the Olympics for the marathon. He was talking smoothly and well, and the audience was fascinated.

When he had finished, I asked him if he would let me record his reminis-cences in shorthand.

"It is the custom of my people," he said, "to tell their stories around the campfires at night, preferably in cold weather."

"Would a fireplace do?" I asked.

"Gallup would be a good place to begin," was the reply.

"Your daughter is going; so is Mrs. Ogilvie. Why don't you join us on this trip to Gallup?" I asked.

"Going to; we're already packed," he replied.

All the way to Gallup I worried about getting rooms for Maude and her father, but they did not seem concerned.

As we neared the Rio Grande Daklugie asked me to drive slowly and stop before crossing the bridge. "It was the custom of my People," he explained, "that when they were trying to escape from a pursuing enemy and they reached the banks of a stream in flood, to stop, sing the hymn to the river, and throw turquoise into the water. That made it go down *thin* so that they could cross." I stopped while he and Maude sang the prayer in their own language, but I refused to throw turquoise into the river.

We arrived in Gallup in time for the parade. To my surprise I found shop windows full of photographs of famous Indians such as Geronimo, Quanah Parker, Chee Dodge, and, conspicuous among them, Daklugie. How this old Indian rated the recognition he was receiving was puzzling to me.

He ordered me to drive to the administration building and bring Mr. Woodward (who had sponsored the ceremonials at Gallup) out to the car. Daklugie's arrogance was offensive, but I meekly obeyed. When I found Mr. Woodward's son, he courteously informed me that it was impossible to grant my request. His father was in conference with the chairmen of his committees and could not be disturbed.

"I quite understand," I told him, "and I hope that Mr. Daklugie will."

"Daklugie!" he exclaimed. "Do you mean to tell me you have the old Apache chief out there?"

When I assented, he replied, "Wait a moment. I'll bring my father."

In ten minutes Maude and her father had been registered for the one vacant room, they had tickets admitting them to the dining room, and I had a sticker for my car. We drove to the performer's village, an area surrounded by a ten-foot-high barbed wire fence. Before the locked gate an armed guard paced back and forth. When he saw the sticker, he opened the gate and motioned us through. We left Daklugie and Maude at their quarters. (Because of a deluge of rain that night, Mrs. Ogilvie and I ditched our bedrolls and slept in the car.)

Local people told me that Woodward had been unable to persuade many tribes to assemble at Gallup because they did not want White Eyes to witness their sacred dances. He had tried to lure them by describing the pleasure they would find in getting together for dancing and visiting. He pointed out that they could enter the products of their artists for prizes and find a market for jewelry, pottery, baskets, and blankets. Still they stayed away. Then he had recalled that Daklugie, whom he had known for years, was a graduate of Carlisle Indian School—as were many other tribal leaders. He had asked Daklugie to intercede for him. To Woodward's delight, at Daklugie's invitation the other tribes finally attended.

After our trip to Gallup, Ace Daklugie came to my house each Thursday at eight in the morning to dictate. But he came well chaperoned. He brought Maude, her daughter Evangeline Kazhe, and the latter's two preschool children. They stayed until three-thirty. I read aloud the dictation I'd taken the preceding week and made such changes or additions as he indicated; then he dictated for the rest of the day.

I made preparations so that getting lunch was a matter of little time; Maude and Evangeline did last-minute preparations, served it, and washed the dishes.

The small children played around the huge living room so quietly that I was seldom aware of their presence. I was so impressed by their remarkably good behavior that I asked Daklugie how he achieved it.

"I just tell them what to do and they do it," he explained.

I was to learn that almost all of the Apaches followed suit when he spoke. I did not know at that time that part of their subservience was owing to their firm conviction that Daklugie was a witch (they applied the term to men as well as women).

I explained to him that when I had his account of an occurrence I would compare it with the record left by army officers, newspaper editors, or Indian agents.

"Why?" he demanded.

"To verify it; to find what new information, if any, you contribute; and if accounts differ, to try to understand where they differed and why."

"Did any white man ever consult an Indian when writing history?" he asked.

I could think of none.

"Then why," he asked, "should I worry? What difference does it make what they think? They won't accept my account, anyway."

"Probably not," I conceded. "But you and I will have it in a form that can be preserved and your children's children can read it when you no longer can tell them your history. It may even bring about a better understanding between your people and mine. I'd particularly like to have mine understand not only what *happened*, but what *motivated* the Apaches. You know they have the reputation of being the most warlike, the most cruel, and the 'fightingest' Indians of the United States."

"I don't want to spoil that image," he replied, "so you tell 'em. Tell 'em that I'm not only an Apache, I'm Nednhi. And we were the worst of the lot!"

Dan L. Thrapp has portrayed in *Juh, an Incredible Indian*, exactly what the title implies. Battling a different kind of enemy under bewildering modern conditions, I found Juh's son, Daklugie, equally incredible. I was well aware of his faults, for he admitted them, but I do not believe that Ace Daklugie ever made a decision affecting the tribe (and he made many, both as chairman of the Tribal Council and later, when, in desperation, he was called in to make the decisions and clear its agenda) that was not beneficial to his people rather than for personal gain. Though he bridged the chasm between primitive and—as he would say—"so-called civilized life"—he did it with equal dedication and unselfish concern for his people.

In obtaining information for this book—particularly for Part One—I followed procedures largely determined by Ace Daklugie. I did not call him by his given name until he requested it. He disclaimed the title of *Chief*, disliked the White Eyes's *Mister*, and insisted that, since Daklugie was his name, he be called that. And though it seemed disrespectful, I complied with his wishes in the matter.

Though he occasionally lapsed into the vernacular of the reservation he spoke very good English, and the errors he made were not those of an ignorant white person. Since this was to be a book about Apaches, by Apaches, Daklugie thought that the spelling of their names should be as they preferred. I explained that when the military officers recorded Apache names they spelled them phonetically, and not all Apaches pronounced them alike. Consequently, there were sometimes several different ways of spelling the same name. For uniform usage, I told him, the University of Oklahoma Press decided upon certain spellings, some of which were not acceptable to the individuals. That, he said, was their privilege, just as was the spelling used by the Apaches.

When reminded that excellent accounts have been written of the Apache wars, Daklugie agreed that good accounts have been written of military campaigns against the Indians, but he stressed that there have been few attempts to give the Apache side of the conflict. Only two books have been written by Apaches—those authored by James Kaywaykla and Jason Betzinez.

I had long been familiar with the Apache word *Indah,* which military officers and historians have interpreted as meaning *White People.* That translation is indirect; the literal meaning of *Indah* is *The Living.*

Until Ace Daklugie used the term *Indeh,* I had not encountered it. Literally it means *The Dead,* and it is the term by which Apaches, recognizing their fate, designated themselves.

This book is not an attempt to write a definitive history of the Apaches from their memorized accounts. There were many important people and events of which my informants had little or no knowledge. Consequently, there is a serious lack of information; and it is lost, I am afraid, forever. Unfortunately, nobody was sufficiently interested in securing it while there were living participants and witnesses to relate their experiences.

Many accounts given by the Apaches coincide with those of recorded history and many are similar. I have concentrated my research on the conflicting reports.

Because no individual could give a firsthand account of all occurrences, different narrators have been used. Each gives the record as he lived it or knew it from those who had experienced it.

Please remember that I do not think that these old people were infallible. I do not think anyone is, including military officers whose reports to their superiors have been, with few exceptions, accepted without question.

I have presented the evidence as I found it, regardless of whether or not it conformed to my own opinions. I am as much or more concerned with accounts that do not coincide with those made by contemporaries of the Apache campaigns as with those that do.

Fortunately, my obligation to the Apaches, who have given me their evidence, is to present it as I have received it. I am neither the judge nor the jury. Though I do have opinions, I leave to the readers the freedom to make their own decisions.

Now only very few of the old Apaches remain, and I am deeply indebted to those who so generously recounted their personal experiences and those of their parents so that their account of the Apaches might be preserved for their children.

To Eugene Chihuahua, his sister Ramona Daklugie, and his wife Jennie (a Mescalero), I wish to express my gratitude. I am also indebted to Eugene Chihuahua's niece, Edna Comanche, and his nephew, Richard Johlsannie (Josannie, Ulzanna), son of Ulsanna.

My good friends Jasper Kanseah and his wife, Lucy, both frequently stopped at my house for visits, as did Amelia Naiche and Isabel Perico Enjady, daughter of Perico, warrior with Geronimo. Christian and Amelia Naiche, grandchildren of both Cochise and Mangas Coloradas and children of Chief Naiche, gave valuable assistance.

George Martine, well educated and well informed as to the history of his people, and his daughter Eveline Gaines, granddaughter of Victorio, were frequent visitors and gave much valuable information. I am also indebted to Evans Istee, grandson of Victorio, and his father, Charles Istee. Information was also donated by Dan Nicholas, a Warm Springs Apache; his cousin Nelson Kedizinne; and Eustace Fatty and Dorland Robinson, sons of Gordo (Old Fatty).

John Ballard, a Chiricahua, and Lena Morgan, daughter of Naiche's half-sister, gave of their knowledge and experience. So, also, did Wynona Magoosh, daughter of Yahnosha, and Lipan Apaches Willie and Richard Magoosh, sons of the Lipan chief who sought and obtained refuge at Mescalero.

Alton Peso, Solon Sombrero, and May Peso Second, widow of Jose Second, a Chiricahua, contributed liberally, as did Old Big Mouth (the Mescalero scout who died when he was about 107), Mack Big Mouth, and Mack's wife Margaret Balachi Big Mouth, daughter of a famous Warm Springs warrior. And I am deeply indebted to those of the sixty-seven Apaches not already named for their trust, information, and assistance.

Now that only two of my Apache informants are still living, historians are conceding that their testimonies are of value and that the people who *made* history sometimes knew something about it. They are coming to the reservation for information no longer obtainable. It's very gratifying to know that the testimony of these people has been preserved and is being accepted.

I wish also to acknowledge my indebtedness to Mrs. James A. Carroll, widow of the Mescalero Apache agent; their daughter, Eloise (Mrs. Theodore Sutherland); Mrs. C. R. Jefferis, widow of the agent who succeeded Mr. Carroll; and John Crow, the agent at Mescalero who gave me access to the records at the agency, many of which were later shipped to Denver or destroyed.

Among my other White-Eye friends who were generous with information, I wish to thank Dr. Harwood P. Hinton, Department of History, the University of Arizona; Dan L. Thrapp, author of *The Conquest of Apacheria*; and Dr. Angie Debo, writer of many books on the Southwest. I am very grateful to Mrs. Pat Wagner, editor of Western Publications, for her gracious permission to use articles written by me and published in *True West, Old West,* and *Frontier Times.* My appreciation is also extended to Gillett Griswold, curator of the Museum of Artillery and Missiles at Fort Sill, for the compilation of the Apache prisoner of war list that names both those who died at Fort Sill and those who elected to come to the Mescalero Apache reservation. To Donald Cline, whose papers containing valuable research were of much assistance, I also give my thanks.

Paramount in importance is my gratitude and obligation to Lynda (Mrs. James) Sanchez and to Nora (Mrs. Walter) Henn. For more than five years these young women have given invaluable assistance in the completion of this book. They have helped not only with mechanical aid in typing, but in highly skilled research and in evaluation of the suitability of material.

During this time Nora was writing several articles as well as a short history of the Lincoln County War, upon which she is an authority. At present she is under contract to the Museum of New Mexico for a comprehensive architectural history of Old Lincoln Town.

Lynda was working on a project in anthropology involving the folklore of

Spanish-American residents along the Bonito and Hondo valleys of southern New Mexico. She, too, has had several articles pertaining to southwestern history published and is at present writing a book about the Spanish-American culture in southern New Mexico.

The interviewing of Apaches had been completed when a visual problem necessitated skilled assistance and I was very fortunate in obtaining it from these two companions and scholars. It is possible to recompense for services but not for ability and dedication. Both Lynda and Nora neglected their own writing projects in order to enable me to complete mine. I am at a loss to express my gratitude.

To Mr. Howard Christy, history editor for Brigham Young University Press, I am deeply indebted. Only one liberal in his point of view and untramelled by centuries of tradition could have realized the value of oral history. It is eminently fitting that the excellent history written from documentary evidence given by enemies of the Apaches be presented formally. But that of the people who made that history was unconventional and is presented so. Not without an understanding of the mores, religion, standards, opinions, and *feelings* of these people, presented in their way, can one understand their actions. Without Mr. Christy's acceptance of this, my more than a quarter of a century of work might have been wasted.

—EVE BALL

NOTE TO READERS:

The material presented in this volume is in four formats of varying style. There are narratives by the author's several oral sources reproduced with little or no editing. Other oral narratives have been rather extensively edited by the author, particularly where accounts of two or more sources have been combined. There are short conversations between the author and her oral sources interspersed throughout the volume where integration into the narratives or reduction to footnotes has been deemed inadvisable. Finally, there are the author's historical narratives.

In order to clearly differentiate between these several approaches, oral accounts are set off by hairlines running the full width of the page, each headed by the name of the source. Author narratives and author-source conversations at beginnings and endings of chapters, and interspersed between oral accounts, are not set off.

BOOK ONE

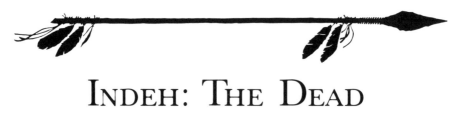

INDEH: THE DEAD

Mountain Spirit Dancers
(Eugene Chihuahua's Motif).

(U.S. Army Photograph)

CHAPTER 1

JUH'S STRONGHOLD

"They come!" exclaimed Daklegon.[1] "Juh and Geronimo. See them, Little Brother?"

We lay prone on Daklegon's blanket at the top of the zigzag trail leading up to the flattopped mountain, our father's stronghold.[2] From that dizzy height the trail winding from the timber along the river and across the plain to the foot of the mountain was barely discernible.

I had to admit that I could not see them.

Daklegon shifted his rifle and, as Apaches do, pointed with his nose. "They are leaving the trees to cross the plain. Look closely."

I could see nothing on the trail until suddenly a movement caught my eye. Tiny things, like a string of ants, were crawling toward us. Surely they were not horsemen!

"But they are," my brother assured me. "They are our father and his Nednhi."

I watched the long line wind across the open country to disappear at the foot of the mountain upon which we lay. There were more horsemen than our father had taken with him, and I asked Daklegon if Juh might be bringing captives.

Daklegon did not know. He thought Juh might have taken Mexican women and children as slaves, but he might also have rescued the women who had not returned after they had gone to the foothills to bake mescal.

"If he brings captives, won't the Mexican warriors come to fight us?"

"They've tried that," Daklegon explained. "Juh let them climb part way up the trail before signalling our braves to topple the stones alongside it down

---

1. Little Dog Collar.

2. Daklugie and George Martine, son of the scout Martine who was a Nednhi and was with Juh, both identified Juh's stronghold as "just west of the Chihuahua-Sonora line in the Sierra Madre, about a three-day walk from Casas Grandes, Mexico."

An Elder Whipple of The Church of Jesus Christ of Latter-day Saints lived at the Colonia Dublan near Casas Grandes when he was a young man, and he hunted over the area west of there. He identified the flattopped mountain described by the Apaches, and said that it is as they locate it.

upon them. You've seen the bones and saddle irons at the foot of the trail. The Mexicans don't want any more of that zigzag trail. I doubt that they'll try it again."

Daklegon continued, "Our father and Geronimo must have taken captives; if so, I hope they got an ammunition train, for we are getting short of bullets." He glanced upward and said, "It is almost midday. The warriors won't get up here before late afternoon, but your mother asked me to let her know when I sighted them, for she wants to prepare a feast. Will you run and tell her?"

My two elder brothers and I each had different mothers. Delzhinne[3] was with the warriors, and this was his fourth raid. Upon their return the braves would sit in council and determine whether or not his conduct merited his becoming one of them. Because our father was chief, he would require more of his own sons than of others. I longed for the time when I, too, could go on the warpath and serve a brave as his apprentice. How gladly would I cook his food, run his errands, care for his horse, and observe the rigid rules of the aspiring warrior!

I thought of these things as I ran toward the long line of tepees silhouetted against the blue-green of the forest. My father's tepees stood in the center, one for each of his wives, with a space between my father's tepees and those of the next warrior's. The others were grouped similarly to afford privacy. They faced the east, as do all Apache tepees.

When I reached Ishton, my tall, beautiful mother, she was standing in the opening to our tepee and her slave women were dressing her hair. My father called her *Ishton;* the name means *The* Woman. She was the first wife—not in order of marriage, but in order of being best loved. She was also dearly loved by her brother Geronimo.

Her slaves had gathered the roots of the amole, pounded them, made a fragrant suds, and washed her hair with it. Now they were combing her hair. One slave had a brush made of cactus fiber, which she drew from my mother's belt. Another slave, kneeling, took the brush and gently pulled it through my mother's hair until the brush was taken by a third, seated on the ground, who unsnarled the ends of my mother's hair, a foot or more of which lay on a hide.

Another group of slaves was working with Jacali's hair; Jacali, my sister, was standing nearby. I knew that when the women's hair was dry it would be braided, and the heavy ropes of hair would be tucked into their belts. Other women sometimes asked my mother what medicine she used to make her hair so long and luxuriant. She told them that she used only the amole as they did.

I stood before Ishton, respectfully awaiting her permission to speak. She smiled and asked if I was hungry. She knew well that small boys are always hungry.

"Daklegon sent me to tell you that my father comes."

"And the others?"

"There is a long line of them, many more than he took with him."

"That gives us time to prepare the feast. Give my thanks to your brother. Will you carry food and a jug of water to him?"

"I can. I'm a big boy now."

"Yes, six winters big," she said, and she smiled.

---

3. Dark Skinned.

3

I trudged back to the observation point and Daklegon. As we ate he gave instructions. When the warriors neared the top and boys ran to line up on either side of the path in order to take the mounts of the returning men, I was to remember that I was the son of the chief and must use good manners. Instead of trying to force my way to the best position on the brink, I was to wait until the others were in line and then take the poorest position at the end.

"But I've done that three times," I protested, "and no warrior has so much as looked my way."

"This will be the fourth," said my brother, "and four is our sacred number. Perhaps this time someone may let you take his mount."

"Delzhinne, perhaps?"

"Maybe. If he is to become a warrior our mothers will prepare a feast for him tomorrow. Caring for his horse will be an honor."

I knew that Daklegon, too, had asked permission to go on this, his first, raid, but that our father had refused him. He had done it kindly and had reminded my brother that being left to protect the women and children in the absence of the warriors was a position of trust to them as well as to the old men who shared the responsibility. Daklegon had been disappointed but was too courteous to protest his chief's decision, for Daklegon was an Apache, and, more important than that, a Nednhi. And the Nednhi, though the bravest and fiercest of all Apaches, were also the most courteous.

The raid was sent out in response to an attack by Mexicans on a group of our women and children who had gone out to gather and prepare mescal. The Mexicans had killed all the older boys and had taken the women and children captive.

Our father had sent Martine, his orderly, and Fun, half-brother to our uncle Geronomio, to the mescal pits to learn why our people had not returned. At the pits they had found our dead in their blankets, killed at night. (We believe that those who kill in darkness must walk in darkness through eternity in our Happy Place.)

Moreover, the Mexicans had scalped our people, something Apaches seldom did. (On rare occasions scalping was done by Apaches in retaliation and occasionally it was done to provide just one scalp for the victory dance; but the warrior who lifted the scalp had to undergo a four-day purification ceremony in isolation, thereby missing the celebration of the victory.)

The scouts had trailed the Mexicans to a village in a canyon where they had grovelled in the earth for the yellow iron sacred to Ussen.[4] There the scouts found our people, with other slaves, imprisoned in a trap made of adobe. An armed guard paced back and forth in front of the prison night and day.

Concealed on a high cliff overlooking the village, Fun and Martine had spied upon the captors. A stream flowed close to the side of the cliff on which they lay. Across it stood the place of imprisonment, and near it a large two-story building. As a boy Martine had been captured and sold to a Mexican family near Casas Grandes, and he knew the ways of the Mexicans. He said that the two-story building was the lodge of the Medicine Man, and in it everyone except the guard assembled on the morning of each seventh day. He

---

4. God, Creator of Life.

identified the building by the crossed sticks on the roof; in addition to the door facing them, Martine said there was probably a door in the rear. An irregular row of small adobe huts followed the river, and toward the upper end of the canyon stood another large, low building, probably a storehouse. Around the building was a corral that housed many mules and some horses. The building might be used to store supplies of various kinds, and it was undoubtedly there that the Mexicans kept the forbidden ore (gold) they took from Mother Earth. There they might also store the white iron (silver) not forbidden to us. Neither metal was of value for bullets as each was too soft, but when the Mexicans had accumulated a huge amount of either, they took it by pack mule to the City of Mules (Chihuahua) to exchange it for money and supplies.

Martine was reluctant to go into the sacred house of the Mexicans, so he decided to scout the storehouse and Fun the prison and church. They lay and watched captured Apache women and children with baskets strapped to their backs be driven with ox goads across the bridge and disappear into a tunnel in the side of the canyon. Some returned with loads which were carried to the storehouse, but many more dumped refuse into the river from the middle of the bridge. The scouts watched a woman fall, unresponsive to terrible blows; contemptuously a guard kicked her body into the stream.

When it began to get dark, the slaves were permitted to quit work. The guard arrogantly threw ears of corn to them. The Apache women disdained to pick them up, but the hungry children did and were ordered by their mothers to throw the corn down. All the women and children were herded into the prison, and the heavy door was locked. The guard resumed his monotonous pacing in front of the prison door.

"The women, first," said Martine. "They may know when the people will go to the church. It is usually there that they take refuge if attacked. If you could just get into that place."

"I think I can. If the roof is of mud, I can dig a hole in it and drop in."

They arranged to meet and agreed that one must then go report to Juh.

When all the fires had been extinguished and the village was asleep, each scout went silently about his mission. Fun crossed the bridge and slipped to the rear of the church. He found a second door but no other openings except a few long slits near the roof that were covered with skins. A tree afforded easy access to the roof. He dug through the adobe of the roof and, suspended by his arms, felt for footing. From a stack of wood, he reached the floor. As he crept around the wall, he found casks of water, stacks of blankets, food, and a great amount of ammunition.

Suddenly his hand encountered emptiness. Reaching below the surface of the floor he found a step. He descended stairs; at the foot was a door that would open toward him. With a stick of wood it could be braced against entry.

Noiselessly he pulled the door ajar. By tiny lights he could distinguish a figure in black kneeling before a man who had been tortured and nailed to large crossed sticks. The Mexican god! No Apache would have killed *Ussen* as the cruel Mexicans had killed their god. As the kneeling figure stirred, light fell on his head. He had been scalped! He stood, took a light, and disappeared through the opposite door.

Fun, too, left the church. In deep shadow he watched the guard, who walked only in front of the place. Fun slipped to the rear of the prison and felt for an opening. When his hand slipped into the slit he sought, he reached for the interior and found that the wall was almost as thick as the length of his arm.

How was he to attract the attention of one of the Apaches who were inside without alerting the guard? What if a child should cry or a woman scream? He took his headband and tied a pebble into one end of it. Holding it by the other end, he lowered it through the slit into the darkness and began swinging it gently back and forth. It was grasped and held by someone inside. A slight tug responded to his; something rustled, and he heard a low murmur.

"My sister, help will come. Soon. Juh will come. You must eat."

"We will eat," was the reply. "Tell him that at dawn on the fourth day from now everyone in the village will go to the lodge of the Medicine Man and close the door. All but the guard. That is the time to strike."

"It will be done."

Suddenly Fun became aware that the regular pacing of the guard had ceased. He dropped and lay flat against the wall. As the footsteps approached, he held his breath and pressed close. When the guard had circled the building and resumed his march, Fun stole away to join Martine.

Martine, too, had been successful. To his surprise, he found the storehouse unguarded. Inside he found large cowhide bags laden with ore. Water jugs and food had been prepared for a journey. Before the mule train bearing the ore and precious metals left for Chihuahua, Martine felt, he must get word to Juh. Fun agreed. Fun would stay at the village and keep watch, while Martine, who knew every foot of the terrain, made the trip back to the stronghold.

When all this was reported to my father, there was no time nor need for a war dance, for the warriors were already at fighting pitch and eager to start. Within minutes Juh, Geronimo, and the warriors had been on their way.[5] Now they were returning.

"And now, Little Brother," said Daklegon, "it will be a long time before the warriors reach the top of this cliff. You may as well sleep until they come."

I was awakened by the impact of unshod hoofs on rock. My brother stood with rifle upraised as many boys scrambled frantically for choice positions. I, too, rushed to the brim and was in time to see my father, riding ahead of his men as a chief should, round a sharp point of the trail.[6] Other boys had lined up on either side, leaving a space through which the warriors would ride. As before, the big boys had the best places. I took mine at the end of the line, farthest from the brink.

Suddenly a head bobbed into sight and Juh's powerful black stallion found footing and lunged to the top of the cliff. Above him my father's eagle plumes

---

5. Juh, pronounced by the Apaches "Hō," is spelled also *Ju*, *Ho*, *Whoa*, and occasionally *Who* (consistent with the Spanish pronunciation). Daklugie says that the meaning of his father's name is "he sees ahead." Because of a speech impediment that occasionally troubled Juh his name has been said to mean "he stammers" or "the stammerer." "Long neck" has been another interpretation. Confusion may result from the fact that, because Apache is a tonal language, different pitches of the same word may have different meanings.

6. Both Eugene Chihuahua and Jasper Kanseah repeatedly spoke of the obligation of a chief to lead his men in conflict. Apaches had great contempt for armed forces officers who sent their men into battle but watched the battle themselves from a safe distance. Apache social custom dictated the position the chief occupied when on the march or when seated in camp. When seated, the chief must be the central figure.

6

waved. His face was smeared with red clay, and he held himself proudly as he rode between the lines of outstretched arms. He ignored all until he reached me. Then he dismounted, smiled through closed lids, and laid the reins in my hand. He lifted me to his saddle and walked beside me past the tepees and to the little stream of water in the pines.

That was the proudest and happiest day of my life.

CHAPTER 2

VENGEANCE OF JUH

By firelight the Nednhi and their guests assembled before my father's tepees. Dressed in her gorgeous beaded buckskin robes, Ishton directed preparations for the feast. Her slaves spread skins and blankets in a semicircle for Juh and his men; the most famous of the visiting chiefs and warriors would be seated nearest my father, with those of lesser fame seated further away. The women and children would sit behind the warriors.

Cooking pots were placed around the big central fire of logs, and meat was laid to roast on small beds of coals. Women baked meal cakes made of sweet acorns and piled them on wooden slabs. Jugs of water and *tiswin* were in readiness for the feast.

The singers and drummers were to file in and take their places, and the warriors were to follow. But not until my mother signalled did Juh, in his best finery, lead the way. He stopped beside Ishton and motioned to Nana, a tall, slender old man, to take the place of honor at his left. Nana waited until Juh had seated himself before dropping beside him. On my father's right he placed Chihuahua, a young and handsome Chokonen Apache warrior. Geronimo came next; and beside Nana sat Kaytennae, a Chihenne Apache and *segundo* to Nana. Then came Fun and Perico, half-brothers to Geronimo. Others took their places according to rank and fighting reputation.

Not until his guests were seated did my father's warriors take their places at the ends of the huge semicircle. I paid little attention to them, for I was watching eagerly to see who would come last. To my delight it was Delzhinne. Though he modestly stayed several steps behind the rest, his pride in having become a warrior was obvious.

Juh raised his hand and there was silence. Not a sound was heard as he rolled a cigarette and smoked it. He used an oak leaf for a wrapper; I do not know whether he had real tobacco or not. When he lacked tobacco, he used dried shrub leaves. Some accounts tell that Apaches smoked a peace pipe; those who wrote such things knew little of Apaches, for they used no pipes. After my father had blown smoke in each of the four directions, he raised his arm and the women began serving the food. Roasted venison, mescal, sweet acorn meal cakes, and honey were provided.

No one started eating before all had been served, then Juh raised his cup. I wondered why the men were not eating until I heard through the stillness that most distressing of all sounds, the Apache death wail. It came from the tepees of families who had lost warriors in the raid. Those families could not attend the feast. The group around the fire sat in silence until the sound died away; then my mother directed the filling of bowls for the women and children. When she handed me one, I asked if those who had lost a member of their family could have food. She told me that she had already sent it to them.

When everyone around the fire had finished eating, my father rose and again there was silence. I knew that he was under emotional strain, for he was tapping one foot on the ground. Ordinarily that meant trouble for somebody—usually me. But I knew, too, that Juh was disturbed about the loss of some of his people. When he began to speak there was no indication of the speech impediment he sometimes experienced. First he named the honored dead who had preceded us to the Happy Place. They, he said, were the fortunate ones, for they had given their lives for their tribe. Henceforth their names were not to be spoken. I knew that if their names were spoken, it would summon their ghosts to the speaker. Apaches were loath to do this because in the Happy Place the one called might be hunting or gambling and not wish to be disturbed. For this reason a dead person was called only in extreme need.

When my father had finished, again he lifted his hand, and from the darkness the young boys of the Nednhi—Daklegon in charge—led a string of pack mules up to the circle. Each animal, heavily laden, was led up to the fire and halted, its burden placed before the warriors. The first mule load contained guns and ammunition (the plunder had been previously sorted and arranged in order of its value.) Juh announced that the rifles confiscated would go first to those most needing them; all ammunition was to be shared equally. Only three needed weapons, but some asked if they might have rifles for wives or sons.

Knives were distributed next; then a second mule load of ammunition was divided. When Daklegon brought a portion to Nana there was much laughter, the first heard that evening. It was well known that Nana had Power over ammunition trains and rattlesnakes; when nobody else could obtain bullets, old Nana could go out and bring home a good supply.[1] Nana calmly accepted the bullets and put them into his leather pouch. Like many others, he preferred a pouch to an ammunition belt. When a share of the ammunition was laid before my father, he asked that it be added to the portions reserved for the bereaved families.

Blankets, saddles, shawls, metal cooking utensils, water jugs, and shirts came

---

1. Few Apaches will discuss Power, and those who do will tell little, possibly because they cannot explain it. Power was often obtained by the adolescent boy during the four-day fast in which he participated preparatory to becoming a warrior. Being deprived of food or water while praying for four days may have caused hallucinatory experiences in which his Medicine appeared. His Medicine might be an animal, a tree, a plant, or almost anything; whatever the boy saw—his Medicine—was to be a sort of guide and consultant for the rest of his life. But Power could be obtained in other ways, for many women had the gift. Power could also be given by one individual to another, as offered by Chato to Dan Nicholas.

For an example of a woman possessing Power, see Eve Ball, *In the Days of Victorio* (Tucson: University of Arizona Press, 1970), pp. 14–15.

9

next. No other articles of clothing had been taken from the Mexican village, because our people did not use them.

The last mule load consisted of two huge cowhide bags full of the yellow and white metals that the White Eyes love. When they were emptied before my father, he was indignant. He asked who had been so foolish as to bring that useless stuff. Didn't we know that bullets made of either were worthless? The stuff was of no value to us except for the making of children's toys.

Nana took pieces of the ore in his wrinkled hands and held them so that they reflected the firelight. "This," he said, referring to the silver, "is the white iron, not forbidden to us. But this yellow stuff is sacred to Ussen. We are permitted to pick it up from the surface of Mother Earth, but not to grovel in her body for it. To do so is to incur the wrath of Ussen. The Mountain Gods dance and shake their mighty shoulders, destroying everything near. The Mexicans and the greedy White Eyes are superstitious about this stuff. The love of life is strong in all people, but to them it is not so strong as their greed for gold. For it, they risk their lives."

"But, my father," said Martine, "I have lived among the Mexicans at Casas Grandes. I know they value this stuff. White Eyes will exchange ammunition, food, anything for it."

Nana nodded, "I know," he said. "Nevertheless, it is this stuff that will bring our people to ruin and cause us to lose first our land and then our lives. But right now, it has value."

"If my father approves, then," said Juh, "let it be divided. Guns last a long time, but ammunition must be constantly replaced. If it will provide for us for awhile, why should we not use it?"

When the women and children had finished their meal, Juh asked that Nana relate the account of the attack upon the Mexican mining village. Nana declined, asking that Geronimo do so. This is the account my uncle gave:

We reached the canyon in which the village is located after dark. Martine guided us to Fun. Kaytennae was assigned the honor of determining when all of the people had entered the church and of killing the guard. He was to kill the guard with a knife, which is noiseless. Fun climbed again to the roof of the Medicine Man's lodge with something wrapped in a bundle. In the upper story he quietly dug a hole in the adobe floor.

At dawn the Medicine Man made lights in the big room. Through a partially opened door we watched him at the feet of his God. He arose, went to a rope, and the pulling sent out loud noises. Many people began coming. We lay hidden until we made sure that everybody in the village had entered. When the door had been closed, we silently carried logs and stones with which to barricade both that door and a smaller one so that neither could be opened from the inside. Juh signalled to Fun on the roof. He had made a chili bomb by grinding red peppers on a *metate* and mixing into the ground peppers a very soft and inflammable wood. He had wrapped the mixture in a piece of his shirt. He quietly enlarged the opening in the ceiling of the big room until it would admit his bundle. With fire sticks he ignited it and, when it was burning well, dropped the flaming bundle into the room below and covered the hole with a blanket.

Soon there were noises of coughing and sneezing, blows on the door, and sounds of frantic attempts to open it. Fun slipped quickly to the ground.

We waited until the noises inside ceased before we released our captive women and children from the prison. But we did not release those Mexicans who were in the church. We left guards at the church while we went through the houses for what we needed. The women and children that we had released from the prison helped us go through the houses and pack the items on the mules. Horses were taken for those who had none. Among the non-Apache prisoners were boys young enough to be trained as warriors. They are to be treated as our own.

My brother Juh, the Nednhi chief, has brought home supplies sufficient not only for his own, but he insists that his guests share them. You know that of all the plunder divided tonight Juh took none. A great chief is one who supplies the needs of his people, not one who robs them of what they have. Let this be remembered and told to your children's children.

But Geronimo had not finished. He went on: "The Nednhi have done well. They have destroyed the enemy with the loss of only two brave warriors. They have avenged the deaths of their people, and much honor is due Juh for his conduct of the raid. Much honor is due Fun and Martine. They have proved their courage and skill as scouts. And let not Kaytennae's good work be forgotten. I have spoken."

The women refilled the small wicker cups and, when the men had drunk, departed from the circle. Fresh logs were placed on the fire and the space about it was cleared for the victory dance. After the singers and drummers again took their places, my father led, followed by his Nednhi. Then came Nana and the Chihenne; then Chihuahua and the Chokonen; and last Geronimo and his few Bedonkohes. Though my uncle Geronimo exercised the prerogatives of a chief, he was never elected to that position. In later days, when Naiche was chief of the Chiricahua, Geronimo continued to direct the fighting but scrupulously required the warriors to render to Naiche the respect due a chief. He acted as leader of war parties, but acted rather in the relationship of general to commander-in-chief. And Geronimo did his share of the fighting.

The long line danced about the fire clockwise, in single file. All joined in the singing, but above the rest I could hear the powerful voice of Juh. The difficulty he sometimes had in speaking did not affect his singing.

The men improvised steps and poses. Some gave pantomimes of their own ideas of fighting, using a rifle to gesticulate. Others knelt momentarily, fired an arrow or a bullet, or mimicked the thrust of a lance. Each performed as he chose, without effort to duplicate the actions of another.

"I am glad," murmured my mother, "that they have brought no scalps. Scalps have always sickened me."

"You have seen them, then?" I asked.

"A few times, a very few. Not until after my brother Geronimo returned to his camp in Mexico to find his beautiful wife Alope, his children, and his mother butchered and scalped did he take one.[2] After that, he did it rarely, and never except in retaliation. I hope that when you become a warrior you will remember that Victorio has permitted *no* scalping and that you will not."

I sat thinking.

"Victorio permits no scalping regardless of the provocation, and he has suffered no dishonor because of that.[3] Other tribes of Apaches do very little of it. You will not lose face by not permitting it. Will you give me your promise?"

I loved my mother, but a promise cannot be broken. I had never seen any

2. See S. M. Barrett, ed., *Geronimo's Story of His Life* (New York: Duffield & Co., 1906); and John G. Bourke, *On the Border with Crook* (New York: Charles Scribner's Sons, 1891), p. 26.

3. Ball, *Victorio*, p. 13.

scalping, but how could I know what I might have to do when I became a man? Apaches must protect their women and children. Ussen commanded that. White Eyes may care nothing about how they go through eternity, but Apaches do. The dead do not suffer by scalping, but they must appear in the Happy Place without their hair. There was no greater punishment for one's enemies. My mother did not press me for a promise, but added, "Do not forget to pray before you sleep."

I was told that the men caused landslides that covered all of that village and made a lake of the river. No White Eye will ever find that gold.

I asked Daklugie if he thought the Mexican mining village might have been the Lost Tayopa for which people have searched for years, but Daklugie had never heard of the Lost Tayopa.[4]

"You have said that Geronimo was never a chief," I told Daklugie. "In the book you interpreted for Mr. Barrett, didn't you make a chief of him?"

Daklugie gave one of his rare laughs. "Not I," he replied, "but Barrett did. You know that Geronimo and I were then prisoners of war, and we still did not know that we would not be killed. There were many things that we could not tell at that time because we knew we were closely censored. Geronimo wanted that book printed and so did I. What Barrett changed to suit himself we could not prevent. But he didn't change much. For the greater part, it is as Geronimo dictated it to me.[5]

"You want proof for everything and that is all right. But don't try burning any chili in the house, or you might kill yourself. I'll guarantee you that a chili bomb will work."

---

4. J. Frank Dobie, *Apache Gold and Yaqui Silver* (New York: Little, Brown and Co., 1930). This book, as its title indicates, is full of references to deposits of gold and caches of ore that are known to the Apache Indians. Dobie undoubtedly knew of the taboo against the Apaches' digging for gold, but he does not specifically address the issue.

5. In Barrett's *Geronimo's Story of His Life,* Daklugie said that at the time he interpreted Geronimo's story they knew that there had been objections to its being published. They still anticipated that at any time they might be killed; consequently, both he and Geronimo were very cautious about making any statements.

CHAPTER 3

CHILDHOOD

DAKLUGIE

I was born in southeastern Arizona not far from Fort Bowie, but since no records were kept at that time I do not know the date of my birth. I do not even know with certainty the year, though I do know that it was during the winter. A birth date was given me at Carlisle, where my age was estimated, but it is not even approximately right.[1]

Ishton, my mother, was a Bedonkohe and the favorite sister of Geronimo.[2] When the time for my birth drew near, my father was on a raid in Mexico. Geronimo came to our camp at the risk of his life to officiate as Medicine Man for the sister whom he so dearly loved.

As was the case with women of her family, my mother had great difficulty in giving birth. For four days she suffered terribly. Geronimo thought that she was going to die; he had done all he could for her, and was so distressed that he climbed high up the mountain behind Fort Bowie to plead with Ussen for his sister's life. As Geronimo stood with arms and eyes upraised, as our people do, Ussen spoke. Geronimo heard His voice clearly, as distinctly as if on a telephone. Ussen told Geronimo that his sister was to live, and he promised my uncle that he would never be killed but would live to a ripe old age and would die a natural death.

There is only one God, and we worship Him under the name in our tongue.

---

1. At Carlisle, the school for Indians near Harrisburg, Pennsylvania, the newly arrived Apache boys and girls were lined up and given names, arbitrarily selected, alphabetically down the lines. "Asa" Daklugie was at the head of the boys' line when names were dispensed to his group.

   Also, the age of each was estimated and a specific date of birth—day, month, and year—was arbitrarily assigned to each. At Carlisle, Daklugie's birth year was estimated as 1874. Later he came to realize that this was incorrect because he remembered, as a very young child, seeing Cochise's tepees; and he decided on this basis that he was probably born during the winter of 1869–70. (Cochise died in 1874.)

2. I asked why it was, if Daklugie's mother was a Bedonkohe, that he also was not a Bedonkohe, since the Apaches are members of the mother's tribe. Though he insisted that his father was a Nednhi, Juh was born a Bedonkohe. The reply was that he married a Nednhi woman and left his tribe to join the Nednhi in the Sierra Madre and that he was elected to the chieftainship. That Nednhi wife was the mother of one of his older sons. Though it was unusual, his first and favorite wife, though a Bedonkohe (Daklugie's mother and Geronimo's sister), was also called a Nednhi.

He speaks to the Apache. But he speaks to any who have faith and ask. You White Eyes no longer have sufficient faith to hear Him. Long ago He talked to some of you; your Book says that He did. If you really believe in Him, He would do so now.

I think that Ussen's promise is what gave Geronimo his wonderful courage. He was by nature already a brave person; but if one knows that he will never be killed, why be afraid? I don't know that Geronimo ever told his warriors that he had supernatural protection, but they were with him in many dangerous times and saw his miraculous escapes, his cures for wounds, and the results of his medicine; so his warriors knew that Geronimo was alive only because of Ussen's protection.

I learned much more from my own people than I did during the many long years I spent at Carlisle. I do not remember when I learned to pray. My mother taught me; all Apache mothers teach their children to pray. We are a very religious people; and each day, sometimes several times each day, we prayed when I was a child. We prayed as I still do, as I shall do as long as I live.

Next to our religion, I learned of my people and their brave men and deeds. As we ate our evening meal around the fire, an older man recited the stories of our people. Sometimes my father recited these stories, or sometimes one of his warriors did; sometimes a visitor was given the honor. We heard these stories until we memorized them. The narrator never deviated by one word. He, too, had memorized the account; each account was a sacred thing that must be handed down word for word as it happened. Occasionally some child went to sleep during the recital, but I did not. My mother had impressed upon me that the son of a chief must stay awake and learn. But I think I stayed awake largely because I loved hearing of the brave deeds of our brave people.

We had no written language and were forced to remember what we heard or were told. Our lives depended on accurate recall of such information, and particularly upon the reliability of messages sent by a chief to his people by runners. They had to accurately record his orders in their heads.

When I was very young I could not distinguish between fictional stories told for entertainment and true stories told to teach.

When my father left Cochise's reservation, he usually went to his stronghold in the Sierra Madres. We call them the Blue Mountains. One morning when my father was working with his arrows, he heard a child scream. He saw Kanseah, Geronimo's orphaned nephew, come running out of a cluster of trees with a bear at his heels. Juh could not shoot the bear because the boy was between them. He yelled for Kanseah to run between two trees that were growing very close together, and he did. He squeezed through, but the bear could not.

There was one story about Mahco, my mother's grandfather, a wise and good chief. He lived far to the north of us on the Río Gila. His were a happy and peaceful people. They obeyed Ussen's commands that they were not to fight unless they were attacked; but if they were attacked, they were to defend themselves. They were good hunters and killed much game. They also planted crops along the rivers: corn, pumpkin, beans, and watermelons. The story doesn't explain where they got the seed, but the crops did not grow wild, at least not after I went into that country. Perhaps seeds were obtained from the Spanish or Mexican people.

Other tribes seldom bothered them, but Mahco told stories about one tribe with whom they had bad trouble. Mahco's people used bowstrings made of yucca fiber; the enemy made their bowstrings of sinew. The sinew bowstring was much better than the yucca fiber. Even though Mahco's warriors did not ask Ussen for help in the battle, He sent it. There came a rain that tightened the yucca fiber but made the sinew stretch. The sinew was so loose that the bows did not shoot well; Mahco won the battle.[3]

After that, other tribes did not cause them much trouble, but the Mexicans who came into the country digging in the mountains for gold did cause difficulty. Mahco did not molest the Mexicans unless they attacked.

Apaches believed that Mexicans grubbing into Mother Earth caused earthquakes, and Apaches feared earthquakes. When the Apaches left their own country to spend winters in the warm part of Mexico, they saw the effects of the shaking of the earth and thought that the Mountain Spirits, who are the servants of Ussen, caused the shaking to avenge the desecration of the mountains.

Once my father took nearly all of the tribe to Casas Grandes for supplies. He had an arrangement with the Mexican people there for obtaining ammunition, and though he did not trust them he went occasionally. He knew that they would give him and his men *mescal* and *tequila*, very strong distillates of the maguey that they would kill them when and if they got drunk. While we were camped outside the town he told us of a trip he made years before when he was a very young man (long before he became chief). On that journey Juh's camp was close to Khonzhalito, a small village, and the Mexicans would come to the camp and have horse races. The Nednhi knew nothing of money, but they would bet horses, game, mules, blankets, hides, or any other possessions so that they could win the strong liquors the Mexicans made.

During the settlement of a bet, two men—a Nednhi and a Mexican—had started to fight with knives. They were separated by their friends, but they wanted to settle the argument with a fight. The Mexicans had always insisted that a pistol is a better weapon than the bow and arrow, but this was when there were only muzzle-loading guns. If an Apache with a bow and arrow had to fight a Mexican with a gun, the Apache lured the Mexican to fire both his rifle and his pistol, if he had both; then the Mexican had to reload before firing again. While the Mexican was reloading, the Apache would run in, firing arrows as he came. If he missed he was killed, but I knew men who could put seven arrows in the air before the first one that was fired fell to the earth. (There was a time that I could do that myself.)

The Mexican fired his pistol, and the Indian ran toward him. The Mexican got an arrow in his back; and when the Apache reached him, the man was dead.

The Mexicans were our enemies, yet unless they outnumbered us greatly we

---

3. Schat-Chen, *History, Traditions and Narratives of the Quares Indians of Laguna and Acoma*, John N. Gunn, ed. (Albuquerque: Albright and Anderson, 1971). Though this reference is not to an Athapascan tribe, the Queres lived under similar conditions to the east of the Apaches. Materials used for bowstrings would have been identical.

Geronimo, ca 1885.

Nana.

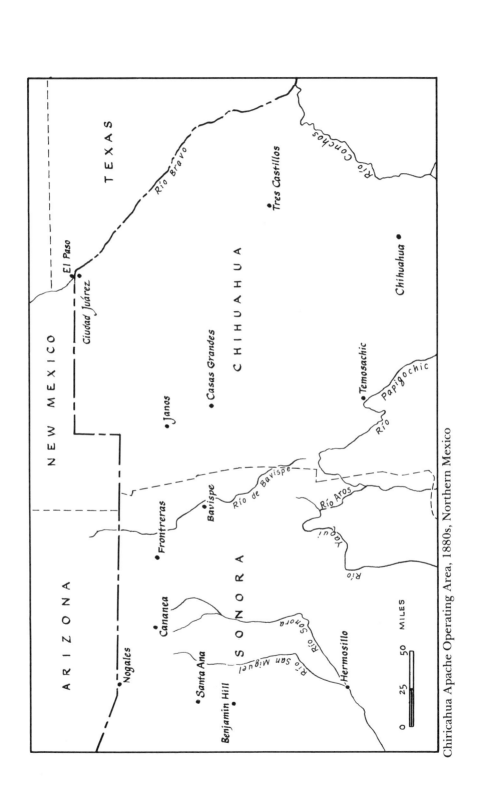

Chiricahua Apache Operating Area, 1880s, Northern Mexico

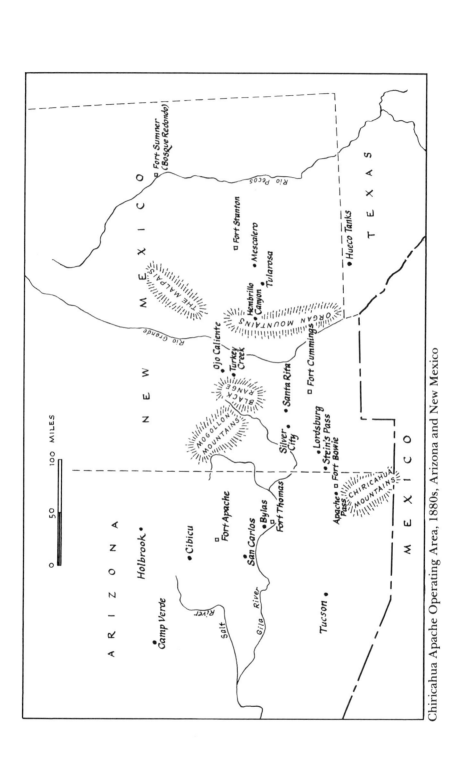

Chiricahua Apache Operating Area, 1880s, Arizona and New Mexico

had no fear of them. They much preferred being on good terms with Indian people of the villages, because then they could trade with them. When a Mexican left his home with a cart, he could easily be killed; but my people seldom bothered them.

As enemies, the Mexicans were nothing in comparison with the White Eyes who came in from the east. *White Eyes* is not the exact meaning of our word for them; a more exact meaning would be *Pale Eyes.* The first white people our people saw looked very queer because Indians have no whites in their eyes: the part around the iris is more nearly coffee-colored.

Next to the eyes, my people were impressed by how much hair they had on their faces and bodies and how little of it they had on their heads. I have seen only one Indian—Chief Magoosh of the Lipans—who was bald. At first we wondered if he had been scalped, for it is possible for people to survive scalping. People with all that hair where it didn't belong were repulsive to us—they looked too much like bears.

At first there were few white people, and they were all going west; then, as wise old Nana knew, the lure of gold, discovered far to our west, brought them in hordes. Though most of them went on, some stayed to burrow into Mother Earth for the ore sacred to Ussen. Nana was right in thinking that gold was to bring about our extermination.

I have heard people say that self-preservation is the first law of life and that the perpetuation of the race is the second. That may be true of Indians. But getting something for nothing was the outstanding characteristic of White Eyes. We cared nothing for gold, yet it is thought that we are superstitious about it. That is not true. It is of little value, even for bullets. I've used both gold and silver ones, and neither is good. It is White Eyes who are superstitious.

It was because of the influx of the white people that Juh sought and held his stronghold in Mexico. He could not trust the cruel and treacherous White Eyes; neither could Nana nor Victorio. Mangas Coloradas had tried, and look what had happened to him. Mangas Coloradas was so eager to secure peace with White Eyes that he made the mistake of trusting their guarantee of safety and went alone into their camp, not far from the copper mine [Santa Rita Mine, near Silver City, New Mexico].

Both Victorio and Nana, each a Chihenne chief, pleaded with him not to go. Mangas Coloradas knew the danger well but wanted peace so badly that he risked his life. These soldiers had invaded his country not from the east, but from California. They had come with Colonel James H. Carleton. Part of his troops had stopped at Tucson. Part went north; and it was they Mangas Coloradas sought. Having invaders constantly coming in from the east was bad enough, but now they had started coming from the west.[4]

Mangas Coloradas had married one of his daughters to Cochise. They then joined forces and enlisted the support of others, including Victorio and Nana. When Mangas Coloradas learned that troops were starting east from Tucson, he determined to stop them at Apache Pass, since it had the only source of

4. David Ellis Conner, *Joseph Reddeford Walker and the Arizona Adventure,* Donald J. Berthrong and Odessa Davenport, eds. (Norman: University of Oklahoma Press, 1961), pp. 36–40.

water available to the soldiers on that route.[5] The Apaches prepared an ambush on the mountainsides overlooking the spring, and my father said that in some places they moved stones to afford shelter where there was little or none. Juh believed that they could easily have defeated the White Eyes had they not used terrible weapons new to the Indians: huge guns mounted on wheels. The Army officers reported later that they had killed many Apaches, but the Indians who participated in that battle denied this. The Apaches realized that they could not compete with cannon, so they withdrew without losing a man. Most of the Indians were armed only with bows and arrows.

Mangas Coloradas had received a very severe wound; his warriors carried him by horse to Janos, where there was a white Medicine Man skilled in healing wounds. Though the Apaches feared that the Medicine Man might kill their chief instead of curing him, they took the risk. They warned the Medicine Man that if Mangas Coloradas died they would kill every person in the village. He recovered.

It was to another part of Carleton's command that Mangas Coloradas went unarmed and alone in order to attempt to establish a permanent peace with them. He went into their camp under a promise of safety. His warriors lay hidden and watched for the safe return of their chief. As they had anticipated, Mangas Coloradas did not leave that place alive. Instead, the soldiers killed him and threw his body out of the camp, dug a shallow ditch, and buried him. That was not the worst: the next day they dug up his body, cut off his head, and boiled his head in a big black kettle. To an Apache the mutilation of the body is much worse than death, because the body must go through eternity in the mutilated condition. Little did White Eyes know what they were starting when they mutilated Mangas Coloradas. While there was little mutilation previously, it was nothing compared to what was to follow. I have seen these things done. Every Apache who lived through those terrible times saw them. I was only a child, but women and children were taken with the warriors; there was no other way of protecting them. But there was no attempt to protect the women and children from knowledge of what occurred. They saw mutilation in many forms.

"You seem to think that mutilation is worse than death, yet a dead body does not suffer from what is done to it. Was torture and mutilation done before death?"

"No. I never saw that. If it had been done I think I would have known. I know about those stories of torture. Most stories about torture were written to make our enemies believe that they might be treated so. Remember World War I? There were stories in circulation about the Germans cutting off the hands of Belgian children so that they would be useless and helpless. When the war ended, did anyone find those handless children? If so, I never read about it. And don't forget that not all the cruelty and mistreatment was done by the Apaches. I do not talk of the indignities my people suffered, and especially the women. I do not like to even think about them.

---

5. Dan L. Thrapp, *The Conquest of Apacheria* (Norman: University of Oklahoma Press, 1967), p. 20.

"Why are White Eyes so squeamish about scalping? It was White Eyes who started it. The Indians of the east and of the plains practiced it a little, but not until both Mexicans and White Eyes scalped some of our people did Apaches resort to it. And anyway, the dead feel nothing. After all, there's nothing to it. You just put your foot on a man's neck (we never scalped women), run your knife around the hairline, and peel the skin off."

"In an issue of *Harper's*," I told him, "there is an article by editor Bernard DeVoto in which he quotes from a letter written by his uncle who has visited Fort Sill. There he was shown a cell with a stone floor. Around the inside along the walls was a path two inches deep, reportedly made by Geronimo pacing around and around his cell. Was that true?"

"About as true as anything else one hears!"

I went on. "The article says that Geronimo had a blanket made of the scalps of white women. He complained about the difficulty of securing patches for repairing it."

As I completed my statement, Daklugie asked me to type a letter for him. The gist of Daklugie's letter was that Mr. DeVoto's esteemed relative was either a liar or a fool or both, as anyone should know.

I did not want to send the letter, but I had committed myself to Daklugie, who had signed the letter. Fortunately for me, it was unnecessary; news of Mr. DeVoto's death reached me before the letter was mailed.

CHAPTER 4

COCHISE

C ochise was chief of the Chokonen, called by the white people Chiricahua, but by us Chihuicahui. There was another band of Chokonen up along the Gila, whose territory extended into New Mexico and the Mogollons, and they were independent. Their chief, when Cochise was old, was the young Chihuahua. Though both military reports and the records of historians classify the Nednhi, Chihenne, and sometimes the Bedonkohe—as well as Cochise's band— as Chiricahua, from our point of view they are mistaken. To us, even today, the classification is objectionable. Only the bands of Cochise and Chihuahua were true Chiricahua.

At times bands joined forces, but not often. And there was no obligation to do so though mutual need sometimes occasioned it. If I understand these writers, white people seem incapable of understanding that these bands were separate, and my people could not comprehend that the villages in Mexico were not so.

Though I have no proof that Cochise was the descendant of Juan José, my people believed him to be. And they say that the Apaches did no scalping before his time. Juan José was a very good and intelligent Apache and had been educated in Mexican schools to become a priest. He made the mistake of befriending two white men, and they eventually betrayed his people and killed him. His tribe was near the copper mine [Santa Rita] when these people came to his camp and were received and treated kindly. The White Eyes said they had brought gifts, and when the people came to get them a new and terrible kind of weapon was fired into the group of women and children, and many were killed. Then one of them, the stranger, attempted to kill Juan José, who called on his white friend for help, but instead was shot by him.[1]

I learned both from my father and from Nana that the governor of Chihuahua offered a hundred dollars, American, for the scalp of an Apache man, fifty for that of a woman, and twenty-five for one of our children.[2] It was not in revenge for depredations made by Apaches that these men killed, but for

---

1. Thrapp, *Conquest*, pp. 10–12.

2. Ibid., p. 9.

the money offered. But they did not stop with Indians, for the government of Chihuahua paid for any scalp with long black hair.

Cochise knew of these things; he told my father of them. They were of common knowledge among our people and added, of course, to our distrust of all white men.

Cochise became chief of the Chiricahua by election when he was a very young man. That meant that his ability as a fighting man was well established and that he was respected by his people. But a chief's election was just the first step toward ruling his people. If challenged for his position, he must fight for it. Most necessary of all was the ability to rule them without creating antagonism and dissent. Moreover, the chief was responsible for not only their safety but for supplies of food, clothing, and weapons and for transportation. All of these things Cochise provided.

I do not know how long he had led the Chiricahua when [in 1858] he took some of the warriors who responded to his call, as did Mangas Coloradas, to avenge the deaths of their people. Though guards were left with the women and children in their camp near Kas-ki-yeh [north of Casas Grandes], Mexicans had attacked it. They had first killed the few men on guard and then murdered the women and children—including Geronimo's young wife, Alope, their three small children, and his mother.

The warriors were almost out of ammunition, and they knew that retaliation was impossible until the supply could be replenished. Mangas Coloradas ordered that they return to their homes, and they did so by forced march. Traveling by night was abhorrent to the Apaches, but when it was a matter of necessity they did it. In years to come Geronimo took ample revenge upon the Mexicans, and as long as he lived he hated them. I sat beside his bed in the hospital at Fort Sill the night Geronimo died and I know.

From the time my father was very young he had known Cochise. Till the great chief died they were friends. The Chiricahua chief was both physically and mentally superior to even the "superior people" [Apaches]. According to our standards he was a very handsome man. That meant primarily that he was of physical perfection, but we did not disregard pleasing features and appearance. Cochise had those, also.

Our people called him Cheis, which is sometimes interpreted as "oak." In a sense it does mean that, though it indicates the strength and quality of oak rather than the wood itself. Who added the prefix I do not know—perhaps some military officer. Our language is a difficult one, and it is not strange that mistakes have been made. I have never known but one white man who really spoke it well, and that was George Wratten.

Usually a chief chose as his *segundo* a warrior whom he wished to train as his successor. This Nana did for Kaytennae, as did my father for Ponce. I think that Taza, Cochise's son, must have been forty-five or fifty years younger than his father, and his son Naiche was younger still.[3] In 1874, Cochise was about seventy; I was about four and do not remember having seen him. Of those of us left, only Kanseah did. I do remember having his tepees pointed out to me, and I heard a man say that it was as much as anyone's life was worth to even

---

3. Naiche means mischievous. His daughter, Amelia, said "like meddling around trying to find something in the tepee." The literal meaning of the word is "digging."

23

Naiche, son of Cochise.   (Smithsonian Institution)

Haozinne, wife of Naiche.   (Smithsonian Institution)

look toward them. Because I was a very small child, I took this statement literally.

Taza was young, but Cochise groomed him for the position. The older son was given much knowledge denied to Naiche because their father did not want dissension between his sons. As were nearly all chiefs, Cochise was a Medicine Man. So was Taza, but Naiche was not. Faith in his Power does much for any man, and especially for a chief, for who can deny the influence of the supernatural?

Then, too, Taza was taught every trail, every source of water, and every secret cache known to his father.

It was when Naiche was a baby that an arrogant young officer did a stupid thing that antagonized Cochise and his Chiricahuas. That was one of our favorite stories. I've heard it about the campfire at night many, many times. A coyote [half-breed] of Mexican and Irish parents was stolen, allegedly by Cochise's men. His mother (Mexican) was living with a rancher named [John] Ward, not far from Fort Buchanan. This boy, later known as Mickey Free, was probably not of as much importance to Ward as were the cattle taken from him, but the man made complaint at Fort Buchanan, and Lt. George W. Bascom was sent to Apache Pass to recover the child from Cochise. He camped near the mail station where fresh horses were kept for incoming riders.

Cochise—with his wife (daughter of Mangas Coloradas), their infant son Naiche, and three of Cochise's close male relatives—came to the station. Ward, in the officer's camp, recognized Cochise and informed Bascom of his presence. Cochise denied that any of his band had done the kidnapping. Ward accused the chief of telling a lie. Cochise was very proud of making his word good, and no greater offense could have been offered to him. Apaches hated liars. If a man was known to be untruthful, even though he had witnessed a murder he could not testify. He could not carry a message from one band to another because the lives of both might depend upon delivery of the sender's exact words. Ward demanded pay for both boy and cattle. Cochise offered to investigate, determine the offenders, and help restore the child.

Unknown to the Apaches, soldiers surrounded the tent in which Bascom and the Apaches were talking. The young officer informed Cochise that he and his party were prisoners and would not be released until the boy was produced. With his knife, Cochise cut a slit in the tent and escaped. The chief summoned his warriors and captured some white men to exchange for his family. Despite the protestations of an experienced old sergeant, Bascom had the men he still held captive hanged, though he released Cochise's wife and child. Cochise dragged one captive to death and had the others hanged in retaliation.[4]

From that time on Cochise harassed the invaders, but I do not believe that he was guilty of all the atrocities attributed to him. Undoubtedly some of his young men ambushed wagon trains and stages without his even knowing of it. In general, my father knew much of his actions and they have been exaggerated by writers.

The mail was sent by pony express. Along the route from El Paso to Tucson there were stations, small fort-like buildings of adobe with high walls and a corral, where fresh mounts were kept for relays. Usually only one man lived in

---

4. Thrapp, *Conquest*, pp. 17–18. Thrapp indicates that Cochise killed his prisoners first.

a relay station and he provided for the riders who needed rest. Some of these were killed by the Apaches, some of whom were Cochise's men. But from Mesilla on the Rio Grande to Lordsburg and sometimes further west, Victorio took care of a lot of the westward-bound traffic.

The engagement in which Juh took the greatest pride occurred at about this time [May 1871]. This is when he killed Lieutenant Howard Cushing.[5] It began over in New Mexico. Some Mescaleros, with their families, left the Mescalero Apache Reservation to camp in the Guadalupes and hunt. (Yahnosha, one of Geronimo's warriors, knows of this.) They returned to find all at the camp dead except for two women. Cushing! Both of the survivors were wounded, each by a gunshot in the leg, but the bones were not broken. When the three Mescalero warriors had buried their dead, they found that their horses had been stolen by the soldiers. They had the problem of getting these wounded women to Mayhill, where their people were camped. Caje was a very strong man, and he volunteered to carry the lighter of the women on his back if the other two, by alternating, would care for the other. The three men toiled up the mountain, following the Peñasco; the route was uphill, and at times the women begged that they leave them, get horses, and return for them. But the danger was so great that the men refused. For that reason they did not abandon their rifles, blankets, nor what food they were carrying. That was a long, tiring trip, and nobody knows how many days it lasted; but they did finally bring those women home to their tribe. And from that time on, Caje was called Packs on his Back.

My father had heard much about this Lieutenant Cushing and his depredations in Arizona.[6] From the time Juh heard of what Cushing did to those people in the Guadalupes he was determined to kill that man. Finally he came into Arizona, and my father kept scouts out watching him. He murdered people up around Camp Grant and Globe, but it was a long time before my father had an opportunity to retaliate. Cushing went in pursuit of Apaches accused of attacking a wagon train and taking much plunder not far from Camp Grant. He attacked and killed many Indians at night. They were not of our band, but they were our brothers. Three times Juh's warriors had skirmishes with Cushing, once after having robbed a paymaster taking money to a camp.

It was out west of Tombstone that Juh finally maneuvered Cushing into an ambush. He lured the officer into a canyon by sending one of the women up the dry arroyo so that the soldiers might follow her. It took a brave woman to do that. I wish I could remember her name; she should be honored.

---

5. For an account of the Cushing fight—and the best description of Juh prior to this publication—see Dan L. Thrapp, *Juh: An Incredible Indian,* Southwestern Studies Monograph No. 39 (El Paso: Texas Western Press, University of Texas at El Paso, 1973). Thrapp closes with what may be the ultimate compliment: "With [Juh's death], the power of the Apaches to make massive war virtually died, for his successor, Geronimo, never became more than a minor guerrilla chieftain." Ibid., p. 39.

6. Bourke, *On the Border with Crook,* p. 29. Cushing "had killed more savages of the Apache tribe than any other officer or troop of the United States Army had done before or since." Cushing was in F Company, Third Cavalry, Bourke's Regiment. Donald N. Bentz, "Sword of Revenge," *Golden West* 8 (January 1972): 40–43.

My father was afraid that the old sergeant might warn Cushing, and he may have; but Cushing was so sure of himself and had killed so many Apaches that he must have thought he knew more than Ussen Himself. At any rate, he walked into the trap Juh set for him.

Other White Eyes were killed, too; I don't know how many. We weren't all the time counting the dead as the soldiers did. Juh wasn't much interested in the troops—just Cushing. And what good does all this counting do? You can't remember the number anyway. Look in the book. It might be right for once.

That payroll money? We were camped near Chihuahua when that paymaster was robbed. Juh and Chihuahua were close friends, but the latter did not want to be sent out to investigate that killing and robbing. To Chihuahua's relief, another scout went with the troops. They reported that the driver and the cavalry escort had been killed and the stage [ambulance] burned. The money was silver dollars, and they are heavy. They, too, were missing.

The guard took Juh to the fort [Fort Apache], and for four days and nights they grilled him. During that time he got neither food, water, nor sleep. An Apache can go without food for days, especially if he isn't exercising. But water and sleep he needs.

My father had great strength and endurance, but in spite of that he would doze at times. Always they waked him and, by turns, through an interpreter, they questioned him. They kept him awake and tormented him in an attempt to get him to admit that he had done this thing. He got so weak and sick that he was afraid he might admit something just to get to sleep; but he did not. They got no confession from Juh; so finally they turned him loose.

As Daklugie and the rest of his party were going out my door, I asked, "Where is it, Ace?"

"Where is what?"

"That money your father got."

"It's probably still in that cave where Juh put it. Now don't you go hunting for that money. You couldn't find it, and if you did, you'd just get yourself killed."

There was a twinkle in his eye when he said, after a long pause, "For a white woman, you're pretty smart."

DAKLUGIE

Tom Jeffords came to the country as a scout. I believe that for awhile he was a stage driver. He became superintendent of mails between Fort Bowie [Apache Pass] and Tucson and sometimes carried the mail himself. He had several riders killed and decided to make an attempt to meet Cochise and try to get his promise to permit the mail to go through.

There are stories of Jeffords having gone boldly to Cochise's stronghold alone. That is not as the Apaches know it. They say that Jeffords was captured by Cochise's scouts, but that he exhibited no fear. The Apaches were so impressed by his courage that instead of killing him they took him to Cochise. My father knew both Cochise and Jeffords well, and he believed the latter account to be true. He knew that the two became very close friends; and in time Juh and Jeffords did, too. Cochise had shut himself off from White Eyes since the Bascom affair, and accepting a white man as his friend was a tribute to a brave man. No greater praise could be given Jeffords than to say that he won the friendship of Cochise. It should be remembered that for about ten years Cochise had no contact with other white men except on very rare occasions and that those he did see seldom lived to tell it. Not even army officers were able to see Cochise. When he was in his stronghold nobody even attempted to effect an entrance. It was not, I think, as safe as was my father's in Mexico, but Cochise could have stood off a big force easily.

But the great chief knew that his men were being killed off and that he was practically a prisoner in his own land. It was Tom Jeffords who persuaded him to agree to a meeting with General Gordon Granger [in September 1871]. This meeting was held near Victorio's favorite camp site, Ojo Caliente.[7]

Cochise agreed to stay near Ojo Caliente and to draw food and blankets. The soldiers tried to persuade him to go to Washington and talk with the president, but he refused. He said that the officers sometimes kept their word, but that no Indian had ever known of the Great White Father doing so.

As Cochise had foreseen, the promises—especially as to the blankets—were not kept. His warriors were attacked by soldiers sent to keep the peace; and though in reality this country was his, he returned to the Chiricahua Mountains in what is now Arizona.

It was not long after this [late September 1872] that another General, O. O. Howard, was sent to the Apache country to attempt to secure peace with our people. General Howard had a meeting with Tom Jeffords and asked if he could arrange a meeting with Cochise. Jeffords thought that he might, provided that the general would go to the stronghold of the Chiricahua chief. Howard agreed to do that and Jeffords got two guides, Chee (Chie) and Ponce. Chee was the nephew of Cochise and one of his highly trusted men. Ponce was said to be the son of Mangas Coloradas. I think that is true. He was my

---

7. Captain Henry Stuart Turrill gave the following account of that meeting. "He (Cochise) was rather tall, over six feet, with broad shoulders, and impressed one as a wonderfully strong man, of much endurance, accustomed to command and to expect instant and implicit obedience. . . . Clad in a buckskin hunting shirt belted in at the waist with a Navajo garter, leggings and moccasins of the same material, the only bit of finery about him [Cochise] was a new and gaudy Mexico poncho, which was draped about him with a careless grace; his face, while at rest, was perfectly impassive. I wish it were within my power to give, as I heard it, this finest bit of Indian oratory that I ever listened to." Turrill's account quotes the speech, which is reprinted here in part.

". . . At last in my youth came the white man, under your people. Under the counsel of my father, who had for a very long time been the head of the Apaches, they were received with friendship. Soon their numbers increaased and many passed through the country. I received favors from your people and did all that I could to return them, and we lived in peace. At last, your soldiers did me a very great wrong [the Bascom incident], and I and my people went to war with them. . . . I have destroyed many of your people, but where I have destroyed one white man, many have come to his place; where an Indian has been killed, there have been none to come in his place, so that the great people that welcomed you with acts of kindness to this land are now but a feeble band that fly before your soldiers as the deer before the hunter. . . . I have come to you not from my love for you or for your great father in Washington, or from any regard for him or his wishes, but as a conquered chief to try to save alive the few people that still remain to me. I am the last of my family. . . ."

Turrill's account was given in his speech "A Vanished Race of Aboriginal Founders," before the New York Society of Founders and Patriots of America, February 14, 1907.

father's *segundo,* and Juh should have known.

These two did guide Jeffords and General Howard to the stronghold. They went by way of Stein's Pass and on to the mountains where Cochise was waiting. Juh was at the stronghold when they arrived.

With Jeffords interpreting, Cochise and General Howard made a treaty, a verbal one, in which Cochise was to have a reservation in the southeast corner of Arizona. It was about fifty-five miles square and included within its boundaries Apache Pass. His people were to be provided with food and clothing, blankets, and other necessities so long as they kept the peace.[8]

I remember seeing Tom Jeffords. But until I read it, I had not known that he was the agent of the reservation first for Cochise and then for Juh. I learned that Cochise had submitted to reservation life on condition that Jeffords be his agent and that he was to have no interference from military or civilians. I do not know that these things were written, but I do know that they were promised. If a man's word is not good, of what value is his writing?

It was, I believe, in 1872 that Cochise's reservation was established. Cochise was old, and even then he was a sick man. Otherwise Juh thought that he would not have agreed to be confined on a reservation. Two years later, Cochise died.[9]

Some time previously, Cochise talked with Juh regarding the next chief. Taza was young [about thirty-three], perhaps too young to have the responsibility of the tribe; but the chief wanted very much that his son succeed him. It took a man, a strong man, to lead the Chiricahua. Cochise knew that well. He asked that Juh give him his word that he would support his elder son for the position. Juh did so; but he reminded Cochise that, not being a member of the tribe, he could not have a vote in the election. Juh doubted that his influence had much to do with the result, but he thought that Taza received the chieftainship primarily because it was the wish of Cochise. Taza was not the man his father had been, but he had been trained by Cochise. And, though it may be unintelligible to White Eyes, he was a Medicine Man. The Chiricahua were by no means easily controlled. Supernatural Power is more potent than is any human force, and who can combat it? Perhaps Taza was a wise choice, but he did not live long enough to be tested.

As Cochise had requested, his burial place was kept secret; only a few of his warriors and Tom Jeffords knew where his body was laid.

The council met and elected Taza.

"Had Cochise no other children than Taza and Naiche?"

"Two daughters. Both came to this [the Mescalero Apache] reservation."

---

8. Howard, O. O., "The Indian, General Howard's Mission," *Washington Daily Evening Chronicle,* November 10, 1872, pp. 1–4. "[Cochise] answered that he was as much in favor of peace as anybody; that he, himself, had not been out to do mischief since his visit to Cañada (the Cañada Alamosa) where he met General Granger and Colonel Pope the year before." Also see Frank C. Lockwood, *The Apache Indians* (New York: The Macmillan Co., 1938), pp. 113–22; and Thrapp, *Conquest,* p. 144.

9. The order creating the San Carlos Division of the White Mountain Reservation was signed in Washington on December 14, 1872. Those lands were returned to the public domain by an executive order signed October 30, 1876.

"No other sons?"

"No other sons. A claimant to being the son of Taza has come to this reservation. The Naiches—Christian, Amelia, Barney, and Hazel—thought him an imposter. None of the older people had ever heard of Taza's son, and none believed that he had one."

CHAPTER 5

JUH

J uh came and went as he wished, but he stayed sometimes for months on Cochise's reservation. Sometimes Geronimo was with us, sometimes not. If Chihuahua happened to be there our families visited or sometimes camped close together. I knew there was something mysterious about Chihuahua, though I did not understand just what it implied. I did realize that, though he was a scout, the chief was respected. At that time, the Apache scouts had not been used by the army against their own people, but even then those who wore the red headband (the insignia of a scout) were regarded with suspicion by many Apaches.

Though I never remember having seen Cochise, I often did see Red Beard [Tom Jeffords]. Every Apache child knew that he and the chief were great friends, though few could understand why Cochise would condescend to acknowledge a White Eye as brother. I could understand even less why my father, who hated white people worse even than I do, could like this man.

I have read this book [*Blood Brother*].[1] You say that a novel need not tell the truth. That I understand, but the writer did know a good bit about my people. Why, then, did he invent a blood brother rite? He must have invented it, for in all my life I never heard of such a ceremony. And why did he have a Medicine Man perform a marriage ceremony? Marriage is something in the heart, not words mumbled by some Medicine Man. Our people gave a four-day feast and at the end of it, at sunset, the marriage ceremony was finished. The young couple's parents had officially announced their marriage; and to the Apaches it was sacred and, except in unusual cases, permanent. There was no marriage rite such as that described in that book.

I saw Captain Jeffords several times. And I knew that he got supplies for Cochise, and, after Taza went to San Carlos, for my father. But not until much later did I know that he was our agent.

So long as Cochise lived, the Chihenne, Bedonkohe, and Nednhi visited back and forth with the Chiricahua, and we went to the homes of the others at

---

1. Elliott Arnold, *Blood Brother* (New York: Duell, Sloan and Pearce, c1950); a novel, but it is valuable for historical and anthropological authenticity except for a few details.

times. Chihuahua came often before he became a scout, and for a while he lived on the reservation. He had several children [five], and until his older daughter was half grown the children of both families were put through a strenuous program of exercises to make them strong and able to take care of themselves. The daughter (later named Ramona at Carlisle) was a beautiful child and a remarkable rider. The Apaches used to say that she could ride anything on four feet.

Our people roamed, following the ripening of foods, so that they could provide a year's supply. They killed deer when venison was at its best, late in the fall. They baked mescal in the spring when the blossom stalk was pushing through the leaves. And they gathered acorns and mesquite beans. They cached supplies in places near water all along the route from Cochise's reservation to Juh's, and sometimes in many other strategic spots.

When we traveled we followed the ridges, usually the high ones, and fortunately for us mountains run generally north and south instead of east and west. Even so, at times we had to cross a plain from one chain to another; and if on the warpath, as we often were, we usually did it at night. If forced to leave one camp without supplies, we knew that at the next stop we had them—not only food, but sometimes blankets, cooking pots, weapons, and ammunition. When we found an overhanging cliff under which there was honey, we spread a hide on the ground, shot masses of comb loose with arrows, and, when it fell on the hides, squeezed the honey out into buckskin bags. It was the only sweet we had except dried fruit.

We either burned the thorns from the fruit of the cacti or got them off by rolling them in the sand. Dried, the cacti were good and nourishing food. But of all cacti we liked the fruit of the giant one, the sahuara, best.

From the older men I learned of other tribes who lived far toward the rising sun. They were fighting men, but not so good as ours. They scalped their enemies. Because of that some of these tribes did not let their hair grow long as Apaches do. We gloried in our long, luxuriant hair, but other tribes cut at least part of theirs off. Long hair all over one's head was an expression of courage and a dare to one's enemies. Of course, when there was a death in the family our women cut their hair short, but it soon grew back. When I went to Carlisle, my hair came down to my knees. I braided it and fastened it under my belt to prevent its catching on brush and thorns.

My wise old grandfather, Mahco, had married his daughters and sisters to chiefs of neighboring tribes, so that if he were attacked he would have relatives to fight for him. Mangas Coloradas, too, did that. And that is what the white rulers over in Europe did. That I learned at Carlisle, where I spent twelve years. They, too, did it so that when they had a war they could get help from their relatives.

When we moved, the coverings of our tepees were rolled and carried on horses or mules. I do not remember having seen lodge poles taken along; I think that because we kept to the mountains new ones were easily obtainable. We had a saying that the Indian follows the mountains and the white man the streams.

My people prepared places where the helpless, the aged, or the wounded, and sometimes mothers of tiny babies, could be left for a time. These were not abandoned to die, as has been written, but they were left to enable them to live. Nor were they left alone. It was the ambition of every warrior to have the honor and responsibility of acting as defender and provider of food for the helpless. So boys were placed with them in carefully concealed places near such supplies.

After the death of Cochise, my father continued to come and go as he pleased, sometimes with Geronimo. Both knew that under Taza's leadership things were not going as they had when his father was living. They knew, too, that it was not by any means the fault of the young chief, who had difficult problems which at that time nobody on the reservation really understood.

Food and other supplies promised to Cochise were not furnished as promised. Some were sent to us, but not sufficient to supply our needs. Years later I learned that Jeffords had bought food on credit and charged it to the government, and when that amount was paid he was refused more credit. Jeffords, from his own funds, bought food for us. That he could not do indefinitely, so he granted permission for some of the warriors to leave the reservation to hunt. Some of them got drunk and people were killed. It was partly because of those depredations that the young agent at San Carlos, John Clum, got permission to take the people from Cochise's reservation to the one on the Gila [San Carlos]. That was a terrible place, the worst in all our vast territory.

When ordered to make the move, the Apaches on the Verde had very few horses, and nearly all had to make the trip on foot. That was a rough and mountainous trail, where there was no game and little water. Driven like cattle by the military, the people started, carrying what they could of their meager possessions. There was one old woman who was crippled and unable to walk. Her husband had no horses, but he was determined to get her to San Carlos alive. He got a large basket, such as we use for storing grain, cut holes in one side, and placed her in it with her feet extending through the openings. He carried her on his back over that long trail, up steep cliffs, through little streams, through forest and desert—until the food gave out. The soldiers sent ahead for more, and the young man, John Clum, sent some to the starving Indians. If he had not, I doubt that his unfortunate victims would have lived to finish that terrible trip. But the majority of them did live through it to be settled in that desolate place in the midst of their enemies.

After the agreement was reached by Cochise and Howard, Jeffords was the agent on the Chiricahua Reservation. Jeffords was to have sole jurisdiction over us. Neither soldiers, civilians, nor government officials were to enter the reservation without Jeffords's permission.

The cavalry had not troubled those at Cochise's reservation, but Juh learned that at San Carlos the agent and the military officers had much trouble, not so much with the Indians but between themselves. John Clum was determined to bring all of the Apaches to his miserable reservation, perhaps for personal fame, perhaps for a bigger salary, or both.

In 1876 Clum came to the Chiricahua Reservation and ordered Taza to take his tribe, and everybody on the reservation, to San Carlos. The young chief attempted to persuade all of us to conform, but many of the Chiricahua were as determined as were the Nednhi and Bedonkohe not to do so. What right had this arrogant young man to tell them what to do? Councils were held. About a third of all on the reservation decided to go with Taza to San Carlos. The others elected my father as their chief and left for Mexico.

I well remember that trip to our old stronghold. For years Juh harried the

State of Chihuahua. At times we returned to our old haunts north of the border, going as far as Ojo Caliente [Warm Springs, New Mexico]. That was Victorio's favorite campsite, as it had been that of Mangas Coloradas. There the spring that bubbled from the foot of Tall Mountain [San Mateo Peak] had cut a channel through the front range and found its way through the Canada Alamosa to the Rio Grande. This gorge ran diagonally through the ridge, and in places it was very narrow. The Mexicans at Monticello, with whom Victorio was on good terms, could drive a cart through the channel and three horsemen could ride abreast through it. The water was seldom more than a foot deep anywhere in it.

Along the rim of the cliffs the Chihenne kept stones for rolling down on an enemy; and if attacked from one side, the women and children waded through to the other, knowing themselves to be comparatively safe.

By executive order President Grant had promised that reservation, including the famous warm spring, to Victorio and his band forever. It was a very small part of the land belonging to the Warm Springs Apaches, but so eager was Victorio for peace that he agreed to live on it peacefully. Loco, leader of another of the Warm Springs bands, realized as had Cochise that his people were already the *Indeh*, doomed even if they had secured peace. Reluctantly he acquiesced. But Nana, *segundo* of Victorio, and much older, preferred death to imprisonment and slavery on a reservation.

Juh had accepted the chieftainship not only of his own band, but of all others who refused to accompany Taza to San Carlos. He talked with the warriors. He told them that he could offer them nothing but hardship and death. He reminded them that no Apache was subject to forced military service; he told them that men impressed as fighters against their will are slaves. And he reminded them of the rigid rules governing the Apache when on the warpath, laws binding on every warrior. He pictured the worst aspects of the life they must lead in the future, that of the *Indeh*. As he saw it they must choose between death from heat, starvation, and degradation at San Carlos and a wild, free life in Mexico—short, perhaps, but free. Hadn't they always been a free people, roaming where they wished and living as Ussen had promised they should, free and in their own land?

If any wished to undergo degradation and slavery, let him speak, Juh invited. He urged that they consult with each other and with their families before making a decision. Let them remember that if they took this step they would be hunted like wild animals by the troops of both the United States and Mexico.

Every man decided to stay with Juh. They were good fighting men, forced by desperation to take this stand. The Mexicans had invaded their country, killed their deer, and driven them from their old homes. Where were they to get food? Did not their enemies have great herds of horses and cattle? Why should they go hungry with abundance of food in their own land?

For other supplies all they need do was watch the pack trains coming from Chihuahua City and, when one left, help themselves. Didn't the Mexicans owe them a livelihood?

And they did just that. Even before a pack train left Chihuahua City Juh knew both the contents and the destination. There were many times that he took an entire pack train without firing a shot.

Juh and Geronimo could always cross into Arizona, and, until the soldiers in the United States made an arrangement with the governors of Chihuahua and Sonora allowing cross-border pursuit, evasion was made easy by crossing back and forth.

Both Juh and Geronimo spoke some Spanish. There were few of our men who did not know a little of it. Many were called by Mexican names (such as Geronimo—from Jerome). But that came later. Meanwhile, he was known by his Apache name which I do not speak.[2]

Juh was so successful in his raiding that the governor of Chihuahua wished to meet with him and have a talk. My father wanted peace as badly as did the Mexicans. He learned that not only the governor but *El Presidente* wanted to see him. So he chose the place of meeting carefully. It was on a mountainside with not one but several means of escape in case of treachery. He demanded that only five men come to his rendezvous and that they come unarmed. He, too, chose five men, all of whom he knew were dependable and could not be bluffed.

And they sat in council. Juh awaited their speaking. It was slow in coming but at last the subject was broached by Díaz [Porfirio Díaz, President of Mexico]. He was very diplomatic in his approach. He asked the help of my father and his band in controlling depredations frequently occurring in Chihuahua, and especially along the trails used for trading. Juh solemnly told him that he would take precautions for the defense of his Apaches. That was not quite the meaning the president intended to convey. Mexican traders as well as many travelers had been ambushed, robbed, and killed. Horses, mules, and cattle had been stolen.

"Our land has been invaded and our deer killed off," replied my father. "Our country has been taken from the Indians and their game destroyed until my people are hungry. Why should my women and children starve with great herds grazing on their land? What are we to do?"

Díaz said nothing for a while. Then he spoke rapidly to Terrazas [Luis Terrazas, Governor of Chihuahua and owner of a huge spread of land and cattle] so rapidly that Juh did not understand all that he said. Finally he turned to my father and said, "If you are hungry, kill cattle. Do not kill mules and horses for meat, but take cattle. Do not destroy the cows, but kill the males. Then there will be increase for all."

My father considered and agreed to this. He sensed that there were more complaints to come and waited.

The president finally said, "This scalping—do not permit it."

"Who started the scalping?" Juh demanded. "Didn't your *gobernador* offer one hundred pesos for the scalps of Apache men, fifty for women, and twenty-five for children?[3] And didn't he get more hair from your own people than from mine? Aren't scalps bringing bounty every day in your City of Mules? If you will stop your people from taking hair, I'll stop mine; but not until you do."

"I want peace," said Díaz, "and will so order it."

---

2. Goth-lyka (Daklugie's preference as to spelling), meaning "To Yawn" or "He Who Yawns." Others spelled it Gothlay.

3. See Thrapp, *Conquest*, p. 9.

"I want peace, too," said Juh. "And you'd better do more than give orders. You'd better see that they are obeyed."

And that ended the conference.

"I'm unable to find a record of your father's having ever met with Díaz," I told Daklugie. "Or Terrazas, either. There may be such accounts in Spanish, of course."

"Juh met with Díaz not only once; there were two or three meetings. I was a child, but I was with him when the one back on the mountain occurred. My two brothers, Delzhinne and Daklegon, sat with them in council at the others."

"Have you any idea as to why no records were made of these meetings?"

Daklugie indulged in one of his infrequent smiles. "Do you think 'El Presidente' of Mexico liked having to crawl to an ignorant 'savage'? And that is how he described my father. Do you think he would have wanted Mexico to know that he had lost face by meeting with an Apache?"[4]

---

4. To an Apache, losing face is an extremely humiliating experience.

CHAPTER 6

SAN CARLOS

DAKLUGIE

S an Carlos! That was the worst place in all the great territory stolen from the Apaches. If anybody had ever lived there permanently, no Apache knew of it. Where there is no grass there is no game. Nearly all of the vegetation was catci; and though in season a little cactus fruit was produced, the rest of the year food was lacking. The heat was terrible. The insects were terrible. The water was terrible. What there was in the sluggish river was brackish and warm. Pools alongside the channel afforded places for insects to hatch. They served, as I know now, as breeding places for clouds of mosquitoes. Insects and rattlesnakes seemed to thrive there; and no White Eye could possibly fear and dislike snakes more than do Apaches. There were also tarantulas, Gila monsters, and centipedes.

At times it was so hot that I am sure a thermometer would have registered well above 120 degrees.

At San Carlos, for the first time within the memory of any of my people, the Apaches experienced the shaking sickness. Our Medicine Men knew of herbs that would reduce bodily temperature but had nothing effective against the strange and weakening attacks that caused people to alternately suffer from heat and cold. At times attacks came that caused people with high temperatures to feel cold and to shake uncontrollably while covered with blankets. And this sickness sometimes lasted for weeks unless the patient died.[1]

At one time, troops had been stationed at old Camp Goodwin, but living at that place was such an ordeal that it was abandoned.[2] It was so unfit for the officers and troops that it was considered a good place for the Apaches—a good place for them to die.

When I was about four years old, John P. Clum became agent at the San Carlos reservation [August 8, 1874].

Clum was an arrogant young man, hardly out of baby grass, but very ambitious not only for power, but also for money. Juh said that this boy thought

---

1. Ball, *Victorio*, p. 28, gives an Apache account of the suffering from mosquitoes and malaria.

2. Thomas Cruse, *Apache Days and After*, (Caldwell, Ida.: The Caxton Printers, Ltd., 1941), p. 31.

that he knew more than Ussen Himself and that he could defy not only the Indians but the army.

Eskiminzin, and the few survivors of his band after the massacre at Camp Grant, came to San Carlos after Clum arranged their transfer and he and Clum were on good terms. And there were the San Carlos Indians too, who were nomadic and, though they sometimes went to that place during the winter, could not be said to live there. They had to do so after Clum came, however. I think that there must have been more than three thousand people in that abominable place. Clum seemed to have been determined to force all of the Apaches to live there under his jurisdiction. Within a year he had moved those at Camp Verde to San Carlos. These he had brought to gratify his ambition and greed. Those on the Verde River had been living peacefully and producing their own food and clothing. They were doing well at Camp Verde until Clum persuaded the government to let him take them to San Carlos.

There were others, too, whom he had brought along from Date Creek, though they and the Camp Verde Indians were unfriendly. A little later he brought in some Coyoteros and White Mountain Apaches from Camp Apache [later Fort Apache] and put them, too, on his reservation.

In 1876, Clum ordered Taza to leave the reservation given to Cochise and his people forever and go to San Carlos. There was dissension on the reservation (there was dissatisfaction with Taza), and I think not more than a third of the people decided to accompany their young chief who so meekly took orders from Clum. Among them were Naiche, his younger brother. About three hundred, perhaps a few more, obeyed.

Those who refused to go, among whom were many Chiricahuas, held a council and elected Juh as their chief. I think that there were about seven hundred of them. They felt fairly secure where they were, for if troops were sent against them they could easily cross the line into Mexico and the military could not follow them.

Still Clum was not satisfied; it was his intention to force all of the Apaches to come under his rule. There were still Victorio's and Loco's bands, and he didn't stop until he had them too.[3]

Geronimo, with perhaps close to a hundred, including women and children, had stolen horses in Mexico and had gone to Ojo Caliente. Part of the warriors with him were my father's. Neither he nor Victorio were camped within three miles of the famous spring. Across the little stream that flowed from it was located the large adobe building used for the agency. When Clum sent word that the leaders were to come in to the agency with their men, all complied. Geronimo, Ponce, Gordo (Old Fatty), Francisco, and several others—thirteen in all, I believe—were arrested, shackled, and put into a corral.

I read the account written by Clum's son of the "capture" of Geronimo at Ojo Caliente.[4] I wonder if that man ever thought that the Apaches might be asked to give their side of that affair. Probably not. It has taken nearly a hundred years for that and even now our story may not be believed. You don't suppose that Woodworth Clum, or perhaps his father, had been reading Rider

---

3. There were other bands of Apaches still on their own reservations: the Mescaleros, the Jicarillas, and the Tontos. See Lockwood, *Apache Indians,* pp. 144–48.

4. Clum, Woodworth, *Apache Agent* (Boston: Houghton Mifflin Co., 1936).

Haggard? Or maybe of the capture of Satanta [Kiowa chief]?

And that scene that he described with the police filing out of the old fort that had also served as the agency—well it just didn't happen; especially the part about Clum's taking the rifle from Geronimo. Would any Indian have told that it had happened? Why not? Geronimo was envied by many; he had enemies among his own people. Had it been true, they would have known it and they would have told it. There were many who blamed him for their being made prisoners of war twenty-seven years, him and Nana. The truth of the matter is that they envied them because they had the fighting spirit and courage to hold out longer than the rest.

Clum did take several of the leaders to San Carlos in chains; among them were Geronimo, Old Fatty (Gordo), and Ponce. I believe that there were eight of them in all. They did not include Victorio and Loco. The shackled ones were hauled off toward the reservation in wagons.

One of my father's men who had gone with Geronimo started immediately for Juh.

Juh, with about ten warriors, started to San Carlos and, upon arriving there, stopped at the *ranchería* of Eskiminzin. My father knew him well and knew of the terrible massacre at old Camp Grant which few of Eskiminzin's band survived. Clum and Eskiminzin had met and Eskiminzin had been friendly to him. Eskiminzin was shrewd enough and was sufficiently concerned for the remnant of his band that he professed great admiration and friendship for Clum.[5]

When Juh reported that Clum was on his way from Ojo Caliente with Geronimo and the others in chains, Eskiminzin agreed with my father that the time to act had come. He warned, however, that they must not be too hasty or they might defeat their purpose.

They put scouts about the agency and on the route they expected Clum to use. When informed that the miserable band was approaching San Carlos, Juh and Eskiminzin rode to the agency and watched them come in. The wretched captives, mostly women and children, came straggling in on foot, carrying their meager possessions. The chiefs, still shackled, were in wagons. Juh noticed the absence of most of the men and knew that if they had left Ojo Caliente with the rest they had slipped away en route.

When the wagon in which Geronimo was hauled passed near my father, neither gave any sign of recognition; but my uncle knew why Juh was there and that he would get help.

Clum made a tribal judge of Victorio, but little good that did the agent, for the Chief of the Chihenne was both unhappy and angry over the injustice done him and hated Clum none the less for his giving him the recognition.

Just how long Geronimo and the rest were kept in the guardhouse, I do not know; but they came in the middle of May and Clum resigned the first of July. Juh said that it was about a half-moon before he and Eskiminzin went to Clum. My father hated talking with White Eyes and Eskiminzin was the

---

5. En route to his post at San Carlos, Clum stopped at Camp Grant and found Eskiminzin in chains there. He immediately arranged for the transfer of Eskiminzin and his Aravaipa Apache band to San Carlos. See Clum, *Apache Agent*, pp. 129–30. Daklugie went on to state that Clum was the butt of ridicule among the Apaches—at least to some extent. Because of his strutting they dubbed him Turkey Gobbler. A common expression of warning among them was, "Look out; he's dragging his wings."

spokesman. "We have come," he said, "to demand that you turn the prisoners loose. We won't stand for this any longer." Clum sputtered and strutted about, dragging his wings while attempting to put them off. But Eskiminzin said, "You will do it, and you'll do it right now or we'll have every Apache on this reservation on your back."

Clum led the way to the guardhouse and ordered the door to be unlocked and the prisoners released. Within a short time their shackles were removed and Geronimo and the others were free.[6] There probably is no record of my father's and Eskiminzin's securing the release of the prisoners. Clum was a braggart and would not have written anything reflecting upon his record and especially since he had been defied by the Apaches.[7] He strutted about with his wing feathers dragging and boasted that he did not need any help from the military and that he could control all the Apaches in Arizona single-handed.[8]

Eskiminzin's threat may have been a factor in Clum's decision to quit. The agent was also disgruntled because he found a military inspector at San Carlos when he got back from Ojo Caliente, and the refusal of the government to give him a bigger salary no doubt had its effect. At any rate, he left.

Why Victorio's and Loco's Chihenne stayed as long as they did during the heat of that terrible summer, no Apache knows. But on the first of September they left. They wandered northeast by way of Horse Springs in New Mexico until they got close to Fort Wingate. (That was old Fort Wingate; it was moved close to Gallup later.) Victorio surrendered to the officer there and was permitted to return to Ojo Caliente.

They were again ordered to leave it [thirteen months later] and orders were also given that any Apaches (men and boys old enough to bear arms) found off a reservation were to be shot without giving them a chance to surrender.

Victorio pled with the young officer [Captain Bennett] to be permitted to stay on his reservation. He begged that his people might keep that small bit of the land that had been theirs. He said that they infinitely preferred quick and merciful death to the lingering one that awaited them at San Carlos. He warned the sympathetic young officer that, though it might be possible for him to take the helpless women and children, the warriors would never go. Then he and his men bolted [October 1878] and they made good Victorio's word.

Loco's band, servile things that they were, tamely submitted to the degradation of the move. Loco had been a brave and fearless warrior; perhaps his spirit was broken. When that happens, a man is finished. Nearly all men occupy about the same amount of space, with some larger than others, but the real difference in them is determined by the fighting spirit within them. Loco's explanation was that the struggle was useless, and that he did not want his people exterminated. That was true. Nobody wanted that. And so far as I know, nobody was critical of Loco. The great Cochise had felt the same way. All of us knew that we were doomed, but some preferred death to slavery and imprisonment.

---

6. Lockwood, *Apache Indians,* p. 223.

7. I find no mention of an attempt by Juh and Eskiminzin to go to Clum and even ask that the prisoners be released; but all of the older Apaches whom I interviewed believed that it was done as Daklugie told it.

8. See Lockwood, *Apache Indians,* p. 224.

My father and Noche stayed until winter. Knowing that they could leave any time they wished, they just took their time. Occasionally they made raids, sometimes to return to the reservation. In winter, life wasn't nearly so terrible as in summer.

Once Juh captured a wagon train, a small one, down near Stein's Peak. There were only three or four wagons. He followed it for days so that he might attack when it was crossing a deep arroyo where he could ambush it. There were only men with those wagons, and no women or children. Juh took the ammunition belts and the shirts from the bodies. On one man they found a belt under his clothing. My father slit it open with his knife and found nothing in it but some long pieces of green paper with a man's picture on them. As he threw them into the bushes, Ponce asked, "What do you suppose they carry that stuff for?"

"To wipe their noses, I guess."

They thought that was funny, for we didn't get colds.

We were living near Bylas [now Geronimo], the sub-agency on the San Carlos Reservation. There was a white man there, one who had been long with the Indians and understood them. Our people called him Ne-go-li, but his white name was Brown. The officers got a report that the Indians of Juh's band were trying to make trouble. Three troops of cavalry came to Bylas and stopped near my father's camp. I do not know whether or not this is on record in the military reports, but I remember it well and know that it happened. All the Indians within miles joined Juh. They did nothing but just come and camp. They were forbidden to have guns and ammunition, but they brought them anyway.

The officer requested a council and my father granted it. When they were seated the officer said, "You'll kill all my troops."

"Not unless they attack us," said Juh. "If they do, we certainly will."

Captain Brown had advised Juh to stay where he was, offer no resistance, and above all prevent the Apaches from doing anything for which they could be accused of starting trouble. He told my father that the army was there to prevent trouble, not to start it. That was a new idea to the Apaches, and especially to Juh.

My father called together his most trusted men, those who had often faced death with him and who had never uttered one word of complaint, regardless of their losses. He reminded them that he had warned them that he could offer them nothing but fighting and death; that he had told them exactly what to expect; and that there was still time, if they wished, to avoid what might come, and without dishonor. Then he asked them to keep the young hotheads, eager to prove themselves in conflict, from firing a shot and precipitating a fight. They promised that they could and would do just that; and they did.

The cavalry had come to force Juh to leave, but it was the military that left.

Daklugie was so extreme in his denunciation of John Philip Clum that it seemed expedient to include some statements and opinions in conflict with his. Having no desire to act as judge or jury, but wishing to present the evidence both pro and con, I reminded him that Kaywaykla had pronounced Clum to have been "the best civilian agent ever stationed at San Carlos." Daklugie

41

replied, "Kaywaykla is a good man and an honest one. But he is receiving a pension from the government for his military service at Fort Sill and he is too intelligent to jeopardize it. I, too, am getting a pension, for we were in the same troop. But that is not going to keep me from telling exactly what I think of Clum."[9]

---

9. For other accounts of the San Carlos experience, see, in addition to Lockwood, *Apache Indians* and Clum, *Apache Agent;* Thrapp, *Conquest;* and John Upton Terrell, *Apache Chronicle* (New York: World Publ. Co., 1972).

CHAPTER 7

CHIHUAHUA

EUGENE CHIHUAHUA

These things I've been telling you for fifteen years are true. I tell you only what I have either experienced or learned from my father or Nana or someone else who knew of which he spoke. You may not find some of my accounts in books; and that may be because the history of my people has been written from reports made by our enemies. Do writers of history never question military reports? Don't they know that the officers told only the White Eye side of the conflict? And if you write ours, do you think you can get it printed? Don't the people who make books realize that there is always more than one side to everything that happens?

I was with Chihuahua and well remember many things that happened before we surrendered and were sent to Florida, St. Augustine.

Chihuahua was the name given my father by the Mexicans; he had an Apache one, of course, but it is not spoken.[1] He became chief of a band of the Chiricahuas when he was a very young man—not of Cochise's band, but of a smaller one. My father's territory was north of Cochise's and was very large. It extended from west of where Safford is now far into New Mexico and the Mogollons. It included the canyon of the blue, and that is the part my father liked best, for it afforded good hunting, good grass, water, wood, and places for ambush. We visited back and forth with Cochise and his people; it was in that stronghold that I first knew Daklugie and Juh's family. Our fathers had been friends for a long time; we camped near the stronghold and had our training together, boys and girls both, for we were small then.

Chihuahua was not a subchief to Cochise. The Chokonen [Chiricahua] had no subchiefs. If he wished, he joined other chiefs, as he had Cochise, but there was no obligation to do so. It was entirely up to him and his warriors whether or not they fought.

We had no clans, either. If those books say so they are mistaken. And what was that other word you said, *gan?* What's a *gan?* I never heard of one. Am I a *gan?* You know very well that I'm a Medicine Man. We didn't have any *gans.*

---

1. Daklugie, Kaywaykla, and Kanseah all said that some names are never to be spoken, though their Spanish or English equivalents may be.

Chihuahua. (Smithsonian Institution)

Ulzanna. (Smithsonian Institution)

And the chieftainship was not hereditary; chiefs were elected. Sometimes sons succeeded their fathers, but not unless they were elected by the warriors as Taza was after Cochise died. Any warrior could qualify for the job, but nobody held it without being elected.

The qualifications for the chieftainship? You think that being a good fighter was all? You just didn't know the old Apache. Every warrior could fight. Anything will fight when cornered, even a rabbit. I don't speak English so well and it is hard for me to put into your words what I mean. I think in Apache. To be a chief a warrior has to be able to draw and hold men. He has to lead those men, not drive them.

This thing that makes a man a great chief—Daklugie's father, Juh, had it. He told his men that he had nothing to offer them but death; but they followed him. They were loyal to him and they would have fought and died, if necessary, for him; but they, as well as Juh, were fighting for their freedom, their families, and their homeland. And their self-respect. Chihuahua and Juh led their men and didn't hide up on some mountain with field glasses like your officers did.

Ulzanna was my father's older brother, and as brave as Chihuahua; but when the election was held it was my father who got the votes. Ulzanna had no resentment toward Chihuahua but became his *segundo* and was a faithful and loyal one.[2]

I did many things as a boy, not all of them smart.

I remember that once I watched the chiefs making Medicine. They rolled tobacco in oak leaves and smoked. My father blew smoke toward the east first, then south, west, and north; then up and down. I watched where he put that tobacco; I thought it must be good because I was not permitted to have any. (Apaches never smoked pipes, so when you read of it, you'll know that the men who made that book probably never saw an Apache.) Well, I slipped out some of that tobacco and smoked it. My mother thought I was going to die, but my father smelled my breath and knew exactly what had happened. And he laughed while I lay there sick.

When I began using blunt wooden arrows for practice, once my cousin [Ulzanna's son] and I shot it at a mark on a tree. My arrow bounced back and struck me on the forehead. See that scar? It knocked me out for awhile and I was afraid to go back to the tepee because I knew I would catch it. When we went, my mother looked closely at the cut but didn't ask any questions. Children had to take some bumps and cuts if they expected to live.

One of my favorite stories was about my maternal grandmother, whose Apache name is not spoken but whose Mexican name was Francesca.

My grandmother was in late middle age when she and Siki (Kaywaykla's cousin) were captured by Mexicans. They got two other young women, too, and sold all into slavery at Chihuahua.

They were taken to Mexico City and bought by a man who had a small maguey farm inside the north wall of the city. He made my grandmother housekeeper and called her Francesca. The three young women worked in the

2. Johlsannie, Richard, son of Ulzana, told of this incident almost identically.

Maguey field. Every day slaves cut the big thorny leaves from a plant with a machete and scooped out the center so that the sap would collect in the hollow. Every day they siphoned out a gallon or more into a goatskin bag. It was a sweet, slightly greenish liquid that, after standing eighteen hours, thickened and looked like buttermilk. This *pulque* was used instead of drinking water because it did not make people sick.

It was five or six years before Francesca contrived the escape of the four. They were wearing the clothes of the peon, and each had a blanket. Without a knife they dared not leave. Francesca finally obtained one.

Their owners sometimes permitted them to attend church. There was one just outside the north gate and she decided to make the start at dusk, as many people were going to the service. They joined them, but instead of entering the building, they walked on into the darkness.

They traveled by night and hid by day. They lived on fruit of the nopal [prickly pear] which was ripe at the time. They knew that as they went north they would find the fruit ripening all the way to Ojo Caliente, their old home.

From the nearby mountains they knew that they were approaching Arizona and they felt that once they were across the border they would be safe. When they reached a small, tree-lined stream, they decided to rest a day or two.

They tied saplings together to form the poles of a tepee and twined leafy branches among them to form a shelter. Though it did not afford any real protection, they felt safer with something overhead. And before going to sleep they collected clubs and stones for use if attacked.

Francesca carried her butcher knife in a scabbard attached to her belt, underneath her long skirt. By lifting her overblouse she could reach it.

Wrapped in their blankets they lay in the brush arbor. It was chilly and Francesca pulled a heavy fold of her blanket tightly about her neck. Then she heard a noise. Something was prowling about the arbor, something heavy. A lion perhaps? Then an animal crashed through the flimsy wall and seized Francesca by the throat. It was the largest lion the women had ever seen! It clawed her scalp partly from her head and tore her face. Then it fastened its fangs in her shoulder and began to drag her out of the shelter. The blanket had protected her throat, and as she tried to grasp her knife the others beat the lion's head with stones and clubs. Finally Francesca reached her knife. She stabbed the lion repeatedly until the knife reached its heart. The others got her back into the arbor and risked the danger of lighting a fire. Her scalp was hanging from her head. They replaced it and bound it with buckskin thongs. They had no herbs but they used a remedy of which they had heard. Two women returned to the dead lion and got sputum, which they rubbed into the wounds. When morning came they cut nopal leaves, burned the thorns, split them, and applied the fleshy side to Francesca's wounds.

It was three or four weeks before she could resume the long walk to Ojo Caliente.

These dances [of the Mountain Spirits] that I have, they belong to Francesca; they are in her honor. She taught them to me. After we went to Florida we danced them in her honor. She used to sing them too. She did not like for anyone to see her scarred face and she kept a scarf over it. When we got to Fort Sill she said that she would not sing for that dance anymore. She sang it the last time just before she died. But before that she married Geronimo.

Apaches like brave women, but she was so scarred that nobody would marry her. Geronimo said that she deserved a good husband because she was the bravest of all Apache women. So he married her. He had plenty of wives, anyway. How many? Oh, I don't know. Plenty.

I remember, once when we were camped down near Fort Bowie, that Mexican troops, under a flag of truce, came to exchange captive Apaches for slaves we had taken from them. My father treated them well and let them go through the camp, though he suspected that they were just spying on his force. They looked around and then said they'd take him and me because we were not Apaches. That may have been because our skins were lighter than those of most Apaches. And Chihuahua's eyes were a sort of gray, sometimes almost blue.[3]

Chihuahua was mad. He was about to order them out of camp when an old woman came to them and told them in Mexican that she had been with his mother when Chihuahua was born and knew that he was an *Indio puro*. And another told them that she knew that I, too, was all Apache. It was lucky for those Mexican troops that they didn't try to take us.

Had I made the four raids preparatory to becoming a warrior before we went to Florida? I hadn't done much else since I could remember. Wherever my father and his warriors went their women and children were taken. We had been chased and attacked; we had fought and run; we had ambushed and been ambushed. Boys my age had received far more training in real fighting than that given in times of peace. But I had not yet been admitted to the status of a warrior as Daklugie had. He is two or three years older.

While at Fort Apache, my father was enlisted as a scout; at that time being a scout was not a disgrace, for they had not been used against their own people. When they were, those who stayed with the army were considered traitors. But even when Chihuahua was enlisted it was a doubtful step. My father was the only chief who became a scout. Chato? That coyote! [This, to the Apaches was a term of contempt; it denoted not only the concept of one of mixed blood, but the traits of a coyote.] Chato, the traitor and liar, never was a chief.[4]

My father didn't like living on a reservation; being a scout let him get away from time to time. And he got a rifle and an ammunition belt—and some clothes. (He wore only the shirt and jacket.) Best of all, my father could leave his wife and children and know that they would be protected.

---

3. I asked Daklugie if he had heard of a report that Victorio was a Mexican—stolen when a child from a big *hacienda* in Chihuahua. "Oh, yes; every Apache, I think, heard that. But nobody believed that story; at least no Apache I knew did. Victorio was a Chihenne. Do you think the Warm Springs would have chosen a Mexican as their chief?" Though it is conjecture, it seems far more probable that if any Apache may have been of Mexican descent it was Chihuahua. Chihuahua's skin was light and his eyes blue-gray; he had a flare for clothes and was polished. But his absolute fearlessness, his defiance of the army, and his fighting ability were typically Apache.

4. Eve Ball, "The Apache Scouts; a Chiricahua Appraisal," *Arizona and the West* 7 (Winter 1965): 327.

One time the war department sent some money, in silver dollars, to Fort Apache to pay the soldiers. Before it got to the fort the ambulance was attacked, the cavalry escort killed, and the money stolen. When it didn't come on time, troops, with my father as chief of scouts, were sent out to look for it. They found that everybody had been killed and that everything that could be burned had been, so that only a few pieces of iron were to be found.

But there were tracks, moccasin tracks. But they were not Chiricahua moccasins. These had no tab turning back over the toes as ours do. Perhaps some White Eyes had worn moccasins to put the blame on the Indians. Chihuahua knew who had made those tracks, but he kept still. He took the troops on the trail leading east. The scouts went out, fanwise, afoot, ahead of the troops on horses, to do the trailing.

He followed that trail a long way, through Las Cruces and east to the water where Alamogordo is now (for there was no town then). From there the trail led to Fort Kow-yu-ni-to [Stanton] where, my father said, he saw the biggest tribe of Indians that he ever saw together [Mescaleros]; they were camped on a little stream [the Bonito] above the fort. That was all Mescalero country and the people were drawing rations from a wagon.

From there he followed that trail into the Sacramentos, away high to where they could look out over the broad, low, flat plain [the Tularosa Basin]. La Luz was there then, but it was only a few little houses. The officer told four soldiers and four Apache scouts to get some food from a nearby store, and they started out, with the scouts, as usual, leading the way. Somebody shot at them, but the scouts went on and motioned for the soldiers to follow. The soldiers told the merchant what they needed and paid for it. With packs they all started back up the mountain. Toward morning they saw a fire at the foot of that high mountain; and then they saw other fires and they knew that Apaches were camping down at the foot.

One of the scouts asked my father how they were to get down to those fires. They must have been almost a mile below, and Chihuahua did not know. He had never been there before and he did not know whether there might be a trail—but he was sure that there was one. And the next day he found it. It was a very dangerous one, going almost straight down. The scouts took the lead, each followed by a horse. Everybody walked, even the captain. He had field glasses and he saw the band crossing over toward the little mountains, where they stopped for water. From there they headed for the Organs.

My father told the officer, "You better stay back and let us use your horses."

"Why?"

"We'll call to the Indians and they won't shoot us, maybe. We might know them."

Years later, some men were talking about that time over at the office one day. Paul Guydelkon, one of my father's scouts, was talking and Kaytennae was listening. He was laughing. Kaytennae had been with Nana that day [it was Nana's band spotted by Chihuahua at the foot of the mountain], but he had stopped to kill some Mexicans coming up from Paso del Norte on the old trail that ran along the west side of the basin, just at the foot of the Organs. He saw these men in a buckboard. His horse was tired out and he needed a fresh one.

But he saw that the scouts were after him, and in his hurry he did not wait to unsaddle his spent horse. He just cut one of the team loose from the buckboard. But it balked. He saw that he couldn't make it go, so he got off and hid in an arroyo. By that time it was getting dark. The scouts knew all the time where he was, but they pretended they couldn't find him. They let him get away and catch up with Nana.

When they got back to the troops, all were out of water. All day and all night they didn't have any. They went on southeast; it was just like crossing a desert. They kept going, looking all over for water until night came again. The horses were pawing and digging for water but could not find any. My father told the captain to turn the horses loose. They started off and the men went after them with canteens. Horses can smell water a long way and will go to it. They began to walk fast, then to trot and nicker. Pretty soon the horses were running. They came to a little lake, a tiny one. The soldiers followed and began to shoot to let the others know that they had found water. They drank, filled their canteens, and started back. The scouts warned them not to drink but a very little at first, for they might get sick if they drank too much. When they met the troops, those White Eyes fought over that water. When they got to the little lake, they lay down and drank until a scout pulled them back by their feet. Then they were mad. They threw that water on themselves and they rolled in it, acting *loco*. They camped there two days. I don't know where it was unless it was Hueco Tanks. I think it was Hueco, because they went on from there to Fort Bliss.

The officer put the scouts on the train and sent them to Fort Thomas, on the San Carlos Reservation, because they didn't have any horses. The troops did have horses, so they rode. That Fort Thomas was a hot, bad place. There was no water fit to drink, no wood, no game, no shade; there was nothing but stickers and insects. It was the worst place in all the land claimed by the Apaches. Daklugie says that they put us there to die. I think so, too, when I think of it.

My father went to Fort Apache where his family was. Then they tried to put all of us, all tribes, on that San Carlos Reservation. We didn't know what the army was going to do with us. They made the ones at Camp Verde go first; then Cochise's band; and then the Warm Springs Apaches. They put us all there with a lot of other tribes that we didn't like.

For awhile we lived at Turkey Creek. Kaytennae and Nana lived right across the creek from the tent where Britton [Lt. Britton Davis] stayed. But my father had his camp away off, close to where Geronimo lived. And so did Mangus. (Daklugie was with Mangus part of the time after Juh's death, and part of the time with Geronimo.) Kaywaykla lived with his mother; Nana also lived nearby.

All this time the scouts had no idea that they would ever have to be used against their own people.

While at Turkey Creek, Chihuahua found that Britton Davis had spies reporting to his tent at night, and one of them was a woman. All of this was bad, but that was very bad. And Chihuahua listened outside Davis's tent and heard Chato and Mickey Free telling the Fat Boy [Davis] that Chihuahua was plotting to kill him. He heard many more lies and knew that they were trying to get him sent to that island like Kaytennae was. After the arrest of Kaytennae, the other chiefs on Turkey Creek fully expected that they, too, someday would be sent to Alcatraz. All believed that Chato and Mickey Free were responsible for Kaytennae's being sent.[5]

My father doesn't sneak around in the dark. The next day he went to Davis's tent, took off all his army things, and threw them down in the corner. And he told Davis, "Now, give them to your spies. I won't scout any longer."

"But you're in the army; you can't quit," said Davis.

"I am quit," replied Chihuahua, and went to his camp and sat down to wait for them to come and take him to be hanged. But they didn't. Maybe Davis was beginning to find out what liars Chato and Mickey Free were. And not long after, Davis quit the army too and went down to Mexico to be manager of a big ranch down there, the Corralitos. Apaches think he knew he had been fooled by Chato. But they liked Davis, because Chato can fool smart people, even Apaches. If Chato was good for anything it was telling lies. That is not quite fair, either; he was a good fighter.

I was just a little boy then. Much more happened, but not until later. I was maybe thirteen or fourteen when my father surrendered and we were sent to Florida.[6]

DAKLUGIE

Chihuahua led the famous raid in which Judge and Mrs. McComas were killed between Lordsburg and Silver City. In history that is known as Chato's raid. It was not led by Chato, though he convinced Britton Davis that he had been the leader. Chihuahua was chief of this band, and it was Chihuahua's raid.

Chato was ambitious to become a chief and, though not descended from one, he was eligible. There is no denying that he was a brave man and a good fighter. He was intelligent, too—intelligent enough to know that he had no chance to succeed Cochise. Victorio had been reported killed at Tres Castillos, though the truth is that he and his little handful of men fought until they had fired their last bullet and the great Warm Springs chief had committed suicide by falling on his own knife. Kaytennae, who gave the body hasty burial, told me this.

Chato had gone to Victorio's band only to find that Nana, old and lame but a superb fighting man, was runner-up for the chieftainship. After the death of Victorio, Nana selected Kaytennae as his *segundo*. Chato could not supplant him, and he must have been desperate when he went to Chihuahua's band. There, too, he was frustrated; for Chihuahua's brother, Ulzanna, older than the chief, was his chosen successor.

When Chihuahua summoned his council to consider a raid into Arizona and New Mexico, Chato, uninvited, joined them. Nana, honored guest, dis-

---

5. Kaytennae was arrested in the spring of 1884, tried by his peers, and sentenced to three years imprisonment at Alcatraz, where he served eighteen months. Davis describes the incident, including warnings in the night by an Apache man and a woman, who informed him that Kaytennae was hosting a tizwin drunk and plotting Davis's death. See Davis, *Truth*, pp. 124–30.

6. Eugene had been about thirteen, he said, when his father and his band of Chiricahua surrendered and were shipped to Florida. If Eugene's estimate of his age was approximately correct, he was ninety when interviewed. In appearance, mental alertness, and dignified bearing he appeared to be many years younger. For Eugene could have been correctly described as "every inch a chief."

approved of the insolence of Chato but knew that every warrior was needed and that Chato, in spite of his faults, was brave and would fight. At the war dance that followed, Chato, without waiting for Chief Chihuahua to call his name, arose and joined the dancers, thereby signifying his desire to become a member of this raiding party. So did Tzoe (Yellow Wolf or Coyote), a White Mountain Apache married to a Chiricahua. These two warriors were permitted to go. Just how many warriors were included I do not know; as many as twenty-six are sometimes said to have been in the raiding party.

I was not with these men, but I knew intimately nearly all of them. Their story is that Chato was with the advance guard when it unexpectedly encountered Judge McComas, his wife, and their small son, Charlie, in a buckboard. Chihuahua was in the rear. The front guard killed the man, but did not mutilate his body, because he exhibited great bravery by jumping from the buckboard with his rifle in order to hold the warriors off so that his wife and child might escape. They killed him and also Mrs. McComas. Charlie, a little boy about six or seven, was brought back to the rest of the raiders by Chato.

There have been many different accounts of the fate of Charlie McComas. I saw that child once, but I do not know what family had taken him and was rearing him to be a warrior. I was not present when the Mexicans attacked that camp, but in the escape Charlie was killed.

Of this I can be sure. When an Apache family adopted a child, it gave it the same care and protection it did its own. Nobody among them would have killed that child. During that attack Apache children, too, lost their lives. That happened after my father's death.

In July of 1960, Ruey Darrow, daughter of Sam Haozous, called at my home. She said that so long as some members of her family lived, they did not want this account about Charlie McComas published, but that now she could tell the story. It is as follows.

Ruey Darrow

When the attack was made on their camp, people scattered and attempted to escape through the dense chaparral. Carrying a baby in a *tsach* on her back, her mother ran with her grandmother who led a small child. In the underbrush they stumbled upon the body of the McComas child. He had been struck, possibly by a stray bullet, and was obviously dying. The grandmother, who had seen many deaths, said that at best he could not live more than a few minutes. Nevertheless, she attempted to lift and carry the boy. Her mother, who in addition to the baby was carrying a rifle, attempted to relieve her mother of the burden. Between them they tried to carry the wounded child until they heard, crashing through the brush, soldiers coming very close. Further attempts to save the dying boy could result only in their being killed and also the children they protected.

They decided that their obligation to the living came first, and they laid the unconscious child on the ground. The grandmother thought that he had stopped breathing but the mother was not sure, and so long as she lived she reproached herself for having abandoned him without knowing. It was her wish that this occurrence not be made known during her life.

CHAPTER 8

CIBICU

DAKLUGIE

I was at Cibicu. I was just a boy and did not see much that occurred except at the camp of Noche-del-klinne, and not all of that. But my father, who participated, witnessed much more than I. And I've had reports from several who saw different occurrences of that massacre—and that is exactly what it was. I have not forgotten that terrible thing; I can never forget it. This is the Apache side of the story.

Of all encounters Apaches had with their enemies I believe that Cibicu is least understood by white people. Writers, using reports of military officers, believed that Noche-del-klinne was inciting the Indians to an uprising. He was attempting to do exactly the opposite; he was doing his best to *prevent* one. He did not invent the Ghost Dance, but neither did Wovoka. Wovoka revived it after it had fallen into disuse. Apache Medicine Men had used it to remind us that Ussen had promised to rid the country of our enemies in His own way and at His own time. That seems to have been unintelligible both to military officers and to historians.

After they turned cannon loose on us at Apache Pass, my people were certain that they were doomed. That was before I was born but my father was there. Mangas Coloradas, Cochise, Victorio, Nana, and other leaders of the Apaches joined forces to stop part of Carleton's California column coming from the West. The Indians were confident of stopping the soldiers bound for the spring until cannons were fired at them. They had known for a long time that the *Indah* outnumbered them by tremendous odds, that they had better weapons, and that they seemed to have unlimited supplies of necessities furnished them, while the Indians were compelled to rustle everything they obtained.

We were on the Apache reservation at San Carlos. In early summer [of 1881], my father learned that the Medicine Man, Noche-del-klinne, was teaching a dance to those who went to him. The participants formed concentric circles with the Medicine Man in the center. Those who could get passes from the agent [J. C. Tiffany] attended it, and when they returned they reported to their chiefs. More and more went, many of them without obtaining passes.

The agent sent for the Prophet, as he was called, to come in and report to him, but Noche-del-klinne ignored the order. Tiffany was the worst agent San Carlos ever had. My people hated him because he was selling the food sent by the government for their use, so that they were compelled to live barely above starvation level. Though he and Colonel Eugene A. Carr at Fort Apache were not on good terms, the officer had orders to furnish assistance if requested to do so by the agent. Carr, too, summoned the Medicine Man to the fort, but again he did not obey.

Then Sam Bowman, interpreter at Fort Apache, was sent to spy on the Indians. Bowman was greatly alarmed and talked of getting out of the service; he thought the rites meant trouble.

Carr, too, became alarmed and decided to go out with a big force to arrest Noche-del-klinne.

At first Juh paid little attention to reports that came to him of the Ghost Dance. But when he heard that great numbers of people were attending, he began to suspect that the Medicine Man might be able to influence the warriors *against* fighting. He knew that Loco would favor nonresistance; but he knew also that if attacked Loco would fight. Still, among Loco's band were a few like Betzinez who would oppose all fighting.[1] Juh did not anticipate that his Nednhi could be swayed to becoming disloyal to him, for he knew their dependability. But when he learned that Chihuahua, Nana, Kaytennae, and more of the real fighting men of the Apaches had gone to the gatherings, he decided to investigate.

The camp had been moved from Carriso Creek to the Cibicu, about forty-five miles northwest of Fort Apache. It was there that our family, with that of Geronimo, camped on the stream not far from the lodge and brush arbor of Noche-del-klinne. Naiche, chief of the Chiricahua, who had succeeded his brother, Taza, had gone ahead with Nana and Kaytennae.

Although none of my father's band joined in the Ghost Dance at first, they were impressed by the Medicine Man and convinced of his sincerity. After watching and listening, and after talking with Nana, Juh and Geronimo accepted his teachings.

That old fire-eater, Nana, told him that he and his *segundo*, Kaytennae, had felt as Juh did until after joining in the dance. Nana recounted that first experience. After performing until almost morning, Noche-del-klinne had terminated the rite, and, accompanied by a few dancers, he started up an incline in the misty light. Before he reached the crest, he stopped and lifted his arms in prayer. Dimly those with him saw the bodies of three great chiefs—Mangas Coloradas, Cochise, and Victorio—rise slowly from the earth.[2] When they had emerged and were visible to their knees, they slowly sank back. Nana said that

---

1. Betzinez was not regarded as a fighting man by the Apaches interviewed. They ridiculed the idea of his ever having done any fighting, and also the title of his book. This may be partially owing to private differences between him and the warrior-type Apaches. They had the utmost contempt for those who would not fight to protect their tribe and their families.

2. James Mooney states: "In June of 1881 he announced to his people that he would bring back from the dead two chiefs who had been killed a few months before. . . . Accordingly Nakai daklinne [Noche-del-klinne] began his prayers and ceremonies, and the dance was kept up steadily at his camp on Cibicu Creek until August. . . ." Mooney, "The Ghost Dance Religion and the Sioux Outbreak of 1890," U.S. Bureau of American Ethnology, *14th Annual Report, 1892–1893*, p. 206.

he had seen this and the word of Nana was not to be questioned.

Juh and Geronimo were greatly impressed. In the past each had held war dances only for the sake of custom; such dances were not needed to incite their warriors to fighting pitch. (Getting an Apache to fight is easy; it is preventing him from fighting that is difficult.) Geronimo told me shortly before he died that he had never understood why he and Juh could have been so easily influenced by that Medicine Man; but he had convinced them that the Apaches should leave revenge to Ussen.

Sergeant Mose, an Indian scout from Fort Apache, came out to Cibicu to warn the Medicine Man that troops were coming to arrest him. The Apaches knew that because Colonel Eugene Asa Carr's orders had not been obeyed they might expect reprisals. So when a scout for the Apaches reported the coming of troops, Sanchez rode out to meet them and to learn the size of the military force. A few others rode with him.

Noche-del-klinne sat quietly in his brush arbor awaiting the soldiers. When told that he was under arrest, the Medicine Man agreed quietly to go in, but asked for three or four days' time to remain at Cibicu so that he might complete the healing of a patient he was treating. Carr said that he must go immediately, and the Medicine Man sent his son for his horse. His wife prepared food for him, both to eat there and to carry with him. I watched from the hillside. We could see Noche-del-klinne eating and we could hear the scouts urging him to hurry. He finished his meal and, surrounded by scouts, left with Colonel Carr and about half of the soldiers. His wife and son followed. Even then I knew how our people detested the scouts who were working for our enemies.

As they rode off many warriors followed—among them Geronimo, Juh, Chihuahua, and Naiche, who had gone along to assure that there would be no treachery. The other half of the soldiers stayed back with us. Two young officers also stayed back; one of them, Lieutenant Cruse, was the officer in charge of the Apache scouts. The second group also left after a while. What happened after the troops got out of sight I learned from warriors who witnessed the murder of the Medicine Man.

The first division of soldiers made camp for the night and were soon joined by the rest. The Apaches did not go close until they saw the Medicine Man in a sort of barricade made of supplies carried by the soldiers. Although the Indians were doing nothing but watching, an officer called to them to leave. This they refused to do.

Suddenly a shot was fired—then many. My father did not know who fired the first shot, but once the fight started, the Apaches got into it. Men were killed on both sides. While the shooting went on, Lozen, sister of Victorio, and Sanchez swooped down on the horse herd and drove a bunch off. They wanted especially the ammunition mules, for they had not yet been unloaded. They got some, but I do not know just how many. I do know that they got a good supply of ammunition. I learned later that Carr and Cruse denied losing any. If they believed that, they were badly mistaken.

Noche-del-klinne was hit. Kanseah told me that when the Medicine Man's wife attempted to reach her husband, she also was shot, as was his son, arriving with his horse. When the wounded Noche-del-klinne got up on hands and knees and tried to crawl to his wife's body, a soldier killed him with an axe.

The bugle call for sleep was blown, but Juh did not believe the soldiers would spend the night in that camp. They stayed long enough to dig graves inside a tent and bury their dead. Some warriors stayed to make sure that the troops would not attack our *ranchería*. Apaches seldom fight at night unless they are attacked.

My father learned later that Carr reported an attack on Fort Apache the next day. If so, it was done by somebody other than our forces. Any sniper could have fired into that fort because it was not walled.

That fall some of the scouts under Lieutenant Thomas Cruse, whom the Apaches called "Nantan Greenhorn" because of his ignorance of the Apaches, were court-martialed for mutiny. They were convicted and some were sent to Alcatraz. Three of these—Dandy Jim, Dead Shot, and Skippy—were sentenced to be hanged.[3] Somebody higher in rank than Colonel Carr must have ordered that court-martial. I never knew an Indian who attended it, but from my experience as a scout at Fort Sill, after my return from Carlisle, I doubt that any but officers were permitted to testify. Would any judge have taken the word of an enlisted man? Would any enlisted man, if permitted to testify, have dared to tell the truth? Carr and Cruse must have needed an alibi to have placed the blame for starting the shooting on the scouts.

Years later, I learned that General [Orlando] Willcox ordered an investigation of the actions of both Carr and Cruse. That was an indication that he was not satisfied that they had acted wisely. It hinged, I think, upon the advisability of Carr's having divided his forces. The reported mutiny of Cruse's scouts also reflected upon his ability as an officer. The Apaches knew that the officers had difficulty in maintaining discipline, and that there were many deserters among the enlisted men. Did that influence the judge and jury to return a verdict of the commanding officer's being guilty of no more than an error in judgment?

General George Crook was also dissatisfied. When he returned to the Southwest he immediately began meeting with the Indians to get their side of the story. Captain John Bourke says, "There was a coincidence of sentiment among all people whose opinion was worthy of consideration, that the blame did not rest with the Indians. . . . No one had heard the Apache's story, and no one seemed to care whether they had a story or not."

Cruse himself tells of his dread of meeting with the general, and of his relief when he got off without as severe a reprimand as he expected. Did even Crook feel the necessity of upholding the young officer?

I enlisted as a scout at Fort Sill and am now receiving a pension for military service. I learned something of military procedures there, and I did not get it from books. But as books came out, those dealing with the Apache campaigns especially, I bought and read them. I learned of officers who got promotions, as Carr and Cruse did—both became brigadier generals—for just such questionable procedures as these men practiced. I am sure that some officers earned and deserved their promotions. I also understand that at trying times such as existed at Cibicu, higher officers must protect those in their command.

---

3. Thrapp, *Conquest*, p. 123. Dead Shot's wife, too, was said to have hanged herself. Daklugie said that because she loved her husband very much she wished to go through eternity with him, even though it might have meant a deformed (elongated) neck.

CHAPTER 9

THE APACHE RELIGION

DAKLUGIE

Without at least a little understanding of our religion it is difficult to comprehend what motivates the Apache. My people have never liked to talk about our religion, partly because they anticipate ridicule, but more because it is the only thing we possess of which the whites have not robbed us. Instead of trying to force it upon all whom we contact, as your people seem to be obligated to do, we preserve it for ourselves and our children. It is the one thing of which we cannot be deprived. You already know much about it. You might as well get it right.

We do not talk it; we believe and practice it. And so long as one of the old Apaches lives, he will continue to do that. Moreover, there is a definite trend among the young men to revive both the customs and observances of the old religion. It is not often organized, as in the Native American Church, but it exists in the hearts of my people.

The Apaches have always believed in one God, whose name is Ussen. The word means Creator of Life. He put the Apache on the land which He had created for us, and He laid down certain laws which we were to obey. These are very much like your Ten Commandments, with the exception of our not being required to observe the Sabbath. Of that we knew nothing.

That part of your religion as told in the Old Testament I think I understand. It seems to me much like what I was taught as a child. But there are some things in the New Testament that I doubt many Apaches understand—like your queer three-headed God. And we make no pretense of loving our enemies as you say you do. Have you ever known anybody who really did that? I have not. Ussen did not command that of the Apaches. He did tell them that they were not to fight unless attacked, but if that should happen he did not forbid them to defend themselves.

Your keeping your God locked up in a trap all week and letting him out an hour or two on Sunday is also strange. To us, instead of being our prisoner, Ussen is free and everywhere, always with us. We obey Him. You say you do, but your people use profane language.[1] We have too much respect to use it; in

---

1. During this conversation Daklugie accused me of swearing—I had said that the way Apaches

our language there is not any profanity.

Apaches believe that the spirits of bad people, very bad ones such as those who betray their tribe, cannot go directly to the Happy Place, but must be reincarnated in the body of a bear—sometimes more than once—before being admitted to our Happy Place, which you call Heaven. If an Apache kills a bear he might be murdering one of his relatives or friends. He may not even touch the hide, and eating the flesh of one is unthinkable.

Our people believe in communication with their loved ones who have gone before them. If they speak in Apache the name of one who is dead, they summon the ghost of that person to them. This person might be hunting, or gambling, or sleeping, and he may not want to come, but he must. In our Happy Place we live just as we do here. Gambling is one of our favorite pastimes, so why not gamble in the Cloud Land?

In our Happy Place, we are to have bodies such as we have on earth, but they will never wear out, tire, or know hunger. Your Book says that in your Heaven there will be no marrying nor giving in marriage. That may be the white man's idea of Paradise, but it isn't Mr. Apache's.

Our Happy Place is much like our reservation, or like Juh's was in the Sierra Madre: trees, grass, game, one's friends and relatives, safety, and a happy life. We have no concept of your queer ideas of Hell. We thought that even White Eyes might eventually be admitted to the Happy Place. Of course that'll never be done now, not with Geronimo there. If even one got in, the first thing we'd know surveyors would be invading and farmers stringing barbed wire over the place.

We have been discussing dead Indians, some by their Apache names. That may mean that those people are in this room right now. I do not know that this is so, but it could be. Before you got that television, you could not see people nor hear the sounds they made, but they were there. You were just unable to see or hear them. Apaches are so in regard to the ghosts of their dead. They are heard sometimes, but I do not know of anyone now who sees them. Kanseah hears them occasionally. Ussen speaks to him as people on a telephone do to you. You people no longer believe in God, and that is why He does not speak to you. If you had the faith of the old Apaches, you could hear Him.

Eugene Chihuahua, too, sometimes hears the voice of his father, the chief, who died in Oklahoma. When Chihuahua attends the white man's church, he sometimes loses the ability to hear his father and he is distressed. But when he makes Medicine and heals the sick, or when he sings for the dances, his father returns to him. I think these spirits guide the Apaches and are something like the guardian angels of the Christians.

With us religion is a personal thing; we have neither an organization nor a minister to intercede for us with Ussen, but we pray directly to Him and He answers us. Not always; sometimes we ask for things He does not think best for us. Each morning as the sun first appears on the horizon, the father of the family stands at the door of his tepee, always facing the east, and with eyes and

---

were treated was damnable. It is true that the Apaches do not swear—in Apache. They swear in Spanish and English.

arms uplifted prays to Ussen—not to the sun, but to Ussen. But he does not attempt to tell Ussen how to run the world as your preachers do. Ussen had the intelligence to make Mother Earth and everything on the earth, but the White Eyes do not realize that He also has the intelligence to manage what He has made. They have to tell Him how. We do not. We pray primarily for courage to meet what must come, and we pray to thank Him for what has been given us.

To us the worst crime of which a man can be guilty is betraying his people. For that he could be banished, and to Apaches that is worse punishment than death. To be driven from one's family, tribe, and country is terrible. Next to being a traitor and being banished, the worst punishment to us is being shut up in a cage [prison]. No Apache was ever guilty of that cruelty.

It is a four-day journey to the Happy Place, and if a chief or warrior dies his war horse is killed for his use on the trip. For those who have no mount, there is a Death Pony. As the body looks when buried, so it looks throughout eternity. So it must be dressed in its best, and every possession that cannot be buried with it must be destroyed. Because the dead leave no property, Apaches have not been killed by their sons to get their possessions.

Some of my people have knowledge of their death drawing near. I do not know how or why this happens, but many times I have known it to occur. Of course, all people of advanced age know that they cannot live long, because that is the way of all life. But sometimes this also comes to the young and the strong.

Ceremonials for the Maidens are the most sacred of all our religious rites, and in the old days they were observed individually when the girl reached maturity. No matter what the situation the rite was held, although sometimes the observance had to be shorter than the customary four days. Once, when my people left San Carlos for their dash for Mexico, they got into the Stein's Peak range and stopped. They knew that the cavalry was after them, but when one of the mothers announced that her daughter had reached maturity, the band had to observe the puberty rite. Women were baking mescal when we were attacked from the north and west. Unknown to us, another troop, led by Forsyth, was coming in from the east to cut us off from Mexico. We had a terrible time there in order to cover the flight of the women. That was just before the battle with the Mexican troops in the arroyo.

Though revenge was part of our philosophy, Apaches believed that eventually Ussen would take vengeance upon our enemies. He would send some catastrophe of nature, such as an earthquake, to destroy human life on this continent. There would be no necessity for any Indian to raise a hand when Ussen deemed the time right to kill. The catastrophe might kill our people, too, but in four days they would be raised from the dead to again possess their land. The buffalo would return to the plains and the deer to the mountains, and life would be as it was before the coming of the White Eyes. And this would last forever. It has not happened yet, but there is yet time. Now we think this might be brought about by an atomic bomb. That would get rid of the White Eyes for us.

I am often told that White Eyes regard us as brothers; but how many of them treat us as brothers? We make no pretensions of brotherhood with white people, for we are a religious and moral folk. In times of death or other tragedy, our people, regardless of church affiliation, usually revert to the solace of our old religion. It comforts us and we see no reason why we should not.

Both Kaywaykla and Chihuahua, his brother-in-law, were members of the Reformed Church for many years. Each acted as interpreter for his minister's sermons. After we came here from Fort Sill, Chihuahua sang in the choir. At that time, by custom, a son-in-law and his mother-in-law were forbidden to see each other. To prevent this a curtain was hung down the central aisle of the church. The women sat on one side, the men on the other. Chihuahua's wife [Viola Massai] had died, so he had no mother-in-law and could be seated with the choir where he could see the women. He had a magnificent voice; musicians said that if trained he could have sung grand opera. He led the singing and got much pleasure from doing so. He often sang solos in our language, and especially at funerals. He translated hymns into our language himself.

Many Apaches, both young and old, are active members of some Christian church. They can do this because they see no conflicts in the two faiths. I have often acted as interpreter to ministers, and I have attended churches for many years, partly because Ramona wanted to go and partly because of my love and respect for Father Albert.[2] Much of his teachings were, so far as I could see, just what we had believed long before the coming of the Black Robes. For those on this reservation who have no transportation and who live a long way from the village, the Christian churches send buses. Often the people spend the day and have a noon meal. They get together, visit, and for a time forget their troubles. Many could get out but seldom except for this.

I have much gratitude, too, for the churches that have, I think, done more to bring about an acceptance of the ways of civilization than has the government. At Fort Sill the Dutch Reformed Church provided both a school and a little hospital long before the government did either. The Naiche children walked eight miles each morning to school and eight back home.

Apaches are sincere in their acceptance of Christianity because in it they see nothing in conflict with their old religion. The trouble with our youth is that they have, to a great extent, abandoned their old religion and are not yet bound by the inhibitions of the new. Between the two they are confused and I fear for them. That is why I am glad to see this Native American Church interest them.

Dan Nicholas, a Chiricahua Apache and one of the best educated and most intellectual members of his tribe, told me the following about the Apache religion.

The Apaches emphasized the life on earth through rites and ceremonies. They wanted to live as long as they could. Nothing was ever said of reward or punishment. They emphasized good behavior. There should be no stealing. One should not tell lies. It was not a matter of future punishment, but of doing what was right because it was right.

All Apaches can go to each other in distress, and if one asks help from another the help must be given. An Apache can turn no one from his house and can refuse no one food, especially if the person seeking help has given the distress signal.

---

2. For an account of this great man, see chapter *The Early Missionaries,* in Book Three.

The role of the Apache medicine man has been both misunderstood and underestimated. It was and still is of great importance. Though his primary function was that of healing, he performed other services and exercised great influence in the tribe.

In their primitive state the Apaches knew little of disease. They feared *viruelos* (smallpox) because they had been decimated by it. They knew that it was caused by their wearing shirts and using blankets obtained from Mexicans.

They knew nothing of children's diseases. They did not know of the common cold. Above all, they were ignorant of social diseases. They rarely suffered from toothache or arthritis. They probably did know malignancy, however.[3]

They were expert in curing wounds; if, rarely, one became infected they treated the wound by burning.[4] Even small children were taught the use of medicinal herbs. Only in extreme cases did they seek the aid of the medicine man; he made no charge for his services but it was customary to reward him with a gift of considerable value.

His treatment was both physical and psychological. To the Apache it was also religious. Without the faith of the patient and his family and friends the herbs would be less effective, or perhaps of no aid. They must believe in Ussen and in the Power he had bestowed upon the healer.[5]

Byron Treas told of his uncle having gone to the cave in the Guadalupes where the puberty rites originated. He heard the songs and the drums but did not enter. He brought back medicine that would cure everything. There is no other that will, but he could never get any more of it.

Elmer Wilson was a good and dedicated man, greatly revered by his people. He presided over the Ceremonials with great dignity. After his death, his son, Woodrow, followed him, but was never as successful as his father. "Once," said Byron Treas, "I sat down on a log and a rattlesnake bit my leg. I tied a thong above the wound and my wife got me to the hospital. A doctor treated my leg, but it continued to swell and get more painful. She [his wife] brought Woodrow. He gave me some herb, then sang and prayed for me. I recovered very soon. We gave Woodrow a Pendleton blanket and later I took some money to him."

"I don't believe in the old ways," said Martine. I am a member of the Reformed Church and have been for many years. But there are some good luck things that work: turquoise, *hoddentin*, and certain shells. In the dances of the Mountain Spirits each young man wears a bit of this shell (abalone) between his eyes. It is fastened by a thin buckskin thong and hidden by his mask. And there is a coarse whitish clay that when exposed to the air gets almost as hard as stone. But I can't tell you about that."

One of the most scrupulously observed taboos among Apaches is one regarding gold. Strangely, it seems to have escaped the attention of anthropologists.

---

3. At age 87 Jasper Kanseah had not lost a permanent tooth; the same is true of many other older individuals. Daklugie thought that Cochise died of cancer.

4. The standard treatment for wounds was splitting the leaf of a *nopal* (prickly pear) and applying the cut side of it to the wound.

5. Elmer Wilson, famous medicine man; Willie Comanche and Fred Comanche, medicine men; interviews.

An Apache may pick up nuggets from the dry bed of a stream but he is forbidden to "grub in Mother Earth" for it. It is the symbol of the sun and hence sacred to Ussen. I have never seen an Apache wear anything made of gold.

Nor have I known of one's making use of a snake skin, or of a snake. They will speak of their attitude regarding gold; but if one mentions a snake it is usually a "slip," and he will not discuss the subject. May Peso Second, who was well informed and gracious about giving information, said their history and traditions should be told only around campfires at night. Otherwise "the snakes would get mad." She would make no explanation. Several others avoid mention of the subject, though all confirmed the necessity of a fire. Only a few were willing to concede that a fireplace can be substituted.

There are medicine women, too. A few years ago an epidemic caused the death of several Apache infants, some of whom were in the hospital. To determine the cause, a biochemist was flown in from Johns Hopkins, but he could not isolate a virus. Catherine Cojo, whose grandchild was a patient the doctors had pronounced incurable, went to one of the doctors. She asked to make medicine for the baby, and consent was granted. She went high on Sierra Blanca, returned with an herb, and made tea for the baby. He recovered. It was administered to other children, and they, too, recovered.

Apaches make medicine for purposes other than healing. *Hoddentin,* the pollen of the tule (cattail) is placed upon the brow of persons who go to the sacred tepee during the Ceremonials. The maidens participating are said to have the Power of White Painted Woman during the four-day rites. Those who have faith may receive healing or any other blessing for which they pray.

P*ower* is a mysterious, intangible attribute difficult to explain, even by one possessing it. It was, even above his courage, the most valuable attribute of a chief.

DAKLUGIE

W*ithout* it, how could he maintain discipline and hold his warriors? You know that Apaches are not easily controlled. Unless they believe their leader has Power he's out of luck. Of all the chiefs I knew, Naiche, when young, was the only one who had no Power. But when Taza was poisoned in Washington Naiche was elected to succeed him.

Juh, my father, had great Powers—several of them. Like Geronimo, he could foretell the future. That is what his name means: he sees ahead. But greatest of all was his Power to handle men. No Apache had to perform compulsory military service. No warrior got pay for fighting. My father told his men that he could offer them nothing but death. It was for them to decide between that and slavery. When he met with Governor Terrazas and Díaz, Presidente of all Mexico, it was his Power that enabled him to bring them to terms. He told them that if they would make their forces quit killing Apaches he would call off his warriors.

Chief Chihuahua had the Power over horses. He could gentle and ride the wildest horses. He could heal them of sickness or wounds. I saw him cure a horse dying of a rattlesnake bite.

And Nana—his Power was over ammunition trains and rattlesnakes. Victorio's bravest, such as Kaytennae, might make a raid for bullets and fail. But when Nana, long past eighty and crippled, rode all night, he brought back ammunition.

Victorio's sister, Lozen, was famous for her Power. She could locate the enemy and even tell how far away it was. Many of the old Apaches today are convinced that, had she been with Victorio at Tres Castillos, there would have been no ambush.

Most Medicine Men acquire Power when they are adolescents. All boys must go alone to the sacred mountains to fast and pray for four days and nights. They can take no food, water, or weapon. They have a blanket, but nothing else. Many do not obtain the gift. The few who do attain it in various ways, usually not until the last night of the ordeal. Then the supplicants may hear a voice; they may see a person, an animal, or even a tree, plant, or stone that is to be their medicine. It talks to them, telling them what they are to use and how. From that time on they carry a bit of it in a small buckskin pouch on a thong around their neck. It is their guide and their help all their lives.

Though I had been very fortunate in obtaining other information from him, Daklugie would not discuss his own medicine nor his Power. It was not until after his death that Maude gave the following account.

Maude Daklugie Geronimo

My father and mother took Eva Geronimo into our home after Geronimo's death. She married Fred Godlie [Godley], though Ramona had warned her that the women of her family had difficulty in giving birth. When her child was due she sent for Daklugie to sing for her. He made medicine and she lived about a year; then she died.

Apaches had been promised by Ussen that without their lifting a hand all of North America would be given back to them. Many thought that this would be the result of a volcanic upheaval or of earthquakes; but my father expected it to come about by an atomic attack. He would sing:

> Ussen gave us this land,
> Through our forefathers
> It has come to us.
> It was our land
> Before the White Eyes came;
> It is still our land.

Robert [Geronimo] and I were both married when we were very young. Each of us was divorced. We were both past fifty when we were married. My father liked Robert but he made us get a divorce. He did it because he believed Robert to be Geronimo's son, not Cross Eyes'. And the marriage of close relatives is forbidden. His mother was a sister of Geronimo. That made Robert and me cousins.

We had to obey him. He was more than my father; he was my chief. I have been very lonely and unhappy. Now my father is gone, but Robert and I can never remarry.

After we came here [Mescalero] in 1913 Daklugie had pneumonia. My mother put up a sing for him. For a short time he died. He saw the death hole open for him; he saw trees and grass down there. Just as he started to go through the opening a four-point buck brushed past his shoulder and the hole closed after it. The deer had taken his place. After that he never killed another deer.

Jasper [Kanseah] says that it was their great Power that enabled them to come through the wars alive. Ussen protected them so that they could be of help to their people.

Robert saw butterflies flitting around him. That means that his first wife is trying to get him back. She's witching him; and if a man is witched he can be made to do anything. If he does not want to do a bad thing like murder, he cannot help himself. But the witch will pay for it. He cannot go to the Happy Place until he has lived again in the body of a bear. If he has done something very bad, such as betraying his people, he may have to come back to Mother Earth several times. That is why we don't kill a bear or eat its meat. We might be eating one of our own family.

My father said that you do not know it but you either have Indian blood or in another life you have been an Apache. That is why he took so much time to tell you our stories.

Eugene Chihuahua was willing to talk about his Power.

EUGENE CHIHUAHUA

I have two—the Owl Feather and the Bear. Not just an owl feather; any will do. An eagle feather is very sacred, and it is best. But even a chicken one will do. I take it in my hand and say, "Feather, I'll take care of you, and I want you to take care of me." And Feather does. He helps heal the sick.

And Bear. I carry a bit of its fur in a little buckskin bag tied to a cord around my neck. And I talk to the bears.

If you meet a bear and he stands on his hind feet and holds his hands up, he is trying to tell you that he is your friend. We kill one only in self-defense as we might a person. We do not eat its flesh nor use its hide.[6] We do not touch a

---

6. Convinced that James Kaywaykla had long since given up old customs—by his own admission—I had an occasion to invite him to dinner, a dinner which had bear roast as the main course. He was taking a third serving of bear meat when another guest said, "Eve, this is the most delicious pork I've ever eaten."

"But it isn't pork," I replied.

James Kaywaykla laid his fork on his plate, folded his napkin, stood, and without a word stalked out of the house. Whether to follow and apologize or to await his return I did not know. I explained to my other guests my embarrassment at having offended him and also that I thought he no longer was bound by the old customs. When, after an hour or so, there was still a light in the guest house, I knew that he had not, as I had feared, started to walk the twenty miles to Mescalero.

The next morning, without being summoned to breakfast, he walked in, smiled, and said, "Mrs. Ball, I'm sorry. As I've often told you, I thought I'd given up all the old customs. I've been a member of the Reformed Church for sixty years, but I've been an Apache much longer."

dead bear. But Bear is my Power and my friend. So I talk to him and he listens. He understands and he helps. Out in the Rinconada, where Jennie used to live, are many bears. We go out there to get apples. They visit us there. They don't talk, but they stand on their hind feet and hold their hands up.

You know Del and Robert Barton, our adopted children, Indian way. They come up from El Paso and take us to their home to visit and tell stories. We have gone two or three times. Bob wanted to take us over to Juárez to eat, but I don't go to Mexico. I haven't forgotten what we did to those Mexicans. That's no place for me.

But our children did take us to eat at that new Fort Bliss. We ate with the commanding general. He is their friend. Can you believe Apaches eating with a general? He had lots of food—good food, I guess. I didn't know what some of it was. I was holding off for pumpkin pie, but they didn't have any. They brought some kind of sweet stuff that I didn't like but I ate some of it anyway. I was scared that it would be impolite not to.

What do you guess that general did? He put up a big military parade for all the Apaches, I guess, but nobody was there but me and Jennie. Maybe it was for all Indians everywhere; I don't know. But I thanked him for all the Apaches. And I told him about seeing old Fort Bliss down by the Río Bravo when it was just two or three old adobes as big as chicken houses. And he laughed and laughed.

He wanted to take me and Jennie up in a plane, but we didn't go. We'll die soon enough anyway. I told the general how a Medicine Man, a long time ago, said that some day wagons were going to run without horses and fly in the sky like birds. How did they know? Me, I don't know—even if I am a Medicine Man. My medicine is not wagons.

Witchcraft is just the wrong use of Power. Like a gun or knife, it can do good or harm. I know that there are witches. People are afraid to oppose them, so they become dictators. They dominate everybody—except White Eyes. If they could do that there wouldn't be any White Eyes.

My Daughter, did you know that I make medicine for you? We make medicine so you don't get sick or have a car wreck. When I make medicine for you I sing prayers to Ussen. If He thinks they should be answered, the coyotes across the canyon howl, and I know Ussen is going to take care of you. If they don't answer I know I've prayed for something He thinks is not good for us. When that happens I have lost my Spirit Guide, and that makes me unhappy. Chihuahua, my father, is my guide. When I come to the fork in the road and don't know which trail to follow, he comes to me and tells me what to do. Then I know I am on the right trail. Then I have to go to my medicine.[7]

Back when we became prisoners of war and were sent to Florida, at first we thought that even Ussen was taken away from us. We had long known that we were *Indeh,* the Dead, but even so, back in our own country we could go to the mountains to pray, and Ussen would answer us.[8]

---

7. An Apache spirit guide is similar to a Christian guardian angel.

8. Eugene reminded me that even a White Eye had written, "I will lift up mine eyes unto the hills from whence cometh my understanding."

And we had His promise that in His own time the world would be destroyed and, though all life might perish, in four days He would raise the Apaches, and all Indians, from the dead and the buffalo would return to the plains and the antelope to the hills. The deer would graze on the mountains and the land would be ours forever.

That is His promise, and it will be.[9]

---

9. A number of those interviewed stated the same belief, one akin to the Ghost Dance Religion belief in such a restoration. See chapter *Cibicu*. This chapter has been pieced together from information given by many of the Apaches I have interviewed through the years. I have made no attempt to pull into the narrative any information from anthropological sources.

CHAPTER 10

BRONCO APACHE

I once committed a blunder by asking what the Apaches did about some minor problem when they were wild.

"Wild!" snorted Daklugie. "What makes you think we were wild? We had a culture of our own, much better than the White Eyes have today. How could you possibly think that we were wild, after what I've told you?"

I apologized.

Somewhat mollified, he conceded that as a small child he had seen an Apache who was really wild.

"What did he do?"

"He went off and lived with the bears."

From my point of view, he qualified.

DAKLUGIE

I saw him only once, but Kaywaykla knew him.*

Kay-se-goh-neh, a White Mountain Apache, once took his wife, children, and mother hunting with him. No others were along. He saw several warriors coming and lifted his rifle. He called to the armed band, "If you want trouble, come on!" I think he must have been very brave to oppose several well-armed men. He undoubtedly recognized them as Apaches, but he also knew them to be strangers. They were Chihenne, of Kaytennae's band, and their young chief was with them. Both Kaytennae and one other warrior in the party wore small mirrors around their necks (for use as signalling devices).

Kay-se-goh-neh kept the strange party off until his family could take cover, but the group kept coming toward him slowly. He fired but did not hit anyone. Then a Chihenne warrior shot back and killed him. Watching, Kay-se-goh-neh's mother saw the flash of light from a mirror around the assailant's neck. All ran to where Kay-se-goh-neh had fallen, where the mother pointed out Kaytennae as the one who killed her son. He had not even fired. Kay-

---

*Kanseah, Chihuahua, and Kaywaykla said that they had also seen this man and had heard his story since they were children. Others of the older people among the Chiricahua and Chihenne knew of him and were familiar with the story.

tennae felt very sorry for the family, but an Apache does not express his sympathy in words. It is too deep for that. Kay-se-goh-neh's mother accused Kaytennae of the murder of her son and he did not deny the charge. To do so would be to throw suspicion upon the only other man wearing a mirror. The culprit knew that Kaytennae was defending him in the only way he could. He did not speak and admit his guilt. He did not even speak.

Head bowed, Kaytennae stood in silence and let the hysterical woman upbraid him. She said, "You killed my only son with that gun. You killed him for no cause whatever and made his wife a widow and his children orphans. Now they have no one to protect them, no one to hunt for them. Your rifle is loaded. Shoot me! Shoot his poor wife! Shoot his children! A quick death is much more merciful than starvation."

When the old mother had finished berating Kaytennae, the man who had done the killing said, "If your son had not fired at us he would have been alive. It was nobody's fault but his own that he died."

His mother ignored him and raved at Kaytennae: "You are very handy with guns. Shoot me! I'd much rather die a quick than a slow death. Go ahead and shoot me."

When the party returned to Fort Apache, the guilty man left. He told nobody that he was going; he just disappeared. Few of the Chihenne had seen him in camp except his wife. He had taken his family to their tepee, but he had not told them of his intentions.

Days later he chanced to meet Gouyen, the mother of Kaywaykla and the wife of Kaytennae. Kay-se-goh-neh's killer saw her, and, contrary to Apache custom, he humbly stepped from her path to let her pass. And he spoke to her. "My sister, there is something that bothers me so much that I cannot sleep. For days I have not slept more than a few minutes at a time." He told Gouyen that he had done something for which he was both sorry and ashamed and that he could not leave his wife and family without telling someone. He had decided to go far away and never return. Gouyen had begun to suspect that, but she was surprised to hear the man admit it.

She replied, gently, "If you mean that you are deserting your family, consider whether or not you are making a mistake. I am but a woman, but I know that other women need the protection and care of a husband. Without you, your wife, mother, and children may go hungry. For one time, listen to a woman who, though she is weak and foolish, is trying to help both you and your family."

The man shook his head and left.

Gouyen was not called Wise Woman without reason. Only a very intelligent woman could have influenced Kaytennae, and even Nana, as she did. It may be that she was mistaken in thinking that the man did not recognize her, for he did a strange thing—he turned back to speak with her again. She greeted him with "I hope you have changed your mind and will stay."

"I wish I might," he replied. "But something stronger than I drives me. I came to ask if you will try to help my poor mother and wife, and my little helpless children, for you have a kind heart. But I must go. At night animals prowl about but do not attack me. Sometimes I think I have been witched. Sometimes a bear stays near my camp, and I hope that he will kill me, but he does not. Perhaps *he* keeps guard over my family. It is well known that bears protect those in need of care."

"That should keep you here."

"If I go it may protect my family," he replied.

Gouyen reminded him that there was a story of one bear who prevented an Apache woman from walking into a camp of Mexican cavalry. She said, "Stay with your family and your tribe and the bear may protect all of you. It may contain the spirit of one of your ancestors."

Again the man shook his head and walked away, this time not to return.

The Apaches think that the man may have been witched, but I believe that he was both sorry and ashamed. He thought that he had lost face both with his chief and the men who witnessed the shooting. And he was probably more embarrassed and distressed over that than he was for having killed the man. After all, Kay-se-go-neh had fired the first shot.

When Kaytennae took Gouyen and Kaywaykla with him to draw rations, they met the wife of the one who had gone, but they asked no questions. Others, not knowing the cause of his absence, did ask questions, but his wife only shook her head without speaking.

The unfortunate man did not return. His family mourned for him as if he were dead. His mother and his wife roamed through the forest wailing and praying. Kaytennae gave orders that men were to keep watch over them and to protect them if necessary, but to remain hidden. Twice his wife found tracks about her camp, footprints that she recognized as her husband's, but not once did she see him. She thought his love for his family was so great that he had to return, but that the agony of a second parting might have prevented him from making his presence known to her.

I saw that man, but only once. Down in Sonora one night, as we sat about the fire eating our evening meal, a voice called to my father from the darkness and asked if an Apache might come to his fire. Juh answered that his brothers were always welcome. A man, clothed in skins from which the hair had not been removed, appeared and dropped beside the fire. My mother handed food to him. When she poured a cup of coffee, he drank it eagerly and extended his cup for more. As he ate, I noticed that his moccasins had the characteristic Chiricahua toe, but this style was common also to the Chihenne and Bedonkohe. He carried no weapons, not even a knife. But he may have hidden them before calling to Juh. It did not seem possible that anyone, not even an Apache, could have survived without a knife.

It was the tantalizing odor of the coffee, he said, that led him to our camp. He had not tasted it for a long, long time, and he missed it more than he did food. He drank four cups. When he had finished, he stood, handed his cup to my mother, and thanked her. My father urged him to join us, but he shook his head. When invited to stay at least one night, he declined politely but positively. He said, "I cannot stay. There is something that drives me and will not let me have peace. I am doomed to be an outcast for the rest of my life. I was not banished by my tribe, but by this thing that nags me. I am the victim of my own mind. I have no companions, no friends, no family, nothing but bears. Always there are one or more with me. They bring me food. If I move they follow. If I sleep they guard me. I no longer fear them, but I dread them as I do the bad thoughts that torment me both sleeping and waking. For me there is no hope, nothing."

"Perhaps here you will not be troubled."

"I might bring trouble to you. That I will not do."

The man's face showed that he really wished to stay, but he had made up his mind and there was no changing it. Without further word he turned and walked rapidly into the darkness. We never saw him again, but when strange moccasin tracks were found about our camp, my mother recognized them as those of Kay-se-goh-neh's killer.

To us it seemed strange that the man wore a small mirror on his chest, for surely he did not communicate with anybody, and that was the primary purpose of having one. This man wore his inside his shirt, but when he leaned forward Juh saw the firelight reflected in it. I, too, had noticed it and wondered why he wore it.

Years afterward, in northern Sonora, we found the skeleton of a man with long black hair and with a small round mirror on his ribs inside his body. The bones still had fragments of skins sticking to them, skins with the hair left on them.

Kaywaykla told me that Kaytennae supplied food to the family of the voluntary outcast but had others carry it to them, for he did not wish them to know that it came from him.

These books all seem to have copied the same mistakes, and especially about Kaytennae. He was a good man.

Chapter 11

Mexican Attack

Daklugie

J uh was in camp south of Janos, in Mexico. I believe that the closest town was Temosachic, but I do not know how far from it we were. My father seldom stopped near Mexican towns, except Casas Grandes, where he had an arrangement for coming into the town for trading. With us were some of the survivors of the Tres Castillos Massacre [October 1880], in which Victorio lost his life.

My father knew that the Mexicans, both cavalry and civilians, were combing the country for us, so he was doubly cautious. He chose a site along an arroyo coming down from a mountain. It had only a trickle of water at that time, but it was sufficient for the needs of both people and horses. The channel provided a protected route of escape in case of attack. Where we were it was deep enough to conceal a tall man standing upright; it got shallower higher up, but it led to what he considered a fairly safe rendezvous. He always selected camps in the mountains, well watered and with good places of concealment.

Guards were always stationed at night, but at this time my father doubled the usual number. Apaches did not make night attacks, but Mexicans had no scruples against doing so. Before dawn, with nobody yet stirring, one of Juh's slave boys, on guard with Kaytennae's men, saw Mexican civilians approaching. The Mexicans recognized him as being a fellow Mexican and beckoned to him to join them. Instead, the boy ran toward camp to warn us. Mounted Mexicans chased him, but he reached our tepee screaming that we were being attacked.

Warriors grabbed weapons and ran to the defense of the camp. By the light of a burning brush arbor, I saw horsemen riding fast. They dashed through the camp firing as they came. I struggled to my feet attempting to roll my blanket as I had been taught. My mother was gathering up food and ammunition. My sister, Jacali, recently married, had rolled up her blanket and was gathering the water jugs. A tepee close by burst into flame and the next thing I knew Delzhinne, my brother, was firing over my head at a Mexican whose horse just missed coming into our door. Jacali's husband, rifle in hand, rushed in and told us to take my baby sister and run for the arroyo.

70

As my mother started to lift the child, a bullet struck the baby and she went limp. Mother then reached for the rifle discarded by Delzhinne and began loading it. I started toward the door and saw mother stagger and fall. Jacali, rushing to her, stopped suddenly, grasped her knee, and sank to the earth. Delzhinne and Jacali's husband continued to fire, with Jacali reloading as fast as she could. They were taking careful aim and riders were dropping just outside. I knew that we had little ammunition and that every bullet must count. I could see flames as brush arbors were set on fire; and I could hear horses running madly.

Suddenly firing ceased and the Mexicans pulled back to reorganize for a second charge on the camp. "They won't be long," said my mother. "Get away before they come back." Delzhinne stooped to lift her but she told him that he must not, that she was dying, and that he must save the others.

"But I can't leave you," he said.

"You must."

Again he undertook to carry her, but she refused to permit it.

"Save your sister," she said. "Carry her to the arroyo. Lower her into it and hide her in a thicket close to the water. Take my blanket and knife for her. And run, all of you!" As the two men attempted to lift my sister in her blanket, her husband fell, mortally wounded. Delzhinne lifted Jacali and carried her toward the watercourse. I followed with food bags and my blanket. He laid my sister on the bank, jumped down, and, with Jacali in his arms, waded up the shallow little stream toward a thick clump of brush. When he had hidden her in it, he laid food, a knife, and a small jug of water beside her. He spread my blanket over her and said, "If I live, I'll come back for you. I do not think they will find you, but if they do, you have a knife."

"They will not take me alive," she promised.

Sounds of galloping hoofs told us that another attack was under way. Delzhinne had no weapon but his knife. We crouched under an overhanging bank on the side toward the camp and hid until the riders left. When he lifted me to the rim I could see a pile of dead Mexicans in front of our burning tepee. When Delzhinne reached it our mother was dead, as was Jacali's husband and my baby sister. There were rifles, but no ammunition. Before we could find some in a still unfired tepee, the Mexicans charged a third time. We raced for the arroyo, with my brother carrying an empty rifle. He dropped into the watercourse and pulled me after him. Delzhinne was determined to get back and hunt ammunition, but after a fourth wave of men and bullets, they began riding up and down the banks, firing into clumps of vegetation.

I gritted my teeth when water splashed very close to the chaparral in which my sister lay. When we thought all the Mexicans had left, I wanted to go to her, but Delzhinne shook his head. He looked over the tracks of horses that had carried our people up the arroyo and identified those of Kaytennae's mount. It must have been carrying double, for its hoofs had sunk very deep in the sand. Beside them were the tracks of a child. "Kaywaykla," said Delzhinne. "Gouyen must have been behind her husband when they overtook the boy. They've escaped."

"But our father?"

Delzhinne shook his head.

"Worthless as a gun is without bullets, I must keep it, for it may be impossible to get another soon. Little Brother, you bring what food we have, and carry two water jugs. And be very quiet."

As we worked our way quietly up the arroyo, the walls became shallower until it was impossible for my brother to walk without being seen. Finally, I, too, had to crouch. Three more times Mexicans rode close; we lay flat by the bank and I held my breath.

We continued to climb. Neither of us had tasted food since the preceding evening and I was very tired, but I struggled along behind my brother, determined to keep up with him. It seemed a very long time that we stumbled along in the dark before we reached an overhanging ledge along a cliff. There a group of wretched people huddled. Protected from sight by the ledge was a bed of coals upon which Gouyen was laying strips of meat.

Kaytennae, she said, had ridden with Juh to avenge the death of his people. My brother Daklegon was with them. Three other men who had fled up the arroyo also had joined them, leaving no men with Gouyen and the few children she had with her.

Our mother? Jacali? The baby? Delzhinne shook his head and she understood. "But the men?" he asked. "Were there enough left to attack the Mexicans? How many had escaped?" She did not know. When he told her that he must return to bring Jacali, she reminded him that she had no ammunition. Neither was there a man left. If it were not for leaving the helpless children and the three women with her, she would go with him and help carry our sister back. But didn't he think it wiser to await the coming of a man with bullets? It was decided that if one man came in during the night he was to go with my brother.

Gouyen gave us food and her blanket. She insisted upon standing guard while we got some sleep. She promised to awaken Delzhinne at midnight, whether or not any of the men came. As we slept, Daklegon, Kaytennae, two wounded men, and other refugees came into camp. Daklegon woke up Delzhinne and they made ready to go back for Jacali. Kaytennae shared a few of his precious bullets with them, and Gouyen had food ready. I waited till all was quiet, and then I got up and followed. I knew that they would not permit it if they knew, so I kept behind them, guided by the soft thud of their moccasins. I feared that I might lose the sound and ran toward them. They must have heard me, for they stopped and called softly. They let me stay with them.

We found Jacali right where we had left her the previous day. She had bathed her wound and had tied a strip from her dress around it. This Delzhinne reinforced with his headband. They laid Jacali in a litter made of lances and one of her blankets and we began the return trip. Not until then had my brothers approved of my coming, but they found me useful for carrying food bags and jugs. The return was slow and difficult. Exhausted and very hungry, we finally made it back to camp. There Gouyen bathed my sister and bandaged her wounded knee. She split the leaf of a nopal and bound it to the leg with thongs of buckskin. Jacali had lost much blood and was very weak, but not once did she complain or make a sound. She was a true Apache.

Juh took vengeance on our attackers. I do not know how many we lost, nor how many were killed in revenge, but there were many lives lost on each side. Most of our dead were women and children. Additionally, we had lost most of our horses and pack mules and our tepees, food, blankets, and weapons.*

---

*Thrapp, in his account of the 1883 attack in *Conquest* (p. 265), cites sources indicating that six

Next morning my father ordered us to be on the move. Nobody questioned the commands of Juh and the miserable people complied, but it was a weary and discouraged band that broke camp. The old and the wounded (including my sister) got the few mounts. The rest walked. Juh kept to the mountains during the day; we crossed the open plains at night. I walked as did every child large enough. I remember trudging across those open spaces without rest in order to reach the mountains before dawn. Once in the hills, in a safe place where there was water, gratefully we would take to our beds. As we gradually acquired food, blankets, and skins, it became necessary to use the horses as pack animals. In time everyone was walking. Even Jacali, with that injured knee, uncomplainingly plodded along with the rest. I know that she walked hundreds of miles with that wounded leg, and when we camped she helped with the women's work as she had always done.

We wandered about in the foothills, picking up horses, replenishing our food and other supplies, and keeping well under cover. Both Geronimo and Chief Chihuahua were with us some of the time. I do not think that there was any difficulty between my father and uncle, but Geronimo wished to go north and Juh decided to stay in the Sierra Madres for awhile. Chihuahua elected to go with Geronimo, and the forces divided.

Though Geronimo had his own band, he acted as my father's *segundo* until this division of forces. Ponce then became Juh's choice for the position. (My brothers were still too young to serve in that capacity.) It was the *segundo* who usually led the advance guard while my father and a few men rode in the rear—the place, in most cases, of the greater danger. We kept away from settlements, but we picked up supplies of various kinds including mounts wherever we found them. In inaccessible camps we sometimes stayed several weeks. I do not know just how far west we went, but I do remember very distinctly having seen the ocean. We first glimpsed it from the top of the mountains. Nana had said that there was no water so wide that his horse could not swim it. And Nana never lied. He really believed that. We went down the mountain toward that water but there were little villages along it, and my father would not permit us to go further.

Juh decided that the band should return to Arizona. But first we would have to acquire horses and other items needed for the trip. Raiding parties were sent out and gradually we collected the necessary mounts and supplies. We were to spend the winter at San Carlos. Hopefully life there would be more endurable in the winter than it was in the summer. At least we knew that we would find friends and brothers there and that when spring came we could leave whenever we wished.

It was while we were at San Carlos that a very wonderful thing happened to me. My father and Chihuahua had talked over the matter a long time before telling me. They had decided that when I was old enough I was to marry Ramona, Chihuahua's daughter. We were both very young, too young to know whether or not we wished to marry. My father told me that but also said that it was his hope that Ramona and I would love each other and welcome this

---

whites and as many as four more Apaches were killed in the Apache retaliatory raid. Of the Mexican attack, Daklugie solemnly commented: "It took a long time for my father to recover from that attack. In fact, I am not sure that he ever did."

marriage. Then he warned me that "from now on you are not to see each other except when her parents or I am with you. Even then, if you talk, it must be with something between you, a bush perhaps, and you must speak back to back. You must respect Chihuahua's daughter and defend her with your life if necessary. And when you are a man and have proved yourself to the satisfaction of the warriors, you may be married with a four-day feast and all the tribe must know of your wedding. That way Ramona will be respected as she should be, and you will love each other and be happy. After your marriage, you will owe nothing to me nor to our family; you will support your wife's family and protect and defend them."

I was very happy; I had always admired Chihuahua's beautiful daughter, but marriage had never entered my head. I had been greatly concerned over becoming a warrior as soon as my father would permit, but marriage—that was the least of my interests. I gave my word to my father, as he asked me to do, and I observed it scrupulously.

The army surgeon at San Carlos had noticed my sister and asked why she limped. By this time the flesh had shrivelled, leaving nothing but skin and bone. He had wanted to amputate the leg, but Juh had not permitted it. A year or so later the same doctor talked with Geronimo about the surgery. [Juh had since returned to Mexico and had left Jacali behind because of her injury.] Geronimo also refused removal of the leg.

Chihuahua, however, agreed with the doctor that the leg should be removed. He told Geronimo that the white Medicine Man was telling the truth as to his being able to cut through flesh and bone without the patient's feeling pain. He had seen it done. A scout had had an arm so badly shattered that the doctor had removed it, and without hurting him. He had poured some queer-smelling water on a cloth and held it to the man's nostrils, and the scout had gone to sleep. When he awoke the arm was off and the wound was dressed. If this were done for Jacali, the white doctor would give her a wooden leg upon which she could walk, and so far as the leg was concerned she would have no more suffering.

Geronimo talked with my brothers. Nobody could question the word of Chihuahua. All agreed that it should be done, including Jacali. The doctor put Jacali to sleep and the leg was amputated. And as he had promised, he provided her with a wooden one.

I never saw my sister again, but years later I learned from a scout that she died at Fort Apache.

74

CHAPTER 12

DEATH OF JUH

DAKLUGIE

Once again, and for the last time, Juh returned to Mexico. At times he went into Casas Grandes for supplies. He rigidly enforced his policy of refusing to let all of the warriors drink at the same time; half one time and the other half next was his rule. Juh knew well that the Mexicans would give generously of their fiery liquor, get the Apaches drunk, and murder them. He had known of some Indians getting drunk and being locked up in a building, and a chili bomb being thrown in—thereby saving the Mexicans the use of even one bullet. They finished those men with knives and clubs.*

On his last trip to Casas Grandes, my father bought a good supply of ammunition, coffee, and blankets. He traded hides and jerked meat for them. As usual, liquor was given to the men and they bartered for some; but most of them remained sober. Among them was Juh. He did drink and sometimes got drunk, but that day he had not had liquor. It was Ponce's time to get drunk. And Juh scrupulously denied himself even one drink. He got Ponce and the ones who were drinking out of town first and sent the sober ones after them. He brought up the rear with Delzhinne and me. Daklegon went ahead with Ponce.

We were riding single file up the Río Aros. The bank was not as high as my head. Suddenly my father's mount shied to the left, the bank crumbled, and he went over into the river. Delzhinne and I followed as fast as we could. The water was waist-deep to me. When I got to them Delzhinne was holding my father's head above water, and he was unconscious.

Whether he had a heart attack or was injured by the fall, nobody ever knew. Water was running from his mouth, and I helped my brother turn Juh's head so that he might expel the water.

The opposite bank of the river had a sandy beach. We pulled him over toward it. Delzhinne and I could have lifted him out of the shallow water, but my brother thought it might help revive him, so he lay in it, face down, with me holding his head out of the water, while Delzhinne rode ahead for help. It

---

*For a corroborative account, see Thrapp, *Conquest,* p. 263.

seemed to me that my brother was gone a very long time. Two or three times I thought Juh was trying to speak. I know that he moved and that his lips moved; but there was no sound. When my brother came with Daklegon, Ponce, and the warriors, he was still breathing, but he soon stopped.

On the west bank of the Río Aros the warriors scraped out a grave, and they wrapped Juh in his blanket and laid him in it.

It was a sober and sorrowing band who rode up the river and made camp that evening.

M y father took his band to visit the great canyon [Del Cobre] and there we experienced a prophetic vision.

There my father's warriors assembled and built their ceremonial fire near the edge of the cliff, overlooking the gorge. Many were seated, but a few stood along the wall. To my people, this was a place sacred to Ussen. They had been fighting, running, hiding, and fighting again until they were war-weary and discouraged. They had come to this place to pray for the guidance of Ussen and to seek His aid in renewing their courage and energy. From the past experiences of our people, we knew that Ussen considers this place sacred and that He answers prayers rising from it.

As was our custom, we looked through the thin blue smoke across that wide, wide chasm. When everybody was silent, my father, Juh, lifted his eyes and arms in prayer, and the warriors did also. When the supplication was ended, our eyes were fixed on the opposite wall, far, far away. At first we could see nothing, but gradually a black spot appeared and seemed to grow larger and closer. It looked like an opening in the immense wall opposite us. It was. It was the opening to a big cave, one inaccessible from the rim and equally so from below. Nothing but a bird could have reached the entrance to that cavern.

As we watched, a thin white cloud descended and stopped just below the opening in the cliff. Every person there knew that this was a message from Ussen.

"We have seen His sign," said Juh.

We watched as thousands of soldiers in blue uniforms began marching eight abreast into the great opening. This lasted for a long time, for there seemed to be an endless number of soldiers. The cave must have extended far into the cliff, for none returned.

The vision, for that is what it was, lasted until dusk.

We returned to the mesa where Juh had camped. The Medicine Men, of whom my father was head, consulted, and one said, "There were many, many soldiers, all Blue Coats. They signify the government of the United States. Ussen sent the vision to warn us that we will be defeated, and perhaps all killed by the government. Their strength in numbers, with their more powerful weapons, will make us indeed *Indeh*, the Dead. Eventually they will exterminate us.

"That is the meaning of the vision."

Juh said, "We must gather together all Apaches—the Chokonen, the Nednhi, the Chihenne, the Bedonkohe, the Tonto, and the Mescaleros. And we must bind them into a strong force, just as these soldiers are strong. With our courage in fighting and our skill, we must oppose the enemy who has driven us from our country. We must not give up. We must fight to the last man. We

76

must remain free men or die fighting. There is no choice."

I did not at first intend telling of this vision, for you do not understand the ways of Ussen. And the White Eyes ridicule anything they do not understand. They have everything in books, but much of what has been written about the Apaches is wrong, for it has been written by our enemies. And you have not asked the Apaches what happened. Consequently, you White Eyes have everything in books and nothing in heads.

On our way north my father was drowned, but his warriors obeyed his wishes and runners were sent to the chiefs of the various tribes to enlist their help in saving our people. But too many, like Loco, had given up, even though they were brave fighting men. They had given up so that those of their tribes who still lived might survive. There was only one leader remaining who did not give up and that was Geronimo. And now the descendants of the faint-hearted blame him for the twenty-seven years of captivity just because their fathers did not have the fighting spirit and the courage to risk death as he did. They submitted to living—or rather to starving—on reservations like dumb, craven things. And today they dare criticize the fighting men.

We were few, and poorly equipped, but we did not quit. Our women and children were butchered and still we did not quit.

You say that finally Geronimo did? You've been reading books! Sometime I am going to tell you just how and why he did give up and how bitterly he regretted having done so. For the time finally came that he, too, knew that the vision must be fulfilled.

CHAPTER 13

GENOCIDE

D o you really think that it was the intention of the white race to inflict genocide upon the Indians?" I asked.

"Genocide?" repeated Daklugie.

"The intention of one race to exterminate another. I never heard the word used until it was applied to the German effort to kill all of the Jews."

DAKLUGIE

I never heard the word before, but I am thoroughly familiar with its practice. It was certainly that in the case of the Apaches.

I have heard a story told that illustrates the procedure. When the white man landed on the Atlantic coast, there was an Indian sitting on a log that extended to the Pacific. The Indian moved over, welcomed his white brother, and gave him a seat beside him. As more and more of the invaders came, the Indian was pushed west until he reached the Colorado River. Beyond that, the White Eyes had already polluted the land, and the Indians' best chance was in Arizona. So the last victim of the invader was the Apache. But he didn't find it easy to get rid of us. We fought him every step of the way.

And he never did whip us.

We had the Sioux beat [for cruelty], especially the Nednhi and Chiricahua. The Warm Springs, too. They were brave warriors and real fighting men, all but Loco's bunch. And they would fight when attacked, as they did in that battle with García's troops.[1]

But I am going back to the terrible massacre at the cave high above the Salt River. The victims of that massacre were not of my tribe, but they were Apaches. That was soon after Crook was brought back to the Southwest to exterminate the Apaches. I have been to that place while there were still bones of my brothers to be seen. There are some who think that one man lived to escape, but I do not know whether or not that is true. If so, that was still extermination of a band.[2] And all of our bands were small.

---

1. Thrapp, *Conquest*, pp. 240–50. For an Indian account see Kaywaykla, in Ball, *Victorio*, pp. 142–45.

2. Thrapp, *Conquest*, pp. 249–50.

And there was Turret Butte,[3] another attack soon after the cave murders, where everybody was killed—women, children, and warriors.

And there was Tres Castillos.[4]

The warriors, at least most of them, were away on a raid for ammunition. And some were hunting. So they were not victims. But more than ninety women and children were driven to Chihuahua to be sold into slavery. There were seventeen survivors of the massacre whom Nana assembled and held while awaiting the return of the warriors.

That was extermination. When either the men or women are killed off, how does a race continue to exist? It doesn't.

It was usually the women and children killed and perhaps the adolescent boys, for your army officers seldom attacked a *ranchería* while any of the warriors were about. They waited until the men were gone and then reported having killed thirty-seven, or whatever the number might be. But they did not consider it neccessary to add that they were all women and children. And they didn't attack Victorio while his warriors were there. It was not just an accident that the men survived.[5]

And there was Carleton and his treatment of the Mescaleros. When he got his forces to New Mexico, presumably to fight the Confederate troops, they had left. Carleton wanted to retain his command, and without somebody to fight neither he nor it was needed. So he trumped up stories of Mescalero atrocities, few of which had foundation. He wound up by moving what he could catch of those unfortunate people to a concentration camp at the Bosque Redondo.[6]

Not satisfied with that, he sent Kit Carson to round up and move the Navajos, thousands of them, from their own land in northern Arizona to the Pecos. They and the Mescaleros were enemies, but that made no difference. He placed the Navajos upstream from the Mescaleros. And they so outnumbered the Apaches that they stole their horses and harassed the Mescaleros until eventually, from contact with the soldiers, the Navajos got smallpox. When the military forced them to throw the bodies of their dead into the Pecos, the water was covered with corpses and was full of maggots. My people knew nothing of germs, but they did know that they could not drink that water. They had been accustomed to the pure mountain water from melting snows. So they decided to run away to their own country near Fort Stanton.

And what did Carleton order concerning the Warm Springs when Victorio was driven from Ojo Caliente to San Carlos? Read it. On his way to reoccupy the fort [Stanton], Carson was overtaken by his final instructions [from Carleton]: "All Indian men of that tribe are to be killed wherever and whenever you can find them. The women and children will not be harmed, but you will take them prisoners and feed them at Fort Stanton until you receive other instruc-

---

3. Ibid., pp. 136–37.

4. I interjected that Victorio's band was attacked by Mexicans. Daklugie retorted, "They were white people, weren't they? . . . They were white; at least they were obeying white officers or *politicos*."

5. Thrapp, *Conquest*, pp. 208–10. For an Apache account by a survivor of the massacres, see Kaywaykla, in Ball, *Victorio*, pp. 88–99.

6. Sonnichsen, *Mescalero Apaches*, pp. 96–98.

tions about them. If the Indians send in a flag and desire to treat for peace, say to the bearer that when the people of New Mexico were attacked by the Texans, the Mescaleros broke their treaty of peace and murdered innocent people and ran off their stock; that now our hands are tied and you have been sent to punish them for their treachery and their crimes; that you have no power to make peace; that you are there to kill them wherever you can find them; that if they beg for peace, their chiefs and twenty of their principal men must come to Santa Fe to have a talk there."

The complete savagery of this order shocked and embarrassed Kit Carson, but he could do nothing but follow orders.[7]

Captain James Graydon, in the last days of October, sallied out of newly occupied Fort Stanton on a scout and before long came up with a band of Mescaleros—men, women, and children. The leader was the aged Chief Manuelito, who came on with his hand raised in the sign that he wanted to make peace talk. Captain Graydon obeyed his orders. He fired into the band without warning and with severe execution.

Manuelito was killed as was his second in command, Juan Largo, along with four additional warriors and one woman.

Carson was appalled and even Carleton had some doubts about the "victory"—especially when word got around that at least one white civilian had made money out of the transaction.[8]

Orders to kill every male is equivalent to an attempt at extermination. In those days women and children could not exist without men to protect them.

[Taking the women to Fort Stanton] was worse than death. They'd have been killed by slow torture and shame. No. That was extermination to an Apache woman. How long do you think any would have lived? Our women were chaste and degradation was much worse than death. The only consolation they had was that it couldn't last long.[9]

It was death to the children, too. Out here at Fort Stanton a soldier took an Apache baby by the heels and dashed its head against a wagon wheel. He said, "Nits make lice." That was a common expression used to explain the murder of children, and it indicated the intention of extermination as did "The only good Indian is the dead Indian." In common use too was this phrase, "He'd killed a certain number of men, not counting Indians."

In Arizona, there was Bloody Tanks, the Massacre at Fort Grant, and the Pinole Treaty. And in Mexico, there was the attack on Geronimo's band at Janos when nearly all the women and children were killed. My uncle [Geronimo] lost his wife, mother, and three children. And there was the attack on my father's band near Temosachic, where I lost my mother, my little sister,

---

7. Ibid., p. 99.

8. Ibid., p. 100.

9. Chihuahua and Kanseah said that the Apache women of that time would have died of starvation before becoming slaves of their captors. See *Condition of the Indian Tribes, Report of the Joint Special Committee of 1867* (Washington: Government Printing Office, 1867), p. 245. This investigation was made while the Mescaleros were incarcerated at the Bosque Redondo. Physician George Gunter gave testimony that: "In speaking of the prevalence of social diseases among the prisoners at the Bosque Redondo . . . the greatest quantity [of venereal disease] existed among the Indians and was imported to them by the troops. In speaking upon the subject, I refer to the Navajos and not to the Apaches. Among the Apaches it hardly exists at all."

and my brother-in-law, and where Jacali was wounded.[10]

Both in this country and in Mexico, a bounty was offered for Apache scalps, just as there is today for those of some animals. And it was collected, too. It was collected until authorities became suspicious, wondering if all that black hair was really taken from Indians. If that were not done for the purpose of ridding the earth of Apaches, why did they waste the money that they love? Why was a bounty offered in New Mexico?[11]

That there were attempts to exterminate the Apaches cannot be denied. Carleton's edicts are well known. Less known is that another American officer, of the Confederate Army, also issued such an order in March 1862. General John R. Baylor, then in New Mexico, ordered the extermination of all Apaches. His men were to entice them with promises of peace and presents and then to slaughter them. Only the children were to be spared and these were to be sold as slaves to defray the cost of the program. (To the credit of Jefferson Davis and his Secretary of War, this order brought an end to Baylor's career.[12])

This should be said: Insofar as they could, the Apaches retaliated. Theirs was not an eye for an eye and a life for a life. If they could, they extracted many lives for each one taken by their enemies. Nor do they regret having done so. As long as he lived, Geronimo regretted having believed what he termed "the lies told by Miles" and having surrendered. Time after time he told Daklugie that they should have stayed in Mexico and fought until the last man had died. Though he did not say so, it was obvious that Daklugie felt much as did his uncle.[13]

When asked what he thought about genocide being the policy of the white race, Frederick Peso, grandson of the last Mescalero chief, replied: "I am sure that that was the intention. The surest way to kill a race is to kill its religion and its ideals. Can anybody doubt that the white race deliberately attempted to do that? That is to kill the soul of a people. And when the spirit is killed, what remains?"[14]

---

10. Ball, *Ma'am Jones*, p. 36, 146–47; Thrapp, *Conquest*, pp. 31, 265–66; Barrett, *Geronimo*, pp. 86–88; Betzinez, *Geronimo*, pp. 101–2.

11. Thrapp, *Conquest*, p. 11.

12. Alexander B. Adams, *Geronimo: A Biography* (New York: G. P. Putnam's Sons, 1971), p. 125.

13. Daklugie and Kanseah, interviews.

14. Frederick Peso, interview.

CHAPTER 14

MISCONCEPTIONS

DAKLUGIE

That's a fancy name for alibis and lies. That's what I call them. You White Eyes have some strange ideas about Apaches.

Writers, when describing us, always refer to our beady eyes. Did you ever see anybody whose eyes look like beads? No. Nor has anybody else. I've seen birds whose eyes might be called beady, but never a human being.

Writers say that Indians are boastful. They are the exact opposite. Apaches dislike a boaster as much as anybody does. We think that if anybody was a braggart it was the officers in the army who wrote of their bravery. If an Indian states modestly his achievements he is boasting; but if an officer makes a hero of himself, as many did, he gets a medal and a star. There were officers who were both honest and truthful, like Crook and Davis.[1] And there was Gatewood who was one of the bravest and most modest of men. And what did he get for it? He was cheated of the credit by that scoundrel, Miles.

Any book you read about the Apache campaigns will tell you that the chieftainship was hereditary.[2] It was not. It was elective. Yes, I know that a son often succeeded his father, but that was not always true. Taza may have been elected because of the great respect and love the Chiricahua warriors had for Cochise. And Naiche may have followed his brother because the Chiricahua thought that Taza was murdered. Many of the old ones still think so. But both Taza and Naiche were elected. Mangus would have been chosen by the Warm Springs to follow Mangas Coloradas, but he did not want the chieftainship. And Mangus was no coward. He was a brave and resourceful warrior. Nor was it necessary for a man to be the relative of a chief to be chosen for that position. He had to qualify for it, regardless of anything else. You think that they

---

1. Crook had such great faith in the integrity of Davis that he accepted without question reports from him. The Apaches think that in most instances the general was justified, but that Davis was completely deceived by Chato. See Kaywaykla, in Ball, *Victorio*, p. 162.

2. Apparently, military experts and historians have misunderstood the requirements for the chieftainship. See Ball, *Victorio*, pp. 162–63; also Miles, *Recollections*, p. 525.

must have been good politicians? There is no such thing as a good politician. The word is an insult.

On the other hand, many leaders are listed as chiefs who had no claim whatever to the position. Some had bands of their own, as did Fatty (Gordo), Mangus, Zele, Sanchez, Pionsenay, Ponce, and a number of others. Nor were there any subchiefs. Each band leader was independent. If he wished he could, and did, join some greater leader, such as Cochise or Victorio, but not through any obligation to do so.

And there are these many stories of torture and mutilation. Well, some of the torture stories are true, but they were done in retaliation for worse crimes. The White Eyes have never understood that bodies were mutilated *after death.* My people believed that the condition in which a body was left when dead was that which he would have through eternity. There was little of it before the treacherous soldiers of Carleton's forces lured Mangas Coloradas into their camp under a flag of truce, promised him protection, and murdered him. His death was bad; but to the Apaches the troops' cutting his head off and boiling it to get his skull were much worse. That meant that their great chief must go through the Happy Place forever headless.

I can think of one Indian who beat Miles and Forsyth, also Carr and Cruse, when it came to boasting and lying. That was a Tarahumara, Mauricio Corredor. He is the one who claimed to have killed Victorio in a hand-to-hand conflict. The City of Mules had a big parade and presented him with a silver-mounted rifle for something he positively did not do. Just before the Massacre of Tres Castillos, the warriors went on a raid for ammunition, for the band had very little. Others of the men were on a hunting trip for food. Victorio and four or five warriors constituted the advance guard; and Nana, with a few more, protected the rear. When Kaytennae, in charge of the raiding party, returned with an abundance of bullets, he found only seventeen survivors whom Nana had gathered—they were awaiting the return of the warriors. Nana sent Kaytennae and a few men, including Jasper Kanseah, to bury their beloved dead. Many bodies had been burned. About ninety-four women and children had been driven like cattle before the Mexican cavalry to Chihuahua. The adolescent boys had been killed. And Kaytennae told me that he found the body of his chief with his own knife in his heart. Victorio and his few men had fired their last bullets at the enemy before falling on their own knives.

Nor did Corredor kill Captain Crawford as he claimed to have done. Kanseah and Charlie Smith were with Geronimo and they witnessed that skirmish. So did several others of Geronimo's band, and they told me positively that it was not Mauricio Corredor who shot Crawford. Again, he claimed the doubtful honor of killing a brave man. The Chiricahua Apaches have always held that Corredor was a liar of the first order. But does any historian question either of Corredor's stories?

And Chato! I don't suppose that any White Eye but you will ever be convinced that Chato was not all he represented himself to be: the leader of Chihuahua's raid, and a faithful and loyal scout to Crook and Davis. If he were the latter, it was simply because nobody else could offer him more prestige. To the Apaches he was the arch traitor—as James Kaywaykla said, a sort of Benedict Arnold to us. But Davis believed what Chato told him, and what Davis believed Crook believed, for Britton was not a liar. He was our enemy but we respected him. And we respected Crook. And we knew only too well how very shrewd and convincing Chato could be when he was ambitious for recognition. He had thought for awhile that he could supplant Kaytennae with Nana. Nana was very old and crippled, and Chato knew that he could not long lead the Warm Springs. But, when he found that Nana had selected Kaytennae, he knew he had no chance there and he hated Kaytennae accordingly. Chato had been Geronimo's man, but he knew that he had no chance with my uncle. Nor did he have a chance with Chihuahua, who hated him for the liar and traitor he was. So—he went to the army.

I think that his success was based on his boasting to the officer that he led the raid known as Chato's. He did not. Chihuahua did, and his older brother, Ulzanna, was his *segundo*.[3]

I don't like the way you white people have Indians talk. Did you ever hear one grunt or say "heap plenty?" No! You've talked to hundreds.

And in the books all Indians are lazy. My people will work if they can do something they enjoy. Regardless of their intelligence and education, the only work open to them now is menial. Of course they don't like to do maid's work in a motel, or clean houses, or rake yards. There is some opportunity for them in civil service if they work on reservations. But if they apply for other jobs there are three strikes against them before they sign an application. There is some opportunity for those who have unusual ability as artists of some kind, but there are few who do.

When I left Carlisle to return to my people they were at Fort Sill, and the government was trying to make farmers of them. They had never done much of that and they did not like it. But they like handling cattle. So I promoted that and got to be in charge of the livestock. When we came to Mescalero they forced us to handle sheep. Sheep! The Navajos seem to like them but not the Apaches. We soon got rid of those sheep—stupid things, and lots of trouble. We got cattle. Eugene and I had much to do with that. Running cattle was more like the hunting we had done before we were forced into captivity. We liked to ride and to work cattle. And the reservation is fit for nothing else. In the almost half-million acres of land there are about five thousand that could be plowed and planted; but unless irrigated they would produce nothing. Many years there is insufficient rainfall to produce anything. So we don't plant the few little fields. And people say that we are lazy.

And Forsyth! I'll tell you of some of his dishonesty. Do you know of the battle of the Arickaree, where Roman Nose was killed? Have you read Forsyth's story? It differs materially from that I heard from a scout, a white scout, who was with Forsyth there.

When I went with Geronimo to the World's Fair I got acquainted with an old man who looked like, and was, a Westerner. He had been a scout and was with Forsyth on the Arickaree. He said that arrogant officer just rode blindly into a trap in spite of anything the scouts could do. They could read signs even

---

3. Richard Johlsannie, son of Ulzanna, gave his father's account of Chihuahua's raid, which Chato claimed that he had led. See Kaywaykla, in Ball, *Victorio,* pp. 147–48.

if he could not. And they kept warning him that they were following an increasingly large number of warriors. The scouts knew that they were not far ahead and that there were many of them. If it had been left to Forsyth they would have made their stand on a hill, but the scouts paid no attention whatever to his orders and took refuge on an island in the shallow stream where there was cover. He went along, of course; he had to. No Indian would have walked into such a trap as Forsyth did. But who can tell an army officer anything? This old scout did give him credit for being game when he was wounded. But he despised Forsyth for getting them into such a trap, for it was just his stubbornness that made him refuse to listen to those who knew. And he made a hero of himself.

We had our own name for him. It was Always Too Late to Fight. Kaywaykla has told you what really happened at Stein's Peak; and you know that Forsyth didn't even show up down on the border till the fighting was over. Do you think that any Indian chief could have blundered as he did and held his men? They expected their leaders to have some horse sense as well as fighting ability.

I said to Daklugie: "Your old scout did give Forsyth credit for being brave under fire and for courage while severely wounded."

"Anything will fight when cornered."

"But your real cause of hatred for Forsyth is because of his attack on the unarmed at Wounded Knee."

"That too; and his turning cannon loose on the women and children. But back of Forsyth was Miles, and back of them Sheridan and Sherman. It was the generals higher up who should have had the blame for much of the attempt to exterminate the Indians."

"And that is where the Ghost Dance ended?" I inquired.

"Ended! Who says it has ended? In every reservation in the United States today it is observed at least once a year. And it is not too late yet for the White Eyes to get just what they tried to inflict upon the Indians—this genocide."

I shook my head.

"You don't believe it! That is because you just don't want to believe it. You think you understand how we feel. Sometimes I really think you do. But—I've told you this before—when the Russians come over here and put you to digging ditches, then you'll begin to know just how we feel."

Maude's hearing was deficient, and she did not understand why her father was indignant; but as Evangeline ushered her little daughters to the door she patted my arm reassuringly and murmured, "It isn't you he's mad at, Mrs. Ball; it's the White Eyes."

CHAPTER 15

MY BROTHERS

After the deaths of my father and mother I was a very lonely child, but old enough to know that an Apache does not complain. My brothers were sympathetic, and without voicing their understanding they tried to make me happy. They assured me that I could stay with them, even though their trail led to the warpath again, and that my training to become a warrior would continue to be under their supervision. They also told me, however, that if we should go near Fort Apache and find Jacali living, I was to stay with her if she needed me.

From time to time we joined my uncle Geronimo's band. When we were with Geronimo, Delzhinne would be away often, but Daklegon seldom left. Whether or not either was in camp, Geronimo personally directed much of the training of the young boys for the warpath. Whether we went to my father's old stronghold or some other secluded retreat, he lined the boys up along a stream, after having them build a fire, and at his command had them jump into the cold water, even when it meant breaking the ice. When we climbed up the bank with our teeth chattering, he let us go to the fire for a short time, but then we had to jump into the water again. Of course, nobody wanted to obey, but one look at the stout switch in Geronimo's hand prevented any refusal. I never saw him strike anybody with it, but that club worked wonders.

We had not been with Geronimo for long when we met the little band led by Mangus, son of Mangas Coloradas. Mangus's band consisted of his wife, son, daughter, and a little boy he was caring for; the wife and daughter of Kedizhinne; an old man; and, to our great surprise and joy, my brother Delzhinne's wife and child.[1]

It was decided that I was to join Mangus's band. Did that mean that Gero-

---

1. Mangus married Dilth-Clay-ih, daughter of Victorio. Daklugie did not explain how Delzhinne had become separated from his family. Faulk states: "Mangus explained his much reduced band by stating that a portion of his followers had been captured by Mexicans and never heard from again; they had been caught . . . and were immediately executed by Tarahumara Indians, irregulars hunting scalps for bounty." Odie B. Faulk, *The Geronimo Campaign* (New York: The Oxford Press, 1968), p. 174.

nimo did not want me? I went to my uncle. He explained that for a while at least my two older brothers were to be attached to Mangus's band, for he needed men. And he did not wish to separate me from them. He assured me that he was pleased with my behavior, that he was sure that I would make a good warrior, and that he believed that some day I would be a chief. I think that even that long ago Geronimo may have known that I was to lose my brothers and wished to prevent the family's extinction. He had the Power of foresight, even as my father had. As it turned out I need not have feared for my training. Geronimo himself could not have been more inflexible than was Mangus.

Mangus's son, Frank, was a year older than I, but we trained together. (We became close, lifelong friends.) We both wanted to become fighting men so we worked hard and we obeyed orders. We learned not to kneel to put our mouths to the water in a stream. Rather, with cupped hands we lifted it to our lips after having carefully looked all about us for danger. Not only did we take precautions against any enemy, but we observed a religious custom—that of not seeing our faces reflected. Before looking into the water, we agitated it so that no reflections would appear. That was because Ussen had made no two things exactly alike, not even grains of sand nor blades of grass. For that reason it was presumptuous for Earth People to have duplications of themselves. That is why many of our people today refuse to have photographs made.[2] Above all, when we camped or drank we were never to lay our weapons out of reach. Loco, when he was young, had once done that. He had knelt to put his lips to the water, and when he raised himself from this position a grizzly bear stood over him with arms upraised. Loco had no weapon other than his knife and with it he stabbed the bear in the heart. But he was mauled so badly that his face was torn and disfigured. I'd seen Loco and thought that he had lost one eye, but he had vision in it. The lid dropped over it, and he could not keep it up without holding it.

As had my father, Mangus taught us to study the animals and their reactions. A horse often gives warning of danger before his rider is aware of it. A dog is also keenly sensitive to the presence of an enemy. The Apaches have a saying, "A man is a fool not to trust his dog." That is true. But other things—birds, rabbits, deer, almost every wild thing—are alert and if watched can give warning of danger.

Mangus did little drinking and he did not permit those with him to do much. That may have been because there were only the four men, including my two brothers, with the band. I was getting almost as tall as the men, yet I was not a warrior; nor was Mangus's son. Neither of us had formally made even one of the raids requisite to being admitted to the rank of warrior. Mangus told us that we might not be required to do so because we had been through several skirmishes with the Mexican cavalry. We'd seen men killed, he

2. Although Daklugie had been photographed repeatedly and with his consent, he refused to look into a mirror. There was a large one in my living room, but he always sat with his back to it. A fellow Apache who worked for me occasionally gave the following explanation: "That man's a witch. He can witch people just by looking at them. No witch will see himself in a mirror." Daklugie had no hesitancy in saying that he possessed Power; but he was careful to explain that, when used beneficially for either an individual or the tribe, Power is not witchcraft. If employed for sinister purposes it is.

Mangus.

Frank Mangus, son of Mangus.

said, and if attacked he knew we would acquit ourselves as braves. No more was necessary.

Without weapons we were not equipped for fighting. Frank and I constantly tried to get some. Once when we camped near Casas Grandes out near the place of the Old Ones,[3] we prowled about in search of something they might have left, such as sword blades. When I found one I was delighted. I don't know how or where it was made, but it must have been very fine metal, for it would bend double without breaking. I knew men who had bayonet blades, but none so good as this. And we liked long sharp points on our lances because they pulled out easily. I put the blade on a shaft about twelve feet long and was very proud of it. Even Mangus approved.

Of course, Frank wanted one like it and we hunted for days. We looked for game as we did so. Once we chased a rabbit into a clump of chaparral growing close to a cliff. We parted the brush and found a small opening into a cave. As it was very dark inside, we got a dry stalk of sotol and used it as a torch. Frank dared me to go first and I told him that I would if he'd hand me burning sotol when I got inside.

I crept on hands and knees until the tunnel emerged into a large room with high ceiling. There were dead bodies in that cave. They were dried up to skin and bones. We do not fear death as I think White Eyes do, but we do fear the dead. We got out of there just as fast as we could, without stopping to hunt weapons or anything else.

One morning I awoke to find that my brother Daklegon was gone. Mangus looked disturbed when I asked if he knew where my brother was. Casas Grandes, he thought. He had forbidden it, but it was probably there that Daklegon had gone. When he had not returned later that day, Delzhinne talked with Mangus, who approved his going into the town. He also instructed Delzhinne to take me along.

The next morning we set out for Casas Grandes. We took along a pack horse loaded with skins and a big cowhide bag of dried venison for trade. We arrived at the town in midafternoon and stopped at the trading post. As we were taking our jerky off the horse a troop of Mexican cavalry rode by and I recognized Daklegon in the ragged uniform of a Mexican soldier. When I glanced at Delzhinne, I knew that he had seen. Daklegon did not even look our way, and Delzhinne gave no sign of recognition. I froze. Our brother would never have joined the Mexican army; he had been captured. To an Apache any enforced military service is degrading. Had it not been for a remote possibility of Daklegon's being rescued, I would have preferred seeing him dead.

Delzhinne calmly began carrying our produce into the post. He did not speak until a man came to him and looked over the meat and hides. Slowly and carefully he traded the hides and jerky for ammunition, a blanket, and

---

3. Harry Sinclair, "Casas Grandes, Mexico", *El Paso Times*, June 10, 1972: "The apartment building was four or five stories high. The walls were plastered and painted white. There was running water. In cold winter nights most of the residents had an early version of an electric blanket to keep them warm—bunk beds with coals underneath. . . . It sounds like a modern apartment development, but it wasn't. It existed—and disappeared—long before the coming of the first Spaniards in 1563. . . . They have learned a lot about the intelligent and skilled early Americans who built the Casas Grandes big houses. . . ."

coffee and sugar. As he was picking up his purchases, the Mexican offered him a bottle of liquor. My brother shook his head, handed me a bundle, and lifted others from the counter. I followed him to our mounts. He took his time loading, and returned once for something that he had forgotten. We did not talk.

I kept wondering what we could do. Mangus had no men with which to attempt a rescue. Now if he were only Geronimo! Regardless of the odds, my uncle would have taken action. But not Mangus. Why had we left my uncle?

As I feared, when Mangus learned of Daklegon's capture, he just shook his head. I had no chance to talk with Delzhinne that night, and when I awoke the next morning he too was gone. I knew where and why. And I was not surprised when, while we were eating breakfast, Mangus ordered us to get ready to move. Going off with no attempt to help my brothers seemed terrible; but Mangus had no choice, now that Delzhinne was gone.[4]

Many years later, when I was living at Fort Sill, an elderly man, Francisco, came to our house. He spoke no English, but in Spanish he told me that he had been sold into slavery and was taken into Baja California. He escaped and slowly worked his way to Oklahoma and to my house. I was puzzled as to why he had gone to so much trouble to seek me out until the realization came to me that he must have known my brothers!

He had known them. Delzhinne, he said, had made an attempt to rescue Daklegon, and he too had been captured. When the two attempted to talk, they were seized and bound. Sharpened sticks were forced between their teeth and imbedded in both lower and upper jaws so that they could not close their mouths. They had to eat and sleep with those devices in their mouths. With other captives they had been fastened to a long chain and forced to walk to the city of Chihuahua. Daklegon was forced to carry a heavy burden for the cavalry, as though he were a pack horse. Delzhinne was given an equally heavy load and placed far from his brother. When a captive fell a guard finished him with one shot and left him where he lay. My brothers had made it into the City of Mules and were then shipped to Mexico City to be executed.

Francisco had never heard of either again. The only hope for either was the thought that, if the Mexicans intended killing them, why did they waste the expense of sending them hundreds of miles by train?

I never heard any more about them until you reported that Sēnor Chavez, in Chihuahua, had found that the two sons of Juh had died of *viruelas*.[5]

---

4. At this point in our interview, the old chief sat without speaking for some time, and there were tears in his eyes.

5. Daklugie was referring to the visit that Dr. Kathleen Doering, Mrs. Zoe Glasmire, Kaywaykla, and I made to Chihuahua, Mexico. James Kaywaykla had long wanted to go there because as a boy he had been told that when the captives taken at Tres Castillos were driven to the city some of the weak had been forced to jump off a high cliff at the edge of the city, to die on the rocks below. There are no such cliffs. Señor Carlos Chavez, who had an office in the State House, dismissed his staff to give us an interview. He told us that while a student at the University of Mexico he had done extensive research in its archives on the depredations of the Apaches in Chihuahua and Sonora, and that he was at that time working on a book on the subject. He told us that he had found evidence of the death of two sons of Chief Juh, of *viruelas* (smallpox).

CHAPTER 16

THE BLACK RANGE

DAKLUGIE

Mangus was camped on the side of Standing Mountain northeast of the peak [Cook's Peak]. While going in we got separated from the women and children.

It got dark as we followed them up the canyon. I think we must have crossed the little stream ten or twelve times. I asked Mangus why we kept going uphill and he told me that the women were intelligent even though I was a fool. They had done as he said and, when they had reached what they thought was a fairly safe place, they had stopped and cooked a meal. We stayed there a long time, but we took care to prevent our presence being known. The cavalry was scouting the country for Victorio's band, but Mangus did not want even the Indians to know where we were.

Mangus permitted Frank and me to put bunches of grass on our heads and to act as lookouts for him. One day we borrowed (without permission) a pair of field glasses Mangus had. From the mountain we could see wagons drawn by oxen going west, many of them. That fort [Cummings] was built for the cavalry so that travelers might have an armed escort through Cook's Pass. The gorge wasn't long, perhaps four miles, but it afforded an excellent opportunity for ambush. Many attacks had been made on wagon trains there. Many white people, and Indians too, had left their bones in that pass.

That site for the fort had been selected because of a spring that furnished an abundant water supply, not only for men and horses, but for the cattle herd kept for beef; it also supplied the people going west. Frank and I watched black soldiers ride out to water the cavalry horses and pack mules. We watched the white men take the oxen to drink and saw them fill barrels to carry with them. Water was a necessity, of course; but what we envied was their equipment. They had good weapons and many of them. We had bows and arrows and lances, although Mangus had both a rifle and a sixshooter (both of which used the same ammunition). Frank and I had only bows and arrows and lances.

When Mangus missed those field glasses, he had a good idea of where they were; and he would not permit us to leave camp any more. It was very

91

tiresome staying in camp. On top of being idle we had to be quiet. And we were tired of shooting arrows at targets.

Mangus occupied his time in making saddles for the band. He was, I believe, the most able of any of the Apaches in that art. We sometimes hunted for days to find just the right shape of tree or limb for making the saddle trees. Cutting saddles was a slow and tedious task; then they had to be dried and shaped to fit. Mangus used both fire and knife for shaping them, and he rubbed them smooth with pieces of sandstone. But when he got a foundation finished, it fit the body of the horse for which it was intended as nearly perfectly as the means of making it permitted. He covered each saddle tree with tanned hide and finished each off with a wide band of cowhide and, if he could get it, a buckle. If not, we tied knots. I was a proud and happy boy when he completed one for me. Mangus said that it was a waste of time because I would outgrow it in a year or two. My mount was a mule—a pack mule—but a good one, and well trained. And of all the saddles Mangus made for the band, mine was the best.

Frank and I became increasingly restless. We were too young to share the confidences of the men, and we were too old to spend our time with the women and children. If we even spoke to Kedizinne's daughter or to Mangus's girl, we could do so only with a bush between us, and back to back. When we were younger we could share in the races and other exercises that we practiced for hours each day with our sisters and cousins, but not now.

We decided to run away. We planned our leaving very carefully. We knew that if we took our mounts we could be easily trailed; we knew, too, that if we took our new saddles we would really be in trouble. That trailing! In a big band, say of fifty or more, there were seldom more than two trailers, and one of those was usually just learning. It takes keen eyes and good thinking to be a trailer. The position of a stone, the breaking of a fallen twig, the angle of a blade of grass—such signs can be accurately read by an expert. A good trailer goes ahead of a band on the move and directs, to some extent, their movements. Of course, if an enemy is in close pursuit, he is not of much value.

We kept a supply of food in our ration bags all the time. Suspended from our belts was a buckskin thong with a small bag at each end. One bag contained dried venison, and the other usually contained mescal or mesquite bean. Even the smallest child wore his at all times—even while sleeping—and all were required to check and resupply their rations every day. But taking additional food would be sure to excite suspicion, and Mangus's wife was intelligent. We would take our bows and arrows, of course, for we carried them all the time. And I could take my spear; that Mangus would expect of me.

One night, Frank and I rolled up in our blankets and, in the dark of the moon after the fire had gone cold, we slipped quietly away and walked until about midnight. We then hid under an overhanging cliff, with our backs to the wall. Frank went to sleep, but I couldn't. I kept listening to noises I'd never felt bothered about when with the others—familiar noises actually, but now strange and menacing. Just as I began to feel sleepy, I heard the hooting of an owl. Bad! Very bad! Every Apache knows that owls are bad luck and that their hooting is a warning of danger or death. That does not mean that the owl itself is bad—just that he foretells something that is. I could not locate the place from which that dreadful sound came, but I was sure that it was getting closer all the time. I felt sure that this one was hunting me, and I wished we had not run away. Whatever I did I must not go to sleep, because then he would work his spell on me.

Suddenly I realized that something—something big—was sitting beside me, and that it was dark and menacing. I was too frightened to do more than pick up my bow when Frank Mangus spoke very low, with his mouth at my ear. "Let's get out of here," he murmured. We scrambled noiselessly to our feet, rolled our blankets, and stole away in the direction opposite that from which the owl's call came. We did not want to travel at night when ghosts are out, but we were too scared to stay. Besides, owls are the harbingers of ghosts and can see things that we cannot. In our fright we stumbled through the dark, having forgotten the *real* danger, which was noise. When dawn began to break we found another secluded spot, under another overhanging ledge, and we went to sleep.

I don't know how many days we wandered. I was getting very eager to return to the camp of Mangus, but I would not admit it. Let Mangus's son decide. I knew that he would when our supply of food was exhausted. We had stretched our supply by collecting the inner bark of trees and some roots that we knew were used by our people. But not one squirrel did we see; nor did we find even one track of a deer. We did find some mescal and we cut some of the cabbages to roast. We carried them up into the timber, scraped out a hole, built a fire of dry wood in the middle of the day, and buried them as our people do. Cooking mescal is a three-day job at best, and the pit must be watched night and day to prevent the escape of steam and heat. We took turns keeping watch, and during my watch on the third day I fell asleep. Awakened at Frank's urging I saw that the whole forest was on fire! Without even getting our blankets we ran for higher ground. It was lucky for us that the wind was blowing the fire away from us and that Ussen took pity on us and sent a rain— otherwise we might have been burned to death.

That was enough. Frank suggested that we had better return to Mangus's camp. Panicked though we were, we still could identify Standing Mountain and make our way back without further mishap.

We found the camp but, exhausted and starved though we were, we were too afraid to enter.

I felt sure that Mangus would beat us for running away; I had never been struck and did not want to be. It was not for running away that I dreaded punishment, but for setting fire to the world. That fire would be seen by our enemies at the fort and by anybody else within fifty miles. I could just hear Mangus. Instead of walking in and taking our punishment, we remained in hiding just outside camp. Frank had an idea that his mother just might know that we were nearby and that she might put food out for us. To our great relief she did. We'd lived on bark long enough. For three days we feasted on the jerky and acorn meal she left by the little stream for us. When it was gone we waited until the good odors coming from the camp tantalized us beyond endurance. When we saw that all were seated about the fire, as casually as we could we walked in and took our customary places. Nobody even looked our way.

Mangus never mentioned our having left, and we didn't either. He did put us on an intensive training schedule, however. Mangus made us practice for hours a day at shooting, using the lance, mounting our horses, and running. Oh, that running! We lined up, took a mouthful of water, and started for our goal, sometimes two miles away. He taught us how to set a pace for that distance, and we were not to spring until we were almost back to the line from which we started. And when we reached it we were to expel the water from our mouths. That was done to insure proper breathing. I hated that practice, but I knew better than to offer any objections.

CHAPTER 17

ROBBING FORT CUMMINGS

DAKLUGIE

Frank Mangus and I wanted nothing so much as our own guns. Mangus told us that, regardless of how many skirmishes we might have participated in, we could never be warriors until we got good weapons. Did we think we could fight effectively with bow and arrow? Or lances? Though mine was a good spear, it would not be effective against the equipment of the cavalry. When it came to war, we would need guns.

How were we to get them? Frank and I talked it over and over. There were good weapons at Fort Cummings. We decided that we would watch and wait for a time when all or most of the troops were gone from the fort, then we would slip in and look for guns.

But that fort had walls. It was the only one I ever saw that did. These were adobe, and I think they must have been at least twelve feet high. We'd have to get over them some way. And there would be guards pacing back and forth inside. We'd be taking a terrible risk.[1]

We were confident that our mounts were well enough trained to do the job. Both had been taught to stand when the rein was dropped and each would come when we called.[2] We also concluded that, although we couldn't count on the animals at the fort not to be spooked, we could at least count on the silence of our own mounts by muzzling them with rawhide thongs. We also planned to tie skins on the feet of our mounts to assure their silent approach.

Our attempt was to be made in the dark of the moon, preferably when most of the troops were away. Now, if we could just get somebody to ride close enough to bait the cavalry into leaving! We concluded that nobody in the band could do it—we dared not tell Mangus or anybody else what we were planning. We asked permission to hunt and were told that we could go but

---

1. Keith Humphries, "Tale of the Pioneers," *New Mexico Magazine,* (April 1939), gives an excellent description of the site and surroundings of the fort. See also Humphries's "They Watered at Fort Cummings," *New Mexico Magazine* (August 1938), which contains a plan of the fort.

2. I questioned the statement that a horse or mule would come when called. Daklugie said that out in Carisso Canyon, where he lived, his horses were so trained and that upon my next visit he would demonstrate. At a shrill cry several came galloping out of the pines to eat from his hand.

that we were not to take the mounts. Mangus went on to tell his wife to let us have food for three days. Committed to go to the fort even if it meant further disobedience of Mangus, we tied our mounts farther away from the rest so that we could more easily take them when we left. I am sure that Mangus's wife suspected that we did not intend returning in a short time because she provided enough venison and acorn meal for ten days or more.

We left after breakfast the next morning and headed for a spot above the fort that we had previously chosen. As was our custom, we hid our animals a mile or so from where we slept. And we stood guard alternately during the day, each with a bunch of grass on his head to prevent the soldiers from seeing us through field glasses. We had none; but Apaches have keen vision, and we were close enough that we could see much of what was going on in the fort.

While we were waiting for the dark of the moon, we did some reconnoitering at night. We took Frank's horse to a bunch of chaparral and tied him. Then, with the mule's feet covered with buckskin and his mouth tied shut, we led him close to the fort. Greatly to our relief, he made no attempt at braying, nor did the animals in the corral seem conscious of his presence.

Finally the dark of the moon came and we made our final approach. We had learned that three walls were lined with rooms but that the corral was just inside the fourth. During the day sentinels paced back and forth both on top of the roofs and on the ground; but at night they seemed to desert the roofs. Near the rear gate there was a blank wall opposite the corral and it was there that we decided to climb over.

We left Frank's mount some distance from the fort and, with the mule's padded hoofs making little noise, we walked beside him to the spot we'd selected for entering the place. I dropped the rein and stood in the saddle. Frank climbed to my shoulders and pulled himself to the top of the wall. He lay prone, listening for the guard. When the man had passed, he slid down the rope to the ground. When he gave a slight tug, I climbed the rope and followed him to Mother Earth. It was very dark and we huddled against the wall trying to see the guard. We could hear him distinctly. When he had passed on his way to the distant gate, we slipped across an open space to a building. It had three windows opening toward the inside. We rounded a corner and found a door, locked. We crossed to a second room, of similar plan, but the door to it was standing open. After listening carefully for breathing, we stepped inside and followed the wall. When we reached a sort of shelf, about three feet above the ground, we felt along it carefully. I don't know what the place was—perhaps a room where weapons were kept ready for emergencies, or perhaps the officers' gun room. At any rate, on that counter we felt rifles standing upright. And by each was a box of ammunition. We had no time to examine the rifles, but we were surprised by the size of the boxes of bullets. Each of us tied a box to his belt. Then we felt further, hoping to find pistols, and we did. We stashed the ammunition for them away in the tops of our moccasins, and with a rifle and pistol each, we retraced our way to the wall. We listened intently, but we could hear nothing but the regular steps of the sentinel. Once he stopped, and I feared that he had spotted us. I think he could not have been more than thirty feet away. Finally the man started back on his beat. We timed our steps with his.

At last I reached the wall, and a second later Frank stood beside me. Which way we should go to find the dangling rope I did not know, but toward our left was the corner, and I tried that first. No rope! Then we must go to the right until I found it. With my left hand on the wall, I moved slowly and quietly until again I heard the returning footsteps of the sentinel. I froze. So did Frank. And again we tried to melt into the wall until he resumed his return walk. He stopped for what seemed a very long time, sensing us perhaps. But at last he started back, and I felt ahead for the rope. And I touched it! I laid my rifle against the wall at my feet and tied Frank's to the rope. He climbed to my shoulders and, with his foot in my hand, he reached for the top of the wall. Without the rope I doubt that he could have made it; but he did, and he drew his rifle up. Then he took mine, and lowered the rawhide for me. I joined him, and we lay flat while the sentry passed close. Then we slid down to the mule. Without attempting to load a weapon, we placed them on him and slowly led him away from the fort. Not yet were we out of danger; the snort of a horse might warn the guard. But we dared not hurry. We went slowly and carefully to where we'd left Frank's mount. Even then we walked and led the animals.

It is strange how badly scared one can be after the danger is over. I knew that we were safe after we'd got to Frank's horse, but I shook. I got to thinking of what could have happened if things had not gone as they did. Suppose the guard had stopped to smoke? Suppose he had sighted the track of moccasins? I thought of such things all the way to Mangus's camp. I tried to picture his pride when he saw our weapons. Two each. That big box of ammunition still worried me, but the more bullets the better. When this was gone we'd have plenty of trouble getting more. Still, I'd never seen bullets carried in anything the size of that box. How did a man carry that thing? Mangus had an ammunition belt, but I intended using a buckskin pouch as many Apaches still did.

When we reached Mangus's camp, the band had just finished eating. Hungry though we were, we first had to show off our plunder. Mangus looked us over and asked what were the queer-looking things that we were carrying. I had not paid much attention to mine until then. The rifle *was* queer looking; it had two barrels. And my pistol—it was small. Mangus opened one of the big boxes of ammunition and took out a big bullet, the biggest I'd ever seen. Perhaps we'd not got the right kind. But they fit. Mangus pointed the rifle at a tree trunk close by and pulled the trigger. That bullet must have broken into a hundred little pieces, judging from the way it speckled that tree.

When I looked around, Mangus was getting up and rubbing his shoulder. The rifle lay on the ground. It was time to leave; I knew it and so did Frank. When we got far enough away that we knew we could outrun his father, we stopped. He shook his fist at us and ordered us to come back. We obeyed, but we did not get close to him.

"Great warriors you are," he snorted. "What do you mean by bringing these worthless weapons here? That rifle—worthless! And those toy pistols—fit for nothing but children."

Those were the first shotguns I'd ever seen. And the first 38s.

CHAPTER 18

FIRST EXILES

EUGENE CHIHUAHUA

After my father quit as a scout for the army, he knew that he would have to leave the reservation. He and Geronimo left at the same time [May 1885].

We went east along the Gila until nearly daylight, then turned southeast across a broad plain. When we got almost to the ridge we saw a cloud of dust and knew that the cavalry was after us. That is when Geronimo and Chihuahua separated, he and Naiche to go south and my father northeast. Chihuahua left the San Francisco to go up the canyon of the Blue where there were very good places for ambush. Then we turned east through a low saddle and on toward Alma. All the cavalry from the forts must have been after us, for we were followed down past Silver City and on south.

I do not know just where it was that we camped on the ridge and spent the night. Before Chihuahua did anything else, he showed the women and children a cave in a canyon in which they were to hide if we were attacked. Then a beef and a colt were killed, a fire made of very dry wood, and the meat put to cook for morning.

Before it got really light, my cousin [Ulzanna's son] and I asked our mothers for our bows and arrows and went down the ridge looking for rabbits. On our left was the canyon where the cave was, and not far from it the horses were concealed. If an attack should come, the men were to draw the cavalry away from the defenseless.

Suddenly, something buzzed by my ear. Then I heard a shot; then many shots. My cousin fell. When I tried to lift him blood ran down my hands. I could not get him on his feet. He told me to leave and save myself. Suddenly a woman came to us. She lifted my cousin to her shoulder and ran along the ridge with me following.

When she reached a place where a shallow trickle of water fell over the cliff, she stopped. The stones were slick. At the bottom I saw a man standing. She put the wounded boy down and pushed him over. The man, José Second, caught him and eased him to the ground; then she shoved me over. She followed, but because she was heavier both she and José Second fell to the ground. Carrying the wounded boy, he led the way to the cave where there were many women and children.

The cavalry did follow the men, but they left a Negro sergeant and troopers to find the women. They rode to the spring to water their horses, saw and followed our tracks, and dragged us out. Three women were wounded, one with a bullet hole through the calf of her leg. My mother was there. I looked for my grandmother, but my mother shook her head. Tears streamed down her face and I knew that my grandmother had been killed. Other women, too, were missing; whether they were dead or wounded we never knew.

The soldiers put my cousin on a pack mule, but he did not live to reach Fort Bowie. Not one of the women, not even the wounded, was permitted to ride. We were herded along like cattle. The one with the bullet hole in her leg limped along as best she could. My mother signalled me and I left the line of march to get a good strong stick for her. With it she hobbled along with the rest. I don't know how long it took us to reach the fort, but when we did we were locked in a building. Some food was thrown on the ground for us as though we were dogs.

After a day or two the children were permitted to play outside and the women were put to digging ditches [latrines].

When Child of the Waters, son of Ussen, came to the Earthland, he gave the Apaches things good for them: herbs, plants for food, and weapons. To the Indians he gave the bow and arrow, the shield, the spear, and the sling. And to the White Eyes he gave the pick and shovel. It was what he gave to them that caused all the trouble. With the pick and shovel the prospectors grubbed in the body of Mother Earth for the forbidden gold and caused the mountains to dance and shake their shoulders. Mother Earth opened up and swallowed whole villages.

Picks and shovels! For the women, and even the wounded ones! They made those women do that digging. They forced the lame one to work with the rest. She bound the stick to her leg for support and worked. When she fell, a soldier prodded her with his rifle and kicked her till she scrambled to her feet. One day she fell and no kicking or prodding could rouse her. We knew that she had escaped and gone to the Happy Place, and we were glad.

One day Perico came into camp (Fort Bowie), but he was not permitted to come near us. I don't know how my mother learned that Chihuahua had surrendered, but he had. He, along with Ulzanna and Nana, after a meeting with Geronimo, decided to surrender to the army. They had been promised that if they did they would be sent away from our country for two years, would be placed with their families, and after two years would be permitted to return to Turkey Creek.

Not long after that, a troop of cavalry rode into Fort Bowie with my father. Neither he nor his people gave any sign of recognition. Some of his warriors were with him, but not all. Some had gone off with Geronimo and Naiche.

Later, Chihuahua was permitted to be with us, and other men with their families. They told us that we were to go to a faraway place called Florida. But my father refused to go until the soldiers went to Fort Apache and brought my brother who was there. That is one time a White Eye kept his word. Soldiers were sent with a horse for my brother and they brought him to Fort Bowie.

From Bowie, maybe twenty miles north of the fort, they put us and some soldiers on the train and started us to Florida.

So Chihuahua was the first of the chiefs to agree to surrender. He did not do this just in order to be with his own family, but so that his men, too, might be reunited with theirs. And he did not decide himself but always consulted with his warriors. The majority of them knew that their wives and children were being held at Fort Bowie and that their only chance to be together was to accept the terms offered them.

With my father was Nana and some women and children from other bands. Among them was one of Naiche's wives and one of Geronimo's. My father, like Cochise, did not want to see his band exterminated; and he well understood what was in store for them if they continued the losing fight.

But he did not do this immediately. He wandered about in Mexico, sometimes meeting with other bands, especially Geronimo's.

That day they put us on that train at Bowie, Arizona, would have been a good day to die. Banishment from our land and the bones of our ancestors was worse than death. Everybody must die sometime; we would have been lucky to go then. We knew that we were facing two years of slavery and degradation, but my father was willing to endure that for the sake of the future when we were to be free again. Chihuahua did not know, nor did anyone else, that we were to be prisoners for twenty-seven years.

It would have been a good day to die.

CHAPTER 19

GERONIMO

DAKLUGIE

Not until after the death of my father, Juh, did Geronimo become very prominent. After that he just took over. He was a Bedonkohe and never was elected to the chieftainship. Naiche was chief, but he was very young—too young for the leadership. It took a man to lead the Chiricahua. Geronimo was of middle age, a well-known fighter and superb leader, and he was also a Medicine Man. No White Eyes seem to understand the importance of that in controlling Apaches. Naiche was not a Medicine Man; so he needed Geronimo as Geronimo needed *him*. It was a good combination. Geronimo saw that Naiche was accorded the respect and recognition due a chief and that he always occupied the seat of honor; but Geronimo planned the strategy, with Naiche's help, and made the decisions. Of course, had Juh or Geronimo been chief, nobody could have usurped their prerogatives. But don't forget that not being a Medicine Man was a great handicap to Naiche.

Several years after our capture, and after I returned from school, I lived in Geronimo's village and was his confidant and interpreter. I accompanied him everywhere he went. When he took pneumonia at Fort Sill and was sent to the hospital, Eugene Chihuahua sat beside him during the day and I at night. And he died with his hand in mine. Even in his delirium, he talked of those seventeen men who had eluded five thousand men of the army of the United States for many years; and eluded not only them, but also twenty-five hundred Mexican soldiers—seventy-five hundred men, well armed, well trained, and well equipped against seventeen whom they regarded as naked savages. The odds were only five hundred to one against Geronimo, but still they could not whip him nor could they capture him.[1]

But I am Geronimo's nephew and there are people who might think that I am biased. Go see Charlie Smith. As a child he and his mother were captured by Geronimo's band. Charlie was with Geronimo and Naiche about a year, I think, before going to Florida.

---

1. For an account of events leading to Geronimo's death, see Chapter 11, Book Two.

CHARLIE SMITH

M y father, Ne-do-bilt-yo, or Conceals His Tracks, was a Chiricahua scout
who was stationed at Fort Stanton for a long time. The officer who enlisted him was unable to either spell or pronounce his name, so he just recorded him as Charlie Smith. In some books he is mentioned as Corporal or Sergeant Charlie; in others he is Alabama Charlie.

While at the fort, he met and married my mother, Cumpah, a Mescalero;
and according to Indian way that made him a Mescalero too. She had a home
at White Tail, and my father went there as often as he was permitted. It was
there that I was born.

There had been no piñon crop in our mountains for four or five years; you
know that the trees don't bear often. My father learned from a scout, who
came in from western New Mexico, that there was a big piñon crop out there.
About forty Mescaleros got passes from the agency for a trip to last thirty days,
and my father's captain let him go with us. To make sure that he did not over-
stay his time, he tied thirty knots in a buckskin thong and each day untied
one.

We went on horseback, of course; there were many more wild horses on the
reservation then than now, and my parents had several. They had given me
the best-broken of the lot, and I was old enough to ride alone.[2] Each of them
had a mount, and they took pack horses. I do not know what year it was, but I
think it was 1885.

We met the others at the Rinconada and rode over the saddle of the Sacred
Mountain [Sierra Blanca] and down past the Shanta place, and then we struck
out between the White Sands and the Malpais [lava flow].

We went on to the Rio Grande, crossed it, and started up the long slope of
the Black Range. We crossed the divide on the old primitive trail and camped
on the west side. From where we stopped we could see the lights at the copper
mine and dim lights as though from small fires further to the southwest. Somebody jokingly said that they might be from Geronimo's camp, but nobody
took it seriously. Still, the next night we stopped in a deep canyon where we
could build a fire for cooking without danger of its being seen. We were still
eating dried food that we had brought with us.

The next morning, usually by twos, the men left to hunt. My father and a
few others preferred going alone. The women also divided into small groups.
With Mother and me were Ih-tedda, or Young Girl, and a young mother with
her baby. We began our harvest of piñons by finding trails of pack rats and
tracking them to their dens. The nests were sometimes two and a half feet
high, and about that in diameter. Sometimes we got as many as two gallons or
more of the tiny nuts from one cache. The rats never carry a faulty piñon to
their hoard. When we could find no more nests, we placed skins under the trees
and beat the lower limbs with clubs; and we even picked up some one by one.

When the men returned in the evening, the women dressed the game and
hung it on bushes and low branches to dry. They scraped the fat from the
hides and pegged them out. The tanning would be done after our return. Both

2. Charlie guessed his age as four or five. Apache children of necessity learned to ride when very
young.

102

meat and piñons were obtained in abundance, and people were thinking of returning to Mescalero when two families asked to stay just one more day to complete their harvest.

On our last evening, as my mother's party started for camp, strange warriors swooped down the mountain and we scattered. I was running toward some chaparral when a bullet nicked the calf of my leg. I still have the scar. The next thing I knew a man leaned from his mount and lifted me in front of him. Riders were forcing the women to mount behind them; and they carried us to the camp of Geronimo.

As was the custom, the chief got first choice of the women; but Naiche was well supplied and yielded to Geronimo. He took Ih-tedda and a warrior named Juan-si-got-si chose my mother and me. What became of the other woman and the baby I don't know.

My mother warned me that I was not to let my unhappiness be known. I was to be very obedient to my stepfather; I was to anticipate his every need. Already I had learned that when he rode in I was to meet him, take his horse, and care for it. I was to build fires, gather wood, and, above all, obey instantly. I was to ask no questions. I was to eat any portion of food given me without complaint. All Apache boys were expected to do these things. My stepfather was a strict disciplinarian but neither mother nor I resented that; had we felt it, we would not have shown it. And I am sure that he liked me. He told my mother that I would make a good warrior and that I must become a good shot. He made a bow and arrows for me—arrows with blunt points—and he required me to practice shooting several hours a day. I was too young, he said, to have real points, but if I continued to gain skill he would provide me with some. Imagine my delight when one evening he rode in with a pony for me!

I'll never forget that winter. Geronimo would line the boys up on the bank, have us build a fire and undress by it, and then make us plunge into the stream, breaking the ice as we went. The first time he did this, I thought that the ordeal would be over when he let us get out of the water. But no—time after time we warmed ourselves by the fire and returned to the icy water. There were times when I just hated him. Geronimo would stand there on the bank, with a stick in his hand. What for, I don't know; I never saw him strike anybody. But we knew he might and that was enough. Nobody defied Geronimo.[3]

Was I present during the fighting? Geronimo had the women and children along, and of course they saw what happened. If pursued, he, as did all Apaches, tried to protect them by sending them ahead; but ordinarily, when fighting occurred, it was because he laid an ambush, and every one of the band was there. Some of the women were very good shots—good fighters, too. Lozen, sister of Victorio, was called The Woman Warrior; and though she may not have had as much strength as one of the men she was as good a shot as any of them.[4]

---

3. Apaches very seldom whipped a child.

4. Lozen never married. She died at Mt. Vernon Barracks. (I am in error in having corrected Kaywaykla in In the Days of Victorio and stating that Lozen married Calvin Zhunni and died on the Mescalero Reservation. However, Zhunni's wife was also named Lozen and she did die at Mescalero. Ball, Victorio, p. 207.)

When actually on the warpath the Apaches were under very strict rules. Even words for common things were different. Women could go with their husbands, but they could not live together. No unmarried woman was permitted to go with them. Lozen? No, she was not married; she never married. But to us she was as a Holy Woman and she was regarded and treated as one. White Painted Woman herself was not more respected. And she was brave! Geronimo sent her on missions to the military officers to arrange for meetings with him, or to carry messages.[5]

When Geronimo crossed the border into New Mexico or Arizona, it was usually to get ammunition. I do not think that he wanted to kill, but there were cases when he had no choice. If he were seen by a civilian, it meant that he would be reported to the military and they'd be after us. So there was nothing to do but kill the civilian and his entire family. It was terrible to see little children killed. I do not like to talk of it. I do not like to think of it. But the soldiers killed our women and children, too. Don't forget that. There were times that I hated Geronimo for that, too; but when I got older, I knew that he had no choice.

Stealing horses was fun. I was not quite old enough to get in on that, and how I envied those who were! It was usually the boys, too, who shot the fire-arrows to set houses ablaze. I never saw that done but twice, though. I did see many, many people killed. I wish I could forget it. Even babies were killed; and I love babies.

But Geronimo was fighting not only to avenge his murdered mother, wife, and children, but for his people and his tribe. Later there were Apaches who were bitter against Geronimo, saying that it was his fault that they were sent to Florida and were prisoners of war for twenty-seven years. Well, if they'd had the fighting spirit of Geronimo, they need not have been sent. The big difference was that he had the courage to keep on and they were quitters. Some of them have "gone white" and blame Geronimo for everything. I don't respect them. They were cowards. I won't name them. I am ashamed that they are Apaches.

And don't forget that Geronimo knew that it was hopeless. But that did not stop him. I admire him for that. He was a great leader of men, and it ill becomes the cowardly to find fault with the man who was trying to keep them free. And don't forget that he was fighting against enormous odds, or that nobody ever captured him.

Jasper Kanseah, nephew of Geronimo, also gave an account.

KANSEAH

My father died before I was born, and my mother died when they drove us like cattle from Cochise's reservation to San Carlos. I had nobody but my grandmother and she had to walk. I was little, and when I couldn't

---

5. I have frequently been asked why nobody but Kaywaykla mentioned Lozen (see Ball, *Victorio*). His explanation was that the Apaches respected her and were protecting her from criticism. Only wives of warriors went on the warpath with their husbands.

Kanseah and Yahnosha.

keep up she carried me. She told me that Geronimo was my uncle, but I didn't remember him till he came to San Carlos. When he came my grandmother had already gone to the Happy Place, and I had nobody. But Indian women were good to me, and even when they were hungry they gave me some of the food their own children needed. We never went hungry till we got to San Carlos; and there we almost died because there was no food.

I think that I was eleven when my uncle, Geronimo, came and took me with him. And he gave me to Yahnosha to be his orderly and learn to be a warrior. I stayed with Yahnosha and cooked his food, and got his horse and fed and watered it; and I never spoke unless somebody asked me a question. And I ate what was left. No matter what happened, I didn't complain. And even when I talked I had to say it differently. (On the warpath we don't talk as we do most of the time, but differently.) I had to think what Yahnosha wanted next and then get it for him before he told me. But I was proud to be taught by a great warrior and I tried to do everything right.

I knew Geronimo and I knew that he was the victim of liars. He was lied about by many of his own people for whom he was fighting. He was betrayed by them. He was betrayed by Miles. I am not sure but that he was betrayed by Crook, though some think not. But I know that he was lied to by Miles. That man did not do what he promised. Geronimo was a really great fighting man, and Miles was a coward. Everything he needed for his troops was provided for him and them, but Geronimo had to obtain food for his men, and for their women and children. When they were hungry, Geronimo got food. When they were cold he provided blankets and clothing. When they were afoot, he stole horses. When they had no bullets, he got ammunition. He was a good man. I think that you have desperados among you White Eyes today that are much worse men and are more cruel than Geronimo.

CHAPTER 20

SURRENDER OF GERONIMO

I asked Daklugie if he knew either Martine or Kayitah, the Apache scouts who were instrumental in Geronimo's final surrender by leading army negotiators to his camp. He had known both, Martine best because he was a Nednhi and had once been Juh's orderly. Daklugie informed me that he had served as interpreter for Martine and Kayitah when they had told their story to a visitor several years before. That account, a transcript of which was with the records at the Mescalero Reservation, is as follows.

MARTINE AND KAYITAH

General Miles sent for us and told us that he had decided to make another effort to get Geronimo to surrender and stop the Indian uprisings. Geronimo had taken a band of his people, 39 in all, and had gone into Mexico. He had made peace with the Mexicans [at Casas Grandes] and was still in a position to quickly cross the line and make further attacks on the American people.

General Miles told us that he wished us to go with a young officer, Lieut. [Charles B.] Gatewood into Mexico, find Geronimo, persuade him to make peace and come back and be delivered to General Miles. Word was sent to Geronimo that he must serve a term in prison when he was brought back to the United States.

We agreed to go with Lieut. Gatewood. There were other persons besides us two scouts and Gatewood, including the interpreter, and the packer in charge of our camp. The name of the interpreter was George Wratten.

We first went into the western part of Chihuahua, coming finally to an old mine near which there were a number of Mexicans packing their burros with acorns which they were carrying away. We talked with these Mexicans who knew of Geronimo and they told us where they believed we could find him. We hit the trail at once, traveling all night long. We came to Fronteras, Mexico, where there was still another party of American troops encamped.

There Lieutenant Gatewood was told that shortly before our coming, two Indian women from the band of Geronimo had been sent into the village with a message from him that he was willing to consider a meeting. These women had been returned to the Indian camp and we did not know whether there was any real truth in this proposed offer of holding a council.

The two Indian women who had been there were Mrs. Hugh Coonie [Dahtes-te] and Lozen who is dead now.

We remained over night in the camp of the soldiers and the following day Lieut. Gatewood led us out to try to locate Geronimo. We came to the top of a mountain near Fronteras where Geronimo's band had just recently camped. We had with us that day ten or twelve additional soldiers which Gatewood had secured while at their camp. We spent the night on the mountain in Geronimo's abandoned camp.

The following morning, we followed their trail down the mountain to the Bavispe River and there we realized that we were very close upon his band.

We spent another night at the river and the next morning Lieut. Gatewood told us two scouts that he wished us to go on alone, try to locate Geronimo and have a talk with him. We therefore left Lieut. Gatewood and his soldiers in the camp by the river, and we two, Kayitah and Martine, climbed another mountain in which we were sure Geronimo was camped. We realized the danger of these proceedings, but we had promised General Miles that we would try our best to bring back Geronimo, and we intended to do it.

At two o'clock that afternoon, we came near the place where his camp was pitched. Between his camp and us, Geronimo had his men stationed out among the rocks with their guns guarding the camp against attack. We proceeded as carefully as we could but they saw us coming. We knew that they might shoot at us at any moment. In fact, there was much danger of their doing this. We learned later that they were doubtful about what they should do as we came up. However, Kayitah had a cousin in Geronimo's camp (Yahnosha) who recognized him and who did not want to see him killed. He therefore jumped upon a rock without permission from Geronimo and called to us and asked why we were coming. We replied that we were messengers from General Miles and Lieut. Gatewood and that we wished to discuss peace with Geronimo.

He then told us that we might come into the camp. We did this and his warriors joined us and together we all filed back to where the real camp was pitched.

We talked over the reasons for which we had come. Geronimo told us that while he had in the past broken faith with the American soldiers, he was now really willing to meet them and make peace.

Geronimo then had cooked some mescal and from this he took in his two hands enough of this mescal to make a lump about the size of a man's heart. This he squeezed together, wrapped it up and told us to take this to Lieut. Gatewood. He said that this was a token of his agreement and that when the mescal had been sent, there would be no reason for Gatewood to doubt his earnestness in planning to make peace.

Kayitah stayed with Geronimo as a hostage. Martine was sent back to Gatewood with the mescal. That same evening, Martine arrived at the river camp and handed the mescal to Gatewood. He took it, sliced it up, and handed it to his soldiers who ate it between bread; they were all very happy for they realized that Geronimo was now in earnest in his plan to end the Indian wars. The soldiers all lay down around the fire that night feeling that there was no danger of an attack.

[The following morning, Gatewood called Martine very early and told him that they would go again for a conference with Geronimo. This time Gatewood, Wratten (the interpreter), and some others went along, but the larger body of soldiers was left behind in a canyon near the river.

Martine resumed his account:] When we had gotten about half way to the Indian camp of the day before, we saw the Indians coming down the mountain to meet us. We were very anxious for a few minutes, thinking that maybe Geronimo had changed his mind and meant trouble for us. We said, however, that the only thing to do is to go on and meet him and when we came nearer we saw that he had Kayitah leading his party. . . . We drew nearer to the Indians coming down the mountain and when we met Geronimo came up and shook hands with the soldiers. We then sat down on the ground together and talked for a long time about the plans for surrender. We then all returned down the mountain to the soldiers' camp.

[There Gatewood made arrangements with them to go in and give themselves up to General Miles. Geronimo refused to give up his guns, and Gatewood told him that he might take them in and hand them to General Miles. Gatewood gave the Indians provisions and sent out men to get a fresh supply.]

From the Bavispe, we started to the camp of General Miles. While we were on the way, at one place we looked across a flat and there we saw 600 Mexicans, soldiers who had come upon us without our noticing their approach. The Mexican officer came to our camp and he was very angry. It seemed that he wanted to take Geronimo from us. Geronimo was angry for he felt that he would be much safer with the American soldiers than in the hands of the Mexicans. We therefore suggested to Gatewood that he take us scouts and Geronimo's band and slip away from the Mexicans while we left still others of the soldiers to talk with the Mexicans. This we did and we were soon away from the Mexicans and they did not trouble us further.

We then went on toward a mountain in the direction we were told we would reach General Miles. Still other American soldiers had come from one of their camps and they followed on behind us, but they did not join Geronimo and Gatewood who were traveling together.

Geronimo and Gatewood both sent out messengers to the camp of General Miles to tell him that Geronimo was coming in for a conference. These were Kayitah, two other Indians, and at least one white man. When General Miles got the word, he started in a wagon to meet us and we were still about 60 miles from his post when he met us. Shortly before he arrived, Natchez [Naiche], who was the other important warrior with Geronimo, became nervous and took a party of the Indians with him to a nearby hill and acted as if he might leave. We called to him and he returned.

When Miles got there, he took Geronimo, Natchez and some of the other Indians in his wagon with him and drove back to the fort [Bowie], arriving there before the remainder of the party. The Indians surrendered their guns at the fort and thus Geronimo's war was over.

It should be noted that Geronimo and his warriors retained their weapons until they reached Fort Bowie. George Martine, Martine's son, who heard his father and Kayitah tell their experiences many times, gave me the following account.

GEORGE MARTINE

Martine was a Nednhi and a member of Juh's band. When a small boy he was captured by Mexicans and sold to a family, elderly and well-to-do, who lived on a *rancho* near Casas Grandes. This couple had never had a child and they became deeply attached to the boy. They had him call them his mother and father. They took him to church and had him baptized in the Catholic faith. He got a saint's name (Martin), which in Spanish is Martine.

When his owner and foster-father became ill, he felt that he had not long to live and wanted to provide for the boy. He gave Martine a good mount and a pack horse, food, blankets, and a paper saying that he was no longer a slave. He took Martine to Casas Grandes to the home of a friend and arranged that, when Juh or members of his band came to the trading post, the friend would be notified so that the boy could rejoin his people.

My father was so efficient and so loyal to Juh that he became his personal attendant—a sort of orderly, we'd call it now.

Martine grew to manhood and married. He did not want to go on the warpath, nor did he want his wife and children to have to do so. He wished to live in peace. On a trip to Arizona he enlisted as a scout at Fort Apache. He knew well how the scouts were disliked by their people, who regarded them as traitors; but he knew, too, that his wife and children could live at the fort and be protected. He was much influenced in his decision by the fact that Kayitah was a scout. He had known Kayitah before being captured by the Mexicans, and the two were close friends all their lives.

Miles promised these two, "If you come back alive and Geronimo surrenders I will have the government give you a good home at Turkey Creek and there you will have plenty of good water, grass, and game. Everything you need will be furnished you. And the government will give you seventy thousand dollars if you are successful; you will get the money as soon as Geronimo surrenders and you get back."

Neither Martine nor Kayitah had any idea of what seventy thousand dollars might be—just that it was a big sum. They had no use for money but they wanted a home at Turkey Creek where they could live peacefully. They had not asked for money; but because Miles promised it, they looked for it until they died. Of course they did not get it.

Jasper Kanseah, nephew of Geronimo and his youngest warrior, was on guard at the top of the trail when Martine and Kayitah came. He gave me the following account.

KANSEAH

I was on guard at the top of the zigzag trail. I lay with field glasses, watching. When I detected a movement on the plain far below I watched it care-

109

fully. Something was coming; something was crossing the plain toward the foot of the trail. No, two things! Might be deer. They got a little bigger; they were not long enough for deer. I called to Geronimo that somebody was coming. He knew that it would take a long, long time for anyone to reach the top. He told me to watch and when I was sure that it was men to let him know. I was already sure but waited awhile before sending word.

As the figures came up the trail I recognized Martine and Kayitah by their walk.

Then Geronimo and the warriors joined me and seated themselves with Yahnosha at Geronimo's right, and Fun and Eyelash at his left. The two scouts kept on climbing. Martine was carrying a stick with a white rag on it. I could see their faces and told Geronimo who they were.

He said, "It does not matter who they are. If they come closer they are to be shot."

"They are our brothers," said Yahnosha. Let's find out why they come. They are very brave to risk this."

"They do not take the risk for us but for the money promised them by our enemies. When they get close enough, shoot."

"We will not shoot," said Yahnosha. "If there is any shooting done it will be at you, not them. The first man who lifts a rifle I will kill."

"I will help you . . ." said Fun.

"Let them live," grunted Geronimo.

The scouts reminded Geronimo of his plight, and of the uselessness of further fighting. They told him that Chihuahua, with his band and with wives and children of some of Geronimo's band, had given up and had been sent to Florida. Among others were a wife of Chief Naiche and one of Geronimo's wives.

They reminded Geronimo that every living thing—Mexicans, White Eyes, and even the beasts—were his enemies. The mountain itself was both a shield and a menace, for if the trail were destroyed he and his men were forever prisoners upon it.

At that time Geronimo's band, including him and Naiche, consisted of seventeen men; he had also Lozen, sister of Victorio and known as the Woman Warrior. Geronimo was handicapped by the presence, too, of women and children who must be defended and fed.

Nobody ever captured Geronimo. I know. I was with him. Anyway, who can capture the wind?

When he learned that Lieutenant Charles B. Gatewood was to be in charge, George Wratten volunteered his services as interpreter and was Gatewood's choice for the task. The young officer, whom the Apaches called Nantan Long Nose, was to take ten soldiers, an interpreter, and a packer.

In his *The Truth about Geronimo*, Britton Davis reported that "it was essential that some officer with authority should be the bearer of Miles' tender of terms; and this officer must be known to Geronimo. . . . Any strange officer attempting to enter Geronimo's camp would be shot on sight."[1] With Crawford dead

---

1. Davis, *Truth about Geronimo*, pp. 223–24.

and Davis having resigned, Gatewood was the best choice. Not only was he respected by the Apaches, but he knew the country in which Geronimo was expected to be operating.

"My father," said George Martine, "knew that Geronimo would not believe that any soldiers could find him. My mother was a daughter of a Nednhi, I am a Nednhi, and Kayitah had married a sister of Victorio."

Each of the scouts knew that he must forfeit the respect of his people by going on this mission; but they were already scouts, and they wanted to see the fighting come to an end because they feared it would result in the extermination of the Apaches. Their greatest fear was that, neither being medicine men, they might not be able to persuade Geronimo. Although Geronimo had never brought attention to it, all Apaches, including the two scouts, believed that his medicine gave him great Power, and they were awed by it.

When they volunteered they had the promise of Miles that they could return to Turkey Creek where they could live in peace and know that their families were protected by the soldiers at Fort Apache. When they reported to the general, he did not realize how little they were influenced by his promise of much money and again he promised seventy thousand dollars for a successful attempt. This was explained through George Wratten, who told them it was a very great sum and that Miles had promised to give it to them upon their return.

Kanseah said, "In the center of the warriors assembled at the rim [at the top of the trail], Naiche, as a chief should be, was seated in the center. Lined up were, besides those named: Chapo (son of Geronimo), Tissnolthos, Onondiah, Juan-si-got-si, Motzos, Sisnah, Hanloah, and Kasegoneh. Lozen, too, was with the men. Except for Naiche, Geronimo was related to every one of them either by blood or by marriage. I think I could not have been more than fifteen, but I had been on the warpath with my uncle for three years."

Instead of being rewarded, Martine and Kayitah were confined with Geronimo's band and sent to Florida. They remained prisoners until freed in 1913 with the rest of the Chiricahuas. Forty-one years later they, with the assistance of Charles Gatewood, were recognized for their service as scouts and received small pensions.

DAKLUGIE

The thing that embittered Geronimo was the promise that Crook made as to his band's going east for two years and then being returned to their homes on Turkey Creek. Crook was our enemy; but though we hated him, we respected him, and even my uncle thought he would keep his promise. I think that he was honest in his promise but that he was not permitted to keep it. That is said to be his reason for asking Sheridan to relieve him from his command. And there is no doubt that, while we were prisoners of war, he did what he could in our behalf.

If Crook was disliked, you should know how much more bitterly Miles was hated; he was regarded as a coward, a liar, and a poor officer. His claim for having captured Geronimo? If any man deserved credit for that, it was Lieutenant Gatewood. Did Miles come within any reasonable distance to confer with Geronimo? He stayed close to Fort Bowie.

And who sent the band to Florida? Unless the President, Sheridan, and the Secretary of War were all liars, Miles did. And we know that he was a liar. In comparison to Crook, he was despicable.[2]

Geronimo died regretting that he had trusted Miles. He did not blame Gatewood in the least; he knew that that young man was just obeying orders, and that if the general was treacherous it was not the fault of Gatewood. The Apaches admired and respected him for his courage in going to Geronimo, and they had contempt for Miles and his officers who played safe by remaining at a distance—with Miles being the furthest away.

KANSEAH

General Miles lied to us. He told us that we were going to be with Chihuahua and his band, but that didn't happen. They were at St. Augustine and he put us at Pensacola. They took the women and children to be with Chihuahua, but not the men. I remember how General Miles put a rock down and said that it was Chihuahua. Then he put two more rocks close by and said that one was for the people at Fort Apache and the other for Geronimo's band. He said that he was going to forget all the bad things we had done and was going to put us with Chihuahua. And he took one rock and moved it, and then the one that was us. He put both right by Chihuahua. It was just more White Eye lies.

Ten days before ordering Lieutenant Gatewood, Martine, and Kayitah south for their fateful meeting with Geronimo, General Miles informed army headquarters in Washington of his desire to have the Chiricahuas at Fort Apache removed from Arizona. As part of his plan he arranged to have representatives of that group, Chato included, travel to Washington and consult as to where their people might go. Travel of the Fort Apache delegation, surrender and travel of Geronimo north out of Mexico, and removal of the Chiricahua people from Fort Apache all occurred at the same time. Having hoodwinked the chiefs remaining at Fort Apache into reporting to the agency—where they were put under guard—on August 20 Lieutenant Colonel Wade telegraphed Miles that the camp was "under control" and that he was prepared to move them to the nearest railhead, this four days before Gatewood met Geronimo in Mexico. Not necessarily by chance, an order for the removal of the Fort Apache prisoners was dispatched on September 3, the same day Geronimo formally surrendered to Miles.

Now orchestrating the removal of all the Chiricahuas, on September 7 army commanders started the Fort Apache group to the railhead at Holbrook and the next day put Geronimo and his contingent on a train at Bowie Station. On

---

2. Every one of the older Apaches interviewed told me that, though Crook was their enemy, he was an honorable enemy and they respected him. And they had no hesitation in expressing their detestation of Miles. Regarding whether or not Crook had also lied to the Apaches, he admitted in his autobiography that he continued to let them believe that his terms had been approved. Crook, *Autobiography,* p. 263.

September 13 the Fort Apache captives boarded their train at Holbrook, two days before the Chiricahua delegation sent to Washington, now also in captivity, was put on a train at Fort Leavenworth. All the movements were kept secret. President Cleveland's wish to have all the Chiricahua Apaches imprisoned in Florida—hostiles, nonhostiles, and army scouts alike—was to be fully carried out.[3]

Eugene Chihuahua gave a brief account of the removal of his people from Fort Apache.

EUGENE CHIHUAHUA

I think it was in September that General Miles grabbed that big bunch of our people at Fort Apache and shipped them to Fort Marion to stay with us. His soldiers didn't get all of the Chokonen and Chihenne because some of them had already escaped and hidden in Mexico. I've always wanted to go down there and hunt my people.

There must have been over four hundred at Fort Apache when the commanding officer [Lt. Col. James F. Wade] sent word that the warriors were all to come in, and to come without any weapons. He told them that they were all to be shipped to Washington to have a visit with the Great White Father and that their wives and children were to go with them. Of course he was telling them lies, and they should have known it.

They had been living peaceably around Fort Apache, making no trouble. Some of them, about forty, were scouts and had served with the army. All were rounded up and held in a corral under guard until the women and children came. You White Eyes don't understand about the scouts. We didn't like them because they had betrayed their people, and the only consolation we got for those terrible twenty-seven years as prisoners of war is that the scouts, too, were prisoners. And we made it miserable for them.

General Miles, who had been contemptuous both of Crook's use of the mule pack train and his use of Apache scouts, had failed to accomplish anything by methods taught him at West Point and had been forced to adopt the use of devices used by his predecessor whom he had surreptitiously connived to supplant. He had said that getting the Apaches together as the result of a lie was contemptible, but that is exactly what he did. And moreover he did it at a safe distance, and by telegraph. By that means he supervised the assembling and betrayal of those Apaches who were giving no trouble. He ordered that the women bring the children and their meager possessions to the corral in which the men were herded. And it should be remembered that his action was approved by Secretary of War Endicott and the President of the United States,

3.   United States, Senate, Executive Document No. 117, Vol. 2449, 49th Cong., 2nd sess. "Surrender of Geronimo," passim. President Cleveland's desires regarding Geronimo apparently were unequivocal. Army authorities quoted him as saying, "I hope nothing will be done with Geronimo which will prevent our treating him as a prisoner of war, if we cannot hang him, which I would much prefer." Ibid., p. 4. For published accounts by the principal army officers involved, see George Crook, *General George Crook: His Autobiography*, Martin F. Schmitt, ed. (Norman: University of Oklahoma Press, 1946), and Nelson A. Miles, *Personal Recollections and Observations* (Chicago: The Macmillan Co., 1897). See also Bourke, *On the Border With Crook*, and Davis, *Truth about Geronimo*, passim.

Grover Cleveland.

Colonel Wade had assembled troops from Fort Thomas, from San Carlos, and from Alma, New Mexico. On September 5 he told the Apaches the reason for their being held and their destination, and on the seventh he started them on the hundred-mile trek to Holbrook. In that long line of prisoners there were some horsemen and some wagons, but most of the prisoners walked. They were driven under guard along the difficult trails for five days and six nights. Wagons carried corn and some other foods but the Apaches subsisted primarily on the cattle that were prodded along with them.

CHAPTER 21

LAST FREE APACHES

Were you with Mangus when he was captured?"[1]
"Captured! What gave you the idea that Mangus was ever captured?
You've been reading books!"

DAKLUGIE

The general [Miles] may have been reporting the information given by the young officer or he may have been lying. Neither probably considered the possibility that anyone would ever ask an Indian what happened. And it has taken close to seventy years for it to be done. But nobody ever captured Mangus. And nobody captured his little band.[2]

Mangus attacked nobody unless forced to do so in self-defense. We could have killed many had we wished. Frank and I wanted to use our newly acquired weapons.

I usually tried to find a flat rock upon which to sleep. I would lay my spear by my side and place my bow and arrow by it. Then I'd adjust my ammunition belts—I had two—and place the sixshooters so that I wouldn't lie on either. If we were attacked at night, we would use bow and arrow first, for they did not betray our exact position. Then, if necessary, we'd finish up with our guns. A lance is also a good weapon at night. Mine was especially good because it would pull out easily.

---

1. I had quoted from Miles's *Personal Recollections and Observations,* pp. 339–47, passim. Daklugie, caustically refuting a number of Miles's statements, asked if his story would be believed. I stated that long-standing accounts in print are difficult to retract. He answered, "But my people were illiterate. They left none but oral records. But those records are true. You White Eyes! Everything in a book, nothing in heads!" I answered that at least we knew where to get information when we needed it. To that he said, "You go to books. And if they are not true?" The question was unanswerable.

2. Daklugie was not alone in having questioned the accuracy of Miles's memory or sources. For example, in regard to Miles's account of Lt. Johnson's following Mangus "down through parts of Old Mexico," Britton Davis comments, "The General's memory has played him false. Johnson saw no sign of Mangus and trailed him nowhere in Mexico. No one knew of Mangus' whereabouts until early in October, 1886." Davis, *Truth,* p. 231.

We filed our arrowheads till they were sharp. They were made of steel. Sometimes we used hoops from water barrels, for they were light and thin and could be easily worked. When I was a boy there were still some stone arrowheads used, but not many.

Armed as we were, Frank and I could have killed many Mexicans if Mangus had not forbidden it. When a *carreta* left a village, we could hear its wheels squeak for miles. Those wheels were just a cross section of a cottonwood log, with a pole run through a hole in the center of each. The holes were burned in and irregular in shape. The only lubricant they used was a leaf of nopal and it didn't last very long.

Once, we ran into Geronimo's band by accident. We stayed together only a few days. I wanted very much to join my uncle, but Mangus objected. It was not that which caused me to stay with him, but his telling me that I owed it to the women and children for their protection. What surprised me was that Geronimo supported Mangus in this. I think now that it was because he knew that I was the last of my father's family and he did not want it to become extinct. And he may have already decided that I was to be his successor.

I respected Mangus, but I wanted him to stay with Geronimo and take an active part in the fighting. That he was brave I realized, because I had seen him in action and knew. I wondered sometimes if the fact that his father [Mangas Coloradas] had been killed treacherously had not caused his attitude. Still, all of us knew that we might die at any time, and I do not think that we dreaded death as white people seemed to do. But why many of them do not fear the dead as we do is not comprehensible to an Apache. Perhaps it is because they do not believe in ghosts.

After the Mexicans had captured some of our band, Mangus turned north. By that time we had lost most of our mounts, and we used the horses and one mule primarily for packing our equipment. We had got away from the mountains, so Mangus decided that we should travel by night. No Apache liked to do that. Mangus sent Frank ahead a mile or so of the little group to scout, and I was the rear guard. Later that night Frank and I traded places.

That was when we ran into those mules. Here was our chance to get mounts. We slipped quietly toward the nearer ones, and to our surprise they did not become frightened as did most mounts when they scented Indians. They let us walk right up to them and stood while we looked them over and selected what we thought were the best. With thongs from our belts we made slip nooses and mounted. They seemed accustomed to Indians, and I thought I recognized some of them, though I was not sure. There was a bell mare, too, and I knew that I had not seen her before.

An idea came, and I asked Frank why we should not take the whole herd with us. "Enjuh!" he said, and we rounded them up. "I'll hold them while you go back for the others," he said. "They might as well ride, too. And these will furnish plenty of food if we run short. Bring my father, too, while you're at it."

I picked the best mule in the bunch and headed back.

Mangus did not approve of our taking the mules, but he permitted it. He explained that they belonged to the ranch where Britton worked as *Nantan.*[3] He

---

3. "Britton" is, of course, Lt. Britton Davis. Many Apaches called this young officer by his given name. In their own tongue he was "Fat Boy." The mules were the property of the ranch he had resigned his commission to manage, *La Hacienda de Corralitos,* in Chihuahua, 140 miles south of

might make trouble for us. He might even warn the forts in New Mexico and Arizona. I recommended that we take the mules and bell mare and head for the border as fast as we could, not resting until we were safe in Arizona.

It was a hard trip. We were worn out and so were the mules. Somebody had to stand guard and I knew that Mangus would expect me to do it, because I was to blame for the whole thing. Frank offered to relieve me and I got the second half of the night for sleep.

We wandered north for several days without being bothered by the army. By traveling at night, following the ridges and building no fires, we managed to get into the mountains east of Fort Apache. We got too close to the fort and ran into trouble. The soldiers had attacked another band—whose I do not know—and they accidentally spotted us nearby. Mangus, the Mescalero, and I held the cavalry off while our women mounted and rode. We were on foot. Mangus and I could have easily reached our horses, but old Fit-a-hat could not keep up with us. We turned back, keeping under cover until Fit-a-hat had got his mule and had ridden ahead. Then I ran like a cottontail. When I jumped on my mule, I was blowing like a horse. Then I had to wait for Mangus because I had outrun him.

We felt comparatively safe until Frank discovered that only a few miles from us there was a cavalry camp. He had slipped close enough to it to make sure that there was an Apache scout with the soldiers.[4] Much as we hated telling Mangus, we did, though we knew that it meant surrender. And I dreaded that more than I did death.

Yes, Mangus said, it meant surrender. I was to scout the camp and, if the troops left, to go in and talk with the cook. The scout was doing the cooking, wasn't he?

"Ow [Yes]," Frank said, but perhaps not all the time. I would see. How many troopers were in the camp? He thought at least fifteen, maybe a few more. Not many.

"Now that we are well armed, even if we are short of ammunition, haven't we a chance yet?" Mangus shook his head.

For three days I scouted that camp, waiting, yet dreading for the troops to leave. At last they rode out. So far as I could tell, there was one man, an Apache, left there. I spoke in his ear before he knew there was anyone about. He gave me coffee and we talked.

"What," I asked, "are we to do?"

"Give up," he said. "It is the only thing you can do. Chihuahua has. All the rest have quit except maybe old Nana.[5] And he may have."

"Not Geronimo?"

"Yes, Geronimo. He and Naiche have already been shipped east on a train from Fort Bowie."

Deming, New Mexico. On October 9, 1886, Davis sent a telegram to General Miles reporting the theft of over fifty head of mules and suggesting that Mangus and his band were probably heading for Arizona. Davis, *Truth about Geronimo*, p. 232.

4. Davis stated that the force, commanded by Captain Charles L. Cooper of the Tenth Cavalry, consisted of "twenty enlisted men and two scouts from Fort Apache." Ibid.

5. Nana had surrendered with Chihuahua. One of Naiche's wives had started with Geronimo's band but attempted to return to the cavalry. Naiche shot her in the leg. She and one of Geronimo's wives were sent to Florida with Chihuahua's band. Ball, *Victorio*, p. 183.

"What will they do with us?" I asked.

"Probably send you after the rest."

"They'll kill all of us."

"Maybe. But I don't think so. Geronimo made some kind of a treaty with them. He wanted to go back to Turkey Creek, but the big Nantan would not permit that. But he promised that the Apaches would not be killed. And he sent the scouts along with them. I was out with this bunch, so I didn't have to go."

He advised me to arrange for a meeting with Captain Cooper under a flag of truce. He said that it would be safe for Mangus to come into camp to talk with the officer.

And that is what was done. *Mangus went in voluntarily and surrendered.* The scout said that it was unbelievable that we had got that far without being caught, for the cavalry was scouring the country for us. Mangus talked with Captain Cooper and agreed to bring in his band and the mules. They had heard about them, of course; they probably wanted them more than they did us.

I was held in camp while Mangus, with most of the troops, went to bring in his band. The soldiers took my rifle, my two sixshooters, and my ammunition belt. They took my fire sticks and the extra soles for moccasins. They even took my blanket. I could do nothing but submit to the search. They took the knife and scabbard from my belt, but I had kept from them a small, thin one that I had hidden in my hair, which was long and heavy. Hanging loose it fell to my knees. I kept it braided and thrust under my belt. (I kept that knife through Florida, Carlisle, and Fort Sill.) The soldiers also took my good bow and arrows. They did not get my war club because I had dug a hole and buried it at the foot of a cliff where I knew I could find it later. I meant to bury my spear, too, but didn't have time. .

I heard the officer say in Spanish to the scout: "Here's this young man; he's the most dangerous one among them." That was true. All young warriors my age were eager to make a good record and be recognized by their people. I think that when he saw that good spear of mine and the over 200 thin steel arrowheads in my quiver he understood the situation. Those arrows would not pull out, you know; you just had to push one on through if it hit you. And it was worse than an operation today. Everybody in that camp took an interest in my arrows. I didn't mind that, but they did not give them back. And they had no use for them.

When Mangus rode in, the soldiers brought also our few horses and the mules. They got my mule, and he was a good one.

They took every one of our mules. Mangus and his band underwent a search such as I had, and everything was taken from them. His wife clung to a leather bag holding perhaps a peck of corn. When it was wrested from her grasp, she begged so piteously to keep it that I was asked to interpret. I told the black sergeant that she so feared starvation that she brought emergency rations, as was our custom. To my surprise, he grunted and returned it to her.

We were taken to Fort Apache. And from there we made the trip to Holbrook by wagon. Blankets were given us for those taken by the cavalry, and except for the scant clothing we wore those were our only possessions. Mangus was seated by the soldier who drove our wagon, and the rest of us sat flat in the bed, huddled in our blankets. Mounted guards rode before, on either side, and behind us. When we ascended steep grades, we were ordered to walk. No talking was permitted, but we were so wretched and unhappy that there was no desire for conversation. I know that the rest felt as I did; we did not dread death nearly so much as we did the degradation of being prisoners and slaves. Death was infinitely preferable to that.

That is how Captain Cooper captured Mangus. That is how "the only Indians really captured by Miles' army of five thousand men" were taken.[6]

Some of these young Indians, born in captivity, have never been on the warpath and know almost nothing about it. They don't understand that the army had offered fifteen hundred dollars for Mangus, dead or alive. That meant that they really wanted him dead. I did all I could to save him from the enemy. Old Fit-a-hat did, too, though he was too old for fighting.

---

6. Of this tiny Apache force—the force Davis gave Cooper credit for "the only *capture* of armed Indian *men* during the entire campaign"—Daklugie scornfully commented: "Great army, wasn't it?" Davis, *Truth about Geronimo*, p. 232.

Book Two

Twenty-seven Years as Prisoners of War

Prisoners of War, 1886.   (Smithsonian Institution)

INTRODUCTION

A ce Daklugie stated: "No Apache was ever cruel enough to imprison any-one. Only a White Eye was capable of that. I hold Nelson A. Miles re-sponsible for making prisoners of war of my people for twenty-seven years. The President of the United States, the Secretary of War, and General Sheridan were parties to that crime. And it had been initiated by William Tecumseh Sherman."

This is the Apache account of more than a quarter of a century of captivity and degradation as told by Apaches who experienced it. It is not an attempt at a complete history of those years because there were many occurrences of im-portance of which they knew little or nothing.

It has been selected from a vast accumulation of interviews obtained from those that give their personal recollections and their reactions. Some material "from the record" has been added to fill the gaps.

This
is
a
sad
and
bitter
place
A place of death
[The cold Atlantic gale]

Apaches
died
here
Alone, in a land of strangers
[The torpid, miasmal swamps]

Seminoles
died
here
Far from the great grass sea
[The icy rains of winter]

Their
rest-
less
spirits
haunt
the
night
At dusk, tourists hurry to escape these evil walls
[In the distance—thunder]

Castillo
de
San
Marcos
Grim sentinel along this dismal strand
[Soon the sirocco steals in across the Sound]

This
is
a
sad
and
bitter
place.

L. S. Fallis

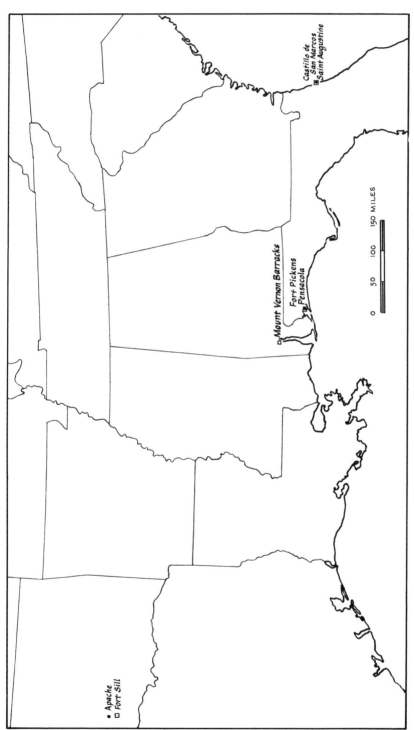

Apache Prisoner-of-War Camps, 1886–1913

CHAPTER 1

FIRST EXILES TO FLORIDA

EUGENE CHIHUAHUA

My father would not leave Fort Bowie until the officer's promise to bring my brother from Fort Apache to us was kept. For once a White Eye kept his word. He sent men and a horse for Tom, and they brought him to us. Then we were hauled to Bowie, the little station on the railroad twenty miles north of the old Apache Pass where they had built the fort. They took everything we possessed except the rags on our backs.

We had seen trains, of course, but I think no member of my father's band had ever ridden on one. I had hidden and watched them go snorting by and wondered what they were like inside. I was afraid of the engine. When it screeched and came snorting to the platform it seemed to me as if it squatted and crouched as though about to pounce on us. I don't know what day it was[1] when they drove about seventy-five of us on that thing. The guards went, too. But they did not ship us in boxcars as has been reported. We were in places with seats that turned down at night and formed a place to sleep. And they gave us food.

Everybody was miserable. Old Nana went about telling us that, though our land and homes had been stolen from us, now families could be together, and that in two years we could go back home. When the wife of Naiche and the wife of Geronimo heard that they began to wail and say that they would never see their husbands again. Nana told them that they should not lose hope, for it was very likely that the others would be put with us, and perhaps before very long. And it comforted them because Nana never lied. It was like going into the Death Hole, for nobody knows what that is like, nor will anyone until he gets there.

The one bit of hope was our faith in the promise made by General Crook. For though he was our enemy, he was an honest enemy. Chihuahua told us that Nantan Lupan did not speak with a forked tongue, and that we could rely upon the word of the Tan Wolf.[2] But Nantan Lupan was not on that

---

1. April 7, 1886.

2. Eugene Chihuahua stated, "You White Eyes think that Lupan means Gray Wolf, but it does

125

train, and nobody knew what those guards might do.

The Mexicans could enslave many tribes, but not the Apache. Nobody could force us to work or to endure slavery. True, sometimes captured Apaches became *vaqueros* for a time, but only long enough that they might escape from their captors. Those forced for a time to grub in the earth starved themselves to death—women as well as men. And now, here we were, going like the wind into what we did not know; nor could we help ourselves if we knew. All we had was that tiny glimmer of hope based upon the word of a White Eye.

I knew that trains had to stop and get water, but not why. I expected that the one taking us away might do that at Lordsburg, but it did not. Deming, then? As we approached the station, guards stood at both ends of the cars with leveled guns. And though the train seemed about to stop as we got near the station, it whipped up and went fast. Years later I learned that a bunch of ruffians had been in ambush there to take us off the train and kill us. To my surprise I learned that the guards were there to help us as well as to take us into captivity.

One of the soldiers who spoke Spanish talked with Chihuahua and told him about Florida. He said that there was a Big Water there, so wide that nobody could even see across it. Nana told us that there is no water so wide but that his horse could swim it, so we knew that the guard was a liar. In fact we thought that, with the exception of Crook, Britton Davis, and George Wratten, all white men were.

My father, before he resigned from the scouts, had been over that country west of El Paso. He had gone that far, walking ahead of the soldiers to do their fighting for them. From El Paso the soldiers had gone back by train and left the scouts to bring their horse cannon. As he finished speaking a cannon was fired and we thought somebody was shooting at the train to kill us. The guards told Chihuahua that it was a salute to an officer on that train but I do not know who he was.

The train was going slowly as we passed Fort Bliss. At that time there were just two or three little adobe buildings, not much bigger than chicken houses. It was not where it is now; it was between the railroad and the Río Bravo [Rio Grande].[3]

I don't know how long we were on that train before they put us off in the night, but we were in Florida, St. Augustine.[4] They put us on a flat place close to a big water and let us camp there, I don't know how long. It was muggy and hot. Mosquitoes almost ate us alive. We were so miserable that we did not care how soon they might kill us. Nana tried to keep us encouraged by telling us that every day brought us one step closer to the time we could go home. He never failed to remind us that no matter how we suffered we were still Apaches and must never complain. Also he said that we were to do whatever we were told and not let anybody know how we hated the White Eyes, because to antagonize them would only make things worse for us.

---

not. They named the general that because of the color of the clothes he wore most of the time, and they were not gray; they were tan."

3.   Richard K. McMasters, *Musket, Saber and Missile, a History of Fort Bliss* (El Paso: Guynes Hunting Company, 1869), pp. 34–36.

4.   The Chihuahua group arrived at St. Augustine April 13, 1886.

That place by the Big Water was bad, bad; but it was not nearly so bad as that old fort where they took us. It looked like something in Mexico and had rooms underground.[5] People have said that the Apaches were cruel, but they never shut people up in traps as White Eyes did. They were merciful and killed them. Those were awful places and smelled bad, but when they put tents on top for us that was much better.

Then they took all the men and big boys away from the women and children and put us on that island. That's when my father gave up ever going back. They put us in a big boat and took us to that island where there was a lighthouse. I think that lighthouse was to scare boats away. It scared me, but I didn't say a word.

A guard told us that there was a boy [buoy] out there but we didn't see one; we just saw a big ball painted red and blue bobbing up and down in the water. The man said that on one side of the line it belonged to one tribe and on the other side to another. But there wasn't any line, either.

They left us on that island with some food; but before they went they showed us how to put oil in the lamps, trim the wicks, and light them. Every morning we climbed up to that light and put it out. Then we had to fill the lamp and light it again each evening. I liked that. There was nothing else to do but fish.

Boys always have to cook for warriors. When we opened those boxes, there was flour, coffee, and some sugar; there were some White Eye beans that we didn't like, but we at least got to eat something. And no meat. What were we going to eat? "Fish," the man said. He brought fishing tackle. The water was full of fish, but we don't eat fish; we don't eat anything that grows under water. And we don't eat pork. (I liked bacon but if my mother had known she would have died. Back home there was a scout we called *Coche* Sergeant because he ate pork.) How long have you ever gone without food? Eighteen hours? Just wait till you have starved eighteen days; then maybe you'll eat anything you can get, like we did.

We were out there a long time. There was nothing to do but fish. A boat came sometimes to bring more food. We couldn't swim back to land; it was too far. We wanted to die.

One day a boat came with food and oil, and it took Chihuahua and me back to that fort. And we saw my mother and my brothers and sister. An officer was picking out Apache children to take away with him. Everybody was frantic! First they didn't let wives and husbands be together; now they were going to take the children away from the mothers.

There were many more people there, mostly Chiricahua, but some Warm Springs, too; they had been rounded up at Fort Apache and shipped out there on a train. There must have been nearly four hundred.[6] That place where they put us was covered with tents till you could hardly move. But at least they were not living down in those damp, dark places under the ground.

Some men were drilling like soldiers. But nobody got enough to eat. And everybody was scared. So were we when we learned why: they were going to

---

5. Fort Marion was originally the *Castillo de San Marcos*. Construction was begun on it by the Spanish in 1692.

6. The Fort Apache captives arrived September, 1886.

take the children away to a place they called a school to teach them how to live.

They didn't take quite all, but every one of Chihuahua's children was to go. My father knew the interpreter—Concepción. My father asked Concepción to tell the officer to leave him one child or he would die. Finally they said he could keep one, just one. Then he and my mother had to decide which one, and that was hard to do. My mother said that it must be a man child because he might be a chief if they ever got back home. So they picked me to stay. The rest had to go.

They knew what White Eyes were going to do to the girls and they wanted to save them, but there was no place to hide them. What were they going to do? Nana told them: One man would take a friend's daughter and say that she was another wife, because wives didn't have to go unless their husbands went too. And they did that and saved some from being taken away.

I had one sister, Ramona. She was about fifteen, almost full grown. When she was just a little girl Juh and Chihuahua promised each other that when she was old enough she was to marry Daklugie, Juh's son. But what was going to happen to her at that place where they were taking her?

They took nearly all away—most on a train, some on a boat.

Then the officer told Chihuahua that his children were going on a train. They let us go to the station when they took my brothers and sister. When the train pulled in we could see a guard standing between two cars. And behind him, who do you think was there? Daklugie. They were sending him, too.

Then we knew that Mangus had given up, too. His group had been sent to Pensacola, where they had been put with Geronimo's band. That meant that, except for a few who had run away to the Blue Mountains in Mexico, all our people had given up.

I don't remember when they took us back to that island, but one day a man came out and told Chihuahua that an officer wanted to see him.

Chihuahua was sent to the officer and I went with him. Whether or not it was a court-martial I don't know, but I don't think so; because if this officer knew my father had resigned from the army he did not say it. Maybe Britton had not reported my father. Chihuahua always thought that when the Fat Boy learned that he had been fooled by Chato and Mickey Free he himself resigned. That's when he took that job managing that big ranch down in Mexico.[7]

The officer asked my father about ambushing and killing a lot of soldiers at a pass. Chihuahua did not lie; standing tall and looking proud, he said, "I did it! My warriors and me, we did it. Aieee! I am proud of it. I just wish that we had killed every one of them!"

"Why did you do this?" asked the officer.

"Why did they kill my mother? Why did they kill the women of my warriors' families? If they wanted to fight, why didn't they fight men? Why just women and children? Your soldiers were not fighting men; they were fighting women!"

And Chihuahua turned his back to the officer and sat down on his blanket. And he sat tall and proud to hear the death sentence.

---

7. See page 116, Book One.

"Chihuahua," said the officer, "You are a brave man. You speak the truth. I like that. I have looked at your record and I know that you are telling the truth. I cannot blame you for what you did. Had I been in your place I hope that I might have had the courage to act as you did. Much as I should like to let you go back to your own country I cannot do that. But this I can do for you: as long as you live nobody can say to you 'Bring wood!' 'Carry water!' 'Dig in the earth!' Nobody can force you to work."

My father answered, "You will not be with me. How will others know that I am not to do these things?"

"I will give you the uniform of a captain in the cavalry. You have been a scout and have worn the uniform."

"Not the pants," said Chihuahua, "Nor the hat; nor the boots."

"But I do this on condition that you wear the uniform, all of it!" He smiled and added, "That includes the trousers."

It was degrading for a Chiricahua to wear the pants, and my father hated them; but he cut out the seat and wore his breechclout over them, so that down the side the stripe showed. The jacket he liked because the double bars of the captain's rank shone on his shoulders.

And nobody bothered Chihuahua. Neither did they Geronimo. He had no double bar, but he was Geronimo; and as long as either lived they did not work. It was not intended by Ussen that Apache warriors work.

Judging by official correspondence, Lieutenant Colonel Loomis E. Langdon, commander at Fort Marion, was deeply interested in the welfare of his charges and strived to support them as best he could. One letter, dated August 15, 1886, is quoted in part.

On May 10th last estimate forwarded by the Commanding Officer of this Post for calico and materials with which to clothe women and children among Indian Prisoners in Ft. Marion. On July 12th a letter from the A.G.O. was sent to the Commanding Officer of this post informing him that the issue of clothing to Indians was authorized by the Hon. Sec. of War and that Quartermaster's Dept. directed to purchase articles required. Up to last night, nothing had been heard of the articles asked for except letter from the Depot Quartermaster asking for sizes of the shoes required.

Women and children much in need of clothing; some women very scantily clad and several children almost, if not naked.

Some charitably disposed ladies in St. Augustine offered to raise money by subscription and pay for material and teach the squaws to cut out garments for themselves and children. I would ask the government to pay for this. If not, we would all divide the expense among us. Twenty dollars will cover the whole expense.[8]

A few days later Langdon responded to a query as to whether an additional four or five hundred Indians (the Fort Apache group) could be accommodated at Fort Marion. He could handle seventy-five more (in addition to the seventy-three remaining after the first contingent of children had been sent to Pennsylvania) but he would need $200 for additional tents. He recommended, however, "that no more Indians be sent here."[9]

---

8. Colonel Loomis E. Langdon, Commanding Officer, Reports to Adjutant General Office, National Archives.

9. United States, Senate, Executive Document No. 117 (Vol. 2449), 49th Cong., 2nd sess., p. 65.

Langdon concluded his August 23 report with the question:

"What is to be done with these prisoners?" In the nature of things they cannot remain prisoners here till they all die. This is as good a time as any to make a permanent disposition for them; or if not a permanent one, then at least one having a more definite purpose in view than their mere confinement here as prisoners. Nor can they very well always remain at Fort Marion without necessitating the constant retention at this post of a battalion of troops, not so much to guard them from escaping as to prevent bad white men's introducing liquor amongst them or bringing them into collision with the disorderly and provoking elements of the contiguous population.

RECOMMENDATION.

Therefore, I respectfully recommend that the *whole* party of prisoners be sent as soon as possible to Carlisle, Pa. There are in the party, as will be seen by reference to the above table, twenty-seven children and youths. The proper place for most of them is the Indian school at Carlisle, and even the youngest will, in a few years, be old enough to attend the school.

I have been told often when these Indians surrendered they were promised by the Government officers that they should not be separated from their children. At all events, these people assert that such a promise was made. A breach of faith in this respect—a separation—is what they constantly dread. Even a present of clothing to their more than half-naked children excites their mistrust and makes them very restless, because it looks to them like preparing them for a journey, a separation from their parents.

I have not consulted Captain Pratt in regard to the practicability of removing the whole party to Carlisle, but if the objection is made that there is no means of guarding them there, I will say that the fourteen adult Indians of the party will be enough guard under the command of Chihuahua, the chief, as the only object of having a guard is to keep the white people away from the Indians, and if there is a reserve of any size at Carlisle, that will be more easily accomplished there than it can be here.

But, and in conclusion, I desire to say that if the whole party cannot go, or at least all of those whose children are with them here, I would not recommend the transfer.[10]

Major General J. N. Schofield, Commander of the Division of the Atlantic, forwarded Langdon's recommendation, concurring to the extent that "the whole number of Indians referred to be removed to some place where they can be given an opportunity to earn their living by their own industry."[11] Five days later Lieutenant General Philip H. Sheridan recommended to the Secretary of War, "The conditions stated by Col. Langdon need not interfere with sending the remainder of the Chiricahua and Warm Springs Indians to Fort Marion, Florida."[12] On September 6 Acting Secretary of War R. C. Drum, by then probably aware of the decision to send the 394 Fort Apache prisoners to join the 73 at Fort Marion, somewhat sarcastically reported to the Secretary of the Interior that "Langdon has been informed that the final disposition of these indians will doubtless be determined by your Department, and that in the mean time all that is expected of him is to hold them as prisoners of war."[13] The next day the Fort Apache prisoners began their forced march to the Holbrook, Arizona, train station.

---

10. Ibid., Executive Document No. 73 (Vol. 2448), pp. 6–7.

11. Ibid., p. 7.

12. P. H. Sheridan to Secretary of War, August 28, 1886, AGO, National Archives.

13. Senate Executive Document No. 73, p. 8.

CHAPTER 2

MORE EXILES

In September two more Chiricahua groups boarded trains for Florida. These were the small band that surrendered with Geronimo and the large group of Chiricahua and Warm Springs Apaches from Fort Apache. Kanseah gave a brief account of the Geronimo group.

KANSEAH

When they put us on that train at Bowie, nobody thought that we'd get far before they'd stop it and kill us. But we kept going till we got to San Antonio and they took us off and out to Fort Sam [Houston]. George Wratten was with us. His tepee was close to ours. They had searched everybody before we left Fort Bowie and taken all the weapons they found. There were three men who had brought two knives each, and when the soldiers found one they didn't look for another. So those three knives were all the weapons we had. Mr. Wratten had guns and ammunition. I don't know how he got them or why he was permitted to keep them.

Wratten tried to reassure us, though he greatly feared that our apprehensions were justified. He talked with Geronimo. "They are not going to kill me," Geronimo said. "I have the promise of Ussen, but my warriors are not so protected. Ussen promised that neither my sister nor Daklugie would die; and he promised that I should live to be an old man and have a natural death. But he made no stipulations regarding the braves. It is for them that I fear. They are unarmed. If we had weapons we would fight it out as we have in the past. Everybody has to die sometime, and regardless of odds we would fight. Haven't we done it for years? And for the last three haven't the odds been five hundred to one?"

Wratten agreed. He deliberated some time before saying, "If an attack is made on unarmed men, I cannot see it without doing what I can to help you. In my tent are some guns and ammunition. Tell your warriors so. And if the attack comes, they are to get them. I can't let unarmed men be murdered even if I have to join them." The word was passed, but the odds were too great for the Apaches to have any hope of surviving an attack. We all expected it, and my mother told me that if it came I was to show these White Eyes how an Apache can die.

131

George Wratten.   (Eve Ball Collection)

They kept us a long time [five weeks], and finally Wratten was able to report that we were to be taken on to Florida. "Ussen has spoken," was Geronimo's comment. The Apaches believe that Generals Miles and Sheridan, the Secretary of War, and even the President lied about being responsible for having put us on that train at Bowie for Florida and that we were held at San Antonio while everybody alibied about ordering it.

Geronimo had been promised that he would be united with his wives and children, and that his warriors, too, would be. One of his wives, and also one of Naiche's, had gone in with Chihuahua, who was the first to surrender. But, of course, General Miles lied. He sent the men to Pensacola and the women and small children to Fort Marion at St. Augustine. After we had been there some time, they did move the women of Geronimo's band to Pensacola. That was after first Daklugie and later Kanseah, Chapo, and Zhunni had been sent to school. And later they sent all of those left in Florida to Mt. Vernon Barracks, Alabama.

It was there that my father had been sent. I do not know when or with whom he went.

Those in the Fort Apache group, after their long and difficult walk from that fort, were held outside Holbrook under close guard until eighteen train cars were assembled. Then they were herded toward the train and forced to board it. Although it was very warm the windows were locked and the doors closed. Armed guards stood outside the latter. When the train started to move the Indians shrieked in terror. In those cars they were confined all during that terrible trip, except when being transferred from one train to another.

The Apaches had no knowledge of the use of sanitary facilities and apparently were given no instructions, though there were both guards and scouts who spoke Spanish and could have acted as interpreters. Conditions became so terrible that the guards said that they dreaded opening the doors. Upon arrival they numbered 381: 278 adults and 103 children.

Eugene tells of the arrival of the Fort Apache group at St. Augustine.

EUGENE CHIHUAHUA

We were at Fort Marion when they were brought there. They were almost dead; they were almost naked; they were hungry; and they were pitifully dirty.

By that time they had two bathrooms for us, one for men and one for women. In separate places they had tubs, but just two. Our people told the arrivals of both facilities and got them lined up. Some of them stood for hours before getting admittance. I don't know how those poor people could have lived through that horrible trip.

That place wasn't much bigger than a football field, and we had been crowded before they came. Tents were placed so close together that they touched and only a narrow path was left between the long rows. There they were quartered, and it was bad for all of us.

Last to surrender, Mangus's group was the last entrained for Florida. Dak-lugie gave an account of that trip.

During that terrible trip to Pensacola, I might still have had hope had I not been told of the surrender of Geronimo. I loved Mangus and had sympathy and understanding for him, but above all living men I respected Geronimo. He was the embodiment of the Apache spirit, of the fighting Chiricahua. Where were they now? Never would he have quit had it not been that the enemy had the wives and children of some of his warriors, including one of Naiche's. As long as Geronimo lived, he regretted having surrendered. He often said that he wished he had died fighting in Mexico.

I had one glimmer of hope: if we were placed with Chihuahua's band I would see Ramona—if she was still alive.

The guard halted outside of the town [Holbrook, Arizona], cooked the evening meal, and we camped, we thought, for the night. They fed us amply, as they had throughout the trip, and we rolled up in our blankets. When we were awakened and ordered to get into the wagon, it was almost dawn. That I knew from the stars. They took us into the town and hurried us into a passenger coach, with double seats arranged so that each of two faced the other. A man came in, laid the backs of the seats down, and we were told to spread our blankets on them so that we could sleep there. We obeyed, Frank Mangus and I together. When all had lain down, the lights were lowered. Guards stood at each end, but there were other guards seated throughout the car.

Frank Mangus and I were at the back end of the coach and Mangus and his wife were at the front. Though we were tired, I could not go to sleep. The unusual noises and the misery I felt kept me awake. For a while a soldier paced back and forth down the aisle, but he finally seated himself. When I raised my head slightly, I could see him nod as though he were going to sleep.

Suddenly I was aware of something rattling softly. The grains of corn! Mangus's wife could not be hungry; she must have something hidden in that bag. She did—a bottle of whiskey. Then I heard a faint sliding noise; it was Mangus and he was raising the window, softly, carefully, a little at a time. The train was moving and to me it seemed very rapidly. Surely he could not be planning to jump from the car! Then I heard a cork being withdrawn from a bottle and knew that Mangus was fortifying himself for the ordeal.

Suddenly Mangus jerked the window fully open and I lifted my head just in time to see Mangus disappear through it. I held my breath while his wife slowly and carefully closed the window. But one of the guards had been awakened by the noises. He quit snoring, gave a grunt, and jumped up to alert the others. The lights went on and the soldiers checked. I pretended to be asleep when one bent over me. At that moment another discovered that Mangus was missing.

Nobody had to tell them what had happened. The train stopped and then began backing. I do not know how far it went. I could see men with lanterns searching the embankment on our side of the coach. Then one signalled and the train stopped. I got just an occasional glimpse out of the window, for I didn't want to be caught watching. Frank, too, got a few glances, and it was he who saw two guards bringing his father between them.

When they hustled Mangus back into the coach, he seemed not to have been hurt except for scratches on his face and arms. He could walk without help and he sat calmly while the guard searched him—for weapons I suppose. Another brought some bandages and applied them. And for the rest of the night a guard stood beside him.

The next morning the guards brought food and again they examined Mangus. His right arm was hurt, but not badly. After that they kept very close watch over us but gave us plenty of food and did not mistreat us.*

I do not recall how many nights we spent on that train, but it seemed a very long time. Every time it stopped we expected to be taken off and killed; but we didn't care much. That was to happen soon, anyway, and at times I thought the sooner the better. An Apache does not want to die, but he does not fear death as White Eyes seem to, perhaps because he really believes in a Happy Place. If whites do, why are they so afraid to die?

There was one consolation for those who had families already in Florida: they would see them soon, provided they still lived. I had no close relatives except for my uncle, Geronimo, so I looked forward to being with him. (Mangus I called "Uncle," but he was not, nor do I know exactly what our relationship was.)

We were taken off the train at Pensacola, Florida. It was there that Geronimo and his warriors also had been taken. They were imprisoned at Fort Pickens, but their families were not left with them as promised; they had been taken to St. Augustine instead. But Geronimo and his men were there, and at least some of the wives and children were brought there later from St. Augustine. One of Geronimo's wives died and was buried at Pensacola. When I saw and talked with Kanseah, he told me with horror that my aunt [wife of Geronimo]'s body had been nailed up in a box and taken away to be put underground.

To my great delight, I was permitted to see and talk with my uncle. I saw Geronimo's son, Chapo, and all of the warriors. What was to be done with the band Geronimo did not know; but he anticipated, as did all the people of our tribe, that we would be murdered. There was, he told me, one chance that I might escape that. There had been a man selecting Indian children to be taken away to a place called a school where they would be taught the evil ways of the white people. The Nantan of this place, Captain Richard H. Pratt, was taking Apache children and some warriors to a place called Carlisle, Pennsylvania, and George Wratten was interpreting for him. He was to take Chapo and, now that I had come, my uncle intended having me go also. I told him positively that I would not. I'd had to decide things for Mangus, but telling Geronimo what I would or would not do was a different matter. My uncle informed me that it was he who made the medicine there and that I was to go to Carlisle.

Not all selected were descended from chiefs, but they might be the leaders of

---

*Mangus, when asked later why he attempted to escape from the train, replied that he overheard the guards planning to attack the women; and because he could not protect them, he preferred death to witnessing the atrocity.

the Apaches in the future—provided that there was any future. Without this training in the ways of the White Eyes our people could never compete with them. So it was necessary that those destined for leadership prepare themselves to cope with the enemy. I was to be trained to become the leader.

"And why not Chapo?" I asked.

"Chapo is my son and I love him very much," replied my uncle, "but he does not have the qualities of leadership. Not many do. Your father possessed it to a great degree and, though I was never elected to the chieftainship, *I* had this thing also, and men knew it. Had Naiche been older, experienced in warfare, and a Medicine Man as I was, he would never have depended upon me to exercise many of his prerogatives. But he was not. And he was wise enough to know that the life of his people depended upon someone who could do these things. And I, rather than see my race perish from Mother Earth, cared little who was chief so long as I could direct the fighting and preserve even a few of our people. You are always to remember that it matters little who gets either the credit or blame, so long as the good of the tribe is hanging fire. And you, you go to Carlisle!"

So I was to have the responsibility and the blame for everything that might happen, but never the credit nor the reward. When I think back over the years, I realize that Geronimo did just that. He had the courage, the fighting ability, the intelligence to outwit the officers from West Point, to fight against insurmountable odds, and to provide for his little band.

I went again to Geronimo. "Chapo is going to this place where we will be taught to lie and cheat. Why can't he learn the things needed by a chief as well as I can?"

"Nothing taught to anybody can put within him the things that are needed to lead a people. Haven't you seen enough of these White Eye nantans? What does Miles, though a general, know about chieftainship? What do any of them know? They are officers because they served their sentences in this thing called a school, not because of either ability to fight or ability to get others to fight. Don't their warriors desert in flocks? Don't their men hate them? Don't they *send* their men into battle instead of *leading* them? And don't they use stupid tactics that cost many lives instead of using strategy in the selection and management of their fights?"

When our train stopped at Pensacola the women and children were not permitted to leave it. The guards, Mangus, Frank Mangus, and I were hustled off and the train pulled out with the rest of our band shrieking and trying to jump off. Later I learned that they were taken to St. Augustine where Chihuahua's band and the people from Fort Apache—which included the scouts— had been taken.

There was just one good thing in the whole procedure; the scouts who had betrayed their people were doomed to captivity like the rest of us. I didn't have to be there to know that the loyal Apaches made it miserable for the cowardly traitors.

CHAPTER 3

LIFE AT FORT MARION

EUGENE CHIHUAHUA

After the officer gave Chihuahua a captain's uniform and bars, he did not send my father back to the island. He did not send me back, either. My sister and three brothers were at Carlisle, and he let me live with my parents.

The women cooked out of doors, when they could find room. It wasn't so bad except when it rained; then it was terrible. We had not had much rain in Arizona, and when our blankets and clothes got wet our food did, too.

In the two bands there were sixty-five men who had served the army as scouts and, after Geronimo surrendered, two more—Martine and Kayitah. Included was Chato.* The others had not betrayed their people as he had. To this day he is regarded by the Apaches as a traitor.

The men were issued uniforms made of heavy canvas, and they did military drill. Every day they marched up and down, but they never got a chance to fight. We thought the drill was the White Eyes' war dance, and we had learned that no matter how long he kept it up he wouldn't fight. When the Apache did *his* war dance he meant business.

Chihuahua was in charge of the Apache guards and of the food issued to us. He saw that the rations were distributed fairly. The adults received the same amount issued the soldiers, and the children received half that amount. Back at Turkey Creek we could kill game and harvest wild food enough to satisfy us, but at Fort Marion we were hungry all the time.

Sometimes we were permitted to go to town, and if we had any money we could buy some food. It didn't take us long to catch on that money would buy things other than ammunition. When we were free we could always rustle food. We never went hungry till we were put in forts or on reservations.

So we began making things to sell—bows and arrows, lances, moccasins, and bead work. We made anything for which we could get materials.

Many people came to the fort just to look at us, as they might look at wild animals. Some of them bought trinkets. The officer told Chihuahua that his greatest problem was protecting us from the White Eyes.

---

*Chief Chihuahua's band and the Fort Apache group combined.

137

Some of Chihuahua's warriors were guards. With them our people could go to town; and they never got into trouble when they did.

Some of the underground rooms at the fort [casemates] were repaired and used for storing supplies. One was made into a bakery and two Apaches learned to make bread like the kind the soldiers ate. We did not like it as much as the round, flat kind [tortillas] the women had learned to make in Mexico; but it was food, and we were hungry.

Some white ladies in St. Augustine brought calico. I don't know where they got it. They taught the women to cut it out and sew it into dresses. They also taught them some English words for clothes and food.

Catholic sisters came too. They taught the children to talk and to be clean. And somebody, maybe the Sisters, got more bathrooms. We had only two before. We liked that. And they told the children about Ussen. They didn't understand that we had always worshipped Him.

Though the prisoners were unaware, efforts were being made by General Crook and others to arouse public sympathy for the captives. Herbert Welsh, Executive Secretary of the Indian Rights Association of Philadelphia, was giving the Indians' condition nationwide publicity. Welsh, along with General Crook, visited Fort Marion in March of 1887. They were particularly concerned with the incarceration of the Apaches who had served the country as scouts. Sheridan, perhaps in self-defense, made an investigation at approximately the same time. Colonel Romeyn B. Ayers reported that, of the eighty-two adult male Indians, sixty-five had served the Government as scouts. Even President Cleveland became aware that noncombatant Apaches and their families, who had been nonhostile before capture, were being held unjustly. Whether he was motivated by conscience or by fear of the effect on his coming race for reelection is uncertain.

The question of moving the prisoners from St. Augustine became acute. Captain Langdon's unsuccessful attempt to have Chihuahua's band transferred to Carlisle has already been discussed. Another unsuccessful attempt was made to remove them to a place perceived to be better—this time to a reservation already occupied in North Carolina. Eugene Chihuahua said that this idea was very repugnant to the band. Having experienced the vicissitudes of being forced as unwelcome residents on the people at San Carlos, they wanted no more of that.

Chihuahua was told of these projected plans for their future. He protested both. They had been promised that after two years they would be returned to Turkey Creek in Arizona, and that was where he was determined to go.

EUGENE CHIHUAHUA

But we didn't go to Carlisle, nor to Carolina, and we didn't know what would be done with us until Chihuahua was ordered to prepare to board a train for Alabama. We were to be stationed at an old army fort near Mobile. It was on the west side of the Mobile River, and about twenty-five miles or so from the Gulf of Mexico. It had been built of brick in the 1830s and had been abandoned. We had thought that anything would be better than Fort Marion with its rain, mosquitoes, and malaria, but we were to find out that it was good in comparison with Mt. Vernon Barracks. We didn't know what misery was till they dumped us in those swamps. There was no place to climb to pray. If we wanted to see the sky we had to climb a tall pine.

pix

CHAPTER 4

CARLISLE AND CAPTAIN PRATT

I was at Fort Pickens a very short time before Frank Mangus and I were again put on a train bound for Carlisle. Chapo, Kanseah, and Zhunni were to come later.

When the train stopped at St. Augustine, on the station platform I saw Ramona, tall and beautiful. Chihuahua and his wife were there also to see their four children board the train. Ramona gave no sign of recognition, nor did I. Two guards, one of them accompanied by his wife, joined us and we were placed together in a coach with no other passengers. Except for the small, sharp knife which I'd managed to keep, there was not a weapon among us. Frank Mangus, though older than I, was much smaller, and the guard who knew some Spanish spoke through me when giving orders.

During that trying ordeal of the trip by train there was little conversation. Once, when the guard had a message for the girls, Ramona, without once glancing up, asked me if I had a knife and if I would kill her if she were attacked. I answered "Ow," and she understood. Beautiful and strong she was, and no man had greater courage. Though we might be going to our death, or into slavery and degradation, my heart sang. I might have to kill Ramona, but while she lived it would be my privilege to defend her and, if it came to an attack, to send her beautiful body to the Happy Place. From that time I had a glimmer of hope.

The train went through the mountains and on the second night the snow came. The boys slept at one end of the coach and the guard's wife and the girls at the other. The soldiers dozed in seats near the middle. I tried to keep awake the first night; but after hours had passed with nothing occurring to disturb us, I slept. I felt fairly secure until I awoke the second morning to find snow falling and the earth covered with the white stuff. I had seen snow in the Blue Mountains before, but not in big heaps as it was here. It might have been that during the winters there were such snows in Mexico, but if so we had been in the low country and had missed it.

140

Before very long the train stopped moving. It did that at some towns, but there was none at this place. When I could see no *rancheria* I asked the guard why we were not moving.

"Stuck," he replied. "May be here a long time."

"Then we must stay until the snow melts?"

"Or until help comes," was the reply.

How could help come? Wouldn't the snow stop them as well as us? There flashed into my memory a story that I had heard as a small boy, one of White Eyes marooned on a mountain in a deep snow—a wagon train on a high mountain with snow over the tops of the wagons. (It wasn't that deep where we were, but looked to be waist-deep at least.) After a long time, perhaps two months, rescuers had reached the people in the wagon train only to find nobody alive. And the bodies, buried in the snow, had had the flesh cut from the bones. There had been a shortage of food; then no food. Then the few left living had killed each other and eaten the flesh of their own dead. No Apache would have done that, but these White Eyes—savages.

If the food should give out, who would be eaten first? The Apache children, of course. Had Ramona foreseen this? What might happen to me mattered little. But if the White Eyes began first on the boys, what then? I would not kill Ramona until it became imperative. Then I would plunge the keen thin blade into her heart and let what might come to me take care of itself.

I was, I learned later, over six feet tall, but not more than seventeen. A man, and especially one destined to be a chief, should be able to find some other solution than death. I had seen what had happened to Mangus; so trying to escape from the train, even when stalled, offered little hope. I would not go without Ramona, and in the deep snow we could not get far. I had a breech-clout, headband, belt, moccasins, and the cheap flimsy blanket provided for each of us. I went over and over the possibilities for three nights before I heard the distant whistle of a train. A guard told me that help had come. And the next morning, for the first time, I ate all of the food that was given me. I had been hiding some of it, as had the children, for a time when no more would be given us.

It did not take the work crew, equipped with a snow plow, very long to enable the train to move. We continued on and arrived safely at the railway station in Harrisburg, Pennsylvania. There we were met by Captain Pratt, who took us to Carlisle. There, desperate to the extent that we did not care whether we lived or died, we were thrust into a vicious and hostile world that we both hated and feared.

Richard Henry Pratt was in charge of the famous Indian School at Carlisle Barracks, Pennsylvania. His experiences with Indians, and his sympathy for them made him an excellent choice for the superintendency of the school. He had served in the Washita campaign in which Custer with his Seventh Cavalry, aided by Kansas militia, had attacked the village of Black Kettle. Pratt had seen those Indians butchered in mid-winter in the throes of a terrible blizzard.[1]

---

1. Richard Henry Pratt, *Battlefields and Classrooms, Four Decades with the American Indian, 1867–1904* (New Haven: Yale University Press, 1964), pp. 1–44.

In 1867 Pratt joined the 10th Cavalry. He served at Forts Gibson, Arbuckle, Griffin, and Sill. He had witnessed the arrest of the Kiowa Chiefs Santanta and Big Tree. All his life he believed in the assimilation of the Indians rather than the segregation of them in prison camps, where, instead of accepting the standards of their captors, they were of necessity forced to cling to their old traditions.[2]

He was assigned to the care of Indian prisoners of war in Florida and he was stationed at Fort Marion. His charges were largely Indians of the Middle West, including Kiowa, Comanches, and Sioux.

He was interested in providing for instruction for both children and adults in learning to speak and read English, in knowledge of sanitation, and in adjusting to the white man's pattern of living.

When it was decided to establish the first school for Indians not located on a reservation, Carlisle Barracks, an abandoned post, was selected for use. It was twenty-seven miles from Harrisburg, Pennsylvania. To the twenty-seven acres two large farms were added so that the children attending it could be taught agriculture. It was primarily an industrial school for both boys and girls.

Captain Pratt was chosen to supervise Carlisle Indian School, which was ceded to the Department of the Interior. He left St. Augustine April 14, 1878 (eight years before the Chiricahua Apaches arrived), and the school opened November 1, 1879, with an enrollment of 136 pupils. (By 1905 one thousand pupils were listed.)

In addition to the curriculum of the elementary school of that time teaching included farming, carpentry, blacksmithing, and household training for the girls. Strangely, the school became famous for its band, which was under the direction of two Oneida Indians, Dennison and James Shulocks.[3]

Captain Pratt remained in charge of Carlisle for twenty-four years.

When the train bearing children of the Apache prisoners of war in Florida stopped at Harrisburg, Captain Pratt and three others were waiting on the platform.

DAKLUGIE

Captain Pratt was not alone. He had with him an Apache from Arizona to interpret for him. He was taller than the officer, who was a small man. There was a lady along, a teacher, to take care of the girls. They had come with wagons to take us to Carlisle.

I will not name the interpreter, because he was much older than I—perhaps thirty—and had never been admitted by his tribe as a warrior. Even the small boys had contempt for him when they learned who he was. But we had no choice but to submit. To my great relief, when we reached the school the boys were turned over to another interpreter.[4]

---

2. Ibid.

3. Ibid.

4. The interpreter was Jason Betzinez. He and Daklugie were enemies all their lives. Daklugie regarded Betzinez as a coward, and Betzinez resented that. For Betzinez's autobiography see Jason Betzinez, *I Fought with Geronimo* (Harrisburg, Pa.: Stackpole Co., 1960).

Students at Carlisle
Top center, *Daklugie;* second row left, *Ramona;* third row left, *Viola Massai;* bottom right, *Kaywaykla.*

(Smithsonian Institution)

The next day the torture began. The first thing they did was cut our hair. I had taken my knife from one of my long braids and wrapped it in my blankets, so I didn't lose it. But I lost my hair. And without it how would Ussen recognize me when I went to the Happy Place?

The bath wasn't bad. We liked it, but not what followed. While we were bathing our breechclouts were taken, and we were ordered to put on trousers. We'd lost our hair and we'd lost our clothes; with the two we'd lost our identity as Indians. Greater punishment could hardly have been devised. That's what I thought till they marched us into a room and our interpreter ordered us to line up with our backs to a wall. I went to the head of the line because that's where a chief belongs.

Then a man went down it. Starting with me he began: "Asa, Benjamin, Charles, Daniel, Eli, Frank." Frank was Mangus's son. So he became Frank Mangus and I became Asa Daklugie. We didn't know till later that they'd even imposed meaningless new names on us, along with the other degradations. I've always hated that name. It was forced on me as though I had been an animal.

Their interpreter conducted them to the dining room for breakfast; he seated himself and them at a table for eight. He placed large and small boys alternately. When a small child was seated by Daklugie he learned that he was expected to assist his charge. This boy was James Kaywaykla, the youngest Apache sent to Carlisle.

DAKLUGIE

There were girls at the other end of the big room and I looked for Ramona, but I could not see her. I did not see anyone I recognized.

Our first instruction began at that table. Our interpreter told us the English words for tableware and food.

Our education proceeded with learning to make our beds and hanging up our new clothes. Our old ones, I learned later, were sent to our families in Florida so that they might know that we were still alive. How they knew from that I do not know. Each student had household chores to do. You know that no Apache wanted to do women's work. Our interpreter told me that it was wise to do everything required, like it or not, and to do it cheerfully. Nobody who had been a warrior three years needed to be reminded of that. We'd been trained more rigidly before we came there than we were at Carlisle.

We liked the outdoor games and contests. We liked the gymnasium, too. And the band. Of course every Apache could beat a drum, but not with two sticks as they did at Carlisle.

Learning English wasn't too bad. There was a necessity for memorizing everything because we could neither read nor write. Before the winter was over I was learning to read. My teacher was a white lady and she was very patient and kind to us. She taught us to write, too, and she was not bossy as most white ladies are. She was polite. She seemed to know without being told that I wanted desperately to be able to read and she helped me.

One day she opened a big book to show me Arizona, and for the first time in my life I saw a map. I was fascinated. When she showed me mountains and rivers I could tell her their names in my language. I knew the Spanish for some of them and a few in English. She let me take that geography book to the dormitory and Frank Mangus and I almost wore it out.[5]

In summer the policy of Captain Pratt was to place Indian children in the homes of thrifty Dutch farmers in the area. Students received a small compensation for their work; probably no one was paid more than five dollars a month. They were taken into the homes as members of the family and helped with any form of work required of them. The boys were taught to do farm work, care for cattle and horses, and to handle simple machinery.

Jasper Kanseah, who came about three months after Daklugie's arrival, was horrified when required to milk a cow. He said, "They do it two times a day, every day. And they drink it too. I thought milk was for babies, but they drink it, everybody! The place where I stayed they had a lady who tried to teach me English but I forgot the words. All I could say was 'yes.' The man sent me to the house one time to get a 'ranch.' I didn't know how I could bring him a 'ranch' but I went anyway. The lady laughed when I told her and she handed me a wrench."

It is interesting to note that in the farmer's report to Carlisle he praised Daklugie for intelligence, reliability, and abstinence from drinking. Evidently liquor had already become a problem among the students.

Daklugie's primary interest was in cattle. Even then he had accepted the fact that the Chiricahua would never become farmers. He eagerly learned all he could about cattle because he felt it was not beneath the dignity of a warrior to do a form of work from the saddle. Unfortunately for him the cattle in Pennsylvania were of the dairy type; but even so they were cattle and he acquired every bit of information he could about them and their care. He foresaw a time when his people might have to depend on cattle for survival.

The girls were taught cooking and cleaning by the Dutch housewives, who boasted that their daily-scrubbed floors were clean enough to eat from. In addition to cooking the girls learned to sew, to care for chickens, to plant and care for kitchen gardens, to make butter, and to can fruit.

When the Chiricahua were finally given refuge at Mescalero in 1913, it was easily discernible whether or not they had had training at Carlisle.

---

5. Daklugie and George Martine read everything in my library pertaining to their people.

CHAPTER 5

LIFE AT CARLISLE

DAKLUGIE

There were times when, if it hadn't been for Ramona, I'd have cut loose and gone to Geronimo. But my first obligation was to her. Juh, my father, had told me time after time that she was one day to be my first consideration. Even as a child I thought that strange. Much as he loved Ishton, Juh put the tribe ahead of her. Geronimo had said that I also must consider my people ahead of all else in the world. But Juh had not said this to me. It was puzzling. At nights I lay awake trying to unravel the problem.

The thing that pulled me through was the athletic training at Carlisle. I enjoyed the sports and, although the conditioning didn't measure up to my father's and Geronimo's training routine, it kept me active and fit.

In bad weather there was always the gym. I was a good wrestler. All Indian boys were good at that; it was a means of survival. But I didn't think much of boxing. That was no way to fight. We had used knives. I could not remember having seen men stand up and fight each other except with knives. They are much quicker and more effective.

I also liked running. I was on the track team, a short-distance runner—five miles. Frank Mangus and I were both good at that. A long-distance event? The marathon. We had a Hopi at Carlisle who was good at it. Lewis Tewanema was the best that Carlisle ever had. Though the Apaches had never considered the Hopis very great warriors, we had to admit that they could run. As we had done in our primitive life, Tewanema could start at that easy jog-trot and keep it up all day. He could outrun a horse.

There was one great advantage in running: we didn't have to wear trousers. Nobody knows how all Indian men hated those pants. The track team wore trunks and we felt like Indians.

On Saturdays Tewanema would suit up and play around in the gym for maybe half an hour after the other long-distance runners had taken off for Harrisburg. No guard went along; they knew that no runaway could get far in trunks. Then Tewanema would start alone and beat the others into Harrisburg. They would all come back in the supply wagons.

Tewanema participated twice in the Olympic Games. In the Marathon he finished seventh, but in the ten-thousand-meter race he made second place.

Years later he was honored with an invitation to attend a reunion with other prize-winning celebrities in New York, all expenses paid. When he declined a reporter was sent to the Hopi Villages to interview the great athlete. He found Tewanema, in native Hopi attire and wearing huge silver earrings, placidly herding sheep. When urged to attend the meeting he just smiled and shook his head. Even when informed that he would go by plane with all expenses paid, Tewanema still refused to make the trip.

I can't say much for our academic standing, but when it came to physical achievements we had the world beat. Our football players were fast and husky. They could outrun, outdodge, and outsmart the players of the big Eastern universities.

Did I play football? Not on your life! It looked silly to me. Why? Well, the only thing that I considered was whether or not a game would help me to survive. Football wouldn't. Leaving a place of ambush to knock your enemy down and sit on him is no way for a warrior to fight.

But I liked to watch the games. We wore our uniforms and sat in the bleachers. A lady teacher herded the girls down in their best clothes. They wore uniforms made at the school. We couldn't talk to them, but we could look at them. I'd stand by the steps so that when Ramona passed we could exchange a silent greeting.

The band played at intervals during the game and we paraded between halves. And afterwards, to celebrate the victory, we had a party in the gym. Some of us did our native dances.

Pop Warner was the coach and he was a good one. He could take a boy who had never heard of football and make a star player of him. That's what he did with Jim Thorpe, a Sac and Fox Indian from Oklahoma. But Thorpe was an all-around athlete when he came to Carlisle. Several times I saw Jim Thorpe play. He was superior at almost all sports.

Margaret Pelman [Pellman], a Mescalero, was in school there. So far as I know she and I were the only ones at Carlisle who didn't like football. She said that all she could see was legs waving in a cloud of dust. However, her feelings about the game may have been owing to a visual problem. She was not a good student until her eyes were examined and the doctor performed a cataract operation. When Margaret got out of the hospital she wore glasses, but most important she could see. Her instructors had thought her to be retarded because she couldn't learn to read. After the operation she made rapid progress and also felt that "Jim Thorpe was the greatest football player of all time."

After I had learned to read a little, I just helped myself. It wasn't until I could read that I found out about my people. The papers reported that Chihuahua's band and that of the people from Fort Apache had been sent to Mt. Vernon Barracks in Alabama. The women and children of Geronimo's band had been left at Pensacola with their husbands and fathers.

It was Sunday morning at breakfast that I learned that Kanseah was in the hospital. At our table I was passing the hot cakes, dealing to the left as one does in a card game. Kaywaykla sat at my right, so he was the last served. He got a plate of buckwheat cakes before the butter and maple syrup were started. By the time the pitcher reached him it was empty. He turned it upside down, but only a few drops of syrup ran out. Then he began to cry. It was the first time that I'd seen one of the Apache children do that. I felt sorry for him. I

Carlisle Barracks.

*Indian Marching Band
Carlisle Barracks.*

knew that it was not just being deprived of the syrup, though we loved sweets and seldom got any. It was because he was the youngest child at Carlisle, and lonely. It was against the rule, but I got more of that maple syrup. As the pitcher reached me the boy who brought it asked very softly if I knew that Kanseah was in the hospital. I didn't, and that was terrible news, for nearly every Apache taken there had died.

I didn't know then that white people, for hundreds and maybe thousands of years, had had the so-called children's diseases, and that their blood had developed an immunity that did not prevent measles and chicken pox but that did preserve them from having them as violently as we did. We'd had none of the social diseases, either, though I had heard of them and had been warned that all White Eyes had them. They, too, were a blessing of civilization that no Indian experienced until the White Eyes took over. We didn't even have colds. One disease we knew and feared was *viruelas* [smallpox]. We had learned that blankets or shirts taken from Mexicans sometimes carried it.

I got permission to see Kanseah. "The others who came here have died," he told me, "but I am not going to die."

"Of course not!" I replied.

"I don't take that medicine," he explained. "I pretend to swallow it but I don't. I hide it and I will live."

And he did, though he was very sick. He was coughing and expelling mucus from his lungs. Few who did that ever survived, but Kanseah did.

When one of the Apaches took that sickness they didn't want him to die at Carlisle. They sent him to his family for that. That is what happened to Chapo, son of Geronimo. That is what happened to many.

About a year after I came, Chapo, Kanseah, and Zhunni had been sent from Pensacola. After leaving Carlisle they, too, were sent to Mt. Vernon Barracks, Alabama. I had a letter from Mr. Wratten, who had stayed with them in Florida and who shared their exile in Oklahoma.

Daklugie continued to learn all that he could about cattle, for he was determined that the government should not make farmers of the Apaches. He had learned about sheep raising, too, and knew that the Navajos practiced it. That, he said, was because their land was too poorly watered and too barren to support cattle. He said, grimly, that despite the attempts to force the Apaches to become sheepherders the government had failed.

Though the Navajos spoke the same language as the Apaches and must be related, nobody could force his people either to farm or to run sheep. Raising cattle was the nearest approach to hunting and fighting that he knew, and it was less degrading to a warrior than any other means the White Eyes employed for making a living. Juh would have approved cattle. Geronimo would have done the same. So Chapo's death might have been a comfort to his father. Think how ashamed Geronimo would have been had Chapo become a farmer.*

Any labor, Daklugie commented, was stupid and unnecessary. Hadn't the Apaches lived off the land Ussen had provided for them without any work

---

*Geronimo relented in time, even to the extent that he did some farming at Fort Sill.

other than protecting it from invasion by their enemies? Already he sensed that the White Eyes would eventually exterminate all game, as the Mexicans had the deer in parts of Sonora and Chihuahua. Already the herds of buffalo on the great plains had been slaughtered. Cattle must be used for food and hides when there was no more game. The Apaches must raise cattle.

During the summer, Daklugie and the others worked on local farms. Daklugie applied himself with intensity to learning about the care and feeding of cattle. Although they were used primarily for dairy purposes, they were still cattle. He asked for and sometimes got books on the subject. And he was fortunate in having a teacher who encouraged him in pursuing his interest.

DAKLUGIE

This lady taught us to use a dictionary. Each day she wrote a list of words on the blackboard. We were required to learn to spell them, learn their meaning, and to write sentences in which we used them. One day I found a strange new one. It was "ferment." I looked for it and took the first meaning given: "ferment, to work." And I wrote "I will not ferment in the house."

My teacher was angry. I did not know why. When she told me I was to remain after the others left and write a sentence using the word a hundred times, I asked why.

"To teach you to use it correctly," she replied.

"But you have told me, and I know. Indians do not need to hear a thing but once. You are not teaching me; you are punishing me!"

"Are you refusing to obey my order?" she asked.

"Ow."

"Go to Captain Pratt's office!" she ordered. "Tell him what you have done."

I did not go immediately. I waited an hour or more. When I rapped on the door he ordered me to enter. After I had done so, he closed and locked the door; then he put the key in his pocket. Next he went to a bookcase, reached behind it, and pulled out a blacksnake [a flexible leather whip].

Pratt was a little man, but he might be armed. I looked for a weapon but could see no sign of a concealed one. I took the whip from him and tossed it up on the bookcase. As I did so he grabbed my collar. I turned, seized his, and jerked him off his feet. I held him at arm's length and shook him a few times, then dropped him to the floor.

"If you think you can whip me," I told him, "you are *muy loco*. Nobody has ever struck me in all my life; and nobody ever will. I could break your neck with my bare hands."

Then he called me Asa and again I saw red; I've always hated that name forced on me by white people. Strangely, he did not get mad. Politely, he asked me to sit down, and I did. He stood. And he asked, "Why did you disobey your teacher?" I knew then that she had told, but I didn't know just what. And I explained. To my surprise he laughed.

"Hasn't the lady been a kind teacher?"

I admitted that she had up until that time, but I added that she had no right to punish me because I had done nothing to deserve it.

"Hasn't she obtained books for you, books that you needed?" he asked.

"Yes, but it was not fair for her to punish me. I did nothing wrong."

150

"If she will admit you back to class will you be courteous as you had been before this happened?"

I thought that one over. Captain Pratt said, "You know that men must be courteous to ladies and indulge them in their whims."

White Eyes! Their men spoil women. No wonder they are all henpecked. No wonder all white women are bossy.

I went back and was never punished again. But I was getting tired of the monotony, tired of being a prisoner, and tired of conforming to stupid customs imposed upon me.

Again I considered running away and going to Mt. Vernon Barracks. Another letter from George Wratten had told me where it was. I had found the place on the map. Geronimo and his little band were there now. I'd go. But when I got to thinking of facing my uncle, I had other thoughts. I had given my word and I must stay. And Ramona was there with me.

Spring had come and gone, and it was during the summer that the disciplinarian took groups of boys to the hills to pick huckleberries for the school. The girls used them for cooking and canning. Sundays we had pie.

There was a Chiricahua boy about fifteen named Jeoffre at the school. He had found a pole to use as the shaft of a lance. He had whittled a barbed, wooden point and had painted it the color of steel. He hid the lance where the wild berries grew. When we got close to it, Jeoffre snatched it from the deep grass and charged the disciplinarian. The man was so frightened that he high-tailed it to the school, Jeoffre in close pursuit. When the Apache explained that he had done it as a joke, Captain Pratt laughed. And he did not punish Jeoffre. That may have been because the boy had begun to cough, and the officer knew that he was going to die. That autumn he did.

The next time we went berry picking I decided to run away. We were in the clothes that we wore to do farm work. They were in common use and would not be noticed as would a uniform. I would travel on foot by night and hide and sleep during the day. I would visit my uncle and my friends at Mt. Vernon. Somebody, maybe Geronimo or George Wratten, would help me get Ramona and take her to my people.

I watched for my chance and slipped away. I hid in a dense thicket and waited for night. They might not miss me until the evening meal was served. Then the Apaches would be questioned. None knew my plans; but even if they did, they'd have faced death rather than tell. I began to worry that Ramona would worry. About midnight I climbed to the third balcony of the dormitory and crawled through a window to my bed.

I was at Carlisle for eight years. During that time I had no further trouble with Captain Pratt. I began to realize that some of the things he required of us were beneficial. It was his intention that all decisions be for our good, regardless of our dislike for them.

In 1894 the prisoners at Mt. Vernon Barracks were moved to Fort Sill. The girls were sent home first. Ramona and Viola Massai went together.

There were some married couples at Carlisle; and it was Ramona's wish that we be married there. I wanted that, too; but I had learned that, before taking on that responsibility in this strange and unpleasant life of another race, a man must have an occupation that would enable him to support a family. Until I had an income our wedding must be postponed.

151

CHAPTER 6

MOUNT VERNON BARRACKS

At one o'clock in the morning on Wednesday, April 27, 1887, the captives left Fort Marion for Mt. Vernon Barracks, Alabama. That evening the train stopped at Pensacola, where the wives and children of Geronimo's band joined them. The combined group arrived at Mt. Vernon the next day and was placed under the charge of Major William Sinclair. Geronimo, the warriors who surrendered with him, and Mangus arrived later.

EUGENE CHIHUAHUA

The buildings were located on a ridge, in the swamp. They were built of brick, in the 1830s, and were enclosed by a massive brick wall.[1] We had thought Fort Marion a terrible place with the mosquitoes and rain, but this was worse. The only way it was better was that it was larger.

The married couples were placed in the tumbledown houses with dirt floors. The unmarried men were housed together. It rained nearly all the time and the roofs leaked. On top of that the mosquitoes almost ate us alive. Babies died from their bites. It was hot and steamy. We had been accustomed to dry heat in Arizona and could take it, but that humidity! It was worse than that at St. Augustine; it was terrible. Everything moulded—food, clothes, moccasins, everything.

But we took it, and without complaining. If the children could stand it, so could the older people. And Nana went about telling us to remember that we were Apaches and that we had been trained to suffer.[2]

They set the men to cutting down trees and building houses. Once they got a roof on those huts we could keep dry, but we still had swarms of mosquitoes tormenting us night and day.

I don't remember any officer's family living there. But it was a good place

---

1. There were 2,160 acres of land surrounded by sandy pine forests and swamps. The soil was not suitable for farming. In the bordering country were a few log cabins occupied by poor whites and blacks.

2. Eugene Chihuahua stated, "It is true that from early childhood Apaches were taught that they must endure suffering without complaint. It was seldom that a child old enough to walk and talk ever cried."

for Apaches to go—and to die. The officers had no screens. I don't think anybody did at that time. But they had a thin cloth tacked over the windows. They had curtains made of it draped over the beds, too. Still, they also probably suffered from the mosquitoes.

Then our people got the shaking sickness. We burned one minute and froze the next. No matter how hot and muggy it was, no pile of blankets would keep us warm. We chilled and shook—not all the time, but every afternoon or every other day. There was an army doctor who gave us medicine, nasty bitter medicine. I don't know whether or not it did us any good. We had our own Medicine Men, but none of them had the Power over this malaria.[3]

Meanwhile, the reports sent to the Adjutant General's Office stated that the prisoners were contented and happy in Alabama. They were, of course, even more miserable and unhappy than they had ever been in Florida. But they went about their routine as usual. They made bows and arrows, moccasins, bead work and other articles for sale. There were few tourists; however, they were permitted to go Mt. Vernon and sell their wares to passengers on the trains.

EUGENE CHIHUAHUA

They soon learned that anything made by Geronimo was in demand and for a higher price than that of others. So many put their products in his keeping. He did not tell anyone that he had made the articles he sold, though a few of them were really his products. Thus, many bows and articles purchasers thought were made by Geronimo are distributed over the country.[4]

My people often gambled to pass the time and forget the misery. They bet on horse races, hunts, almost everything. And they played cards a lot. Before our capture we got decks of cards from the Mexicans. They made them of cowhide, much larger than the usual size. Clubs, spades, and so on were designated by paintings instead of symbols.

In the old days a band seldom numbered more than fifty and all were related by blood or marriage. That meant ten or twelve men. If one killed a deer everybody ate; the next day someone else would get game and all would share. It was the same with gambling. The women, too, loved it. If one person won nearly all the band's possessions today, somebody else got them tomorrow. So it mattered little who claimed ownership. But in big groups such as were imprisoned in Alabama it made a great difference.

But people went on dying from "consumption" and weakness.[5] After they moved into the log cabins they were more comfortable. The houses had two

---

3. So called from *mal aire*—bad air. At that time the knowledge of how yellow fever or malaria was transmitted had yet to be discovered. The discoverer, Walter Reed, was researching the problem; in fact he visited Mt. Vernon Barracks while the Chiricahuas were there.

4. Eugene Chihuahua stated: "After we were sent to Fort Sill, he [Geronimo] continued this practice; it paid him well when he and Daklugie attended the world's fairs."

5. Eugene Chihuahua stated that nearly all of the prisoners were weak, and some of them were

rooms with dirt floors and a "dog-trot" between. This space had a roof and was cooler than the small rooms.

Teachers came and started a school. We were afraid that they wanted to take the children away from their parents as had been done in Florida. Some of the men believed that they were to help us, but Nana never did. Still, he advised us to be courteous and not to show our distrust. We also thought that Geronimo would oppose the school, but he was wise enough to know that we needed the white man's weapons in skullduggery just as we did for fighting. He acted as disciplinarian for the boys and was very strict, just as he had been back home.

When General Howard came for an inspection Geronimo welcomed him just as though he liked the man. When Howard told of losing an arm in the Civil War Geronimo asked, "What did you expect? Do you think war is a picnic?"

Chapo, son of Geronimo, was sent to his father to die of the coughing sickness. At that time, because of the sputum we thought that the patient had worms in the lungs and that they caused the illness. The Medicine Men put up dances for him. I think that the army doctor, too, tried to cure Chapo. But as did many others, he died. Lozen, sister of Chief Victorio, died of the same sickness. She also died at Mt. Vernon.

Chihuahua had been promised by the officer at Fort Marion that he would "never be forced to bring wood nor to carry water." He didn't like being idle, so he was employed in various supervisory tasks. So was Geronimo. They made him a tribal judge and he was harder on the Apaches than were the officers.

I remember well when General Crook came to visit us in Alabama. Two others were with him.[6] My father took me to the meeting. He respected the general but thought that he had lied when he had promised that we would be returned to Turkey Creek in two years. But everybody treated the visitors well until Crook was very rude to Geronimo. He repulsed Geronimo's attempt at courtesy and friendly conversation. Crook seemed to think that my father would take his part; but Chihuahua also believed that, instead of Crook's capturing the band, they had captured Crook.

Crook could see that nobody liked his insult to Geronimo, and that was that. It was cowardly, too, because Geronimo was an unarmed prisoner and could not retaliate. I still think that Crook hated Geronimo because he couldn't whip him.

During the period of incarceration at Mt. Vernon Barracks the prisoners attempted to resume their lives according to the customs they had followed when they were free. They gathered the children about the campfires at night and repeated over and over much of the history and many of the traditions of their people. They trained the dancers and performed the rites of the Puberty Ceremonials. They celebrated weddings according to tribal custom. And they

---

dying of tuberculosis. They hadn't had enough to eat and the post doctor was not able to do much to help. "Finally the War Department ordered that full army rations be given."

6. Crook visited Mt. Vernon Barracks in late December 1889. See page 158.

required the adolescent boys to make the four-day fast and prayer ordeal in order to get the vision or instruction that would be their medicine throughout their lives.

When the army announced that those who wished might enlist in the infantry, many joined. The compensation was minimal but it did bring a man a pittance. Fighting had been their primary occupation, but best of all it relieved them of day labor. Fun, one of Geronimo's most trusted warriors, was one of those who joined.

At the time of surrender, Fun had advanced to be next in rank to Geronimo, a distinction earned by his furious counterforays during the disastrous attack by García's forces during their flight to Mexico.[7] Fun's party, already being pursued by Mexicans, blundered onto another Mexican force. Joined by the rear guard attempting to protect them from the pursuing Mexicans, the Apache party engaged in a desperate battle for their lives. During the encounter, Lozen, sister of Victorio, attempted to pick up a much-needed bag of ammunition inadvertently dropped as the warriors scurried to find defensive positions.

During her attempt, Fun, with bullets between the fingers of his left hand, leaped to the bank toward the Mexican troops and singlehandedly attempted to stem their attack. Dodging from left to right he managed to delay the charge long enough for the ammunition bag to be grasped by the desperate woman who attempted to drag it to the brink of the arroyo where the warriors were positioned. Unable to make the remaining steps, she fell and was dragged to safety with the precious supply of bullets.

Fun enlisted in Company I, Twelfth Infantry, at Mt. Vernon Barracks, along with several other prisoners. On March 31, 1891, First Lieutenant W. W. Wotherspoon reported to the Post Adjutant as follows: "Corporal Fun killed himself in a fit of jealous insanity, after shooting and slightly wounding his young wife. The wife has now recovered and is back in the village."

Perhaps the obligation of the Apache husband to either kill or cut off the nose of the unfaithful wife was not known at that time to any white people. That did not make it any the less obligatory to the Indian. Neither was he famliar with many of the bewildering requirements of the White Eyes' laws. So sometimes when breaking their laws he was simply obeying his own. Since he did know that no killing was permitted by the army—another bewildering prohibition—he took the almost unknown means of escape: suicide.

Fun thought that he had killed his wife. He knew that the Apaches would approve, but he wanted to escape the terrible death and mutilation of hanging. For as the body is buried it must go through eternity. So Fun used his rifle as his means of escape. He took off his shoes, leaned against a tree, and placed the barrel against his head. Unable to reach the trigger with his fingers, he pulled it with his toes.[8]

Communication with the children at Carlisle was restricted to infrequent replies to letters written by the interpreter, George Wratten. They respected and trusted him. When he sought permission, "Indian way," to marry an Apache

---

7. James Kaywaykla; interview. Fun is shown next to Geronimo to his left in a September 1886 photograph. In Apache protocol this indicates Fun as next in rank. See page 121.

8. George Martine and Eugene Chihuahua; interviews.

girl, the tribe feasted, danced, and engaged in contests for the four days of the marriage rites. Two children were born to the couple, Blossom and Amy.

One morning as Wratten passed the house of the scout Martine, he met the beaming man of the house. Martine informed the interpreter that during the night a son had been born.

"Have you named him?" asked Wratten.

"Not yet," was the reply.

"Then why not name him for me?" asked Wratten.

"And," said the son of Martine, "I am George Wratten Martine. And I am one of the few who know the date of my birth. I was born August 15, 1890."

No names of children born were recorded. Military reports list the number of males and females born each year, but not the names of the parents. The last year the Apaches were at Pensacola, records show that one male child was born there. The following is the account as given by members of the tribe.

Shortly before Geronimo and Naiche were informed that they were to be moved to Mt. Vernon Barracks, a son was born to one of Naiche's wives. It was a difficult birth and the army surgeon was asked to attend. He told Naiche that the child was too weak to live if he were moved with the rest. What were the parents to do? They could not desert the infant. "Get a nurse or a family to care for the baby until he is strong enough to be brought to you. The government will pay a woman to care for him and bring him to you."

Finding such a person was difficult, but a civilian nurse by the name of Wells (given name unknown) was secured to keep the child until the Naiches were resettled. Nurse Wells took the baby and cared for him for several months. She became so attached to the boy that she dreaded giving him to his parents. She disappeared and took the baby with her. Representing herself as a widow she named the boy George Wells (after George Wratten) and moved from Florida to Pittsburgh, Pennsylvania, where she reared and educated the child with apparent love and care.

Not until Grorge had grown to adulthood and married did his "foster" mother reveal to him his real identity. George took on his wife's last name, de Marinella, and the couple named their first child Mark de Marinella. When old enough to understand, Mark was informed that he was the grandson of Chief Naiche.

When Mark Naiche was in high school he wrote to every reservation in the United States and inquired if there were any Indians named Natchez (the spelling used in military reports) enrolled at the agency. Not many replies were received, and not one of them reported a Natchez. Significantly, there was no answer from the Mescalero Apache headquarters.

Many years went by. Mark Naiche, now of early middle age, had established his home and dental laboratory practice in a suburb of Philadelphia. He had continued the search for his forebears, but had been unable to learn if there were any of Chief Naiche's descendants living. Then he read *In the Days of Victorio* and found his name. By a telephone call to this author he learned that Naiches were still living on the Mescalero Apache Reservation. Upon learning that the Puberty Ceremonials were to be held the first week in July, he drove to Ruidoso to attend the rites and to find his uncles, Christian and Barnabas, and his aunt, Amelia Naiche.

Several years previously a man whom the Indians considered an imposter had come to Mescalero to attempt to have the Naiches identify him as the son of Taza, older brother of their father, Chief Naiche. Wary of another such attempt, they asked Mark de Naiche for identification and proof of his claim for relationship. They felt that such a request was both reasonable and just, and he agreed. He had no birth certificate, but he did possess his baptismal certificate, which gave his name as Mark de Naiche de Marinella. After some further doubt and delay he was accepted by the Naiches as the grandson of their father.

To a considerable degree white friends of the Indians had been responsible for pressuring the president and the administration to move the Apaches to what they had hoped was a better place in Alabama. Such pressure continued when the problems at Mount Vernon Barracks began to surface.[9]

In December 1887 a party consisting of Miss Richards, Parker West (an Apache from San Carlos in school then at Carlisle), and Miss Isabel B. Eustis visited Mt. Vernon Barracks to observe conditions. Miss Eustis, in a letter of January 5, 1888, described the reservation as containing three square miles of land twenty-eight miles north of Mobile and three miles from the Mobile River, on high ground above the rich but malarial river-bottom land.

Calling on Chief Chihuahua, Richards and Eustis found him tenderly caring for a sick child he had taken to the doctor. Upon learning the purpose of her visit he expressed approval and offered to call the men into council.

Richards and Eustis found that they approved of the advantages their children were receiving at Carlisle; there was only one request that a child be returned.

Only old Nana refused to be reconstructed. He was "near a hundred" and bent with rheumatism. He spoke long, and Parker said that he asked if *they* loved *their* homes. The visitors acknowledged the appeal of his speech and question. Sympathizing with the old man, Miss Eustis took a small globe and explained to Nana that the United States was getting more and more people from other countries of the world. As a result of these crowded conditions the Indians could no longer have their territory to roam over as they had done in the old days. The Apache had to work with his white brother, side by side. She placed the globe in his hands, but Nana said that she should give it to a younger man. He was, he said, too old to learn.

Previous to this interview Nana had retained his hope for freedom, and he had been a constant source of encouragement to others. This is the first occasion upon which any Apache or white man knew of his seeming to resign himself to the fate of his people. Kaytennae, Nana's chosen successor and devoted friend, quietly removed the globe from Nana's hands.[10]

In 1889 General Oliver O. Howard, commander of Headquarters Division of the Atlantic, ordered that a detailed report be submitted on the Apache prisoners of war at Fort Mount Vernon Barracks. The report, signed by his son

---

9. For an excellent treatise on white efforts to assist the prisoners of war, see David Michael Goodman, "Apaches as Prisoners of War: 1886–1894" (Ph.D. diss., Texas Christian University, 1969).

10. Eustis to Hemenway, January 5, 1888, National Archives, Record Group 689, Reel 191, pp. 464–77.

and aide de camp, First Lieutenant Guy Howard, on December 23, 1889, contained the following information. Of a total of 498 Apaches imprisoned between April 13 and November 7, 1886, 119 (24%) had died: 49 at St. Augustine, 50 at Mt. Vernon, and 30 at Carlisle. Eighty-one babies had been born during the same period, and the present total number was 460. Lieutenant Howard stated that:

The normal death rate of civilized people is less than 2 percent. per annum. That of these people, including those at school, is more than three times as great, or 6.8 percent.

A number equal to one-quarter of those brought east has died in three and a half years. Consumption has fastened itself among them, and has been rapid and always fatal where it has attacked.

Lieutenant Howard went on to give as reasons the degrading status as prisoners, malaise, sickness and depression, long-deferred promises of a permanent home, unnatural moist atmosphere, and forced removal of children to school. Lieutenant Howard closed his report with the recommendation: "That application be made to Congress for a suitable tract of land and the fitting out of these people with materials and tools to build cabins, with simple farm utensils, cattle, and seeds, and that they be put on such land by the first of March, 1890. Another year's delay would be criminal."[11]

General Howard forwarded the report with the added comment. "The innocent have suffered with the guilty, and I see no possible way of relieving the situation than by adopting the course within recommended, and, I hope, in the interest of justice, as well as of humanity, that speedy action be taken." The report was endorsed in turn by Major General J. M. Schofield, Commander, Headquarters, Army of the United States.[12]

At the same time, responding to orders by Secretary of War Redfield Proctor, Major General George Crook left for an inspection of possible sites in North Carolina. Impressed enough with possibilities there to state that the country "seems to be fairly well adapted to the needs of the Indians," Crook went on to Mt. Vernon Barracks, where he inspected conditions and had a meeting with, among others, Chihuahua, Naiche, Chato, Kaetennae, Toclanny, and George Wratten.[13] He found the prisoners ill, depressed, and discouraged. At that meeting, Chief Chihuahua made the following appeal.

I am getting so my limbs feel as if they were asleep. I would like to have some place better than this. I would like to have a place where I could have a farm and go right to work so that my children can have plenty to eat; and I would like to have tools to go right to work with. I have a daughter away at school and two other near relatives. I want to see them soon. Won't you make it so I can see them very soon? I didn't get any of the money that was to be sent to me; I never said anything about it. Sam Bowman knows about it. I thought when I saw you I would tell you about it. I never said anything about it. I am just the same now as when I saw you last going along the same road. There are trees all about. I would like to go where I can see.[14]

---

11. United States Senate, Executive Document No. 35, Vol. 2682, 51st Cong., 1st sess., pp. 9–11.

12. Ibid., p. 12.

13. Ibid., pp. 2, 5. Crook pointedly refused to allow Geronimo to have a part in the meeting. See Goodman, "Apaches as Prisoners of War," p.177.

14. Ibid., p. 8.

Crook, also concerned about the alarming death rate, commented in his report that it "would seem due to home-sickness, change of climate, and the dreary monotony of empty lives." He concluded:

I cannot too strongly urge that immediate steps be taken to secure a reservation for them where they could be settled on farms of their own, to work for themselves, and to receive for themselves the full benefit of their labors, for with red people as well as white, self-interest is the mainspring of progress. . . . I would recommend that if possible they be sent as soon as practicable to some point in the Indian territory.[15]

Secretary Proctor forwarded the reports of both General Crook and Lieutenant Howard to President Harrison on January 13, 1890, recommending that "those Indians be transferred to Fort Sill in the Indian Territory." Only a week later the President "earnestly" recommended to Congress "that provision be made by law for locating these Indians upon lands in the Indian Territory."[16]

Unfortunately, the timing was bad. In addition to strong opposition to removal to any location contiguous to New Mexico and Arizona, the move to open up Indian Country had begun in Congress. The Apaches had to wait three more years for relief. Finally, on August 6, 1894, Congress enacted legislation allowing for removal to Fort Sill of all the Chiricahua Apaches, at the same time alloting $15,000 for the "erection of buildings, purchase of draft an imals, stock, necessary farming tools, seeds, household utensils, and other articles needed for said Indians and generally for their support and civilization."[19]

---

15.   Ibid., p. 4.

16.   Ibid., pp. 1–2.

17.   United States House Report No.724, Vol. 6132, 62nd Cong. 2nd Sess., p.7.

CHAPTER 7

VILLAGES AT FORT SILL

EUGENE CHIHUAHUA

The Comanches, Kiowas, and Kiowa-Apaches hauled us and our handful of possessions to Cache Creek. What blankets and other things we'd put in the baggage cars were destroyed. So we set to work to make brush shelters the old way. Where saplings grew close together, we cut those in the way and tied the tops of growing ones together to form a framework. And the army gave us some canvas to use as covering. We'd lived in houses for almost eight years and learned to like some kind of roof. But, Indian way, we made use of what we could get and we were happy.

Captain Scott had not lied to us.*We could see the mountains. They weren't tall like ours but they were mountains. There were trees, and we didn't have to climb one to see the sun. There was water in the creek—clear sparkling mountain water. There were mesquite beans, and we began gathering and shelling them. We hadn't seen one since we were taken to Florida. We gathered several hundred bags of them. And there were deer—not so many as at Turkey Creek, but a good many.

You'll laugh at this, but I don't mind. The best of all was to hear the coyotes sing, and the cry of the quail too. We hadn't heard them since we left Fort Bowie. And the smell of sage was good to us.

Captain Scott, as he had promised, issued food to us. He sent blankets, too. And he managed to supply some clothing. They took the children away from their parents and placed them in school at Anadarko. That was more than thirty miles away. At first the Apaches had no horses, and many of them walked to see their children.

George Wratten, with his Apache wife, was there; but we had a bad time talking without an interpreter because he lived so far away. The Kiowa-Apaches could not understand much of what we said, but there were some

---

* Captain Hugh L. Scott, Seventh Cavalry, in command of the prisoners at Fort Sill. Although Scott did not remain in command throughout the period of the Chiricahuas' imprisonment at Fort Sill, in 1911 and 1912 Scott, then a colonel representing the war department, was instrumental in negotiating with both the Mescalero Apaches in New Mexico and the Chiricahuas in Oklahoma the removal of the Chiricahuas to the Mescalero reservation, which finally occurred in 1913. See United States House Document No. 1249, Vol. 6503, 62nd Cong., 3rd Sess., pp. 1–5.

Comanche and Kiowa boys who had gone to Carlisle who were a great help. And some of us spoke a little English. Many of us also had a knowledge of Spanish, but the people at Fort Sill couldn't understand it.

We got there too late to begin building houses, so we had a hard first winter. The next year we constructed two-room houses built by standing boards up and down. In most of them the rooms were separated by a "dog-trot"—between them and under the same roof—wide enough that a wagon could be driven through it. They afforded shade in hot weather.

Captain Scott knew Indians and understood much of our needs. When the homes were built he let each chief, famous scout, or headman have a village far enough from others that he and his followers would have some privacy. These little settlements were strung out along Cache and Medicine Bluff creeks.

They were located so that friendly people were close together and the scouts we disliked separated by distance. Nobody liked Chato. He was not far from Four Mile Crossing where Geronimo lived, but he knew better than to try anything with Geronimo. Everyone did. And he had sense enough to stay away from him.

Many of the prisoners had served in the infantry [Company I, Twelfth Infantry] and most of them enlisted in the Seventh Cavalry at Fort Sill—Custer's old regiment.

Nearly all the village headmen enlisted in the army, and many who were of lesser rank served also. Some headmen were too old for military service but were recognized for service as scouts and paid to maintain village order.

James Kaywaykla was grown when he returned from Carlisle and did not live in a village. He married Dorothy Naiche and they had a house by themselves. Daklugie and Ramona too were married and lived near the fort. Eugene Chihuahua, still single, also lived apart—near Daklugie. Each wife of a polygamous marriage had her own house.

Although there was little mention of polygamy, it was the Apache custom, and the consideration shown by Captain Scott for the wives indicates a deep understanding and a dislike for the breaking of family ties. That the missionaries did not share this point of view undoubtedly did not contribute to their success in securing converts. They concentrated their efforts on the men, having determined that the women and children were apt to follow the lead of the man of the house. When the husband was ready to accept Christianity and was informed that he must choose one wife and her children and abandon the rest, the minister's task was a discouraging one. Many Apaches refused to comply. How could a woman and children exist without protection and support?

In accordance with President Grant's "peace policy" attempts were made to secure ministers or church members as agents, and a certain denomination was given charge of a specific tribe. That selected for all Apaches was the Dutch Reformed Church, the Dutch branch of the Presbyterian Church.

Frank Hall Wright, a Choctaw, was the first missionary assigned to the prisoners at Fort Sill. He came in 1895 and was joined later by Dr. Walter C. Roe, who had worked among the Cheyennes.

CHAPTER 8

CATTLE

D aklugie returned to his people at Fort Sill in 1895. Having spent over eight years at Carlisle, he was shocked and angered at the conditions he found at Fort Sill. What he disliked most was the labor exacted of the Indian women. Greatly as he hated white people, he had, probably without realizing it, accepted Captain Pratt's admonition as to treating women with more deference. At least he resented their being forced to perform tasks that, from his point of view, should have been assigned to the soldiers.

He lived in a house apart from the villages and closer to the fort. Ramona, of course, was with her parents. She wished to marry immediately but he would not consent to that until he could make a sufficient income to support a family. Much as he disliked customs forced by necessity, he made some concessions. He went to George Wratten, manager of the trading post, who did some of the hiring. He told the interpreter of his years of study of cattle and said that those he had seen on the reservation were inferior and that the herd should be improved.

Wratten sent him to Captain Scott. Daklugie made no effort to conceal his dissatisfaction with conditions on the reservation, and a scuffle ensued. The officer was a small man, and it was an unequal bout. Captain Scott dashed from his office, mounted a horse, and galloped away.

For an hour or more Daklugie stayed, expecting the arrival of the military police. To his surprise nobody came, and he rode to the trading post. There Wratten told him that Scott had come to him.

"Who is this ruffian who wants to run the reservation?" Scott asked.

Wratten replied, "He is Geronimo's nephew, just back from Carlisle. He is well educated and deeply interested in the welfare of his people. He doesn't want to run the reservation; he wants a job. He knows more about cattle than anybody here does. And he can handle men. He wants to marry Chihuahua's daughter and to be able to support her."

Captain Scott sat a few minutes without speaking and Wratten continued, "He will have the support of every chief and influential man among the prisoners with the exception of Chato. And he is young and educated. He could be very useful to you if he respects you. He may dislike you, and you him. But to an Apache, respect is more important than liking. There is no real friendship without it."

162

After Wratten's explanation Captain Scott agreed to put Daklugie in charge of the cattle. Scott admitted that there were some good cowboys among the Indians, although their overall management had been inefficient.[1]

Daklugie

So I took over. The government had given the prisoners a start in cattle, and in one year some of the men had become fairly good at handling them. All were good horsemen, but they had to learn how to rope and to flank calves. I had not done that either and I had to learn with the rest.

When I saw Captain Scott again it was in his office. He stood and we shook hands. I had come to ask for good bulls and he approved the purchase. After that I worked hard to make that herd the best in Oklahoma, and when we left for Mescalero in 1913 I think it was.

The range had not been fenced. We cut posts and set them. The government provided wire and the Apaches built the fence. But we had to have gates because the road crossed our reservation and there was much travel through it.

Nearly all of the older men, and some of the younger men, were farming. They raised some corn, Kaffir corn, and sorghum. All are good feed for both cattle and horses; Kaffir and sorghum stand drouth better. Cattle were our main source of income but hay came next—hay and fodder. We sold it to the cavalry.[2]

We were paid for our work—not very much, but enough that we didn't have to run to the government with our hands out for every pound of sugar or coffee.

When the race for the strip was run, I put extra guards on duty, night and day. Perico was a very efficient scout and he and I spent several nights riding fence to see that cattle weren't stolen.

At another time we had to keep careful watch after I began missing cattle. They were going—sometimes two or three at a time, sometimes just one. Some had been butchered on the reservation; there was evidence of that. Every cowboy watched both for offal and tracks of strange horses. By that time most of our mounts were shod. A white man might have been unable to identify tracks, but Apaches could.

Night after night I kept watch, and sometimes I had Eugene or Perico with me; sometimes others volunteered and stayed. What sleep I got was in the daytime. But it was during the day that by accident I rode by an abandoned well

---

1. The army was to have further altercations with those returning from Carlisle. In 1896 a "Carlisle boy" reportedly attacked a soldier with an axe. He was disarmed and tied. Another prisoner, also returned from Carlisle, came on the scene and attempted to strike at one of the soldiers with a pair of reins. Both were jailed. Apparently Captain Scott's confrontation with Daklugie went unreported as the above incident was reported as "the first disturbance that has taken place since the arrival of these Indians at the Post." The report went on to state that the "Carlisle boys [are] greatly condemned by the older Indians...." H. L. Scott, August 31, 1896, AGO, National Archives.

2. Scott reported that "Apache Prisoners of War have been engaged during the month of August in putting up hay to the amount of 350 tons—this hay is extremely scarce requiring a large area to cut over to secure a ton and as there is a scarcity of hay reported in Northern Texas, Oklahoma, and Southern Kansas it is likely to be very valuable during the coming winter." Ibid.

about which I hadn't known. There were sixty-seven hides in it with Apache brands. Some suspected our neighboring brothers, the Comanches, Kiowas, and Kiowa-Apaches. However, though they didn't like us, they had given part of their range to us and I felt sure that they were not stealing our cattle. We had many good friends among them. There are bad ones among all people, but at that time Indians weren't stealing from each other.[3]

As I had suspected, the thieves were White Eyes. They were sent to the penitentiary for fifteen years. That was the first time I'd ever known of a white man's being punished for robbing Indians. Usually they steal by means of dishonest laws and crooked lawyers. (At least these thieves had the courage to take some risks.) Yet, there are a few honest attorneys and they can do a lot of good, and have. We had one prosecute those thieves and they got what they deserved.

The responsibility for the tribe's herd was great, but I liked it. I looked forward to a time when we must depend upon our own resources—and be free of orders. And to me raising cattle was the answer. I knew very well that the government couldn't make farmers out of us, though at that time some of our people were raising crops. Even though they disliked cultivating the soil they did it. But I didn't know a man who didn't like riding a horse and working cattle.

One thing that happened was very disturbing to me. In a tribal meeting the men elected me as "working chief." Though it was, I felt, an honor, I declined it. Why? We had a chief, one elected to the customs of the Apaches; and he had been a good and efficient one. Young though he was when his older brother, Taza, died, Naiche had wisdom far beyond his years.

When I had earned enough money to get a house and support a family Ramona and I were married. Ramona would have been willing to camp under a tree, if necessary, but I wasn't. She and her mother made a beautiful beaded buckskin dress for the wedding feast. We wanted to be really married, Indian way, and we were. But Ramona wanted the respect of the White Eyes, too; so we had two ceremonies. For that one she made a beautiful silk dress. She still has both.

Never, I think, have I ever known a happier marriage than that of Ramona and Ace Daklugie. Though Daklugie talked freely about his youth, I sensed that his reluctance to speak at length concerning this great love was owing to his reluctance to betray his emotions.

After Ramona's death, Daklugie, with the assistance of Eugene Chihuahua and other close relatives, insisted on digging her grave. It was a very large and deep one in order to hold the many prized possessions buried with her. Daklugie got down into the excavation and personally arranged the platform of boards upon which the casket was to be lowered and lovingly placed each personal treasure. Ramona was buried in her buckskin wedding dress.

---

3. See Angie Debo, *Geronimo: The Man, His Time, His Place* (Norman: University of Oklahoma Press, 1976), pp. 369–70.

Daklugie and Ramona
Wedding picture.

CHAPTER 9

AN APACHE IDYLL

EUGENE CHIHUAHUA

When I was a boy I wasn't interested in girls. All I loved was horses and baseball. The minute I got off from work I got on a horse and rode to Chihuahua's village, and then I played ball. I played even if I had to play alone. I practiced pitching with the barn for a backstop so that I didn't have to chase the ball far. I was left-handed, and I could put that ball right where I wanted it.

I was the only one of my father's children who did not go to Carlisle, but he wanted me to learn things, too. And when the interpreter [George Wratten] took over the store, my father went to him. "I want my son to learn to read," he said.[1]

"But I'm no teacher; I'm a busy man." He was a good man, though, even if he was a White Eye. He went from San Carlos to Florida with the Chiricahua; he stayed with us there and in Alabama; and when we came to Fort Sill he was our agent, I guess, and he was a good one.

So George Wratten took me into the trading post to help him. From the names on the things I learned to read. I learned "sugar" first; I liked it. And I learned English, too. All Apaches can count; our way is better than yours, but I had to learn your names for the numbers, and how to make them.

And Mr. Wratten taught me to write so that I could make bills for the things people bought. It is a quick way to learn. And it is handy for keeping the score in ball games—yet I could always keep them in my head.

I was grown when we went to Fort Sill, and very strong. I could run fast, I could dodge well, and I was a good ball player. Even the young officers said that. They put me on the Fort Sill team. I was the only Indian on it. Wherever they went, I went; and they were proud of me. I worked hard to be a good player. When they needed a pinch hitter, they'd say, "Let's put the Chief in; he won't let us down." And I didn't. One time when we were playing Oklahoma City, they were one ahead in the last inning. We had two men on bases

---

1. Wratten got a primer and taught him to write, to make a statement of articles charged, and to make charges.

Eugene Chihuahua
Scout at Fort Sill.

and two outs when I came to bat. On my third strike I hit a home run. You ought to have seen those officers! First thing I knew I was on their shoulders and they were carrying me in front of the grandstand and everybody was standing up and screaming. At first it scared me, but they were yelling "Chief! Chief!" It made me feel like a real chief, not a prisoner of war.

The Fort Sill officers' team played some of the big teams of the Middle West; and Eugene's fame grew. He was a handsome young man, much lighter in color than the average Apache and much more approachable. (This quality at ninety-three he still retained. He met people well and mades friends effortlessly.)

On one occasion they were playing in a small town in southwestern Oklahoma, largely to keep in practice for a difficult game that they had scheduled in Dallas. They ate their evening meal at a big circular table in the hotel dining room. There were no screens, and occasionally a fly got into the room. As the waitress stopped opposite Eugene, a fly alighted on his eyelid and involuntarily it closed. He looked up to see the girl smile, nod, and go out of the room. When they had finished eating, she was waiting at the front door. She had changed into a street dress and was waiting for him.

"Ready?" she inquired.

"Ready for what?" asked the bewildered Indian.

"The Carnival, of course," was the reply.

EUGENE CHIHUAHUA

I didn't know what a carnival was, and I'd never been alone with any girl in all my life.[2] I didn't know what to say. When I get scared, I think in Indian. The captain of the team stepped up and said, "Go ahead, Gene; take her to ride the chalk horses. Here's five dollars."

She took hold of my arm and pulled me along to where the shows and the merry-go-round were. She rode it, but I didn't. And I didn't go into any of those tents. I shot at those things where tin rabbits go past and hit so many that the man wouldn't let me shoot any more. Every time I hit something he gave that lady a doll or something.

Before it got dark I took her back to that hotel. I had business downtown.

Bad as we thought of white people's ways, I did have dates later. I worked for Lieutenant Allyn Capron as a sort of orderly.[3] I helped him at his place in the officers' quarters and sometimes at his home. He and Mrs. Capron were old people, I thought—maybe forty-five. She was a good lady and she was not afraid of Indians. And she gave me pie. Sometimes I drove for her when she

---

2. Apache custom forbade "dating" as practiced by White Eyes. Brother and sister adolescents were not even left in camp without an older person.

3. Allyn Capron was well liked by the Apaches. He was in charge of the military escort from Mount Vernon Barracks to Fort Sill in 1894. At Fort Sill he served as assistant to Captain Scott until 1898, when he left for duty in the Spanish American War. Reportedly he was the first American officer to be killed in the Cuban campaign. See W. N. Nye, *Carbine and Lance: The Story of Old Fort Sill,* 3d ed. (Norman: University of Oklahoma Press, 1969), pp. 297–300.

went somewhere. And when she had company come in on the train, I met the lady at Lawton and took her to the Capron home.

Mrs. Capron teased me about not having any dates. I couldn't tell her how we looked at that; it might have hurt her feelings. One time she had a party at her house and sent me to bring one of her guests. She wrote a note and put it in an unsealed envelope. I felt bad because it looked as though she couldn't trust me to deliver the message.[4] She told me that it was just the white way. Well, whites have many funny ways, so I took the note. And when I got there, an Indian girl all dressed up like the whites came to the door and said, "Hello, Eugene; nice of you to come for me." Mrs. Capron had tricked me.

I took that girl to a show a few times. But all the time I thought of what would happen if Chihuahua found out that I went out with girls like that. He might think that they were bad girls. But she wasn't. She was a very nice girl; she was just going down the white man's trail, which wasn't good. Her name was Sophy; she was Toclanny's daughter and Uncas Noche's sister. She wanted to marry me. I was afraid of that.

One evening, when I was staying at the Lieutenant's, I was to take Sophy to a party at a place where the Caprons were also going. When I came in, ready to go, Mrs. Capron said, "Whooee! Is that you, Eugene? Lieutenant, look what a handsome boy we've got." She reached around and took some flowers out of a vase. She wrapped something around the stems so that they wouldn't drip and handed them to me. "Take them to your girl; she'll like them."

And she told me to go ahead and marry Sophy; she and the Lieutenant would take us both to Chicago when they went. And they would help us. Indians don't want anybody to help them. Anyway, I didn't want to get married. All I loved was horses and baseball.

Then my sister, Ramona, came home from Carlisle and brought a friend for the vacation. Mrs. Capron invited them to stay with her. They couldn't stay at my father's house; having a strange girl was not proper. She was a Shoshone, and she was beautiful. Her name was Belle Kenoi.

Mrs. Capron told me, "No wonder you don't want to marry Sophy. Belle's a beautiful girl; and I think she likes you, Eugene." Belle told my sister that she wanted to see all of Chihuahua's sons; and my brother came and brought two friends. She didn't know which was my brother. But she told my sister that she didn't like any of them but me. I couldn't talk to her; that was not the Indian way. But I wanted to marry her, and she wanted me. We didn't say it, but we knew in our hearts—Indian way.

I went to my father and asked him to arrange with her parents for the marriage. Chihuahua said, "That girl's going to take you away from us and take you to the Shoshones; you will no longer be a Chiricahua. And I picked you for the next chief. You can't marry her."

He was not just my father; he was my chief. And I am a Chiricahua. So she went away; but before she went she sent me her picture so that I wouldn't forget. And I tried to forget but I couldn't. I had made fun of people who fell in love, but I found out that it was *not* funny. I didn't like anything anymore. I didn't even like baseball.

---

4. Carrying messages was restricted to those who were reliable and trustworthy. As in the old days messages were memorized and delivered orally; being requested to carry a written message concealed even in an unsealed envelope would have been considered an affront.

Nearly all of the Chiricahua children sent to Carlisle had come home. My sister married Ace Daklugie; they married the Indian way, and because Ramona wanted it they married the white way too—with a preacher and a piece of paper. Both ways they were happy. And my father was happy because Daklugie was a real warrior besides knowing white man's ways. And he was a chief's son. Ramona and Ace knew before they went to Carlisle that they were going to marry, but they waited till they got home to their people.

I thought how happy Belle and I would be if we could have married. Now I didn't even know where she lived, nor if she was still alive. I became sick. I got sick slowly. First I didn't want to play ball, then I didn't want to ride horseback, then I didn't want to eat. Chihuahua got worried and thought that maybe I had that sickness that white people get [typhoid].

Skil-yoh-ge, came to Oklahoma to visit his relatives. He was a Ben-et-dinne [San Carlos] Apache, and he was a Medicine Man. My father put up the prayers for me for four nights, and he got Skil-yoh-ge to sing. He sang all night for four nights. He told my father that I was not quite gone yet but that I would go soon if something was not done. And he told Chihuahua that he hoped he could bring me back from under the earth where they were waiting for me. And all my relatives came. Ramona and Ace came. And friends—I didn't know how many friends I had till then. Everybody slept out side my tepee in blankets. In the morning, and at night—all night—they sang and danced for me.

And I remembered who was there and what they did till my spirit got to going around. It left my body and I didn't know anything. But the Medicine Man knew everything that was going on. They thought that I was dead, but Skil-yoh-ge knew that, though my spirit was gone, it would come back. And he knew because there was a sign: on the floor of the tepee he had put a basket, turned upside down, resting on the handle so that something could get under it. And while he was singing he saw a tiny little grass snake, green, glide into the tepee and go under the basket.[5] And he talked to Chihuahua and told him that it was not any disease that made me sick. "Chihuahua, your son is in love and you won't let him marry. That's what has hurt him. But he is going to live. His ghost will return to him. You'll see."

And when it did, Ramona ran and threw her arms around me and cried. And she told my father that she knew where Belle lived.

But Chihuahua still wouldn't let me marry Belle. Nor would he let me marry a white girl. If I had he would have died of shame.

Then the few Chiricahuas still at Carlisle came home.

They were dressed like white people, just like Ramona and Ace and the others who went there. But when they got home they dressed like Indians—all but one girl. I saw her one time at the store and George Wratten told me that she was Viola Massai.[6] She was a nice-looking girl, but not beautiful like Belle.

---

5. When asked about their religious beliefs Apaches will seldom tell much. It is when relating incidents that they reveal such things as these. And they are very superstitious about snakes. No Apache will use anything made of snakeskin.

6. Viola Massai was the daughter of a notorious union between the Chiricahua brave, Massai, and the woman he kidnapped in the Sacramento Mountains of New Mexico. See Chapter *Massai*, Book Three, for that tragic but beautiful story.

And she kept wearing clothes like a white girl. They were all right for white girls, but not for Indians.

One day my father came to my tepee and said, "My Son, Saturday you are going to get married. I am putting up the feast and for four days we will dance and sing. And I will bring you beaded buckskins; your mother will make new ones for the wedding feast." I thought that he was sorry because he was the cause of my almost dying and that he had arranged a marriage for me with Belle Kenoi.

But when he saw the happiness in my face he said, sadly, "My Son, you are to marry Viola Massai. She has been away to school. She has learned the white man's ways. She is, like your sister Ramona, a good cook and a good housekeeper. She will be a good wife. And think how proud all are of Ramona. They will be equally happy with Viola."

"But I don't love Viola. And she doesn't love me."

"That you don't know. The marriage is arranged."

I did come to love her very dearly. And she loved me. But we were never *in love* with each other as Ussen wanted people to be. It was for that reason that each of our six children died young.

Viola accompanied Eugene to the Mescalero Reservation in 1913. There she found relatives. And there she died.

For several years Eugene Chihuahua remained unwed; but his father had died in Oklahoma and could no longer forbid his marriage with his first love. He made a trip to Apache, Oklahoma, to ascertain, if he could, Belle Kenoi's whereabouts and her marital status. To his distress he learned that she had died several years previously. He remained in Oklahoma for some time, and upon his return he brought a new wife—the widow of Hostosovit, a Comanche, and her three children. Perhaps she resented the fact that Eugene preferred living in New Mexico to remaining with her people, as is the custom. At any rate, this marriage terminated in divorce; and though her children remained on the Mescalero Reservation she returned to Oklahoma.

For a long time Eugene was single. He had a magnificent voice and sang in the choir of the Dutch Reformed Church. There the prohibition of a married man seeing his mother-in-law, and vice versa, caused the congregation to hang curtains in the aisle dividing the sides upon which men and women sat.[7] Eugene, being without a mother-in-law and sitting with the choir, was allowed to see the women. Among them was a widow, Jennie Peña, also a widow with three children. She was a pleasant, modest, refined, and respected person, noted for her abstinence from liquor and her ability as a homemaker.

Though their association was limited to speaking as they passed, Eugene decided to ask her to marry him. He went to her oldest son, Marcos, and made known his wishes. Marcos assured him that such a marriage would be favor-

---

7. The mother-in-law taboo is a well-known custom but is not in practice today. James Kaywaykla, who thought he had discarded all of the old customs, said when asked about Naiche's wife, "I didn't talk with her. She was my mother-in-law."

ably considered by his brothers but that Jennie must be consulted. Marcos presented Eugene's proposal to his mother and she consented. The first date they had was one chaperoned by Marcos and his wife—a drive to the county seat of Otero County, Alamogordo, where Eugene and Jennie secured a marriage license. Again, there were two ceremonies—that of the Reformed Church, and the feast that was the Apache custom. And again, there was a happy and serene wedded life.

CHAPTER 10

HIGHLIGHTS AND HIGH JINKS

DAKLUGIE

On top of other problems was that of interpreting for Geronimo. S. M. Barrett, Superintendent of Schools at Lawton, Oklahoma, wished to write a book about my uncle.[1] And strangely, to me, Geronimo consented. Why he wanted it done I still don't understand. It was not our way of preserving our history and traditions. Always the older people had gathered their young about the campfires at night and told repeatedly the stories of our people until the children memorized them. That is the best way for a race to know itself. But my uncle wanted the book done, and he wanted me to act as his interpreter. Busy though I was, I could not refuse.

There were many things to be considered. We were prisoners of war, and I believed that at any time a change in military command might mean massacre for us. Nobody had any sense of security.

There was a chance that Barrett was a spy and the book a device for getting information not obtainable by any other means. We understood that there was a difficulty in obtaining the government's consent for the project and that Barrett had to appeal to the president for approval. That seemed to indicate that they wanted Geronimo to admit something.

We talked it over. Geronimo was shrewd and cautious. Also he had great Power, much greater Power than I.

As you know, Geronimo could foresee what would happen. I relied upon that and upon his habitual caution to keep us out of trouble. So he began dictating and I began interpreting for Barrett.

Geronimo's warriors had been loyal during the campaigns against them. Common danger necessitated that, but their absolute confidence was the

---

1. S. M. Barrett, ed., *Geronimo: His Own Story* (New York: E. P. Dutton & Co., Inc., 1970). For a complete and up-to-date biography of Geronimo, see Angie Debo, *Geronimo: The Man, His Time, His Place* (Norman: University of Oklahoma Press, 1976).

primary cause. Then, too, his ability to foretell what would happen was a very compelling factor. There was also the blood tie, always a very strong tie among Apaches. Now there was no immediate danger to hold them together as there had been in the past. When they learned that Geronimo was dictating his story, the younger men (but not Kanseah) were influenced to some extent by Noche and Chato. Of course Geronimo knew this, and he was very guarded in what he said about them.

Both Kanseah and I felt sure that this was responsible for Eyelash's accusation that Geronimo had witched his daughter to prolong his own life. [Geronimo had hired Eyelash to make medicine for an ailing daughter.] Eyelash had never set himself up as a Medicine Man until then. Why Geronimo hired him to make medicine for his daughter we never knew, but it was probably because he loved his daughter so deeply that for once he wasn't using his head. Why didn't Geronimo make medicine for her himself? What do your Medicine Men do when one of their own family needs treatment? Don't they call in somebody else?

Geronimo wanted to keep peace among all the prisoners and especially those who had been his warriors. Of the younger ones, Perico was most faithful to Geronimo.[2]

Geronimo was very careful in what he told Barrett; and I was just as careful in interpreting. Barrett didn't write shorthand; he took notes. He couldn't write as fast as I talked, so he had to depend on his memory for part of what I told him. But I've wondered if he didn't try to make Geronimo's accounts conform to the books. Nothing could have made my uncle angrier than that. He knew how unreliable military reports sometimes are.

Yes, Geronimo knew much that he didn't include.[3]

Even though we were prisoners of war, there were some rewarding experiences. We got together and held our tribal dances as we had when we were free people. There were attempts made to stop the observance of our Ceremonials but we paid no attention to them.

Geronimo was without doubt the most famous Indian in the United States. People flocked to the reservation to see him and to buy something he had

---

2. Fun, Eyelash, and Perico were brothers.

3. I mentioned Barrett's having written of Geronimo as chief. Daklugie responded, "Well, Geronimo never told him that. Neither did I. It was Barrett who made a chief of my uncle. As you know, Naiche was chief." I went on to remind him that at Fort Sill the warriors had elected *him* (Daklugie) as chief. "They did, but neither Geronimo nor I attended that meeting. Naiche was chief and I refused that honor. It was an honor; but even had there been no Naiche it should have been Geronimo's title, not mine. If anyone ever earned it, he did. Do you think, when Cochise was old, unable to fight, and suffering from cancer, that one of his men would have taken the chieftainship? If you do you just don't know Apaches." Upon Geronimo's death Naiche remained chief and Daklugie took Geronimo's place as the "power behind the throne."

When I remarked that there were other questionable statements in the Barrett account, Daklugie answered, "I know, but Geronimo didn't put them there. Neither did I. Barrett either misunderstood or thought that Geronimo did not know what he was talking about. There are many errors in that book. And Geronimo was far too wise to tell all he knew." Mentally I noted that Daklugie, too, knew what information to withhold.

made or owned. When he ran out of bows and arrows they would pay outlandish prices for anything—a feather, a hat, or even a button from his coat.

When we went somewhere to lead a parade, as we did several times in Oklahoma, he would start with one dollar in his pocket—and a supply of hats and buttons and photographs. Crowds would go to stations to meet the trains, and when we returned Geronimo would have a supply of good clothes and plenty of money.

One of the highlights was our trip to Omaha to the World's Fair.[4] Naiche and others went; but, as usual, attention focused on Geronimo. It was there that he had an encounter with General Miles. Promoters, in their desire to create publicity, felt that this meeting between Miles and Geronimo would attract more people. Apparently Geronimo had always wanted such a meeting, and this was his chance. It must have been difficult for the old warrior to face his enemy, an enemy who had lied and deceived the Apaches in order to obtain their surrender. They exchanged some bitter words and each taunted the other with being a liar.[5]

Miles smiled and freely admitted that he had lied, and then he stated, "You lied to Mexicans, Americans, and to your own Apaches, for thirty years. White men only lied to you once, and I did it."

Geronimo then made his plea to return to Arizona. "The acorns and piñon nuts, the quail and the wild turkey, the giant cactus and the palo verdes—they all miss me. I miss them, too. I want to go back to them."

Miles chuckled again. "A very beautiful thought, Geronimo. Quite poetic. But the men and women who live in Arizona, they do not miss you.... Folks in Arizona sleep now at night, have no fear that Geronimo will come and kill them." And he mimicked the old warrior's style, repeating his enumeration: "Acorns ... palo verde trees—they will have to get along as best they can—without you."[6]

Though his appeal to Miles failed, it brought attention once again to the plight of the Apaches.

DAKLUGIE

In 1904 we went to the Exposition in St. Louis. This was to celebrate the anniversary of the Louisiana Purchase. We stayed there for a long time, and we led parades as we had in many other places. They had an Indian village and brought people to demonstrate Indian craft work. There were weavers, basket makers, pottery workers, and silversmiths. There Geronimo sold bows and arrows—enough to stock a big tribe for a raid. Some he really made himself; but by far the greater number he sold were the products of others who gave him a rake-off on them. He didn't tell anybody that he made them—people just assumed that he did!

There were famous Indians of many different tribes. There were also many foreign people, and among them some from the Philippines. They wore very

4. The Trans-Mississippi and International Exposition of 1898.

5. Debo, *Geronimo*, pp. 405–6.

6. Ibid.

little clothing, such as we had in our primitive life. Geronimo found them very interesting but disapproved of their dress.

It was there that I met a scout who had been with Forsythe on the Arickaree. He told a very different version of that affair than did Forsythe, who possibly became a brigadier general as a result of that affair.

The trip that I enjoyed most was the one we made to Washington for Teddy Roosevelt's inauguration. He was a showman, almost equal to Geronimo. When he was traveling by train in the Middle West, crowds would flock to railway stations to hear him speak from the rear platform of the coach. He would, with an assistant, raise a copper wash boiler and say, "I represent the party that stands for the full dinner pail." Geronimo, too, had promised his followers food, but he made good his promises.

The government paid all our expenses, including transportation for our mounts. We took our finest, those we would have considered our best war horses in the old days. We also took our beaded buckskin suits, but we wore only the breechclouts, belts, moccasins, and our medicine hats. The hats were tightly fitting ones made of skin and covered with the breast feathers of the eagle, so arranged that they stood up. From the crown of these caps dangled two long strips of buckskin, each covered with two hundred eagle plumes, on either side, which hung below our stirrups. Our horses, too, had silver and beads on the bridle and straps.

Along the street bleachers had been erected. People paid high prices for places from which to get a good view of the parade.

Roosevelt, in an open black car, led the way. He was followed by the band.

Then came the Apaches. As Geronimo's *segundo* I rode at his left. Other Apaches followed. And after them came famous men of the Sioux and other Midwestern tribes. Our horses were well trained and we put them through their paces. They pranced, stood on their hind feet, and pivoted like those in a circus.

Spectators seemed to lose interest in Roosevelt. They left their seats and followed us for blocks along the streets. We were told later that Roosevelt said that he never wished to hear the name of Geronimo mentioned again. If this was true, he must have changed his attitude, because four days later Geronimo received permission to see the president. His primary purpose in going had been that he might make a plea that would induce the president to permit him and his people to be returned to their homeland on the headwaters of the Gila, to the canyon in which he was born.

This moment had so greatly moved Geronimo that he spoke some of his most eloquent words. In part he stated:

Great Father, other Indians have homes where they can live and be happy. I and my people have no homes. The place where we are kept is bad for us. . . . We are sick there and we die. White men are in the country that was my home. I pray you to tell them to go away and let my people go there and be happy.

Great Father, my hands are tied as with a rope. My heart is no longer bad. I will tell my people to obey no chief but the Great White Chief. I pray you to cut the ropes and make me free. Let me die in my own country as an old man who has been punished enough and is free.

Roosevelt listened courteously, then he told Geronimo that he harbored no dislike for him but that he would not grant his request because of antagonism against the Apaches by citizens of Arizona. Though he had concluded the meeting by refusing the old man's request, he did promise to meet with the commissioner of Indian affairs and the secretary of war. "That is all I can say, Geronimo, except that I am sorry, and have no feeling against you."[7]

DAKLUGIE

Many people believed that Geronimo and my father, Juh, were born near the present site of Clifton, Arizona. That was because of Geronimo's statement that he was born near the headwaters of the Gila. They assumed incorrectly that the river rises there. It does not. It has three forks two hundred or so miles northeast. It was on the middle fork of the Gila that the canyon in which they lived is located. It is a deep gash on a plain. It is usually with a shock that people first realize its existence. It is perhaps three hundred fifty feet in depth with almost precipitous walls. But they are not so steep that the Apaches could not make zigzag trails leading to the little stream formed by springs gushing from the walls.

Down these hazardous trails they took their horses and their women.[8] They took the covers for their tepees and their children. Slipping, sliding, and bracing themselves, they turned corner after corner while gradually working their way to the lush grass on the floor of the gorge. There they were safe from attack. There they had cold clear water from melting snows. There they found an abundance of game. Moreover, there were trees—stately oaks and graceful willows—to provide shade and fuel.

It was for this peace and beauty that Geronimo spoke so eloquently to Roosevelt. It had been his one hope during those long years of imprisonment— to return to his homeland with his people.

EUGENE CHIHUAHUA

The penalty for buying liquor for an Indian, or for even giving it to one, was severe. That made it all the more desirable. Of course, we liked it anyway.

Kent Kayitah, son of the scout, and I couldn't get any at Lawton; so we decided to ride to a small village about fifteen miles away and buy some. We went horseback, got a quart each, and started home. On the way we took a few nips. The last thing I remembered was approaching the cemetery. It had a

7. Ibid., p. 421.

8. Those trails are still plainly visible. On the headwaters of the Gila there is now a hunting lodge operated by Mrs. Mattie Hulse and her son, Quentin. The Hulse family at first descended into the depths as the Apaches had. They dragged stones from the shallow stream to serve as foundation and fireplace for a cabin. They cut and peeled oaks for the walls as well as for floor and ceiling. Every piece of furniture, including a large black cookstove, was packed upon mules for the descent.

When one is awakened by the song of the birds he does not wonder that Geronimo and his people longed to return to their homeland.

high barbed-wire fence with an extension on the top projecting toward the road. It could be climbed, but getting over that three-foot overhang looked impossible. There was a gate, but it was protected like the fence and was kept padlocked.

When I woke up it was beginning to grow light. I couldn't figure out where I was at first. When I sighted a headstone I knew. I was stretched out with my head on a grave and my knees over another. Kayitah lay with his head across from my knees and his feet across from my head.

One bottle, half-full, was sticking up between us.

I nudged him. "Brother, wake up. Just look where we are!"

He sat up, rubbed his eyes, and groaned. Then he picked up the bottle and took out the cork. He poured some on the head of the grave and said. "Here, Brother, have a drink. We ain't botherin' you. Now don't you bother us." He then turned to the grave upon which his head had lain and gave him a snort.

How we got in I never knew. I don't think anyone could have done it when sober. There was a key on the inside, so we had no difficulty in getting out.

CHAPTER 11

DEATH OF GERONIMO

EUGENE CHIHUAHUA

I feel that I am responsible for the death of Geronimo. It wasn't intentional; and if I had refused his request somebody else might have bought the whiskey that caused it. But I didn't refuse.

I was in the Seventh Cavalry and in uniform when we met in Lawton. He called me grandson because he had married my mother's mother, Francesca. He said, "Grandson I need some whiskey. Take this money and get some for me." It was a penitentiary offense to sell whiskey to an Indian, but I knew several soldiers that I thought would buy it. But how was I to carry it without getting caught? Those army coats fit so tightly that if I'd had a wart it would have shown! But I hunted up a White Eye friend and he said hc would buy a quart. The saloon was on a corner with a high paling fence on two sides. The uprights were nailed to two-by-fours on the inside. This fellow said, "Got a good fast horse?" I didn't; mine was just an ordinary pony. But Geronimo was riding his best and fastest mount. So I went back and traded mounts with Geronimo and returned to town.

The soldier told me that he would put the bottle on the four-inch board inside the fence at the corner. I was to ride by fast, grab the bottle, and hightail it out of town. I made the getaway and we struck for Cache Creek, where there was some timber. We watered our horses and hobbled them on good grass. Then we drank the whiskey and went to sleep with no cover but our saddle blankets.

Toward morning I was awakened by a cold, drizzling rain. Geronimo was coughing. I felt his face and it was hot. He said that he'd been sick all night. I saddled the horses and got him to the hospital. When the doctor came he said that Geronimo had pneumonia. I got a man to ride over to his house and tell his wife. On her way to the hospital she told Daklugie. It was not long till both came.

I stayed with him that day and we arranged for Daklugie to stay during the night. Geronimo was never left alone. People came but the nurses would not permit anyone but his wife, Daklugie, and me to come into the room. Daklugie and I alternated in twelve-hour shifts.

Geronimo was a very sick man and I asked Daklugie to make medicine for

179

Geronimo
Near end of his life.

Daklugie
Fort Sill.

his uncle. Geronimo also took the medicine the doctor left. At times he was delirious, but sometimes he recognized us. We interpreted for him when the doctor came, and they let us sleep at the hospital, time about. I, too, made medicine [by praying]; but my medicine was not nearly so strong as Daklugie's. But neither White Eye nor Indian medicine did any good. It was Geronimo's time to go.

When Daklugie was born his mother was sick for four days. Her husband, Juh, was off on a raid in Mexico and Geronimo made medicine for his beloved sister. He thought that she was going to die and he went up to Mount Bowie to pray. Ussen heard him and spoke: "Go back to your sister. Both she and her child will survive. And you will live to be an old man, and you will die a natural death." And it was as Ussen said. Daklugie was born, and his mother lived. Geronimo had been wounded several times, sometimes severely, but he hadn't died. Now, instead of giving his life for his people as Victorio had, the brave old warrior was dying, like a woman, in a hospital. I knew when Daklugie relieved me at his bedside that Geronimo probably could not last through the night.

DAKLUGIE

Death was not new to me. I had seen hundreds of people die. But Geronimo's death hurt me as had those of my mother, father, and brothers. As I sat beside my uncle I thought that he would never speak to me again and that the Apaches were losing the best they had. Even though he was old he had more influence than had any since Cochise. Now that we needed him most he was slipping away from us. Soon he would ride the ghost pony to the Happy Place. I would see that he went as becomes a chief. He had never been one, but he had wielded more authority than did any chief. He had kept up the struggle, knowing only too well the futility of it. He had fought a good fight and he had lost.

Repeatedly during my vigil he had expressed his regret for having surrendered. He wished that like Victorio he might have died fighting his enemies. Time after time he spoke of the warriors who had been so faithful to him. He even mentioned those whose loyalty had waned. Old, feeble, and dying, he had not lost his fighting spirit.

He moved. I bent over him and took his hand. His fingers closed on mine and he opened his eyes.

"My Nephew," he said, "promise me that you and Ramona will take my daughter, Eva, into your home and care for her as you do your own children. Promise me that you will not let her marry. If you do, she will die. The women of our family have great difficulty, as Ishton [Daklugie's mother] had. Do not let this happen to Eva!"

He closed his eyes and again he slept, but restlessly. When he spoke again he said, "I want your promise."

"Ramona and I will take your daughter and love her as our own. But how can I prevent her from marrying?"

"She will obey you. She has been taught to obey. See that she does."

He died with his fingers clutching my hand.

We could not burn his house; and, though he had not died in it, that should have been done out of respect. We could not bury his best war horse with him, but I saw that he had it for the journey. We placed his most treasured possessions in his grave—and he had some very valuable jewelry and blankets. He walks through eternity garbed as a chief in his ceremonial robes and his medicine hat. He rides a fine horse. He has his best weapons.

We stood guard over his grave every night for months. Not one of his warriors, including Eyelash, failed to volunteer to take his turn guarding that grave. Many who had never been with him on the warpath joined in the lonely vigil. There were so many that we usually had at least two every night. Why? Our most valuable possessions were buried with us. Those that could not be placed in the grave were burned. Many graves had been robbed by greedy traders and White Eyes who have no respect for either Ussen or the dead. And there was another and more important reason; we had not forgotten what happened to Mangas Coloradas. The soldiers who murdered him treacherously buried his body in a shallow grave. The next day they dug it up, cut his head off, and boiled it to remove the flesh. Then they sent the skull to the Smithsonian Institution.

Time went on, and there was no attempt to molest Geronimo's grave. We gradually limited guard duty to two nights a week. Then came a report that the body had been dug up and decapitated—and by Apaches. Suspicion fastened upon two men. They were good men, but greed is a powerful thing, even among Apaches. Those men were watched for years. If they were guilty they would have to dispose of their loot. And so far as anyone knows, they did not. What we anticipated was that the skull of Geronimo would be taken over the country and exhibited to make money for the ghouls who stole it. That, so far, has not been done. But if anyone attempts it in this part of the world there are still men with Winchesters. They'll be used.

CHAPTER 12

A PERMANENT HOME

In 1913 the Chiricahua Apaches were finally given back their freedom. For most of them freedom also meant one last removal—to the Mescalero Apache Reservation in New Mexico. Three primary factors influenced this all-important turn of events. First, the many appeals for freedom by the prisoners of war—supported by an increasing number of whites—had its effect. Second, Geronimo's death, in 1909, removed what little justification might have remained for continued or permanent imprisonment[1]. And third, the United States Army decided, also in 1909, to convert Fort Sill into a field artillery school of fire.

Fortunately, this time the timing was right for a solution that would be satisfactory to both sides. On one hand, the government had the will to approach the Chiricahuas in an attitude of fairness at a time when the prevailing attitude of the American people was also one of fairness. On the other hand, the Chiricahua leaders, in their desire to attain freedom in a permanent home, were ultimately willing to give up their demands for a return to the reservations taken from them in Arizona. And, as important, the Indians in both Oklahoma and New Mexico made a solution possible by graciously agreeing to share some of their land with the exiles. With the majority of all concerned thus committed to a just and workable solution, it was possible for the principal parties to forge ahead through a four-year period—albeit fraught with problems and complicated requirements—to a successful conclusion.

Negotiations began in 1909. Several official documents had clearly implied that the Chiricahuas would remain at Fort Sill permanently, and the government was reluctant to effect another removal without consent. Government negotiators therefore approached the Chiricahuas carefully, offering the possibility of freedom in reserves very near their old homes. Offered as possible options were sharing privileges and rights in the Mescalero Reservation, and purchase of individual lots in severalty in the vicinity of the old Chihenne reservation at Ojo Caliente, an area that had since been opened to the public. As a first step it was agreed that delegations representing the prisoners inspect the lands in question.

---

1. Geronimo died February 17, 1909. The other principal prisoner of war, Nana, died in 1896. Chief Chihuahua died in 1901.

I was not in Alabama but I knew most who were. They looked forward as eagerly as I to eventually having a permanent home with assurance that the government would not take it away from us as it had both Cochise's and Victorio's reservations. Both had been promised to them, and to their people, in perpetuity. That was done by Executive Order, which is the equivalent to a treaty and is the supreme law of the land. We learned that an Executive Order was as worthless as any other piece of paper. If a man's spoken word is worthless, so also is his written one. Who but an Indian ever kept a promise?

In 1909 I made a trip to the Mescalero Apache Reservation. I went during the hunting season when the venison is at its best. I had two distant relatives there, John and Sam Chino. Just what the relationship was I never did know, but they were brothers and called me cousin. I arrived shortly after the death of a member of John Chino's family and so saw little of him. He had gone into the forest alone and was wailing. I could not intrude on his grief, for that is not the Indian way.

The Chinos were Chiricahuas of Cochise's band, but they were pacifists. When the chief called the warriors together for volunteers to go on raids he danced around the fire and called once upon his *segundo*. If joined by him that man in turn called once upon the next warrior in rank. If he did not respond the man next in order was called. There was no enforced military service among the Apaches.

I knew several Mescaleros and rode over the reservation with them, hunting. But I had a much more important objective: I wanted to know its resources and possibilities. What I saw made me very happy. If I could make those at Fort Sill realize what was here it might influence some of them to come. There were almost a half-million acres of land that would support many more people than were living on it without depleting its resources. Less than five thousand acres were tillable; and the seasons were very short. Unless the flat places along the streams were irrigated it was doubtful that crops could be produced. But we did not want to farm; we wanted to run cattle. For that purpose the reservation was ideal. The mountainous area could be grazed during the summer and herds could be driven to the foothills and lower land during the winter.

Mountains in which to pray, wood, water, grass, abundance of game—and no White Eyes! Best of all, we would live among our own people and worship Ussen according to our own religion. There might be missionaries, but not many; and we need not let them spoil it for us. They meant well and no doubt thought their religion better than ours. Of course White Eyes are not close to Ussen as Apaches are.

EUGENE CHIHUAHUA

I was a member of a committee selected to visit the Mescalero Resevation and Ojo Caliente.[2] I rode over the Mescalero reservation and found it better

---

2. Of the committee, Eugene Chihuahua and Goody represented the Chiricahua; Kaywaykla and Toclanny represented the Chihenne (Warm Springs). An army officer completed the five-member group.

than Daklugie had described it. It is much like the mountains at Turkey Creek and in other areas of our homeland. There were thousands of deer, some elk, and wild turkey and other small game.

The winters are long and cold—very cold—but there is plenty of wood. But it is a still, dry cold with little wind, and though they have no houses the Mescaleros live comfortably in skin tepees. In the old days they left immediately after the hunting season and spent the cold months in the warm part of Mexico where there were wild bananas, dates, and other fruit. They cannot do that now, but there are native foods such as we lived on in Arizona: mescal, the fruit of cacti, wild berries, and sweet acorns.

The first time I rode through Dark Canyon to Apache Summit the trail was so overshadowed by pines that I knew how it got its name. Wagons could go through but at places could not pass.

In many places the grama grass was belly deep to a horse. Everywhere it was good; and there is no better feed. It dries standing and cattle and horses eat it all winter.

Then we had to go by way of El Paso to get a train north to Ojo Caliente. (It was the first time that I'd seen Fort Bliss since they took us to Florida.) At the little village where the track crosses the Rio Grande we hired a wagon and team. We went by way of Cuchillo to Monticello on the Cañada Alamosa. There was nobody at either place but Mexicans.[3]

On August 22, 1909, in a shady grove on Cache Creek near Fort Sill, the following debate took place.[4]

Minutes of a conference held at Fort Sill, Oklahoma, August 22, 1909, by 1st Lieut. Geo. A. Purington, 8th Cav., with the Geronimo Apaches (Apache Prisoners of War) with reference to their removal to the Mescalero Indian Reservation, New Mexico.

Geo. M. Wratten, Interpreter

LIEUT. PURINGTON: I understand that some of you sent Asa Daklugie to Mescalero to arrange the details of a transfer of yourselves to that reservation. Is it so?

Answer—Yes.

LIEUT. PURINGTON: I will now read the results of that conference and have it explained to you and afterwards we will talk it over.

Conference of a copy of exhibit "A" was explained.

NAICHE: There was no agreement about any cattle or any money made with Asa Daklugie before he left here. We don't agree to that.

ASA DAKLUGIE: These Apaches talked to me about the cattle before I went to

---

3. At Monticello they inquired for and found older men of whom Kaywaykla had heard his grandmother speak. They interviewed Srs. Chavez and Sedillo. Both remembered Victorio and the friendly relationship between the chief and their headmen.

They camped at Ojo Caliente and found that only a few sections of land were available to them. Their reservation had been returned to the public domain and most of the land had been purchased by white families.

As the members of the Committee anticipated, the people from Ojo Caliente preferred the very small amount of land available on their old reservation to the ample amount at Mescalero. Consequently the last requirement—the consent of the prisoners—was a difficult problem.

4. I am indebted to Mr. Joseph D. Thompson, who furnished me personal copies of the August 22 meeting and follow-up report. Mr. Thompson read one of my articles about the Apaches at Fort Sill and contacted me by mail. These minutes, and the report accompanying them, are in my Apache file.

Mescalero. They said if we are set free we want all our cattle and everything that belongs to us that is here, including all implements used to work with. But it to be left to the Government. If the Government would give us these things, all right; if not, and they would buy them from us and deposit the money to our credit, all right. I told them that just the cows and young stuff to be moved but the steers all should be sold here so the Indians could pay their debts. That is all I said to them here and they to me. I took their words to the Mescalero Agency and gave it to them as I received it. We want to go there but not all of us—maybe a little more than half. Counting the men, women, and children, one hundred and fifty-two of us want to go to Mescalero. Just want to go there because they have friends and relatives among those people and they want to see them and be with them. It is true that the Mescaleros there were willing to have us come. I was there and saw them, saw their mouths move when they talked, and they saw mine. When I gave them the words of these Apaches they said we could come there and live inside their lines of the reservation whether with the Mescaleros or by themselves. I was willing.

There are mountains there and all kinds of timber that can be used. They can cut the timber to make lumber and build houses, or make fences, posts, and railroad ties. There is lots of water all over, and streams and springs. Dig a well three hundred feet and get water that never fails. It is that way all over the reservation. There are places on the reservation, valleys in the mountains and along the streams good for farming where one can get a farm of ten, twenty, fifty, or even a hundred acres. The Indians said that whatever was planted would grow, whether vegetables or grain. I went down there to see what kind of a country it was and if we could make a living on it. The white man first goes and looks at a country and if a certain spot, whether trees or rocks, suits him and he thinks a living can be made, that is where he wants to go. We are the same way ourselves now. Of course it depends upon the Lord whether a living can be made on that ground or not. It might not rain the same as it has not rained in this country this year and then nothing would grow however rich the land. But we don't depend entirely upon farming to make a living. We have cattle, horses, sheep, pigs, and chickens from which to make a living. Lots of us may not have learned yet but we all have brains and anxious to work. Some of us are old and crippled and not able to work; we who are strong can take care of them. Your white people, when a family is poor and unable to earn a living, others will give them something to feed them, also build a house. We are that way now ourselves. The meanness that was in us is all out now—all gone, none have any more.

A great many years ago the Government commenced feeding us and clothing us. Do they want to keep it up until our children's children and their children's children are old men and women? No, we don't want it so. We think we have been given enough, meaning rations and clothing. We want to be free now. We want to be turned over to the Interior Department. When this paper goes to Washington we want its words to set us free. Those who want to stay here, let them stay; those who want to go, send them.

LIEUT. PURINGTON: From what Naiche has said and what was written by Superintendent Carroll in regard to the agreement about the cattle, or its equivalent, can you tell me just what agreement you made out there?

ASA DAKLUGIE: I told them some of the Apaches wanted to come to Mescalero to live—some had brothers and sisters there. I told them that is why they wanted to come there; they wanted to eat together, live together, sleep together and work together. That is why I come here to talk to you. What do you think about it? Are you willing for us to come? Can it be done soon, or don't you want us? It is with you. This is your decision, you have been here a long time. We live some other place, but we have nothing. We have no home, no land. We have been moved about among white people, caused to work here and there and other places while you have lived here always. You are born here and you die here. You must like it for you stay here so long. You think a great deal of your land but we would like to come and live with you and bring all our property. Do you want us?

186

LIEUT. PURINGTON: What did the Indians say when you asked them, "Do you want us?"

ASA DAKLUGIE: "Come to us."

LIEUT. PURINGTON: What promises did you make those people about the distribution of the cattle?

ASA DAKLUGIE: I told them for this privilege that our cattle, those that belong to us that would go there, should be divided among all of them, or the Government could sell part of them and use the money to ship the balance, and they to be divided among all of the Indians there in lieu of land given us.

LIEUT. PURINGTON: I will now ask all of you that want to go to Mescalero if you are willing to divide the proceeds of the cattle, if they are sold, or if you are willing to divide the cattle with the Indians out there?

Count was taken and thirty-eight agreed to divide the cattle with the Indians on the Mescalero Reservation, there being one dissenting vote against the division of the cattle.

LIEUT. PURINGTON: Have you anything more to say?

Answer—No.

LIEUT. PURINGTON: Now we will hear from the people who do not want to go to Mescalero to live.

TSO-DE-KIZEN: We want to stay here until they can send us to Ojo Caliente. They want to be sent to that place but do not want to be moved from here until they can be sent there. We think everything is there by which we can make a living. That has been our home ever since we can remember, we like it, and that is the reason we want to go there. We understand how to work, we have in our heads that which teaches us how to make a living. I am the only old one in this party; the rest are all young men. Of all the places there be to put us, do not send us anywhere but to our old home. There is the only place we want to go. That is all I have to say.

TOCLANNY: I want to stay here but not because I want to make my home here. My people long ago had something that belonged to them; that is why I think and act good. Ojo Caliente! I was born close to there and raised there. That is a good country. There are mountains on this side and on that side, and on the other side. In the middle there is a wide valley. There are springs in that valley, fine grass, and plenty of timber around. Dig a well and get water in forty feet. These people who want to go there will get old pretty soon. They want to be there and get settled so their children can grow up there.

The soil is good there—you can raise anything. Even when I lived there and planted seeds by digging a hole in the ground with a stick the corn grew up very high and pumpkins got very large. Horses and cattle will not freeze there. It is a healthy place for man and beast. Women nor children get sick there. Neither do animals. Don't send me any place except there. For years I have been on other people's ground and trouble has always come of it. Somebody has always bothered me. That is why I want to go to ourselves in our own country. That is why I have always been a friend to the white people. I thought that when the time came and I would ask for something I would not be refused. Since I was a small boy I have been a friend to the white. The white people have accomplished many things that were hard—that were difficult; I ask for something that is not hard for them to grant. I beg it may be granted me. If what I say here will be the cause of my removal to my old home I will be very grateful. Food and water will taste good to me. I will be happy again in my old home.

LIEUT. PURINGTON: Toclanny, for how many Indians do you speak who would like to be removed to Ojo Caliente?

TOCLANNY: Seventeen, with myself, and families.

LIEUT. PURINGTON: Toclanny, you say for years you have been on other people's ground and trouble has come of it. That somebody has always bothered you. What do you mean by that?

187

TOCLANNY: I mean I have been on reservations belonging to others and not my own, and there has always been friction.

LIEUT. PURINGTON: Has any other Indian who wants to go to Ojo Caliente anything to say?

TALBOT GOODY: Ojo Caliente is my home. All of my people so far as I can remember have lived there. It has been a great many years since I was taken away from there. Whoever officer come to talk with the Apaches I have always spoken about that. It is my country. I have not forgotten it. I have asked them to give me back my home. I was taken away from there for no reason whatever. Loco, who was my grandfather and a chief, was moved from there for no cause. From that time until the time of his death here at Fort Sill he always asked to be sent back to Ojo Caliente. Now I am asking for that country myself. I have just a few people here now, relatives and friends, eighteen of us I think, and families, some children—some boys are small yet.

From San Carlos they took me to Fort Apache. We had trouble at San Carlos and Fort Apache both. Both of those times we were on land belonging to other Indians. From Fort Apache I was sent to St. Augustine, Florida. At St. Augustine I was told that my way was a bad one, that my thoughts and life had been bad, to put it away from me, get away from it and go to school and learn the ways of the white people. They sent me to Carlisle, Pennsylvania. At Carlisle they sent me to my people in Alabama. When I got back to Alabama I found lots of my People from Ojo Caliente there. In Alabama lots of them died. They brought us from Alabama to Fort Sill and there was lots of them died here. But they gave us strong words, strong thoughts and some of their writings. And they stayed in our hearts and are there today. From what they gave us we have been able to learn to work and are able to work intelligently. We are not afraid to work and we are not afraid to do right. We are like the white people. We have talked with many generals who have visited Fort Sill and have pleaded with them all to send us back to our old homes. We plead once more to be sent back to our old home. I talked to Secretary Taft when he was here, held him by the wrists, and with tears running from my eyes begged him to send me back to my own country; to send my cattle, my horses, my tools that I used to work with. I still remember that talk. I told him all the Indians had land of their own. They had Agencies for them, somebody to look out for them. That is what I want you to do with us. I have not forgotten that talk.

It has been a great many years that the Government has been our father. We are still looking up and it doesn't matter where they put us, what they do with us. We will still belong, in a sense, to the Government. We are getting along all right here, but we still pine for our old homes. Put us there. Make an Agency there. Build a school house there for our children. We want to live like they live. That is the reason we ask for this. Most all of the Indians originally from Ojo Caliente are dead. Just a few of us left now and we beg to be sent back there. They (meaning the Government) have had us in many different places. They were not satisfied I guess because they kept moving us, and we were not satisfied. All the Indians have reservations, the Mescaleros, the Cheyennes, the Arapajoes, have extra land. Do not put us on land belonging to other Indians but on land that will be our own. The Government goes according to law. If a man owns a piece of property or is given an allotment it can't be taken from him, if he should kill somebody they could not take his land. The Government has been good to us but we want land like that nobody can take away. We have been moved around for twenty-six or seven years, have been taught to do all kinds of work, have done as we have been told to do and now we want to be sent back to our old homes and given land that cannot be taken away. If the Government will put us back at our old home in Ojo Caliente we will stay there and be happy.

LIEUT. PURINGTON: Goody, in case the Government would not move you back to Ojo Caliente would you be willing to go back to the Mescalero Reservation and give half of your cattle to those people as was agreed upon by Asa?

TALBOT GOODY: If they don't send us back there right away we want to stay here until they do, and if in the end they refuse we want to ask for some other place.

OSWALD SMITH: If I am not sent to Ojo Caliente I want to go to Mescalero.

VICTOR BIE-TE: If I am not sent to Ojo Caliente I want to go to Mescalero.

LIEUT. PURINGTON: Goody, I am asking this question just to make it plain to you people so authorities in Washington can make a decision.

TALBOT GOODY: If they do not send us to Ojo Caliente we want to stay here, except for Oswald Smith and Victor Bie-Te. If they do not send us to Ojo Caliente we want to stay here and keep asking until they do.

LIEUT. PURINGTON: Does anybody else in this Ojo Caliente crowd want to say anything?

Answer—No.

LIEUT. PURINGTON: Does anybody else want to say anything?

JASON BETINEZ [sic]: These few men that are here want to stay here—fourteen of us want to stay at Fort Sill. We are poor and want something for ourselves, that is why we want to stay here. I talked before and asked to be left here. I talked with President Taft who was then Secretary of War and asked to be left here. He made a note on paper of what I said and may have it yet. I told him then that I wanted my farm here at Fort Sill. I didn't want to go to Arizona nor New Mexico. And now that these Indians have asked for different places, I still ask to be left here at Fort Sill and given land here for myself and these few people who are with me. I like this country; I like to live here. If a man wants to farm here the land is good and he can raise anything. If he doesn't want to farm here he can make a living at other things. The Government has given us cattle, we have them here, we want to be given land here on which to graze our cattle. They wanted to teach us something and they have taught me something and we are grateful to the Government for having taught us what they have—for teaching us these things by which we can make a living. Help us to get land here at Fort Sill. The land is here, the Comanches gave it to us. If they will to give us land here on this reservation because there are lots of people living outside of the reservation on farms who are our friends and will help us. We beg of you to help us also.

We are very grateful to the Comanches for having given us this land. They thought when they gave it that it would be for the poor Apaches to make a living on. So we have. Our cattle are all over the reservation. We make hay; we have our farms. They gave it for us to make a living and we are doing it. That is all; maybe somebody else will want to talk.

JAMES KAYWAYKLA: The Indians assembled here today to talk. They have had their say, now I want to talk a little. They haven't any home, no place they could call their own. Today it appears as if it was right in front of us awaiting. I know this country around Fort Sill. I know the land because I have seen it. I have thought about it and I am going to talk about it today. We have thought of this land here and want it. They say sometimes that it can't be ours—that they are going to put a lot of soldiers here. Even if they put soldiers here, give us our home here. Before they were sent here, the Comanches, Kiowas, and Apaches were called into council and were willing that these people should be brought here. After their arrival they were again called into council and they, the Comanches, Kiowas, and Kiowa-Apaches, set aside certain of their lands for the Apaches. Though some of these Apaches want to leave here, we want to stay on these lands. We don't ask for something we have not seen—something that is over the hill and out of sight we don't want. What we ask for is land that we have seen and is right here in front of us. If a man lives he must have something to live on, something that will take care of me. Make a strong plea for this land for us.

LIEUT. PURINGTON: Anybody else want to say anything?

LAWRENCE MITHLOW: There are a few of us here who like this country. We worked very hard on this reservation and that is why we like it. We worked hard and like this place and think why should we go away and leave it without making something from that labor. Please give it to us and make it so that it is ours—nobody else's. We think that you think it is time for us to be free. That is why we want this land upon which to make a living. The white people around the country here have farms and they came here since we did, but already they have lots of things and we have nothing. The white man has his farm, has a house on it, a barn and chicken house close to it, and fields not far from the house, and that is the way you want us to be.

LIEUT. PURINGTON: Anybody else have anything to say?

Answer—No.

LIEUT. PURINGTON: I am directed by the Secretary of War to make a report fully as to the present condition of these Indians, their progress, resources, and whether it is the desire of the majority of the band to join their relatives in New Mexico. I have a hard task before me because you people are not all of one mind. Some want to go to Mescalero and give those people an equal share in their cattle, some do not. Some want to go to Ojo Caliente, others want to remain here. I have to make a recommendation, and I will say this: I will recommend that those who want to go to Mescalero be sent there, but not to give those people a share of your cattle. I will recommend that the cattle belonging to the Indians that want to go to Mescalero be sold and that these people be required to pay you all debts that they have contracted in Lawton or elsewhere, and that these debts be paid out of the proceeds of the sale of these cattle. I would like to see you people, if you are moved, leave the Fort Sill Military Reservation as men free from debt and take up the new life with a clean record.

Following the meeting at Cache Creek, First Lieutenant George Purington made the following report.

A conference was held with the Apache Indians under my charge August 22, 1909, copy of the proceedings of which is enclosed marked exhibit "D." In compliance with the 2nd Endorsement, Headquarters Department of Texas, August 16, 1909, I have the honor to enclose exhibit "E," which sets forth the present condition of the Apache Indians, their progress, resources, and the desire of the majority of the band to join their relatives in New Mexico. The Morning Report of August 25, 1909 shows the following:

-Vital Statistics-

The Apache Indian Prisoners of War now number eighty men, sixty-four women, twenty boys over twelve, forty boys under twelve, fourteen girls over twelve, and forty-one girls under twelve years of age. The sixteen Indian Scouts on duty here all belong to this tribe and the aggregate of the tribe is consequently two hundred and sixty-one persons.

-Health-

The health of the tribe has been in general, much better than during the preceding years. This is accounted for partly by the fact that they have been prohibited from having dances in cold and inclement weather during the past few years. Some of their dances during the preceding winters were noticed to be followed by epidemics of cold and pneumonia.

-Clothing-

No clothing has been issued gratuitously to these people by the Quartermaster's Department since 1900. They are, generally, better clothed than formerly and do not sell or gamble away their clothing as much. Not a case of destitution has occurred.

-Agriculture-

These people now have under cultivation about fourteen hundred acres of land which is about the same amount as cultivated the preceding year. Their crops were good last year raising about thirty thousand bushels of corn which was mostly sold in Lawton for forty-five cents per bushel. This year the crops are almost a failure on account of the protracted drouth and hot winds although well cultivated, and the Indians are noticeably discouraged by the failure. Their crops were in good condition and the land clean and well cultivated up to July 1, when the hot winds started. Only about ten thousand bushels of corn will be raised this year and the crops of many individuals failed entirely. The fodder is used to feed the cattle during the winter.

Twelve mowing machines and six bailers were used in putting up the hay although the grass was short and thin on the ground. About six hundred tons of hay is to be sold to the Post Quartermaster this year and about the same amount is to be put up for the cattle during the winter.

-Cattle Raising-

The principal wealth of these people is in their cattle and the industry upon which they chiefly base their hopes of becoming self-supporting. The Indians have about seven thousand head of cattle on the Reservation. In 1898 about one thousand head was issued to them by the Government. These seven thousand cattle are the natural increase under careful management from those given them. Each year about one-half of the increase is shipped to market (steers shipped when three years old). This money is distributed among the owners of the cattle. A marked improvement is noticed in the grade of the herd owing to the improved bulls purchased four years ago.

-Horse Raising-

Twenty-two young brood mares of improved stock were purchased for the Indians with their own money by the Officer in charge and two good stallions (all purpose horses) for use with mares belonging to the Indians. It is required of the Indians to castrate their own stallions or keep them off the range. A good jack was purchased for breeding purposes and the Indians have some of the best young mules in the country.

-Labor-

The men of the tribe are kept continually busy except Saturday afternoons and Sundays. They are employed either in the care of their cattle, the planting or cultivation of their farms or other useful labor for which they are detailed daily. The usual detail follows: seven men to herd cattle, five stable police, one orderly, one blacksmith, one wheelwright, repairing fences, etc.

-Schooling-

The smaller children have attended school at a Mission of the Dutch Reformed Church on the Reservation during the year. The school has accommodations for about fifteen boarders but most of the children take their breakfasts and suppers at home and the Mission prepares the noon-day meal. There are a number of children who have not good homes and the Mission makes good homes for them. The attendance at school was better this year than ever before. An Indian Scout is detailed to compel attendance of all children able to attend. The results accomplished by this school are excellent. Too much could not be said in praise of the women who live alone at this Mission and devote their lives to the education and improvement of this tribe of Indians. The larger children are sent to Chilloco, Oklahoma, to school.

-Hospital Care-

The hospital consists of a woman's ward and a man's ward. A woman nurse is provided for the women and a Hospital Corps man is detailed to attend the men. The work of the hospital is satisfactory in every respect. Too much praise can not be given Miss Agness Deary for her untiring efforts to attend the sick Indians.

-Conduct-

The conduct of these Indians has been generally good. The opening of the surrounding country to settlement by the whites has made whisky easy of access to the Indians and from whisky comes nearly all of the trouble and disorder that arises among them. Whisky is sometimes brought on the Reservation and given or sold to them and they have no difficulty in getting it in the towns nearby.

-Land-

This Reservation (The Military Reservation of Fort Sill) belongs to these Indians. The War Department made several efforts between 1889 and 1894 to select a suitable reservation for them, and conferences were held with them by Captain J. C. Bourke and General G. A. Crook in regard to it. The Indians knew that a reservation was being sought for them and when this reservation was finally selected for them and they were established here by the Secretary of War under authority of an Act of Congress in 1894, they were told that this was their reservation and that they would not be moved again. The fact that they were "permanently established" here has been repeatedly affirmed by Acts of Congress. As their reservation contained only thirty-six square miles (twenty-three thousand two hundred and forty acres) and the tribe numbered over three hundred, the reservation was increased in 1897 through a treaty with the Kiowa and Comanche Indians in order to give sufficient acreage to the reservation to provide one hundred and sixty acres for each individual of the tribe (G. O. No. 14, A.G.O., 1897). Shortly before the Kiowa and Comanche Reservations were opened for settlement, application was made for the thirty-seven fractional pieces of land adjoining the old reservation on the north and south and these tracts were withheld from homestead entry and finally added to the Military Reservation for the use and benefit of the Apache Prisoners of War. (G. O. No. 128, A.G.O., Sept. 27, 1901). These tracts contain about twelve hundred acres and the chief value of the addition consists in grazing land and ridding us of thirty-seven possible neighbors. The Apache Prisoners of War have a most valuable property in this reservation, which should not be taken from them without regard to their best interests. They have been and are at the present time more prosperous than at any time since their surrender in 1886.

The Board of Officers appointed by Special Order No. 205, Headquarters Department of Missouri, November 6, 1902, recommended that "the rights of using this land (Fort Sill Military Reservation) for military maneuvers and exercises be reserved by the Military authorities." These recommendations were made by officers of rank and experience who had personal knowledge of the actual conditions.

-Resources-

There are now on the reservation about seven thousand head of cattle. Placing a conservative value of twenty dollars per head, one hundred forty thousand dollars; one hundred bulls at fifty dollars per head, five thousand dollars; implements such as bailers, binders, movers, plows, etc.—four thousand dollars; buildings—four thousand dollars; fifty miles of fence—six thousand dollars; wagons—one thousand dollars; total— one hundred and sixty-two thousand dollars, not including the land, individual horses, and wagons.

-Recommendations-

That the Indians who wish to be sent to the Mescalero Reservation be sent back and given full membership in the tribe out there without any cost to themselves for the land in lieu of the land on the Fort Sill Military Reservation that they held an interest in; that they sell their cattle to the best advantage, likewise the implements and other stock that they hold a common share in; that they be required to pay their debts that they have contracted here and elsewhere.

In the strongest terms I recommend that the cattle be sold on this market for the following reasons: they are not prepared out in that country to take care of them; that these cattle would take Texas fever going to that range; that during the winter the cattle would die as these Indians would not provide for them here, were they not required to do so. They do not provide for their horses here, some die of starvation, or become so poor that they can not be used during the winter. It would be only a short time until every head of their cattle was butchered by the Indians out there. After their debts are paid they could be given the remainder due them and they could invest it in horses, sheep, or other cattle.

The Indians owe merchants in Lawton for horses, wagons, harnesses, and buggies. I do not believe that the Indians clothed Asa Daklugie with the power to give half of the cattle, or its equivalent, to the Indians on the Mescalero Reservation in exchange for the land. As soon as that part of the letter was explained, Naiche said there was no agreement about any cattle or any money made with Asa Daklugie before he left here. I have talked with some of the other Indians and they tell us that nothing was ever brought out in that meeting about the cattle except that they take the cattle with them. Somehow Asa Daklugie has a power over these Indians that follow him and he will bear watching.

I make the same recommendations in regard to the Indians that want to return to Ojo Caliente, in regard to the cattle.

For the Indians that chose to stay here, I would recommend that the Government buy from the Comanche, or some other tribe what is known as *"Dead Indian Allotments"* and put them on it. Give them some good bottom land claim and not some rough and broken piece land. Handle the cattle in the same way as recommended for those going to Mescalero.

At the conference thirty-eight Indians wanted to go to Mescalero, New Mexico, eighteen wanted to go to Ojo Caliente, and fourteen wanted to remain here. If the Indians are to be alloted anywhere soon, the heads of the families could go to New Mexico at any time and select their allotments, return here, or stay out there. Their interest would be taken care of here were they to remain here. The cattle are the best in the country for a herd of this size.

-Disposing of the Cattle-

Each animal is branded "U.S." on left side, with each individual's number, the numbers ranging from one to one hundred and thirty-four. Some cattle are branded straight "U.S." which belongs to the fund, so each Indian can receive just what was due him and his family.

Now that the cows are well along in calf, it would be detrimental to ship them at this time. The bulk of the calves come during the winter and spring months, that is, during February, March, April, and May. If these cattle are to be shipped next spring after the calves come, the calves could be shipped to market and the cows allowed to grow fat. The bulls should be disposed of this fall. The mares and colts could be better disposed of next spring than they could this fall as the farmers do not wish to carry them through the winter.

If the Indians are moved I would respectfully recommend that the cattle be handled as I have recommended and time taken to send them to market. This movement could be accomplished in good shape by December 1911, and maybe before. 1909 has nearly passed and everything has been carried on as before.

If these cattle are not handled to the best interest for the Indians, many thousands of dollars will be lost for them. I am interested in these Indians and as they have made a fine showing under the Military, I hope they will do likewise under the Department of Interior, under new conditions.

> Respectfully submitted:
> [George Purrington]
> First Lieut. 8th Cavalry, U.S.A.
> In charge of the Apache Prisoners of War

Once again the prisoners of war were moved. But this time was different. All were removing to freedom in permanent homes, most to go to Mescalero to join their brother Mescalero Apaches in reservation life in New Mexico, the others to stay on individual lots in the vicinity of Apache, Oklahoma, on lands purchased from the Comanche and Kiowa-Apache holdings there. The Chiricahuas were never to have to move again.

BOOK THREE

COVETED HAVEN

Sierra Blanca.

(Courtesy Vic Lamb)

Introduction

No period of transition is easy. To advance from the Stone Age to the Atomic in the span of a lifetime requires adjustment for which the white race needed many centuries. It occasions problems of great difficulty.

Book Three concerns the Apaches' life on the Mescalero Reservation from before the time of the Chiricahua arrival in 1913 until 1955, the year of Daklugie's death. It consists of a series of occurrences regarded by both the Chiricahua and Mescalero Apaches as significant. Additionally, stories of individuals, both admirable and rebellious, who exercised great influence during this time are presented.

PART ONE

THE MESCALEROS

INTRODUCTION

When the Chiricahua refugees who had chosen freedom in New Mexico stepped off the train at Tularosa, they were met by fellow Apaches, but Apaches of another tradition. The Chiricahuas, whether or not they located in an area removed from the agency village, were now sharing the homeland of the Mescaleros; and in due time the two peoples would integrate almost totally with each other.

From their village at White Tail, the Chiricahuas went to Mescalero for supplies and, because of poor roads and distance, usually stayed at the village at least two nights. The Mescaleros visited the "Fort Sills" at White Tail when hunting and harvesting piñons. As a result of these contacts, the refugees from Fort Sill heard accounts about the Mescalero past from their hosts. It was primarily from Big Mouth and his son, Percy, that the Chiricahuas learned of the terrible ordeal that the Mescaleros had suffered at the Bosque Redondo and of their experiences after their escape from that concentration camp. And from such master storytellers as May Peso Second and Alberta Begay they heard the stirring legends and hero stories that formed the rich Mescalero heritage. Part One is an episodic account of the Mescalero story up to 1913, the year of the Chiricahua arrival, told by the Mescaleros—and whites—who lived that story.

A piecing together of the whole Mescalero story from oral sources has not been attempted. Therefore, it is suggested that readers consult C. L. Sonnichsen's *The Mescalero Apaches*, second edition (Norman: University of Oklahoma Press, 1972) as an important corollary.

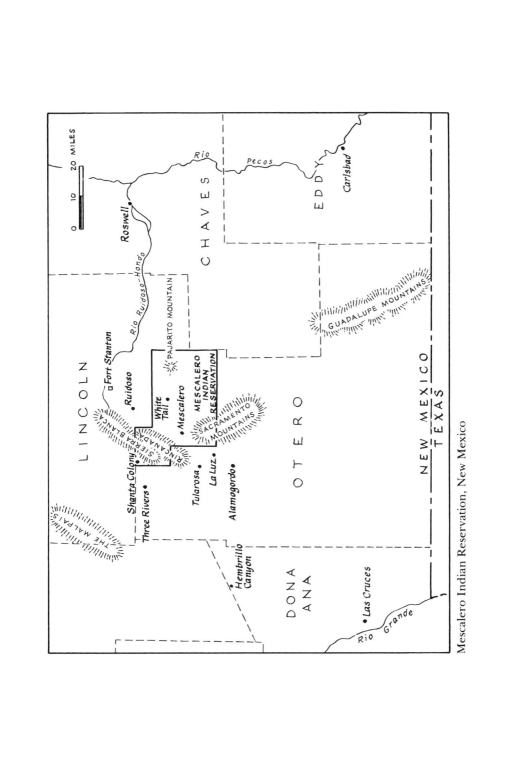

Mescalero Indian Reservation, New Mexico

CHAPTER 1

BIG MOUTH, LAST LIVING SCOUT

BIG MOUTH (INTERPRETED BY HIS SON, PERCY)

I am Big Mouth, last living scout of the Apache wars. I served in the campaigns against Victorio and Geronimo. I do not know my exact age, but I was six or seven years old when my people, the Mescalero Apaches, were forced into captivity at Fort Sumner in 1863.[1]

I was born on the Río Bonito, a few miles above Fort Stanton in southeastern New Mexico. I live near Mescalero, on the reservation belonging to my people. The reservation is a very small part of the vast territory belonging by ancestral and immemorial right to my tribe. Our land lay between the Río Pecos and the Rio Grande. It extended from the high mountains in northern New Mexico far below the Mexican border. And my people spent the winters in the warm country. In the spring they returned each year to the headwaters of the Bonito on the White Mountain. That was their favorite camping place. And they considered it their homeland. When they returned to it they found supplies immediately available.

There were a few Mexican families in the valleys of the Bonito and Hondo, but we had little trouble with them. We traded skins and venison for guns and ammunition. When White Eyes began coming in, trouble ensued. We learned that they fought each other, just as Indian tribes did. They were greedy and cruel people; they had no respect for the rights of others. They hunted us through the forests—our own forests—like wild animals. And they spared nobody. We did not understand why they acted so savagely. We only knew that they did. Always we had respected the rights of the Lipan Apaches to the east and south of us, and of the Warm Springs and others west of the Rio Grande. But these strange people respected nothing and nobody

Apache mothers quieted their children by telling them that the soldiers

---

1. James A. Carroll, *Apache Census* (Mescalero, 1901). Carroll listed Big Mouth as having been born in 1863. Of course, this was an estimated age. Big Mouth was small, and this could easily have been in error, as were many of the estimated ages of Indians. Big Mouth distinctly remembered the 1863 trip to the Bosque Redondo.

would find and kill them if they were noisy. Even babies dared not cry. And the old men told stories about the camps at night—stories that I never forgot.

A great chief of one of the seven Apache peoples, Mangas Coloradas, had been promised safety in order to get him into the White Eyes' fort. He had gone, hoping to make a treaty of peace. And he was treacherously and brutally murdered. One of our warriors had gone to Fort Stanton on a promise of security. The soldiers were butchering hogs and had a big kettle of boiling water. They threw him into it. A drunken soldier had taken an Apache baby by the heels and crashed its head against a wagon wheel. These things and many more we knew.

We had a few guns and at times a little ammunition, but our weapons were mostly the Stone Age arrows and spears. For a while my people held out, but many warriors were killed and women and children needed protection. Our great chief Cadette called his head men and warriors into council and he let them decide their course. Our people were hungry and almost naked. The soldiers had killed the deer about the fort—not for food, but just because they liked to kill. They had used neither meat nor hides. Meanwhile, we starved and froze.

We fought them as long as we could. Though my father was killed before I was born, my mother and I went with the warriors as did all the other members of the tribe.

I do not remember this, but I heard it many times about the camp fires: The cavalry chased my people into Dog Canyon when there were only three braves with them. Two stayed behind to enable the women and children to climb the steep walls; one man fell, wounded, at the entrance to the canyon. The soldiers killed the rear guard and advanced upon the canyon.

The dying warrior had fired his last bullet but he was determined to save his people. He waved his red blanket in the faces of the horses and they would not advance. While the soldiers tried to ride over him, he held them at bay until every woman and child had reached safety.[2]

When the band rejoined Cadette and his braves, they were in desperate condition. It was decided to send men to Fort Stanton to hold a council with "Keet" Carson, the Nantan there. He told them that he was a subchief under another Nantan, Colonel Carleton, who had commanded that every male Apache be killed on sight, regardless of age, upon attempts to surrender or any other condition. But "Keet" Carson said that if the Mescaleros would go to the Bosque Redondo, near the new Fort Sumner on the Pecos, they would be spared and given food until they could raise crops. He promised safe conduct to the Bosque; and he promised blankets and food. "Keet" Carson said that we were to bring all that we had and come to the fort on a certain day. Cadette agreed to do this thing.[3]

My mother had two horses, and upon one of these we packed our tepee and other scanty supplies. I rode this horse and my mother rode the other. Very few of the Mescaleros had mounts, so they had to walk and carry their meager belongings. At times my mother and I let others ride and we walked.

---

2. Carisso Gallarito (Crook Neck), interview, with his son John Gallarito interpreting, corroborated this.

3. See Sonnichsen, *Mescalero Apaches*, pp. 110–33. This was one of the most tragic and disgusting travesties in the annals of Indian-white relations.

We started north through Capitan Gap and then northeast toward the Pecos. It was a terrible journey, for the women were attacked by the soldiers, and no officer did anything to prevent it. Mescalero women were chaste and very modest. The men could not look at each other; they could do nothing to protect the women and were ashamed. They wished that they had chosen death in the land given them by Ussen, but it was too late; they were now captives.

That place at Fort Sumner was what is now called a concentration camp. There was nothing there for us except misery and hunger. There were no pines, no streams except the Pecos, and no game. There was no water fit for drinking. We had been accustomed to the clear, cold water from the melting snow of the White Mountain [Sierra Blanca]. We had to drink the muddy, ill-tasting water from the Pecos. It made us sick; it even made the horses sick. But can one live without water?

They put men and women to work digging ditches and digging up ground with shovels to plant corn. And once a week the soldiers gave us enough food to last perhaps two days. We were not farmers—we were fighters and hunters! Above all, we were free people; and now we were imprisoned within picket lines and made into slaves. The Apache does not mind work, but he does not like slavery. We were cold, hungry, and miserable. Above all, we were home sick for our country and our freedom.

We stayed there three years, I think.[4] I know that we planted one crop that produced much food. But the next one failed, and we were desperate.

To add to our misery, the soldiers brought in many Navajos—maybe nine thousand—and put them above us on the river. There were only four hundred of us, and the Navajos were our enemies! They fought us; they stole our horses and our food. But worst of all, they got a sickness from the soldiers—smallpox, I think. They died by the hundreds, and the soldiers made those who were left throw the dead bodies into the Pecos.[5] They drifted down past our camp into stagnant pools where we had to get our drinking water. There were worms [maggots] in the water—many, many worms.

One night we left; we slipped away, very quietly, and started back to our mountains where there was pure, cold water and plenty of wood and no worms, no bad smells, no Navajos, and no soldiers. It took us several days to reach our old camp in a hidden valley in the Guadalupes. Death meant nothing to us if it could be in that good place which Ussen had given us.

The deer had been killed by the soldiers and we killed some of their cattle to stay our hunger. What man can bear to hear his child crying for food and do nothing? And why was it any worse for us to kill the White Eyes' cattle than for them to kill our deer? And did not Ussen put food on the earth for our use?

Goaded by hunger, we went to the Pecos in hopes of intercepting the migrant buffalo herds. We had horses but few wagons. One man had a sixshooter

4. Carleton's orders establishing the Bosque Redondo prison were issued on November 4, 1862. By March 1863 over 400 Mescalero Apaches had been incarcerated there. On November 3, 1865, exactly three years later, the Mescaleros slipped away in the night. Sonnichsen, *Mescalero Apaches*, pp. 113, 133.

5. Of the 8,200 Navajos ultimately imprisoned at Bosque Redondo, at least 2,321 perished from smallpox, most of them in 1865. See Edward H. Spicer, *Cycles of Conquest* . . . (Tucson: University of Arizona Press, 1962), p. 220.

and two or three others had muzzle-loading rifles; but all were adept with bow and arrow and used the lance and shield to an extent seldom realized by the white man.

We crossed the Río Pecos and struck the buffalo trail on the Llano Estacado, followed it south to Monument Spring near the present site of Hobbs, New Mexico, and traveled on south to Comanche Spring near Fort Stockton, Texas. But we were perhaps a week late for the buffalo migration. Even so, there were usually stragglers unable to keep up with the herd. Their meat was good, especially that of the calves, but on this hunt they did not find even one decrepit animal! And that was strange, for I have seen the moving mass of buffalo come from the north like a great flood. I have watched for hours while it passed. And I've hunted, years later, and helped kill a supply of meat sufficient to last us for a year. People may tell you that they never came west of the Pecos, but that is not true. It was unusual, but I have killed buffalo west of that river.[6] But this time we did not see one of the huge animals. But we killed antelope, many of them. The women jerked the meat and we carried it in huge skin bags.

Gradually the white men killed off the buffalo as they did the deer. Hunters built little rock houses at the water holes from which they could shoot not only the buffalo but the Indians who followed them.[7] White Eyes killed the buffalo for their hides—just wasting the meat. On my last trip I saw men gathering and hauling away the bones in wagons.

Near Monument Spring the Mescaleros found a Lipan who had escaped from the Comanches and was attempting to find his own people. This boy, when a small child, had been a captive with the Mescaleros. He and his mother had gone with many of that tribe to a camp on Pajarito Peak to gather piñons. While the men hunted, women and children harvested the tiny nuts for winter use. One day Comanches swooped down on the camp near the spring and took several captives. This young man and his mother had lived so long with the Mescaleros that, like the rest, they did not want to go with the Comanches; one at a time the captives straggled back to their people.

---

6. Daklugie said several times that the Chiricahua and Nednhi Apaches had tepees made of buffalo hide when he was a small child. If so, they must have obtained them by barter, for I find no record of their having hunted buffalo east of the Pecos, and only stragglers crossed west of it.

7. Mrs. Billy Weir, interview. She told of her husband's following wild horses to the famous spring. She showed me the one-room house built of rock there at the time.

CHAPTER 2

THE VENGEANCE OF GOUYEN

MAY PESO SECOND[1]

The Apache girl lay in the brush arbor of her mother-in-law waiting for the older woman to sleep. Her name is one the Apaches are forbidden to mention and she is known today only as Gouyen, Wise Woman, a term reserved only for the intelligent and chaste. To Apaches the terms were synonymous, and why not? Did not the unfaithful wife suffer the punishment preferred by her husband, death or having her nose cut off? And what wise woman would have risked either?

Gouyen's heart burned like a coal of living fire, a fire that could be quenched only by avenging her husband's death. It had been little more than two days since she had seen the tall Comanche chief stoop over his prostrate body, wave his bloody scalp high, and leap to the back of a black stallion with three white feet. The girl could never forget that murderer; nor could she ever blot from her memory the black horse.

Since her father-in-law had returned with the three whom he had selected to bury his son, Gouyen had not eaten nor slept. Because her father-in-law was on guard with the horses, his wife had taken the young woman to her own temporary shelter. Her husband's father was old, too old to attempt to avenge the death of his son. And the Apache code demanded an eye for an eye and a life for a life. Not infrequently, many lives were exacted for each taken by an enemy; but the girl had decided that since there was no strong man in the

---

1. Over the years I had many interviews with May Peso Second, teller of this classic story. May, daughter of Chief Peso, had always been greatly interested in the traditions and history of her people and had memorized accounts told around the fires at night by the older Apaches. I heard her tell this several times, for I took people to her home to hear it. She would sometimes deviate in the use of a word or two, but never in relating details. Fred Pelman, grandson of Gouyen, read this chapter and seemed surprised to find that it was written authentically until I told him of getting it from May. "It's every word true," he said. "I'm glad that at last some White Eye has come to the Apaches for information. They wouldn't write so many incorrect reports if they would do that."

family she would be satisfied with one life—that of the Comanche chief.

The Comanches had made a surprise attack on the hunting party and killed her husband. They had been raiding in Mexico and were northbound when they discovered the presence of the Mescaleros, who were camped on the Pecos. They had been surprised because of the negligence of two young boys who were making the first of their four apprentice raids with the warriors. Big Mouth, nephew of Chief Peso, and another lad had gone into the foothills looking for game and had left the line of march unguarded.[2] The girl knew well that if her intentions were suspected she would be watched and prevented from leaving camp. She waited. Before she could leave camp she must be sure that her mother-in-law slept soundly. She would also have to wait for the moon to set, for she dared not risk being detected by the guards with the horses. And somewhere, somehow, she must secure a butcher knife. Hers had been taken from her after she had cut her long black hair to shoulder length, as was the custom of her people who had lost a relative. And she must, if possible, get a horse. That she doubted she could do; and she had decided to walk, regardless of distance or difficulty.

She wore the garb of the Apache woman, a two-piece dress of buckskin treated with *hoddentin,* the sacred pollen of the tule. When rubbed into the white deerskin and subjected to a very slow heat, it changed both the color and the texture of the leather. It became medium brown instead of snowy white; it also took on a certain quality that made it repellent to water. White buckskin is easily ruined by rain and is reserved for wear for ceremonial occasions. Her beautiful beaded and fringed dress, made for her Puberty Ceremonial, had been worn twice, once for the presentation of the maidens and once for her wedding feast. Contrary to custom, she had brought it with her, carefully wrapped in a protecting skin. The ceremonial robe was heavy, but by binding it to her shoulders she would free her hands for her water jug. An emergency food bag was filled with dried venison and attached to her belt, along with a bone awl and sinew for repairing her moccasins. But a knife—dare she risk taking the one from the older woman's belt? To an Apache a knife was the essential item necessary for survival. She could go without her blanket, but, somehow, she must obtain a knife.

There were other risks; Kahzhan, the Medicine Man, slept little. Neither he nor her father-in-law seemed ever to relax their vigilance. And the Medicine Man seemed to have miraculous foresight. It was the fourth day of her wedding feast that she saw him join Peso at the council fire. To her great joy her young husband had been bidden to join the warriors; and while they were assembling, she had seen Kahzhan take oak leaves and his native tobacco from his medicine pouch and prepare them for smoking. Only when making medicine did the Apaches smoke—and never a pipe, but always a cigarette. As there was no sickness, Kahzhan must have anticipated fighting. How right he had been! Not only her husband, but three others had also been carried away to a secret place, laid under an overhanging bank, and covered with stones, and the graves concealed by collapsing the bank above them. As Kahzhan solemnly puffed smoke in each of the four directions, she remembered that it was the

---

2. Bessie Big Rope, an aged Mescalero and daughter of the Medicine Man Kahzhan, and Percy Big Mouth both corroborated this.

Comanche moon [September], the month in which both tribes made their raids into Mexico for horses. And if her husband went, she as a faithful and loving wife might accompany him. And she might fight beside him as other brave Apache women had done. She might even attain the coveted title, Gouyen; for it was an honor reserved for the very good and brave Apache wife.

Kahzhan had been given his Power at a very early age. So great was it that his predictions never failed. For that reason he accompanied Chief Peso on every important raid or hunting trip. But it was admitted that occasionally things not foreseen by him came to pass. Many times had she heard of how he received his great Power. When he was very young, so young that his parents went with him up the White Mountain to the huge spruce where his ordeal was undergone, he told them that he was to lie under it for four days and nights without weapons, food, or water. During that time he was not to sleep but to pray to Ussen for wisdom and Power. They were to cover him with buckskin only and leave him. Much as they feared for the boy, Ussen had spoken and they must obey. For four days they prayed for his return.

For four days the boy prayed. He became so exhausted that he was not sure whether or not he slept. And on the fourth night Somebody spoke from the Cloudland. He opened his eyes and saw a sheet of something thin and pink floating from the sky. It was much like the mysterious stuff at Fort Stanton, upon which the Nantans made words, words that other White Eyes understood. When it floated to his side he saw that it, too, had signs upon it. Though he could not read he knew what they meant, and he made a song. He made the melody and, though it had no words but syllables only, it meant "With this I go to the Happy Land, for Ussen has spoken, and I obey."

And his ghost left him and went to the Cloudland. There he saw *sillas* [seats], many of them, like those upon which the Mexicans sit. But he saw few people, just a very few. And he heard a voice—not that of Ussen, but of his son, Too-hab-che-che-ehn [Child of the Water]. It was he who had come to the earthland to give law to the Apaches. And these laws he repeated four times to the boy.

Then Kahzhan returned to his sleeping body and he awakened. He returned to his parents and asked them to go to the chief and request that he call the tribe together to receive orders from the Cloudland. They were the old orders which had been broken and which must be obeyed. They were not to kill one another. They were not to fight other tribes unless attacked. They were not to get drunk on *tiswin*. And they were to pray to Ussen each day. Especially they were to pray when the sun first broke the darkness.

And, young though he was, from that day on Kahzhan had been a powerful Medicine Man.[3]

Could she evade his vigilance? If he knew her intention how would he regard it? And what would her punishment be? Would she be condemned and punished as had been the few old women who were outcasts with disfigured faces from which the nose had been cut?

At last came the slow, regular breathing of the older woman. Through the

---

3. Bessie Big Rope, interviews.

withered leaves of the arbor she could see that the moon was sinking behind the horizon. Did she dare risk taking the knife? She crept softly toward her mother-in-law; but the woman turned and she abandoned the attempt.

The girl bound the bundle to her shoulders and crept softly from the arbor. Keeping in deep shadows, she stole from the camp. She dared not risk an attempt to take a horse, but she stopped at the waterhole and filled the jug. And she stole silently along the broad trail left by the Comanches and toward The Star That Does Not Move. And the stars that revolve about it told the Apache girl that it was after midnight.

Enjuh! It would be five hours before her absence was discovered. She must make good use of those five hours. She fell into the little jog trot of her people, a gait that looks so easy that it seems effortless. Yet that gait enables the Apache to cover many miles in a few hours. It enables him to run down a horse. It can be maintained for many hours even by one bearing a burden. And that on the girl's shoulders was much lighter than the one she bore in her heart. Only once did she pause, and then to drink from a trickle of water.

When she felt the advent of the dawn, she began searching for a hiding place in which to rest. Under an overhanging bank in an arroyo she slept until evening. Upon awakening, she drank from the jug and ate a handful of pounded, dry meat from the bag at her belt.

And for three nights she followed the trail, sleeping by day, running by night, and keeping a constant watch for both pursuers and enemies.

Toward midnight of the fourth night she saw it—a glow in the north; the light of a fire, a big fire. No such fire was required for cooking; she knew it to be that of a dance, the Victory Dance. Very faintly she felt, rather than heard, the rhythm of the drums. And as she neared the camp, the voices of the singers became audible. She slowed her pace and approached cautiously. When she could see the gleam of firelight on the tepees, she began circling the camp. Silently she stole from one clump of vegetation to another, keeping always in the shadows.

From the protection of the darkness she watched. As she anticipated, many of the Comanches were drunk. The older people were leaving the circle about the fire for their tepees. The younger would continue, at intervals, dancing until dawn.

She noted well the position of the tepees, and the thicket in which she was concealed; then she sought to determine the location of the horses. She noiselessly changed from her soiled buckskins into the beaded ceremonial dress she had carried upon her shoulders. Instead of donning the high moccasins she fastened them to her belt. She threw the brown skin, in which her robe had been wrapped, about her and stole cautiously toward the sound of the horses.

Her greatest fear was that the animals might betray her presence by snorting, but they did not. Perhaps to them Indians smell alike. The black one was easily identified. She crept close to the stallion, close enough so that she could lay her hand upon his neck. When she patted his nose he sniffed at her but made no noise. To her great relief she found that he was not hobbled but was staked to a bush with a rawhide rope. Quietly she untied it and led the horse eastward, away from the camp, for some distance before turning south. With the fixed star at her back she walked about a half mile before striking high grass that indicated a low place. Beyond it she ascended a hill upon which she found a clump of vegetation. And there she tied the horse.

As she retraced her route, she debated her procedures. Should she attempt to retrieve the water jug and worn garments she had left in the thicket? Or was it time for her to join the dancers? And would the Comanche chief be among them?

As she drew close to the tepees she stopped, removed her worn moccasins, and replaced them with those made for wear with her robe. She shook her head, smoothed her hair as best she could, and slipped the beaded buckskin band about her head.

Then she sought the identity and position of the chief. He, like the rest, would be wearing his finery for the celebration of the victory. And unlike his warriors, he would not dance continuously. After opening the rites and receiving the ovation due the victor, he would sit in the place of honor until some maiden invited him to be her partner. Perhaps that had already been done. If so, it was her privilege to keep her partner as late as she cared to dance and to receive a generous gift from him.

But, no! He sat on a colorful blanket in the shadow of the ceremonial tepee, watching the dancers. The girl crept near, apparently unnoticed by the spectators. Occasionally the chief's head drooped as though he were sleepy; then it would jerk and be held erect. Enjuh! He was lifting a jug to his lips. He was drunk. And obviously the dancers, too, were intoxicated. Nothing could be better. Now was the time.

She circled the drummer and singers to approach the chief. As she stood before him with arms outstretched he recognized the universal invitation and staggered to his feet. As the firelight illuminated his tall form, she saw the scalp dangling from his belt. But she smiled and again extended her arms. He stared at her, blinked, but made no other response. Was he sober enough to recognize by the face that she was a stranger, an enemy? Desperately she summoned her courage to give the third invitation, and to smile. Again, no response. Four is the sacred number of the Apache, and in the fourth gesture was her final request for acceptance. Once in the circle, dancing with the chief, no Indian dared challenge her. To her great relief the Comanche chief took her hand and pulled her into the circle that was moving around the fire.

As they fell into the simple step of the social dance the scalp, swinging with the movement, steeled her to her purpose. She must remain with the dancers for a few rounds, but she selected a spot near the clump of vegetation in deep shadow from which she could leave the circle when she chose.

Carefully protected as were the maidens of the tribe, the Apaches permitted a widow to make her own decision as to chastity. If she wished to retire to the bushes with the victorious warrior, necessity for preservation of the tribe condoned the act. But she had not yet adjusted to the idea of being a widow, and she thought of the few noseless old women and their loss of the tribe's respect. But she thought also, of the still-damp scalp and she steeled herself for the ordeal. If she succeeded in her attempt, undoubtedly the Comanches would kill her, and that would be merciful.

Though in other dances the Indians do not touch each other, in the circle they stand side by side with arms brushing. Deliberately she snuggled close to the chief, and occasionally she feigned stumbling and grasped his arm as though to regain her footing. He turned his face toward hers and she smiled invitingly. As a couple beside her slipped quietly from the circle, he grasped her hand and, when they neared the thicket, drew her toward the shadow. She jerked away from him and ran. He stumbled awkwardly after her and she slowed her pace sufficiently to permit him to come close enough that she could keep just out of reach. Still easily evading him, she ran toward the swale with the tall grass; and the angry Comanche followed.

Now, if she could just get his knife! She pretended to stumble and his hand brushed her shoulder. Quickly she dodged and turned. She grasped for the knife in his belt but it slipped from her hand. Too late she attempted to escape. The chief's hands closed on her shoulders and he drew her toward him. Visions of noseless women, scorned by their people ... she lifted her head and, as he bent over her, she sank her strong teeth into his neck and locked her arms above his elbows. With bulldog grip she held on, heedless of the hands tearing at her, pounding desperately to loosen her hold. Blood streamed down her throat, streamed down her dress, dripped upon her feet.

How long she maintained her grip before the Comanche, staggering and fighting, fell, she did not know. But in the fall she was unable to retain her hold on his arms and he began tearing at her throat, unable to loosen her teeth. His struggles became weaker, feebler, until finally they ceased. Even then she feared releasing her hold. When she finally did so, she realized that the Comanche was dead.

Now for the knife! She felt about the ground for it and finally her hand closed upon it. First, his heart! She braced a foot upon his chest and pulled it out. Then, with her foot planted firmly upon the torn throat, she ran the blade around the dead man's hairline and peeled off his scalp. Next came his head band, then his beaded breechclout and moccasins. She fastened his belt about her waist, and she stumbled toward his horse on the hill. She released it, tied a loop around its nose, mounted, and headed the stallion south. And the darkness and wind slid past as she urged the horse as fast as she dared. She had a long trip ahead and must make the best of her steed. Only too well did she know that she would be followed and the death avenged. She didn't have much time. At dawn she stopped long enough to let the mount drink and graze. She too drank, but she had no food. She looked down at her beautiful buckskin, stiff with brownish stains. She mounted and let the horse walk and occasionally take a bite of the short grass. When he breathed easily she again put him to a gallop.

For two days and nights she let the animal rest only long enough to graze and drink. She had drunk but had neither food nor sleep. To her surprise she found it extremely difficult to mount after her stopping, and she realized that she might not again be able to do so. If she could get the horse into a shallow arroyo, perhaps . . . .

She awakened with a start; and she saw that the stallion was headed toward the Fixed Star. He was, of course, going home. She turned him southward and fought desperately to avoid going to sleep. She began seeing and hearing things—horsemen in pursuit, ghosts barring her path, moans and shrieks. The Apaches are not afraid to die; but they are afraid of the dead, even of their own beloved dead.

Twice more the horse turned, and how far back he went she did not know. But she rode southward until she began to recognize familiar landmarks. Perhaps if she dismounted and walked she might keep awake. Perhaps she could find a hiding place, one in which the pursuers could not find her. And if her own people did, they might kill her—and the horse, too, was tired, stumbling. . . .

Then, from behind a point of rocks in her path, rode horsemen; Kahzhan, Peso, her father-in-law, Big Mouth, others. She looked back to see more Mescalero warriors cutting off her escape. If they would just kill her—they were coming close, dismounting. . . .

When she regained consciousness she lay, not in a brush arbor, but in the tepee of her husband's parents. His mother laid loving hands upon her. She turned and beckoned and her chief entered the tepee. Behind him came the Medicine Man. They smiled at her.

Then Peso went to the opening and held up garments so that those outside might see. And he spoke: "My daughter," he said, "is a brave and good woman. She has done a braver thing than has any man among the Mescaleros. She has killed the Comanche chief; and she has brought his weapons and garments to her people. She has ridden his mount. Let her always be honored by my people.

"And let her name be Gouyen!"

CHAPTER 3

NATZILI AND THE SOMBREROS

Before the invasion of the white people, the Mescaleros had been widely scattered. Some, under the belligerent chief Juan Gómez, lived much of the time in the Davis Mountains and harried the travelers on the San Antonio-El Paso trail.[1] Some preferred the Guadalupe Mountains in New Mexico, and still others frequented the Sacramentos.

A very large band under the leadership of Natzili claimed a great extent of land about the present site of Amarillo, Texas. Natzili was a large and powerfully built man, much taller than the average Apache, many of whom do not exceed five feet six inches in height. He was so strong that, like Ulysses, nobody else could string his bow.

In the old days this band had roamed about Bent's Fort on the Arkansas River and had raided the Jumanos villages of Abo and Cuarai in New Mexico. On one of these expeditions, Chief Peso had found fragments of a chain-mail shirt. It was found near the *ranchería* of stone and adobe, the walls of which still stand. What had become of the original inhabitants no Apache knows.[2]

Natzili and his people depended almost entirely on the bison for their livelihood, much like the plains Indians further north. In addition to using them for their personal needs, Natzili's people also traded hides with other Indians. The Western Apaches especially liked buffalo hides for covering their tepees. Daklugie said that when he was a child even the Nednhi in the Sierra Madres used them. The hides could be obtained only by barter, since few bison crossed the Pecos and, on the rare occasions when they did, they never went farther west than the Tularosa Basin.[3]

---

1. Sonnichsen, *Mescalero Apaches,* p. 60. Much of this chapter has been compiled from information provided by Solon Sombrero, son of Sombrero (Indian name not spoken) and grandson of Natzili.

2. Daklugie, interview.

3. Big Mouth, interviews.

Natzili.

Natzili's band followed the spring and fall bison migrations and killed enough animals to supply their needs until the next return of the huge shaggy beasts. But the Comanches, Kiowas, and Kiowa-Apaches also lived off the bison. They, too, felt that the land was theirs, and there was dissension and conflict between the tribes over their mutual source of sustenance.

The Comanches were especially belligerent and had frequent encounters with the Mescaleros. The people of Natzili's band have a legend of a prolonged conflict, one lasting perhaps ten days, in which they were almost exterminated by Comanches; but they know neither the location nor the date of the encounter. They also have a legend of a fight in which they were the victors and which only one Comanche survived to report the defeat to his people.[4]

It was after the former engagement that Natzili and the remnant of his band took refuge with the Mescaleros in the mountains where they were better protected than in their open, native habitat. They lived on the slopes of the Sierra Blanca and intermarried with the Mescaleros, who acknowledged and respected Natzili as a great chief.

The buffalo herd did not cross the Rio Grande, but the Indians did. Across

4. Ibid.

the river, the *remudas* of the *hacendados* were very enticing to all the tribes, and they were accustomed to making raids deep into Mexico. The wise *ricos* [rich men] were shrewd enough to understand the Indians' ways and could afford to keep their corrals filled with horses for their raids. They knew that if the Indians met with no resistance and got a good supply of mounts they would not disturb the *hacienda* nor its inhabitants. The Indians preferred to let the cooperative Mexicans live in order to provide them with future supplies of horses. If the Mexicans were uncooperative or too poor to cooperate, the Indians stole their women and children. If the boys were young enough, they could make good warriors of them. The little girls were also important because Apaches usually spaced their children from four to five years apart and the tribe did not increase rapidly.

On one of these annual autumnal raids into Mexico for horses and slaves, the son of Natzili, whose Apache name is not spoken, sighted a *rico* mounted upon a superb animal. The young warrior immediately desired the mount for his own war horse. The magnificent saddle, bridle, and bit gleamed with silver: even the spurs were inlaid with it. The *rico*'s hat, adorned with four pounds of silver, glittered in the sunlight. The son of Natzili killed the Mexican and returned to his camp, superbly mounted and equipped. He wore the *rico*'s belt and, though it was of little use to an Apache warrior, he carried the large glittering hat. From that day forward, his name was Sombrero.

When Sombrero's son was born, someone at the Agency must have been familiar with the classics, for the child was christened Solon Sombrero. Before Solon was old enough to enter school, his father was injured when the horse he was riding fell with him. As many Apaches do, he seemed to know instinctively that he was not to recover. He called his small son into the tepee and, in the presence of his wife and other relatives, asked that the articles he designated be brought to him. He lifted the Chihuahua spurs, hand-forged and glittering with silver, and presented them to his young son. The belt followed. He called attention to the shape of the conchos; instead of being oval they were round, as were those made, albeit rarely, by certain Apaches. So, it was as though the boy were receiving a genuine Apache belt. The saddle and blanket and the large sombrero were buried with their owner, as is proper; but Solon kept his gifts, as also was their custom.

So long as Solon and his mother lived in a tepee, these gifts constituted the major portion of their treasure; and Apache treasure hangs in a buckskin bag over the entrance to the tepee, on the outside. In case of attack, the owner first had to make sure of his horse and his family. He might have to abandon his tepee and stores but never his treasure. That, being on the outside, was easily accessible without his dismounting. He could rest assured that no other Apache, under any circumstances, would touch his buckskin bag of treasures.

Nor would any Apache enter the tepee of another if even a small switch were laid on the earth across the opening. That meant that the family desired privacy, and that wish was always respected. No stick indicated that anyone was welcome to enter. Even today there are Apaches who do not like rapping or pressing a doorbell.[5]

---

5. If I answer a knock or ring and see no one upon opening the door, it is likely to be an Apache; they always stand to one side.

When the Apaches were rounded up at Mescalero following the outbreak of Victorio, Natzili—as did Chiefs Roman Chiquito and Magoosh of the Lipans—feared that they, too, might be forced to go to the San Carlos Reservation. All were determined to resist any attempt to drive them there. Natzili and Santana aided the cavalry in rounding up the other Apaches and getting them to agency headquarters at Mescalero, where they were held in a corral in filth and forced to live upon ears of corn thrown to them.

Before Solon was old enough to have completed the six years of schooling available at Mescalero, his grandfather, Natzili, died. The old chief had been detained by troops and questioned—nobody knew why—and placed in the adobe building at the agency used as a jail. In a blizzard he managed to extricate some iron bars from the adobe walls and escape. The jail had been thought to be so constructed that a breakout was impossible; but Natzili was a very strong man, even when old. He knew that the rapidly falling and blowing snow would conceal his trail, as it did. Three weeks later hunters found his body, frozen, near a spring on the reservation. The old chief had died as a result of an unjust suspicion and the desire by some shavetail fresh from West Point to show his authority.

Solon Sombrero was sent to school at Albuquerque and became an apt pupil. He was deeply desirous of improving the wretched conditions under which his people lived and did much study and research not required of him. It must have been in Albuquerque that he became a convert of the Dutch Reformed Church, for before his going they had no mission at Mescalero.

When this church built a mission and a school at Fort Sill, it was decided that a similar effort should be made at Mescalero. A women's organization of the church sent a missionary to Solon Sombrero, who acted as interpreter and guide for the minister. Together they rode to the most remote canyons and visited the people. It was Solon who interpreted the missionary's sermons and who was largely instrumental in enabling him to establish a permanent residence in the village of Mescalero.

Solon Sombrero was elected to the tribal council, served as chairman of that body, and was, through his great influence with the tribe, largely responsible for the adoption of the system of tribal government in use today.

He married Catarina, daughter of Chief Peso, and they reared a fine family.

As had many other White Eyes, I found him hospitable and cooperative. He and Catarina visited in my home occasionally until Solon, almost eighty-seven, no longer wished to drive. When he came later, it was usually with a grandson at the wheel of his car.

Once, when I returned their call, Solon asked that I write some things that "he meant to tell me but had forgotten to do it." He told me of the "Indian post office" and how it operated. He knew the primitive trails and could read the messages left by those who traversed them. If a party of hunters or of any travelers moved over a trail, it was their custom to leave information for those who might follow. A stone for each person was selected and arranged in single file, with the largest indicating the direction taken. Smaller ones were used to designate children. When and if the party separated, that, too, was shown by a division of the file. And any Apache could, by reading signs, tell approximately how much time had elapsed since the trek was made.

He told me of the time that Agent Carroll had taken Natzili to Washington.

When the chief was told of his invitation to meet the president, he dressed as he would had he been the guest of a great Indian chief—in his best beaded buckskin breechclout and moccasins. He carried his famous bow and arrows; on his arm was his shield. When the large and powerfully built Natzili attempted, Indian fashion, to embrace his host, the president was frightened and called for help. Natzili was so embarrassed that he never permitted anyone to mention the incident in his presence.

Solon told me of his father's going to Mexico and killing the *rico*. He brought out the belt and the Chihuahua spurs. Solon was a very devout member of the Dutch Reformed Church but he, like James Kaywaykla, had been an Indian much longer; and I had learned how offensive it is to an Apache to ask if he would sell his treasures. He must have sensed my thoughts, or have seen a covetous gleam in my eye, for he said, "I do not want these things to be buried with me, or to be destroyed. I'd like to know that someone had them who would appreciate and keep them and not buy them just for profit, as most people would. When I am through with them, would you like to have them?"

"If you should ever decide to sell them, I would like very much to have them," I replied, "but surely you will not be doing that for a long time."

As I left Solon said, "My Sister, I know that you like old things as I do. I can tell by your house; it is built of adobes from Mother Earth and has wooden beams from the forest." He went on, "Your furniture, too, is old, and I like it. You will treasure my father's spurs and belt and not sell them to make money. I want you to have them."

Some time later, when he was past eighty-seven, Solon had a young man drive him and Catarina to visit me. They brought the Chihuahua spurs and the belt that he had promised I should have. Had Ussen spoken? I could not ask, but the Apaches seem to know when they are about to leave Mother Earth for the Happy Place.

A week later Solon died.

CHAPTER 4

DR. BLAZER AND THE MILL

During the brief stay of the Chiricahuas at the village of Mescalero in 1913, Ace Daklugie had been puzzled by the great trust and respect shown by the people on the reservation for Dr. Blazer. He disliked white people, but he had recognized and understood the high regard in which James A. Carroll had been held. He also appreciated the attitude of Carroll's successor, C. R. Jefferis. There were, he reluctantly conceded, a few White Eyes worthy of friendship—but very few. Consequently, he needed time to come to accept Dr. Blazer as the Mescaleros did.*

Almer N. Blazer wrote that his father, Dr. Joseph C. Blazer, was born near Pittsburgh, Pennsylvania, in 1828. After Joseph's father's death he and his mother, with the younger children, moved westward and started a farm in Illinois. There they raised cattle and hogs, and hay and grain beyond their needs. With logs cut from their timber they built rafts for transporting their surplus to New Orleans and floated their cargo down the Mississippi. Then Joseph and his older brothers walked back to Illinois.

In St. Louis Joseph completed studies in dentistry, passed his examinations, and opened a practice at Mt. Pleasant, Iowa. There he remained until the beginning of the Civil War. At that time he joined the First Iowa Cavalry, and after a few months of service in the war he was wounded and sent home. When he attempted to rejoin his regiment he was discharged for disability. Later he secured a commission as sutler to his old regiment and remained in that capacity until the war ended and his unit was disbanded at Shreveport, Louisiana.

In Louisiana he bought four six-mule teams and wagons, and at a quartermaster's sale he purchased a large stock of discarded supplies. He then hired drivers and, leaving his wife and three children in Iowa, set out for El Paso. By the time he reached that city he had sold out his cargo in villages along the way.

In El Paso he got a contract with the government to haul supplies to the Mescalero Apache Reservation and to several military posts, including Forts Stanton and Sumner. On his first trip through the mountains to Fort Stanton,

---

*This brief account is compiled from interviews with and documents provided by Paul Blazer and Emma Blazer Thompson.

216

Blazer saw the sawmill being operated by three whites at Mescalero village.

ALMER BLAZER

At the time [1867] there were three men, late of California Volunteers, who were in possession of lands which are now within the Mescalero Apache Reservation, and they and their assignees had occupied them since 1863. In the year 1868 Blazer purchased an individual one-fourth interest in the land ... including improvements on same among which was a sawmill, and he and his partners continued to occupy and hold said lands until 1870, when their sawmill was burned, presumably by Indians.

In the preceding year Blazer had returned to Iowa to attend the funeral of his wife, and during his absence the Navajo Indians stole his freighting outfit, sixty-one head of mules worth $150.00 each.

In 1870 Blazer returned with machinery for a new mill, which, however, was burned before it was ready to run.

The partners were thereby so reduced financially that they were unable to rebuild their mill and they thereupon turned their attention to farming for the purpose of supplying forage to the military posts then engaged in an attempt to get the Apache Indians onto a reservation at Fort Stanton.

The Indians about that time made friendly advances to the partners [who] furnished several hundred of them with supplies in the shape of green corn, pumpkins, beef, etc., for some time; and [Blazer and his partners] were thereby enabled to render considerable assistance to the military arm of the government in persuading the Indians to go upon the reservation. . . .

In 1871 one of the partners withdrew from the business and the others obtained the required financial assistance and again rebuilt their sawmill. . . .

Subsequently another of the partners, a man named Nesmith, took a portion of the partnership lands and improvements and withdrew from the partnership. He subsequently sold his improvements to the government and abandoned his claim.

In 1877 Blazer bought [sole] interest. . . . He therefore set apart a portion of the lands to a married daughter, Mrs. Ella B. Hedges, and so continued to hold and occupy the remainder with his son, Almer N. Blazer. He was appointed Forage Agent and continued to furnish forage for the troops enroute and stationed at the Agency until the forage agency was discontinued.

He also furnished lumber for the Indian and Military service at Forts Stanton, Sumner, Seldon, Bliss and Davis, and the Mescalero Agency until 1896, and furnished considerable lumber to the settlers in the surrounding country.

A considerable portion of the lumber cut and not furnished to the Government was culls and other portions used to improve the property at Mescalero. Blazer also paid the Government "stumpage" under special permit to cut logs on the Indian Reservation.

During the work of getting out logs it was necessary to construct about sixty miles of road into the mountains in various directions and what is now the Mescalero Reservation, and there are now about thirty miles of these roads in constant use by the Indians in getting to and from the agency from various parts of the reservation.

Joseph Blazer's daughter, Emma Blazer Thompson, reported that his family—consisting of his wife, an older daughter, a son, and herself—lived in Mt. Pleasant, Iowa. Her father would not send for his family until he felt assured that their coming to the mill would not entail much danger, nor until he had built a suitable home for them. While Blazer was thus employed Mrs. Blazer died; the day his letter enclosing money for their train trip arrived his wife was buried. As a result of her death the children were to wait another five years before making their new home in New Mexico. In 1877 they arrived by train at the Trinidad, Colorado, station, accompanied by their aunt. Dr. Blazer was loaned an ambulance from Fort Stanton and a cavalry escort for the trip to Colorado to bring his sister-in-law and the children to the Mescalero Reservation. The aunt did not stay long, and upon her leaving Dr. Blazer hired a governess for the children. It was difficult to find a replacement when she left. There were few women in the country, so he first found a man to instruct them; but finally another governess, Miss McWade, took the position and later married Dr. Blazer. This marriage proved to be a very fortunate one for everybody concerned.

Almer, Emma's brother, was not strong and was encouraged to be out of doors as much as he could. He roamed the forest with both white and Indian boys, learned to speak the Apache language, and became almost as expert as his Indian companions at trailing and shooting arrows and in his knowledge of plants and animals. Later he was sent to school in Santa Fe. For a time he also attended school in Las Cruces and lived in the home of a widow who had a son about his age.

Paul Blazer, Almer's son, continued the family account. He reported that Nellie Munger was his grandfather's first housekeeper after his children came. About eight months after her arrival she fell from a horse and was injured. She recovered, but shortly afterward decided that the reservation was too remote and too wild for her to stay.

During his first months at the mill Dr. Blazer tried hard to win the confidence of the Apaches, but they were wary and shy. For a long time not one showed up at the little commissary that he maintained. Finally two old women came timidly to the door but would not enter. Dr. Blazer asked the wife of a Mexican employee to give them some cooked meat, bread, and pieces of striped peppermint candy. They eyed the food suspiciously, but finally one of the women tasted and began to eat. The Mexican woman spoke to them in her own tongue, which they understood, and told them that they were not to be afraid, for nobody there would harm them. Gradually they overcame their fear and distrust of the white people and began bringing tanned buckskin to barter for coffee, knives, blankets, and metal cooking utensils.

Trust and friendship were enhanced as the result of an epidemic of smallpox. Immune to the disease, Blazer took the chief, who was very ill with it, into a small building beside his home and nursed him back to health.

The Joseph Blazer family consistently acted with honesty and friendship and gained the respect of the Apache people. The family is still held in highest esteem by the Apaches today.

CHAPTER 5

SCHOOL

In 1884 a school was established at Mescalero.* A long crude adobe building was erected. It had a dining room and kitchen in the center, with a basement beneath for storage and baths. On either side was a dormitory—one for girls, the other for boys. A disciplinarian was employed to preserve order during the day and to sleep on one of the cots in the boys' quarters. A matron stayed with the girls.

The primary function of the instructors was to teach the children to speak English and to establish habits of cleanliness. The pupils were required to make their beds, wash their clothes, and do a few light tasks in the preparation and the serving of meals. The cook was to wash the dishes.

The big problem was obtaining pupils to attend. Very few parents permitted their children to be taken from their homes. Many lived at long distances from the village. They used many devices for concealing their children; but eventually nearly all between the ages of seven or eight and sixteen were rounded up and incarcerated in the boarding school. Many of them were taken forcibly.

To prevent their escape the windows were nailed shut. At that time the necessity for ventilation was little understood by the white race. The Indians liked sleeping out of doors and still do. The "superior race" knew little of how diseases are spread. They attributed malaria to the condition of the air at night, not yet understanding the part played by mosquitoes.

The Apaches had developed no immunity to diseases as had the whites. Consequently, when exposed to disease germs in the classroom many Apache children died.

Bertha, youngest child of Andrew Goode, said that five of the older children of her family were victims. Her father protested losing his youngest, but she was forced to attend.

---

*This chapter was compiled from interviews and correspondence with Percy Big Mouth, Peter Gaines, Katherine Peso Sombrero, Maudie Platta, Bertha Tortilla, Eric Tortilla, Sam Jones, Bill Jones, May Peso Second, Seth Platta, Mrs. James A. Carroll, Jessie Lee Hawkins, Eloise Sutherland, Mrs. William J. Atchison, and William J. Atchison. Mr. Atchison was four years old when his parents left Mescalero, and he was eighty-five when we corresponded (in 1974).

Andrew Atchison.   (Courtesy Wm. J. Atchison)   *Mrs. Andrew Atchison.*   (Courtesy Wm. J. Atchison)

Mescalero Agency and School, ca. 1893   (Courtesy Wm. J. Atchison)

In 1892 Andrew Atchison became superintendent of the school and his wife became the primary teacher. They found that the school was hated and feared by the Apaches. The children had no summer vacation because the authorities feared that they would revert to the mores of the tribe. Parents, however, were permitted to see them.

That the children were doing creditable school work by 1893 was demonstrated by an exhibit of letters and drawings sent to the World's Fair in Chicago. It contained letters written by Seth Platta and Albert La Paz. They were well worded and written in beautiful Spencerian script.

Ten years after the school was founded some parents were still opposed to their children's attendance. One family concealed a small boy in a basket of shelled corn. He might have escaped had he not sneezed. He was found and dragged away.

The children were required to have a bath once a week in warm, soapy water, in wash tubs in the basement. They carried water from the kitchen, and it provided enough warm water for about twenty baths each night. It was not until Mr. Carroll's administration (1901–11) that showers and toilets were installed.

Each year an additional grade was added until it consisted of all six primary grades. Some of those who completed the elementary courses were sent away for advanced instruction at Albuquerque, Phoenix, Riverside, St. John's, Fort Lewis, Haskell, and Carlisle. In 1893 there were 94 children of school age enrolled and 529 members of the tribe on the reservation. The Atchisons recorded students ranging from six to twenty-two years of age in the third grade. They found the "children" friendly and usually cooperative. They formed friendships that lasted for many years.

WILLIAM J. ATCHISON (SON OF ANDREW ATCHISON)

The law applying to the reservation was administered by an army captain with white hair and a white beard. What I can remember of him and comments that I later heard make me think that he was a kindly gentleman. However, what the law required sometimes stirred up the Indians' ire. This happened on one occasion when an Indian was jailed for drunkenness. A dozen or so of his friends spent the afternoon on the far side of the creek shooting at us. I think that no one shot back. We all stayed inside and the thick adobe walls were perfect protection. Our only casualty was a hog.

The friendliness of the Indians was demonstrated by their bringing a young fawn for my sister Marjorie and me. It became very friendly. The room in which we slept had windows that came to the floor. They were often open and the fawn would come in and get in bed with us. The fawn had an interesting way of entertaining himself. As you have no doubt observed, two valleys come together at the agency. The fawn would attract the attention of the Indian dogs and then start up one of the valleys with the dogs after him. He could easily outrun them and would go around the mountain and back down the other valley and be waiting for the dogs when they got back.

The genuine desire of those at the agency to help the Indians and their honest conviction that their methods were both beneficial and justifiable are indicated by the following.

Mrs. Andrew Atchison

It must be distinctly understood that we were not in the employ of any church and were not missionaries in name at all, but were in the U.S. Indian School Service under orders and pay from "Uncle Sam" of Washington. But I verily believe that if any of you had spent a week with us at the distant station in New Mexico you might have guessed that we were a modern Aquila and Priscilla with a church in our house or that our quarterly reports went to some church board rather than to Washington.

To reach the school we left the railway at Las Cruces, the last town on the Santa Fe [railroad] in New Mexico. There we had our first experience in the old Mexican mud-house, which for cheap ugliness heads the list of architectural designs in the civilized world. We did not know then that we would find one of those a very acceptable home for the next two years.

Taking a carriage and a Mexican driver whose recommendation was that he knew the road and nothing else, we took our journey eastward from the Rio Grande River, over the Organ Mountains, across the White Sands desert, and through a waterless, treeless region, alive only with prairie dogs, antelopes, and jackrabbits. Thus, after a delightful two-days' drive we reached the school high up in the Sacramento Mountains near the head of the Tularosa River, one of those small mountain-fed streams which run bravely down to the mouth of a canyon and then, at the sight of the desert, hide themselves in the earth again.

We found the Indians to be Apaches, to be sure, but fifty percent better than most Indians in approachability and sociability. While the Apache is cruel, he knows better how to laugh than any other red man. We found them like all wild Indians—a roving, houseless, long-haired, lousy, dirty, lazy set. But they were glad to see us and we had not been there twenty-four hours till the old chief of many battles and more feasts called upon us and begged the loan of $6.00 with which to buy a burro.

As evidence that the Indians were wild the following may suffice: This branch of the Apache tribe numbered, since the Geronimo War of 1886, only about 650 people. The tribe, although small, was divided into smaller clans of a few families each. Such is the tendency to selfishness, jealousy, and hatred in the wild state that a clan rarely holds more than ten families together. Just the week before our arrival among them, two of these clans made a settlement for hard words spoken; and when the sun shone down into the canyon the next morning three men and two women lay dead around the little campfire.

During our first year with them, when one of the clan was off on a hunt, one of the squaws gave birth to a child; through exposure the mother died some days after and the child was buried alive with her.

Women as well as men went armed with hatchet, knife, or pistol. Before we had been long with them an old squaw stopped a little schoolboy from his work of yard sweeping near the kitchen door. When Mr. A. stepped up to her and pointed the way to the gate, quick as a flash her long knife came from under her blanket in a very threatening manner. During our second year on the reservation we had the excitement of witnessing an Indian battle, in which all their tactics were shown, though on a small scale. The police had been ordered to arrest two men for drunkenness. They had got one into the guard house and the other, joined by a few friends, drove off the police and liberated his comrade. The rebel band, reaching a bluff about three hundred yards from the agency and school buildings, made a stand and gave us an exhibition for half an hour of a dancing line of battle. Then I was very glad that our best buildings were of adobe walls, behind which it was easy to keep the Indian children and my own. One man was severely wounded; our best swine was killed; bullets came through the doors and were buried in the walls and posts all around us; and one squaw was captured and imprisoned in our cellar. These were the casualties of the battle. But they were enjoyable, compared with the suspense of the next night and day.

To be sure, we have taken their land from them, but in its place we have given them something worth infinitely more. We have given the Indian a new religion and a Savior, and through this gift we have given him a welcome share in the legacy of the Christian Church, treasures collected in a double thousand years of struggle of all the white nations. Then we have given him knowledge and education by which a single Indian may train his mind so as to accomplish more than his whole race of brutish ancestors had done. If wealth is the measure of good things, we have made them more in value, if less in area, and given them protection of life as well as property. And it is only reasonable that we expect them to return these favors by loyalty and industry.

When James A. Carroll became agent in 1901, his wife, Eloise, became the primary instructor. She taught three grades, and another instructor taught the other three. Both saw that their pupils were permitted to take long walks—and they insured their return by accompanying them.

Families of office employees took their meals in the dining room of the school, which was called the mess hall.

Mr. Carroll had heavy wire mesh placed over the windows so that there could be both security and adequate ventilation. Even so, there were some families that feared the school. It took many years to overcome that.

223

CHAPTER 6

JAMES A. CARROLL
APACHE AGENT

The term *agent,* as applied to one in charge of an Indian reservation, has long become a term of opprobrium. Perhaps that accounts for the title's being changed to superintendent. But it is not true that all Indian agents were dishonest and oblivious to the welfare of the unfortunate people who were their charges and responsibility. James A. Carroll, agent of the Mescalero Apache Reservation from 1901 to 1911, was one of those exceptional agents who respected the Indian people he served and who strived hard to improve their living conditions and general welfare.[1]

After several years of experience on other reservations, including the Rosebud, he was transferred to Mescalero. With his wife and three small children, he arrived at the agency in July 1901. They established themselves in a small adobe house vacated by the previous agent, Dr. Walter M. Luttrell. Though he had realized that this would be no easy assignment, he was unprepared for the wretched conditions under which he found his charges living. He found the Apaches half starved, insufficiently clothed, and miserable. It was no wonder that his predecessor had left under charges of abuse and dishonesty. Of most concern to Carroll was that Luttrell had been instrumental in discontinuing rations to all but a few of the old and blind. He wrote to the Commissioner of Indian Affairs: "The Indians are no longer receiving rations. I ask for a little cloth and some washboards for the old and indigent Indian women. In reply I am informed that my predecessor required that these articles be cut off and that he should know better than anybody else what supplies should be given the Indians." His first official act was the purchase of thirty-seven thousand pounds of dressed beef.

Carroll turned up problems everywhere he looked. Undaunted, he continued

---

1. Mrs. C. R. Jefferis, wife of the chief clerk who worked with Mr. Carroll and who succeeded him as agent, numerous interviews; Daklugie and Solon Sombrero, interviews over a period of ten years; and interviews with Clarence Enjady, son of Scout Enjady [Mighty Hunter], who was employed by the cavalry to provide meat for the company. Throughout this chapter I have relied heavily upon information graciously provided by Mrs. James A. Carroll in many interviews.

to send off requisitions to Washington. He asked for a farmer to direct any Indians willing to plant crops. He complained of a vital need for a sewage disposal system at the agency village. He asked for two dormitories, a mess hall, and adequate water facilities. He listed as essential a laundry and a storeroom. At the suggestion of the resident physician, Dr. Howard Thompson, he asked for vaccination of all persons on the reservation; and he added that ten dozen fine-toothed combs were needed badly and immediately. He requested that a brick mason be employed and that paint be provided. An estimate of $35,000 was submitted for the entire program.[2]

Miss Mary Barclay, field matron, made a report to the commissioner: "In order to be efficient, one has to learn and speak the language for a 500 word vocabulary. Conditions are wretched; in winter they would starve without the sale of things made. They make exquisite lace with bobbins on pillows. A little blanket weaving is done."

Carroll recommended that "Buck" Prude be admitted to the reservation as trader. The Prudes had a trading post at Cherokee Bill Spring, a few miles out on the Fort Stanton road. The next closest place for purchasing merchandise was the town of Lincoln, some thirty miles distant. Prude was given a license to trade with the Indians and he made application for the rental of a condemned cottage, provided certain repairs were made, and agreed to pay a rental of fifty dollars.[3]

In April 1902, Mrs. Agnes Cree of the Angus VV Ranch was issued a grazing permit for thirty-five hundred cattle and Charles Bremond was issued one for eight thousand sheep. Until shortly before that time, the neighboring ranchers had run animals on the reservation freely for many years, entirely without recompense to the Indians.[4]

Carroll was not unmindful of the fact that, with the exception of possibly three agents, those of the Mescalero Apache Reservation had been notorious for selling for personal profit supplies furnished by the government for the use of the Indians.[5] Not only was this true on the Mescalero Reservation, but it had been a general practice. He had been sent to the Kiowa-Comanche Agency at Anadarko, Oklahoma, to check on the conduct of the agent there. He had found that the incumbent bought almost nothing through regular channels. He furnished his home with china, glass, linens, and other luxuries at the expense of the Indians over whom he had charge. Even food for his family was so purchased. Mrs. Carroll recalls a conversation she had there with her hostess, the agent's wife:

"You're a Southerner, ain't you?"

"I was born in Virginia," Mrs. Carroll replied.

"Then you dip snuff."

"No, I've never used snuff." said Mrs. Carroll.

"If you're a Southerner, you dip snuff. Of course you dip snuff." And she

2. Letters of Apache agents at Mescalero to the Commissioner of Indian Affairs, courtesy of John Crow, agent at Mescalero. After he was transferred by the BIA, Walter C. Olsen, who succeeded him, would not permit access to the public records at Mescalero.

3. Ibid.

4. Ibid.

5. Sonnichsen, *Mescalero Apaches,* pp. 165–66.

James A. Carroll. (Eve Ball Collection)

Mrs. James A. Carroll. (Eve Ball Collection)

offered her box. Dipping snuff, Mrs. Carroll said, was a minor offense in comparison with stealing one's household goods and sustenance.

This agent had been appointed to the post at Anadarko by Senator Charles Curtis of Kansas, who was part Indian. When he was dismissed, Senator Curtis attempted, unsuccessfully, to retain him in the Indian Service.[6] By contrast, when government authorities offered Carroll the choice of a new home for the agent or a hospital for the Indians, he did not hesitate. His concern for the Apaches was of greater importance than his own comfort.

MRS. JAMES A. CARROLL

Shortly after our coming to Mescalero there was a *tiswin* brawl. The Indians lay around behind rocks and trees and shot at each other. Old Not-a-gah-lin and his son, Lewis, were killed. Mr. Carroll called in the Indian police and told them to order that all the Indians were to come in and bring their guns. He had the support of the chiefs in this decision—Peso, Sans Peur, and Magoosh. The police took the guns and locked them in the commissary. Some of them did not get them back for a year.

There was no church on the reservation, but Father Migeon came up from Tularosa once a month and said mass in Captain Miller's home. Captain Miller was a white man employed on the reservation. Later, the school and at times the living room of our home were used for services. All who professed Christianity were Catholic. Six years later the Dutch Reformed Church established a mission. Mrs. Page, of Doubleday and Page, donated money, and a little church was built.

Miss Barclay, Field Matron, did a great service to the Apaches by teaching the women to cook, sew, and care for their children. Later she went abroad. She met and married a widower with a title and a castle. So far as I know, nobody heard from her afterwards. She was a very superior woman and very sincere in her attempts to help the Indians.

Mr. Carroll was very fortunate in securing the services of Ah Wan, a Chinese, as cook. He prepared food for both the children in school and the employees. Meals were cooked in the kitchen and served in the dining room between the boys' and girls' dormitories. Some of the older children, both boys and girls, were paid for assisting him in preparing food, clearing the table, and washing the dishes.

Ah Wan was invaluable to the Carrolls. When he learned of Babs's birth, he asked Mrs. Carroll, "How little new missy want her eggs cooked?"

"Oh, you won't need to worry about that for a long time," she told him.

"When I see little new missy?" he asked.

"Not today, but soon," she replied.

But Ah Wan did see the baby that day. When admitted to Mrs. Carroll's room, he looked at the sleeping infant, picked her up, and danced about the room till Mrs. Carroll feared that the baby might be injured.

---

6. Lawrence L. Mehrens, "A History of the Mescalero Apache Reservation, 1869–1881" (Master's thesis, University of Arizona, 1968).

When Ah Wan had accumulated funds sufficient to enable him to return to China and live well, he gave notice that he was leaving. Much as the Carrolls disliked losing him, they understood his need to be with his family and people.

He was replaced by a Japanese man who turned out to be arrogant and demanding. When Mr. Carroll had succeeded in making him understand his duties, he became sullen. After the evening meal he sent an Indian boy to ask who was to wash the dishes. "You are to wash the dishes," Carroll informed the cook.

"The Indian brats can do it," he replied. He stalked out of the room and before long the Indian children told Mr. Carroll that the cook had packed his belongings in a flour sack and had struck out on foot for Cloudcroft. Mr. Carroll dispatched Indian police after him with instructions to bring him back. They obeyed gleefully. When they returned with the cook in tow, Carroll made him wash the dishes, and the next morning he paid off the cook and sent him, under Indian escort, to the train station at Tularosa.

The old people came in every Saturday and got food—usually meat, flour, corn, coffee, and sugar. Sometimes they were given blankets. They made baskets and beaded buckskin articles which they sold to the store, but they were paid very little for their products.

Mrs. James A. Carroll

I had two Indian girls who helped me in our home. Just as soon as school closed at four, I went home to see how Bunch [her youngest child] was. Then I saddled my horse and rode for an hour. Before Babs was born I had a month's leave from teaching. Saturday morning I went for a walk to Sulphur Springs beyond the church. I told the doctor that I felt as though I'd need him that night.

"You won't need me for three weeks."

"Yes, I'm pretty sure I may."

"You're just nervous; now forget it."

After I had read aloud to the children, as was my custom, I put them to bed and got out what supplies I would need—clothes, etc. Then I settled down with *The Houseboat on the Styx.* Before midnight Mr. Carroll went for the doctor, who had promised to give me medication to put me to sleep. When they reached the house, Babs had already discovered America.

I resumed my work at the school and left the baby with an Indian nurse. I loved my pupils. They were shy little things, very responsive to kindness. They were very obedient and intelligent. Among them were Victor Dolan, May Peso, Maggie Lester, Clarence Enjady, Louise Shanta, Bessie Big Rope, and some of the Littles. Fifty years later, when I visited my daughter, Mrs. Ted Sutherland, at Ruidoso, they came to see me.

Theodore Roosevelt may have been a good president in some respects, but he did some things that were very questionable. Some of his appointments were very bad for New Mexico—that of Pat Garrett as collector of customs at El Paso was one example. Roosevelt also turned over the timber on the reservation to the Department of Forestry—property valued at that time at six and one-half million dollars. It would be worth many times that today. Men from the forest service came in and were very arrogant. The Apaches were indignant and appealed to Carroll for help. He took Captain Miller to act as interpreter and with Chiefs Peso, Sans Peur, and Magoosh went to Washington. By that time Taft was president.

They stopped overnight in Chicago to buy clothes for the chiefs. Carroll took them to Marshall Fields. It did not occur to him that they had had no experience with elevators. All three were brave men, but when they got on the elevator and it began to move Carroll saw for an instant the look of terror on Magoosh's face. Magoosh immediately regained his customary lack of expression, but Carroll knew that the others had seen it too. They were probably as startled as Magoosh.

They spent the night at one of the best hotels. The criterion by which the Indians judged the place was the size of its steaks. Upon reaching Washington the Indians were assigned to much less adequate accommodations. They were indignant.

When the Indians were received by President Taft, they were very much pleased with his appearance. He looked well fed, as they thought a chief should. The Great White Father should not be skinny. He listened to their appeal and quickly agreed to restore their timber. After he signed the order, the president gave the pen to Carroll, who in turn presented it to Peso.

Mr. Carroll was firm with the Indians and he kept his word with them. If he promised anything they knew that it would be done. They trusted him; and consequently they liked him. When unpleasant things were necessary he consulted the chiefs and usually took their advice. When he could not, he explained his reason for his decisions and tried to show them that eventually what he did was for their benefit, though it did not always bring about immediate results.[7]

Mrs. Carroll took a group of her pupils for a walk one Saturday afternoon. They were looking for wild fruit. As they neared a tepee on the side of a hill, she heard groans and sent one of the children to investigate. When the girl beckoned, Mrs. Carroll went to the entrance. Inside lay Old Domingo on a bed of skins. He was very ill and his three wives feared that he was dying. Because of their fear of death, they had attempted to leave. The old man lay with his sixshooter aimed at them to prevent their escape. He explained through the child interpreter that his wives' place was with him, regardless of his condition. And he asked her to have the priest come to him. Father Migeon happened to be at the Carroll home and Mrs. Carroll sent the children for him. Old Domingo wanted "the water on the head." Because a sponsor was required and no one else was available, Mrs. Carroll acted as his godmother. Two days later he died.

Soon the three wives came to Mr. Carroll with requests for food and blankets. Of course, everything in the tepee had been destroyed or buried with Old Domingo. Mr. Carroll explained that because they were neither old, blind, nor helpless, he was forbidden to give them supplies.

"But," one said, "your wife is now our mother. That makes you our father. And a father cannot refuse his children."

---

7. Sonnichsen, *Mescalero Apaches*, p. 285.

Their reasoning appealed to Mr. Carroll's sense of humor as well as to his generosity, and he gave them the items they had requested.

Mrs. Carroll had no fear of the Indians and never locked the doors of the house. Once she answered the back door to find a strange Indian in a blanket with his hair in braids standing there. He said, "Me give wood." He had brought her a load of wood and wanted his pay. She invited him in.

"Me Sioux." he said.

"*How, Cola!*" she replied.

"You Sioux, too. Me Sioux. Friends."

Mr. Carroll had been on the Sioux Reservation in Minnesota for a while, and she had learned a few hundred words of their language. Mrs. Carroll brought a peace pipe and showed it to the Sioux visitor. The Sioux didn't use tobacco but substituted the "rabbit" kind. The caller smoked the pipe and talked. She sang the Ghost Dance song of his people.

> "Where do you come from,
> You wonderful shade?
> Whom do you seek?"
> "Like master to slave
> I seek the Great Spirit.
> Whom do you seek?
> Father, I come to seek eternal life."

When he arose to leave he said, "Me Yellow Bull."

It was during the administration of Mr. Carroll that arrangements were made for the Chiricahua to be moved from Fort Sill to Mescalero. Daklugie came to Mescalero as a representative of the Fort Sill Apaches. Mr. Carroll summoned the chiefs and Daklugie appealed to them for asylum. Both Mr. Carroll and they were willing to take the Fort Sill exiles as members of the tribe, with equal rights with the Mescaleros.

Mr. Carroll stayed at Mescalero longer than any other agent, and he saw the condition of the people on the reservation improve greatly under his care. When the Apaches learned that he was to be transferred to Pawhuska as agent of the Osages, they wept and begged him to stay. To this day they speak of the Carrolls with affection and appreciation.

CHAPTER 7

THE EARLY MISSIONARIES

A s early as 1869 priests from Las Cruces and El Paso had made occasional trips to the Mescalero Apache Reservation, but none had stayed more than two or three days.[1] Previously the nearest church service was held at La Luz, a quaint Mexican town ten miles south of the village of Mescalero by the old trail. There was a resident priest there when the fight occurred between the Apaches and the people of Tularosa.

There are conflicting accounts both of the skirmish and of the building of the church. One version is that the Mexicans made a promise to St. Francis de Sales, promising that if their lives were spared they would build a church in his honor. Another is that it was done in gratitude for their having survived.

In 1902 Father Migeon, a French priest stationed at Tularosa, began making a trip each month to Mescalero. He usually said mass in the living room of the home of the agent, James A. Carroll, but sometimes conducted services in the school. Occasionally visiting missionaries from Manzano or Las Cruces came for a Sunday service. In 1914 the parish at Tularosa came under the jurisdiction of the Order of Franciscan Monks, and Father Ferdinand Ortiz became the resident priest at Mescalero. He was of an aristocratic Mexican family that traced the Indian line of its ancestry back to the Aztecs. He was a man of culture but, having taken the vows of poverty, he adjusted remarkably to the primitive living conditions of the reservation. The only available building for both religious worship and his dwelling was a dilapidated adobe with leaking roof, no floors except earth, and crumbling walls. It was a long, narrow structure, and a curtain was hung to partition his living quarters from the front part used for the sanctuary.

In 1916 Father Albert Braun completed his schooling for the priesthood and

---

1. The primary source for this chapter was Father Albert Braun, with whom I have had many interviews. Others consulted were Dorothy Emerson, author of the biography of Father Braun (manuscript at the cathedral archive, El Paso, Texas); Mrs. James A. Carroll; Eloise Sutherland; Ted Sutherland; Paul Blazer; Alexina Chase, daughter of A. B. Fall; Eric Tortilla; Ralph Shanta; Phoebe Wilson, daughter of Shanta Boy; Michael Davalos; Solon Sombrero; Alberta Begay; Catherine Cojo; Jenni Carillo Chihueschua Carillo; Peter Gaines; Gertrude Torres, daughter of Roman Chiquito; Alton Peso; Maudie Platta; Lena Morgan; Jasper Kanseah; Willie Magoosh; Ralph Shanta, Jr.; Mack Big Mouth; Lucius Peso; Dan Nicholas; and Frank Love.

was ordained in his order, the Franciscan Monks. His first assignment was to the isolated reservation occupied by the Mescalero Apaches. He had been born and reared in Los Angeles. He left the train at Tularosa carrying his meager equipment and walked to the church. The next morning he was taken to Mescalero in a buckboard drawn by a pair of Spanish mules over the worst road he had ever seen. But he was enchanted by the beautiful country through which he passed and, if he was repelled or discouraged by his first glimpse of the building that was to be his church and home, he did not reveal it.

Upon finding that very few of his parishioners spoke a word of English, at the suggestion of Father Ferdinand he engaged the services of an Indian as an interpreter. Later, Eric Tortilla, recently returned from Carlisle, was hired. Eric spoke excellent English and Father Albert began immediately to learn enough Apache to allow him to communicate somewhat with the Indians.

He celebrated his first mass and collected his first offering—seventeen cents. The Order required its missionaries to subsist upon what their members could contribute, and the young priest realized that he must produce by himself sufficient food for his needs. Game was abundant, but without a mount he could do little hunting. Nor could he visit the Indians, who were scattered over a mountainous country of approximately a half million acres. His parents sent money for a horse, and he purchased a wiry pony roped on the slopes of White Mountain by an Indian. One of his flock loaned him a primitive handmade saddle. He began making trips outside the village. He visited the Apaches living in the little canyons nearby and gradually increased the distance of his trips. With bedroll, ammunition belt, rifle, and some food, he carried the small bag in which he kept the accessories of the altar for celebrating mass. He was away from the village three or four days at a time, but he always returned for his regular Sunday services.

Always as he rode he watched for game. If he could ride up to a tepee with a deer or even some rabbits, he was assured of a welcome. Unless invited he did not spend the night or even share a meal, but when hospitality was offered he accepted it gratefully. Before eating he said a prayer. The Apaches were greatly impressed by his "making medicine" and listened respectfully. When the meal was finished he repeated the rite; and while his way of worship was new and strange to the Indians, it indicated to them that not all White Eyes are irreligious. His being an expert shot and his ability to adapt to their customs and etiquette won the respect and friendship of the Apaches and they began riding long distances to the village to attend church.

As more and more came, Father Albert determined that he must have a more suitable building. He wrote to the Order of Franciscan Monks for permission to erect one. They replied that, judging from the reports submitted, the Apaches would be unable to finance such an undertaking and that he must wait until they could do so.

At that time the Apaches lived along the little streams of the reservation and planted and harvested crops of corn, beans, pumpkins, and squash. Nearly all owned sheep which, of course, were herded, usually by the women and children of the families. While they had little money, they had existed for centuries without even knowing of it and still produced much of their sustenance. There was an abundance of game, and they harvested and stored much of their primitive food such as mescal, acorn meal, mesquite beans, piñons, and berries. Twice a year they sheared their sheep and sold the fleeces. They culled their flocks and sold the animals, too. Sheep at that time averaged two dollars a head.

A few families could have been considered comparatively affluent. For example, Shanta Boy had five thousand sheep, some cattle, and many horses. He and his sons also raised corn, beans, pumpkins, and squash and, though they had little cash, they had no want.

There were Mexicans at Tularosa and a few more in the canyon of the river. Regardless of the abundant pine on the mountain, nobody had used logs for a habitation. The Mexicans had come from a treeless country and they brought with them the habits of their people. They made adobe houses. There is no better insulation than the good earth; it is cool in summer and warm in winter. And handled by people with an apparently natural bent for design and utility, it is beautiful. The Mexicans could make adobes; the Indians could learn from them.

Prophetically, an unusual accident occurred. There was an explosion and the wall of the wretched building used by Father Albert was blown out, apparently by a blast of powder. (Nobody ever learned the identity of the culprit.) Father Albert and his parishioners began making and drying adobes under the direction of a Mexican skilled in the art. They erected a comfortable building with one large room for religious meetings and, jutting from one side, two smaller ones for living quarters. And they did it at a minimum of expense.

Father Albert found the young Mescalero chief, Roman Chiquito, receptive and they became very close friends. Once, as they followed turkey tracks through a light snow, the priest asked the chief how it happened that the Apaches so firmly believed in Ussen before the coming of the missionaries.

"You see the tracks," replied the Apache, "and you don't ask if there is a turkey ahead. You know that there is. We see Ussen in the mountains; we see Him in the trees, and in the flowers, and in all beautiful things, and we know that they are evidence of Him as the tracks are of the turkey." Not long afterward Father Albert baptized a small son for Roman Chiquito. The proud father said, "See how perfect he is! He has eyes to see, ears to hear, a mouth to eat and speak and sing, hands to hunt and work, feet to walk. Could anyone ask better proof of the existence of Ussen? You call Him another name, but ours is better, for it means Creator of life."

Father Albert tried to say mass at the Shanta *ranchería* once a month. To do so, he had to ride forty miles in order to reach that location, which was only ten miles as the crow flies but was on the far slope of Sierra Blanca. On the way, as he rode past the Three Rivers Ranch of A. B. Fall, the family saw him pass. Fall sent his daughter Jewett after the priest with an invitation to spend the night with them any time he was making the trip to or from the Shanta place. He gladly accepted their hospitality and from that time on was a frequent guest. The family and he became very good friends.

He felt the need of a chapel at the Shanta *ranchería* but had not the finances to build one. When word came from his superior that two charitable young women of a wealthy family in New York had contributed two thousand dollars for the building of a church, he hoped to obtain that aid; but it was decided that a pastor in Arizona was to receive it. When the donors learned that the money had not been used as specified by them, the women protested; and the superior wrote to Father Albert that he could have the money, but only under the stipulation that the structure be built of stone and have stained glass windows.

All for two thousand dollars! Father Albert was discouraged. With an additional thousand he might be able to comply with requirements, but where was he to get the other thousand? He went to Shanta Boy. The Apache meditated for some time. Finally he replied that there was stone available—quantities of it, of good quality. There was also material for burning and making lime. And there was timber. How about labor? Shanta Boy said that he and his sons John, Joe, and Ralph were available. Others, too, might donate their services. And Shanta Boy had a wagon and teams. What was to prevent them from building a church when most of the material and much of the labor would cost nothing?

Although it was a labor of love, the effort was grueling. The building had to be finished before the winter set in or it could not be completed before the coming spring. But the windows? "Well," said Father Albert, "we will build the church; the windows will come." Through friends in St. Louis they did. An old church there which contained beautiful stained glass windows made in Europe was being torn down; the windows were available at a reasonable price. That challenge met, the main structure was complete. Only the pews and altar remained to be constructed. These were fashioned from lumber found and hand hewn at the site.

Father Albert reported to his superior that the little building was completed at a cost of nineteen hundred ninety dollars. Enclosed with the report was a money order for the remaining ten dollars. The money was returned to sender.

World War I interrupted his work at Mescalero when he asked and finally received permission to enlist as a chaplain. He ministered to the dying soldiers, under fire, in some of the worst battles of the war—including Argonne and San Mihiel. For this he was decorated—and promoted—for service beyond the call of duty. When the war ended he returned with the rank of lieutenant colonel to his beloved Apaches and resumed his work among them.

During the time that he spent in Europe, he studied the architecture and the primitive methods of constructing the magnificent cathedrals he visited. He hoped that upon his return he could build another church, bigger and more beautiful, as a memorial to all soldiers of all nations who had given their lives in the service of their country. He met a fellow chaplain who was also an architect. When Father Albert explained his limitations both as to finances and equipment for building, this generous chaplain offered to contribute his services as architect. He drew up plans for the edifice.

Father Albert purchased two heavy trucks, discarded by the army, and combined parts of the two for hauling the rock and beams. He and the Apaches again quarried the stone, this time hauling it to a small mesa overlooking the village, a site fitting for such a memorial.

They were ably assisted by a stonecutter from Santa Barbara whose wife had died and who wished to devote his remaining years to the Order. This lay brother gave not only his work but his life. As he was helping unload some of the heavy stone, a piece slipped and he was crushed to death. He was buried at the right of the entrance of the new St. Joseph Mission.[2]

2. Father Albert has the promise of the Order that he will be laid to rest at the left of the entrance.

Father Albert Braun.

St. Joseph's Mission.

The first protestant minister to be stationed at Mescalero was the Reverend Mr. E. H. Pincher, who was sent by the Women's Organization of the Dutch Reformed Church to establish a mission in 1908. Pincher came from Fort Sill. Solon Sombrero acted as guide and interpreter for him. They rode over the reservation, visited the tepees, and attempted to induce the Indians to attend the services of the minister's church. He, too, found that his work was no bed of roses. The following is from his diary.

Jan. 15 [1908]. Stopped at Marion Simms's camp and spent an hour talking to Indians. Catherine Cojo interpreted.[3] Visited Joe [José] Carillo. He has two Indian sons-in-law who do not support their families. His son John has sore eyes, and says that he is witched by Shosh [Shash, Apache word for bear]. Could not convince him to the contrary. He is intelligent and has been off to school for four years. This is a strange delusion but they hold to it tenaciously.

Slept alone in cabin with White Mtn. glistening in moonlight keeping watch, and the noisy Rinconada and a friendly owl to sing me to sleep. It was my first night in the mountains many miles from any pale face. Rose at daylight and fed pony. Made coffee, cleaned cabin and climbed into saddle for busy day. Started for camp and located camp—blue column of smoke from among the pines. Felix Palmer talked for me.[4] People had goats. The men were pleased to hear me speak a few words in Apache. Penn Schott went with me to hunt up Chief Peso's camp.

Found his camp after a long hard ride and talked to his wife concerning the Kingdom.

Started for home from mouth of Dry Canyon. Met Man Maxwell who told of the murder of McKlean.[5] Was riding hard and got home before night. Saw two tepees and thought once that I would not stop, but my good angel prompted me to not go by. Had a most pleasant talk. Frankie was there and spoke well.... Camp was Roman Chiquito's. He escaped from prison and started home (from the Federal Penitentiary at Leavenworth, Kansas).[6] Kept looking for White Mtn. Saw it at last and it guided me home.

Jan. 20. Took breakfast with Roy McClean, and Ward and the boy with bloodhounds. Indians were trailing Kedinchin the murderer. They overtook and killed him in a fight on the [indecipherable].

January 30, 1908. Rode to mouth of Silver Canyon. Took dinner with Mr. Walker. Had blessing at meal. Helped bail straw and had an opportunity for speaking a word for the Master. Spent night with Roy McClean whose brother had recently been murdered by Kedinchin, an Indian. Asked blessing but did not talk much about Christ. Brought Jesus before Jim Banta while we were washing dishes.[7] He was ready for message. He stopped runaway team in Roswell by roping both horses and making his pony hold them by horn of saddle. He swam into middle of Gila River to save two women whose boat had turned over. He was running cows in the mountains of Arizona alone. His horse fell and knocked him unconscious, breaking his leg and shoulder. After 18 hours he came to himself and saw a pack of coyotes sitting near and waiting. First thing he said was, "I'm not dead yet." He rode 85 miles with foot tied to horse's neck and had leg and shoulder bone set without chloroform.[8]

---

3. Marion Simms is the brother of Zan-a-go-li-che, kidnapped and subsequently married to Massai. See Chapter *Massai.*

4. Felix Palmer is the father of famous Mescalero artist Ignatio Palmer.

5. Don McKlean was killed by Kedinchin in 1908. See Chapter *Kedinchin.*

6. See Chapter *The Shantas.*

7. Jim Banta was a white man who lived on the reservation.

8. Reverend E. H. Pincher Diary, Archives, Dutch Reformed Church.

For many years the Catholic and the Dutch Reformed were the only denominations with missionaries on the reservation, but eventually The Church of Jesus Christ of Latter-day Saints established one; so also did the Assembly of God and the Baptist church.

The early missionaries had talked to their congregations about the dignity of labor; and apparently they believed what they taught, for they worked with their hands and they worked hard. While in their primitive stage, the Apaches' first obligations were protecting and providing for their families. Now that they were partially relieved of these obligations, they were willing—at least many were—to do the type of work that they had considered degrading.

When later ministers came, insisting as strongly as had the earlier ones upon the necessity of men's doing manual labor, the Apaches were critical because some of the new missionaries did not practice what they preached. The Indians were far more impressed by what the ministers did than by what they said. Some forbade their wives to clean the church without being paid. Why, asked the Indians, if work is not degrading, did not the preachers sweep and clean their own churches?

Seldom did a Protestant minister stay more than a year or two. Very few had had experience with Indians. None spoke their language. All quickly learned, however, that their efforts to convert the Apaches should be directed toward the man of the household, because if he decided to become a member of the church his wife and children would follow.

The trouble, for the ministers, was that almost all Apache men had more than one wife. Before one could be baptized he must decide upon which wife and children he could keep. The others must be renounced and left to shift for themselves. The Apaches strictly observed their unwritten law regarding a man's obligation to support his families; failure to do so would mean loss of face in his tribe. Many warriors weighed the decision in the balance and decided in favor of their families. This was very discouraging to the ministers and probably was a primary reason for their short terms of service.

Father Albert also had to deal with the problem of the church versus established families. How he solved it is a matter of conjecture; but that he did was obvious. Did he ignore the existence of plural marriage in preference to breaking up homes? Perhaps. But the old members of his church are certain that had a married man asked him to perform a marriage service for another wife he would have refused.

After there were four or five missions established the ministers came to Father Albert and asked for his cooperation in abolishing the observance of the annual Puberty Ceremonial, the most sacred of all Apache rites. It was, they insisted, a pagan ceremony and they were forbidding their members to permit participation or attendance. Father Albert asked that he be given time to consult his immediate superior before giving his decision. He did so with the result that the next in rank felt that the other missionaries should be supported in their stand. Father Albert deliberated on his quandry, then he decided that before he acquiesced he would invite his bishop in El Paso to visit him during the celebration and to say mass Sunday morning.

When the bishop arrived Friday he found the village full of visiting bands. All the Indians were out in their colorful native garbs feasting and dancing. The bishop asked for an explanation of the gala occasion and Father Albert explained. He asked if His Excellency would like to attend. They went. When the bishop asked the purpose of the rites he was told that it was to impress upon the maidens their sacred obligation to be chaste. Only a virgin could participate. If a girl did so unworthily her action might bring disaster to her, to her family, and to the entire tribe. She was, as a future mother, to be faithful to her husband.

"It sounds," decided the bishop, "as though their objective is similar to ours. It seems to be a beautiful and effective ceremony. It is certainly conducted with impressive solemnity and reverence." He made its observance the primary theme of his sermon.

Attempts by churches to discourage participation in the Puberty Ceremonials have continued in recent times.

In 1969, Frank Love, an Omaha Indian, was assigned as pastor to the Reformed Church at Mescalero. He encountered a distressing conflict between the Christian and primitive religions. Shortly before the observance of the Puberty Ceremonials, he received instructions from his superiors to forbid the participation of any girl of his congregation in the rites and to allow none of his members even to attend. Further, he was instructed to purchase, at the expense of his local church, a large tent and erect it in the churchyard. He was also to pay an evangelist and a song leader who would be sent to aid in a revival meeting.

Frank Love was young, devout, dedicated, and enthusiastic; but he was also an Indian. He obeyed, but he regarded the procedure as ill-advised. The last night of the Ceremonials a frail, elderly Apache woman stopped at the tent. She explained that she had attempted to walk to the feast ground where the Ceremonials were being held, but she could go no further. She was the only one who had appeared during the four-day rites.

The next year the orders were repeated. The young pastor was distressed. He had been unable to complete payment for the previous summer's expense, and he was at a loss as to what to do.

"Have you considered an appendectomy?" I asked.

"It isn't funny."

It wasn't and I apologized. He was so obviously distressed that not until he asked for a suggestion did I ask when he had last visited his parents on the Omaha Reservation. It had been, he said, more than three years. Frank Love and his family took their vacation the week of the Ceremonials.

He finished the term of his contract and returned to Omaha. When next I heard from him he was director of a service club for Indians in Omaha. It had, he said, been the only decision he could make after a prolonged inner conflict. Though he saw no significant difference in the church's theology and the primitive religion, his superiors did. He could not be dishonest to his convictions and had regretfully renounced the ministry.

CHAPTER 8

JOSÉ CARILLO, INTERPRETER

José Carillo was not *Indio puro* but, as his name indicates, part Mexican. When he was a small boy in the State of Chihuahua, the Navajos raided northern Mexico for horses. They returned with many, and with one captive—José. Because he was part Indian and not yet five years old, they thought it not too late for him to develop the skills, endurance, and courage to become a warrior.[1]

José did not disappoint his captors. They were delighted with the alacrity with which the child adapted to their mode of life and learned their language. He became an expert horseman, a master of the bow and arrow, and, though not the equal of the Navajos, an expert trailer.

Though he was a slave he was treated as a member of the family that owned him until an offer came from a wealthy Mexican on the Río Bravo to purchase him. The sum offered was so great that the Navajo accepted. He did not dislike his Mexican owner, but he bitterly resented being forced to labor in the fields; he shared thoroughly the Indians' dislike for what they considered degrading work. Rather than be so debased, he decided to escape and return to the Navajos.

The tribe learned that there had been a big crop of piñons in the Capitán Mountains of southeastern New Mexico and decided upon a hunt. They did not go primarily for the succulent little nuts but for the deer that fattened on them. There were perhaps sixty people in the party, many of whom were women and children. While the men hunted, the latter harvested piñons and butchered and dried the meat.

They took José with them; and he learned that on the Hondo there were people who spoke Spanish. He decided to run away and join them. He timed his departure in the dark of the moon and planned his escape very carefully. Though the Navajos used rifles, they did not permit him to have one. He had to rely upon primitive weapons; and to avoid being trailed easily he had to go on foot. With his blanket, a knife, his bow and arrows, and an emergency ration bag filled with dried meat, he crept out of camp about midnight. He moved slowly and cautiously, lest he break a twig or dislodge a stone, until he

---

1. Interviews with Jennie Chihuahua, Sedillo Sixto, Mrs. James A. Carroll, and Paul Blazer.

was perhaps a half mile from the Navajos. When he reached a rocky ledge sloping gradually uphill, he followed it to the summit. Having left it, he settled down to the steady jog trot used by the Indian to cover many miles in a few hours; he made no effort to hide his trail until dawn. He then used every device taught him by the expert Navajos.

When José thought that he was getting close to the Río Hondo, he saw that he must pass through ledges of rock, always suitable for ambush. He approached very cautiously, looking carefully for the prints of moccasins, reckoning without conscious thought on the superior skill of his instructors, until suddenly something struck the back of his head. When he awakened, he was conscious of a great weight upon him, then the sensation of pain throughout his body and of blood trickling down his face. It was some time before the bewildered young man came to the realization that he had been buried under a pile of rocks!

The Navajos had struck and continued to stone José until they thought he was dead, then they had heaped stones on his unconscious body and left him.

Again José lost consciousness, and when he awakened again he lay on the bank of a little stream with water trickling on his face.

"Enjuh!" said an Indian, bending over him, "he lives."

At the time, it did not occur to José that it was strange that he could understand the words of his rescuers even though it was obvious that they were not Navajos. Their language was so similar to Navajo that he understood without difficulty and answered their questions about what had happened to him.

These strangers were Mescalero Apaches who lived on the little streams flowing from Sierra Blanca; and they, too, were hunting. Upon hearing groans coming from a new burial, they had dug him out and carried him to the Hondo. They offered him membership in the tribe; but if he still wished to join the Mexicans on the Hondo, the choice was his.

José decided to do the latter and for three years he remained with the Mexicans. During that time he married a beautiful girl, but when she died he was no longer happy there. The lure of the old nomadic life returned. He told his friends of his intention to go to the Mescaleros, and he left.

Again he settled into the Indian way of life. And again he found the Indians hospitable and friendly. He married a Mescalero and lived with his wife's family. They had a camp in the Rinconada. The agent learned of José's knowledge of both the Apache and Spanish languages. To his delight, José spoke English also, but not so well as he did the other tongues. He arranged for José and his family to live near the agency so that, when occasion necessitated the aid of an interpreter, José would be available.

José was a great help, though he blundered occasionally. Once, when asked to send word by runners to the chiefs of the different tribes, he informed the messengers that they were to bid them come to the agency for a "meet," which to José had but one meaning—food. To be invited to a feast and not go was unthinkable to the Apaches, and they flocked to the feast ground in numbers. Such a large assembly aroused the curiosity of the agent, and José explained that they had come to be fed. The agent very wisely decided that, though it had not been his intention to furnish provender, it might be wise to do so, thus assuring the Apaches' attendance when summoned in the future. He ordered that several steers be butchered and distributed, along with coffee, sugar, flour, and beans.

When the agent began to use Apaches as police, José doubled in that capacity. He considered it an important responsibility and both he and the others who served as tribal police took their duties seriously and seldom failed to apprehend offenders.

One of the first times José Carillo was mentioned in the records of the reservation was in connection with the killing of Morris J. Bernstein, clerk at the agency, in 1878. Bernstein was in the office "up on the hill where the preacher used to live." Among several people present was José Carillo, who had ridden up, tied his horse, and gone into the office. The men in the office noticed three men riding up the canyon, driving some horses toward a pond situated just below the building.

Bernstein went outside, saw the horses drinking at the pond below, recognized them as belonging to the Indians, and decided to stop the riders. He jumped on Carillo's horse, pulled the carbine from its scabbard on the mount, and fired before riding out of sight down the slope. Those remaining at the office vainly called for him to come back, to no avail. They heard several shots and waited. About a half hour later they went to investigate and they found him dead.

The killing of Bernstein has been attributed to Billy the Kid. He and his *compadres* were accused of being on the reservation for the purpose of stealing the Apaches' horses. But according to Frank Coe, one of the Kid's *compadres* who was there that day, Billy was on his knees drinking from the spring that falls over the bluff below the present site of the Catholic church when the fatal shot was fired.[2]

The first physician stationed on the Mescalero Apache Reservation was Dr. Howard Thompson. Thompson lived in a small three-room house, known locally as a shotgun type. It consisted of a room which he used as his office, a middle room in which he slept, and another which was the kitchen. One evening, rather late, he was called to the door by José Carillo. He found José on the doorstep clad only in breechclout and moccasins. Without speaking, José turned his back, and Thompson found wounds in his shoulders and blood streaming into his moccasins. He took José into his office and, without asking questions, began working. He cleansed the wounds and found one so deep that he feared the heart might have been touched. It was necessary to sew up several of the gashes. When the doctor had finished, José rose to leave. The physician advised him to remain for the night, but José protested. He said that there was a reason why he must return to his home. Thompson, who knew the Indians, asked what had happened.

"Indian drunk."

"Well, did you arrest him?"

"No got gun. Jump on horse; go tepee, get gun; drunk—he go too; ride hard. Jab me in back with spear."

"And you put him in jail, José?"

2. Anne Titsworth, daughter of Frank Coe. While driving through the reservation in July 1960, she pointed out the spring from which Billy the Kid was drinking when the shot was fired that killed Bernstein. This was told her by her father who was with the group. Mrs. Howard Thompson (Emma Blazer), interview.

José lived on the reservation for many years and reared a family of fine children. When James A. Carroll was appointed as Apache agent in 1901, José was still serving occasionally as interpreter. Nobody was employed regularly; as the need arose, any man known to be competent was called in. Once, Carroll employed his services to ascertain the business of a young Apache who came to him. This boy wished to be married and was indignant because the agent required those who contemplated that step to have a ceremony such as the white man considered necessary. It had taken years to teach the Apaches that without a bill of sale he was not secure in his possession of a horse. Now it was being required for women!

José made a detailed and apparently convincing explanation, and the young man reluctantly gave the name of the woman he wished to marry. Mr. Carroll completed filling out the form of application for a marriage license before realizing that the woman named was old enough to be the boy's grandmother. Carroll remonstrated: Surely he didn't want to marry an old woman?

"Good woman," interpreted José. "Cook good; wash shirt."

Carroll shook his head, but he performed the ceremony and gave the aged bride a certificate of marriage. Then the "happy" couple underwent the four-day ceremonies of their tribe. A week after the Apache marriage, the groom returned. Again, José interpreted. The young man untied the buckskin bag at his belt, produced the marriage certificate, and poked it at the agent.

"Here," he said, "you take her!"

CHAPTER 9

KEDINCHIN

The last killing of a white man by a Mescalero Apache occurred on their reservation January 12, 1908.[1]

For many years the ranchers adjacent to the reservation had run cattle and sheep on its excellent grazing land without paying fees. A charge of a dollar a year for cattle and twenty-five cents for sheep was levied but was evaded by many who made use of the range. It is not strange, then, that Apaches felt that they were entitled to eat beef when and if they could butcher one without being detected in the act.

Had it not been for the ignorance of a youth who knew almost nothing of the customs of the West, neither the youth nor Kedinchin need have died so tragically. The youth, Don McLane, the younger brother of Roy McLane who was foreman of the Flying H, was totally unfamiliar with the range. As tenderfeet usually did, he seemed to think that the possession of the costume and accoutrements of a cowboy qualified him for the role.

Roy McLane lived in the ranch headquarters of the Flying H—near the house in which John Tunstall had settled when he undertook to run cattle in Lincoln County. McLane knew the Apaches, paid his grazing fees, and was on good terms with them. When his younger brother came for a visit he attempted to explain the customs of the country but, unfortunately, the lad took the matter lightly.

Don McLane did what nobody familiar with conditions in New Mexico would risk even today. He rode up on a man in an isolated spot who was butchering a beef. Ted Sutherland, first superintendent of livestock on the Mescalero Apache Reservation, said, "I've ridden miles out of my way to avoid just such a situation many times. I knew very well no Apache was killing one of the tribal herd; and I knew, too, that if he was hungry he was going to eat. And if he ate beef belonging to an adjoining rancher, I was for him."[2]

---

1. Information gained from interviews with Paul Blazer, Mrs. James A. Carroll, Ted J. Sutherland, Percy Big Mouth, Willie Magoosh, and Carisso Gallarito was used in the interpretation of this rather well known story. For a melodramatic and highly slanted contemporary white account see the *Cloudcroft Silver Lining,* January 25, 1908. For a more even-handed account, see Sonnichsen, *Mescalero Apaches,* pp. 256–58.

2. Ted J. Sutherland, interview.

When he did not return to the ranch on the Feliz, Roy waited until morning and took his brother's trail. Don's horse was shod and the tracks were easily recognizable. At the village of Mescalero he learned that his brother had stopped at the trading post and post office. He had then crossed the Tularosa and followed the road down the canyon. Paul Blazer had noticed him when he passed the famous mill. That was the last time he was seen alive.

Roy searched alone until dark. The next morning he acquired the services of two experienced Apache trackers and the three followed Don's trail into the mountains. In a patch of thick brush further on they found Don's horse, which was still saddled, its trailing reins entangled. Nearby the party found Don's frozen corpse. He had been shot through the head. Beside the body was a partially butchered beef.

To Roy McLane's discerning eye the explanation was plain. Don had ridden up on a man who had stolen and was butchering a beef far off the beaten path, which indicated plainly that he knew the penalty for the act. Roy realized that his brother had ridden up to the culprit with no idea that he was acting foolishly. He also knew that at that time (1908), no Indian would kill a white man without provocation. There must have been an element of surprise. But how could an Apache have been surprised?

If the Apache trackers suspected the killer's identity, true to their instincts, they protected him. The Indians helped place the frozen body upon a packhorse, and with it the three descended to the agency. There McLane reported the death of his brother to James A. Carroll, one of the few wise and understanding agents ever stationed at Mescalero. Six years of experience with the Apaches had taught him much of their habits and reactions. Only under unusual circumstances could this thing have happened, and the agent felt that, in all probability, Don had precipitated the shooting. In this his brother concurred.

If the officers at the county seat were permitted to handle the case, Carroll could count on serious trouble. An organized police force of Apaches was used for law enforcement on the reservation, and the agent permitted little interference from outside. This he explained to the dead youth's brother, who appreciated the wisdom of relying upon Indian police.[3]

The population of the reservation was mixed. In addition to the Mescaleros there were Lipans. Magoosh, their chief, who as a boy had witnessed the fall of the Alamo, had brought the remnant of his people to the Mescalero Reservation and received refuge. He cooperated with Peso, leader of the Mescaleros, and with Sans Peur, chief of another band of Mescaleros. Carroll called in the three for conference. If he asked it, he knew that they would apprehend and bring in the man who had fired the shot.

The agent inquired if any of their men were missing and was told that one man was—Kedinchin, about middle age. His wife, Minnie, was absent from their tepee, also. And Kedinchin was deaf. In addition, he had lost an eye. He, the chiefs admitted, would butcher a beef if hungry; but kill a man without provocation, no. Young McLane had probably ridden up unheard and, if he approached Kedinchin from the blind side, unseen. The sudden realization of such a confrontation could well have brought an automatic act of defense.

---

3. Mrs. James A. Carroll, interviews.

Kedinchin.

Of course the killer would have to flee. Where? With Minnie also missing it was apparent that he had come back for her and the two had fled together. The Apache police took the trail. Sans Peur directed the search, and with him rode his brother, Crook Neck. Elmer Wilson, Comanche, Sam Chino, Muchacho Negro, Dana Evans, and Caje were also members of the police force.[4]

Roy McLane accompanied the police in their search. They picked up the trail at Kedinchin's tepee and followed it easily. It led south. Had he remained on the reservation Carroll might have been able to protect him. But he left it.

Now off the reservation, a county sheriff's posse joined the Indians. But if the Apaches resented the intrusion they did not indicate it. It is possible that they welcomed it, for the officers were well supplied with food.

---

4. Caje had been hunting to supply meat for the Warm Springs Apaches when Victorio's band was practically exterminated at Tres Castillos in 1880. When the Mescaleros who escaped that terrible massacre returned to their reservation they camped on the Penasco. They were attacked by cavalry who fired into their camp at night and shot several of the party. In addition to the women and children killed, Caje's wife, a Mescalero, received a bullet in the lower leg, as did another woman of the group. Their horses were captured by the soldiers. The injured women were unable to walk, and the men carried them until they found horses for transporting them the long miles up the Penasco and north to Mescalero. For that task Caje received a new name—Packs on His Back.

The trail led through rough and mountainous country. From time to time the Apache trackers found bits of calico, perhaps torn accidentally from the woman's dress by thorns. Or could they have been left intentionally so that the inevitable pursuit would end quickly?

It was evident that the horses of the fugitives were worn down and that the quarry could not be far ahead. But the white posse, unskilled at tracking, became discouraged and returned to Alamogordo.[5]

Early the next morning the pursuers closed in on the hunted. Kedinchin's wife had built a tiny fire in a deep canyon and was cooking meat when they first glimpsed her. As she stooped to take it, one of the police called to her very softly and told her not to move or give any indication of their presence, that a rescue party was at hand. She was to stand, take the meat to her husband, and then go to the opposite side of the fire and remain motionless, well away from him. Apparently she had hoped for rescue; otherwise she would have warned her husband. She obeyed and moved to the opposite side of the fire.

The Apache police also obeyed—a determination to carry out justice in their own way. They brought Kedinchin's body back to Mescalero.[6]

---

5. Ted J. Sutherland, interview.

6. Carisso Gallarito, interview through an interpreter.

PART TWO

THE EXILES

CHAPTER 10

MASSAI

ALBERTA BEGAY

My father, Massai, was a Chiricahua Apache, the son of White Cloud and Little Star. He was born at Mescal Mountain, the home of my grandparents.[1]

White Cloud took great pride in the education of his son. He carefully trained him for survival—something that can't be said for the White Eyes. White Cloud taught Massai to use the bow and spear and to go for a long time without food or water. He taught him to run long distances while holding water in his mouth until his return—this to insure proper breathing habits. By the time Massai was nine years old he could run to the top of the mountain and back. After that, he had to run with a burden on his back. The weight was gradually increased until he could carry many pounds with ease, although he was small of stature.

The next step in his education was training as a horseman. In this he excelled. Marksmanship came next—first with the bow and then with the rifle. To insure his being a good shot, White Cloud suspended a small iron ring from the branch of a tree. Through this ring Massai had to shoot. If he missed, he was sent to his mother in disgrace. The distance was gradually increased until Massai could shoot at a hundred yards without missing his target.

"Enjuh!" said White Cloud at this accomplishment of his son. "It is well. Now you can shoot well enough to kill game for food and protect yourself against men."

Massai's closest friend was a Tonkawa lad whose name in English was Gray Lizard. He and his parents had come from the flat lands of the east and had joined the Apaches. They loved the mountains, and they lived among my

---

1. Mescal Mountain is near Globe, Arizona. Alberta Begay's account, previously published by this author as "Massai—Bronco Apache," *True West* 6 (July–August 1959), by design briefly summarizes the entire story of the Chiricahuas from the time of Mangas Coloradas to surrenders and imprisonment in 1886 and beyond. That account is reproduced here essentially the same as Alberta Begay gave it in the earlier version. The closing paragraphs of the chapter have been added, the additional information having been compiled from subsequent interviews with Alberta Begay; Eloise Carroll, daughter of Mrs. James A. Carroll; and Mrs. C. R. Jefferis.

father's people. White Cloud instructed Gray Lizard with his son. It is well known that the word Tonkawa means coward. But nobody ever mentioned that to Gray Lizard. The Apaches are people of good manners.

White Cloud often sent the boys for game, and they knew better than to return without it. It was a hard lesson that they must learn—that of survival—and there could be no failing it. From rabbits and birds they progressed to deer and mountain lions. Once, before they were fully grown, they were attacked by a bear. Regretfully, they killed it. The Apache does not kill a bear except in self-defense. Under no circumstances does he eat its meat.

The boys trapped and broke wild horses. Sometimes they lay hidden at a water hole and roped the broncos about the neck. They were dragged over rock and cacti until the animal was choked down by the burden; then they rode him home in triumph.

Before Massai had completed the four raids necessary to become a warrior, a visitor came to the *rancheria*. His party halted at the mouth of the canyon and he rode alone toward the camp holding a white cloth. The men of our camp beckoned him to come. When he got close, some of them recognized him.

"Geronimo."

"Yes, Geronimo," he answered grimly. "The Mexicans have given me that name—I who was named Goyahkla. I have come to meet with you in council. I have come to remind you that the White Eyes have invaded our land. They have murdered our chief. They killed Mangas Coloradas after promising him their protection when he went to their camp to treat for peace. They have murdered my wife, mother, and three children. They have killed your people. They have killed our game, and they have taken our land and all that is ours. I come to ask that you join me in fighting them—that all Apaches join me. We must drive them out before it is too late."

"There are too many," objected one man.

"They must have litters like dogs," said another. "Or how else could they multiply so rapidly?"

Geronimo went on, unheeding. "Cochise died of a broken heart because he foresaw the extermination of his people. Taza, the son who succeeded him, trusted the White Eyes. He went to Washington and they poisoned him. Juh, the Nednhi chief, is dead. Naiche and Mangus have seen what happened to their fathers and they do nothing!"

Geronimo paused and fixed us all with his fierce eyes.

"Who will join me in driving out the White Eyes?"

"You are not a chief," said one man.

Geronimo whirled on him. "I have been the war leader for Cochise. I have led a band for Mangas Coloradas. I will lead you!"

"We are a free people," said White Cloud calmly. "Among the Apaches there is no compulsory military service."

"So be it," replied Geronimo. "Let each man decide for himself."

White Cloud agreed. "We will hold a council and let you know our decision."

Massai and Gray Lizard wanted to go with Geronimo. They asked permission of their fathers and were told: "You are almost men. You must decide for yourselves."

They and others told Geronimo that they would join him.

"The time is not yet ripe," he answered. "It will take two summers, perhaps more, to prepare and store food."

"For what?"

"For emergencies, you impatient ones! To fight the White Eyes we must travel fast and ride light. When we reach a hiding place we must have food, clothing, and, especially, moccasins there. We must have cooking pots. We must have ammunition. It is for you to secure and place these things where I shall direct. I know every waterhole between Fort Wingate and Casas Grandes and between Silver City and Chihuahua. I know hidden caves where supplies can be cached. Then, when we have supplies to last for many months, we will strike!"

Our people were not all in favor of joining forces with Geronimo, but all thought his idea of preparing for war to be good. They began killing deer, drying meat, and tanning hides and storing them in safe places. As the cactus fruit ripened they gathered and dried it. They baked great quantities of mescal, stored large supplies of mesquite beans and acorns, gathered piñons when the trees bore. They worked so hard at storing food for the future that the supply close to them was made scarce.

Massai and Gray Lizard got their fathers' permission to make a journey to the west in search of food. Each led a packhorse behind his mount. They rode far toward the west, crossing a high range of mountains and a wide valley, then another range from the top of which they could see the Big Water. Between them and the ocean were some low hills, which concealed a Mexican *ranchería*. But they did not know of this and so set to hunting without fear of being discovered.

There were many deer on the ridge, and there was a cave on the west slope with a grassy bench and a spring. They settled in that place and began preparing meat and hides. They saw no one, but their training required that one keep watch while the other worked. Soon their supplies exceeded their means of carrying them. They wrapped jerky in a buffalo hide that they had brought with them and hid it in the cave. Loading all four horses with food and buckskin, they left for home. Massai spoke to his friend as they rode away: "Now we must remember this place and how to return. If you should come alone the supplies are yours, and the same for me; but I hope we are always together."

"It shall be as you say," replied Gray Lizard.

When the boys reached Mescal Mountain they found that those who had wished to join Geronimo had gone to Ojo Caliente, so they followed. There they found that the troops had arrested Geronimo and taken him to San Carlos. He and his people, along with Victorio and Loco, the Warm Springs leader, and his assistant chief, had all been driven like cattle to San Carlos. And as every Apache knows, that is the worst place in the world.

No White Eyes could have captured Massai and Gray Lizard; but Chiricahua scouts, some of their own people, had joined the White Eyes. Had the boys known of their treachery they could have escaped. But they thought them men and brothers and permitted them to walk into their camp. The scouts took them, too, to San Carlos.

"Well, it is one way to see Geronimo and learn his plans," said Massai. "When he is ready, he will leave. The troops cannot stop him. Meanwhile, the stupid White Eyes will give him and his people food and clothing."

"If they are alive to use it," said Gray Lizard. "Don't you know of the terrible heat, insects, and sickness at San Carlos? The soldiers could not live there. They are putting the Apaches there to die!"

"We can leave when we like," replied Massai. "Neither the soldiers nor Geronimo can hold us. We will talk to him."

Geronimo bade them to be patient and await his word.

I do not know how long they were at San Carlos. The hot summer weather was almost unendurable at that place, so it is probable that they slipped away at that time. Geronimo, with his band, usually left at the beginning of summer. When winter set in and his people needed clothing and blankets, he brought them back. The White Eyes gave them some food, but never enough. All the while Geronimo was scheming, planning, and recruiting men for his band, getting ammunition from the soldiers.

At San Carlos Massai married a Chiricahua girl and they had two children. He paid this girl's father with horses, as an Apache should. She became the friend of Gray Lizard and welcomed him to their tepee as Chiricahuas do.

Geronimo had demanded that his people be removed from San Carlos and finally got them settled at Turkey Creek, near Fort Apache. That was a mountainous country, with good water and grass and plenty of game. The band planted corn and raised crops, and for a time things were peaceful and pleasant. But the Chiricahua scouts constantly stirred up trouble with the people on the reservation. They lied to Chihuahua and Naiche; they told Geronimo that he was to be hanged. Geronimo took his warriors and left. My father stayed with his family. He did not join in the fighting that followed.

Once a week a member of each family went to the agency for supplies. Orders were issued to bring everybody, and this made the Indians suspicious. But they went to the agency, unarmed, and mounted soldiers herded them like cattle into the corral. Then they were put into wagons and hauled north to Holbrook, in Navajo country. There they were driven onto the train and told that they were en route to Florida to join Geronimo, who also had been captured. Chihuahua and many Warm Springs Apaches had also been shipped to Florida. All Chiricahuas were to be sent as prisoners to Florida, whether or not they had been at war with the soldiers. The scouts too were herded aboard the train, headed for exile in Florida. So did the White Eyes reward those Apaches who had betrayed their own people.

From the first moment he was aboard the train Massai was planning to escape. Massai's wife knew that she could not leave the children and escape with her husband, but she urged Massai, and Gray Lizard, to attempt it.

"We will have to loosen the bars on the window when the guards are not close at hand," Massai said. "We will have to choose a time to escape when the train is going up a long slope. Like a horse it will have to slow down. We cannot jump off with it going like the wind, on the level or downhill."

There seemed to be no place suited for the escape attempt, yet they spent three days cautiously loosening the bars when the guards' backs were turned. Then one morning Massai saw low mountains in the east. They were, he guessed, almost a day's journey away. That evening, if ever, he and Gray Lizard must make the attempt to leave the train.

A Chiricahua scout went through the car. A prisoner himself, he taunted the other prisoners. "When you get to Florida, the soldiers will chop your necks

251

off," he gloated. "All who wear red handkerchiefs around their heads will have their necks chopped."

"You wear a red *cord*," retorted Massai. "If the soldiers do not get you first, I will strangle you with it!"

All the scouts wore the red head cord.

When food was brought at noon Massai pretended to eat, but he concealed most of his portion in his breechclout. His wife gave him her share; she would get more that night. Gray Lizard, too, did not eat.

The train began laboring up the slope, moving more and more slowly as it climbed. Massai looked for a place where there was much vegetation in which he could hide. They came to clumps of bushes, with rocks. The train slowed almost to a stop, and Massai and Gray Lizard slipped through the window and dropped to the ground. They rolled down the slope into the thick brush and lay still. Neither was hurt. The train did not stop. They saw it disappear over the hill, then they wriggled through the vegetation to thicker shelter and hid there until dark. Then they walked toward the low mountains to the southwest and by morning had crossed the little valley and were halfway up the slope. There they ate, drank, and slept.

They had hoped to find Indians on those mountains, but they saw no sign of any but white people. When they came near a log cabin they circled around it. They avoided lights until they saw the smoke of a campfire. That might indicate Indians, so they crept close enough to the blaze to smell mutton cooking and coffee boiling. That night, instead of moving on, they lay hidden near the camp.

At daybreak they saw that the campers were white men and suspected that they were miners. If so, they would leave the camp during the day, leaving their supplies unguarded.

Massai and Gray Lizard watched the three men cook breakfast. They could smell the *coche* frying, and the odor made their mouths water. Finally the men finished their breakfast, took their picks and shovels, and went up the mountain.

When they were out of sight, Massai led the way to the camp. There was cold mutton and bread, and even some hot coffee left in the pot. Best of all, there were rifles. Massai and Gray Lizard each took a .30-30 and all the ammunition they could find. They took cartridge belts and two knives. They cut meat from a sheep hanging in a tree and put the food in flour sacks. Each carried one.

They headed ever toward the west, walking until they were tired and hungry, traveling mostly at night until they were out of the wooded country. Still sleeping or resting during the day, they moved on at night through open country. They found a trail where the deer came to water and killed one. They took all the meat they could carry and buried the rest. The stomach of the deer was cleaned for use as a water bag.

I do not know how long it took them to get back to Río Pecos, but it was a long time. Gray Lizard, who was carrying the water, fell against a prickly pear and tore a hole in the bag. Now they had no water, but they kept moving. They hoped to kill an antelope but did not see any although they were in antelope country.

Massai was making medicine, and so was Gray Lizard. And Ussen heard, for soon a heavy rain began to fall. They made a hole in the ground to catch it.

252

After drinking all the water they could, they kept walking to the west. Their guide was the Dipper, for Indians know the stars and use them for directions.

Finally they came to the Pecos. They recognized it by the bad taste of the water. Now they were sure that they were not far from Mescalero country. Next morning they saw a dark cloud looming to the southwest, a cloud that they gradually recognized as distant mountains. The Capitans! They were almost to Apache country. They prayed to Ussen, thanking Him for giving them the strength and courage to reach their homeland. That is the Apache way. There are many who make medicine when they need help, but few who remember to thank Him later, even for saving their lives.

In the Capitans they stopped for a day's badly needed rest, for they knew that the White Eyes could not catch them there. Later they killed a deer and feasted. Some time later they crossed Capitan Gap and saw the beautiful White Mountain.

"It is not far now to Mescal Mountain," said Gray Lizard. "We can make it easily."

"It is there that the soldiers will look for me," Massai said. "I will stay on the White Mountain, at least until the search is ended."

"It will never end," said Gray Lizard. "Our people are there. You want to see your parents, don't you?"

"Yes, but I do not want to be captured and sent away."

"Nor do I. But the scouts said that all but the Chiricahuas are to be turned loose. I am Tonkawa and they will not take me."

"Go to your people, then, if you are so sure that you will not be hunted. I will stay on White Mountain until the search is ended."

But Gray Lizard persisted. "The White Eyes will not know how you look. Your wife said that after our escape she would tell the guards that you are a big tall man like Naiche when they called your name and you did not answer. Maybe that will keep the White Eyes from finding you."

"Perhaps," replied Massai wearily. "But I will stay here awhile. We will go to the north of the White Mountain, and around to the west side. There we will part. I hope that some day we may meet and again be as brothers."

The next day they divided the food and ammunition and filled their new deer-stomach water bag for Gray Lizard. They prayed to Ussen for their reunion and then, in the Apache custom, they embraced and parted.

M assai stood on the slope above Three Rivers and watched Gray Lizard walk away toward the White Sands. He would go, he knew, by the Malpais Spring and our sacred peak in the San Andreas. Then, since he was not a Chiricahua, Gray Lizard would be safe with our people at Mescal Mountain. But Massai would be an exile hunted like an animal as long as he lived.

Heavy-hearted, Massai climbed the ridge of the White Mountain and descended the slope into the Rinconada. It was well named, for it is so secluded that to this day few people have seen that beautiful valley, nestled high on the peak.

In the Rinconada there is a little stream, grass, piñons, mesquite, and greasewood. Game abounded there. Difficult to reach from any point, it was a good place for Massi to hide. He found a cave near a little pool where the deer came to drink and began preparing for winter. He knew that he was not out of danger even in this wild, lonely spot, for Fort Stanton was only a few miles away and the cavalrymen liked to hunt. The report of his rifle might disclose his hiding place to a wandering hunter, so he made a bow and arrows for killing deer. He dried meat and tanned hides until he had a good supply. He was free—but terribly lonely. He knew that he would never see his wife and children again and also that his wife would think him dead and marry again.

So it was with great happiness that he saw the ripening of the piñons that fall. Piñons bear perhaps one year out of four or five, but that fall there was a big crop. Massai knew that the Mescaleros would come to harvest them. They were Apaches and his brothers. They would not betray his presence to the soldiers unless they happened to be scouts. He would recognize the scouts by the red head cords and ammunition belts they wore. Badly as he needed ammunition, he would not kill a scout unless attacked. Even if a scout were ambushed and killed silently with arrow or knife, his comrades would miss him and track down his slayer.

One morning from his lookout ledge, Massai saw Mescalero women and children riding up on horseback to camp only a short distance from his cave. For three days he watched, but no men joined them. He had food, but the smell of their boiling coffee tantalized him. More than anything else, he craved association with his people. Finally, on an evening when he could stand his loneliness no longer, he slipped quietly toward the camp.

Two women sat by the fire. Little children, wrapped in their blankets, lay with their feet toward the warmth. One of the women was telling them the legends of their people. The scene was so sweet and homelike that Massai felt his eyes mist and a lump come into his throat. He called to the women. They stood in alarm, and the children sat up in their blankets.

"Do not be afraid," he said softly. "I will not harm you."

He arose and walked toward them. When they saw that he was an Apache they were not afraid. The children smiled and the women stood with shyly downcast eyes.

"Will my brother sit and eat?" invited one of the women.

"I have eaten, but I have not tasted coffee for a long time."

She poured the hot liquid into a gourd and handed it to him. He drank slowly, enjoying the delicious flavor.

"Enjuh!" he said. "I cannot say how good it tastes."

Then he sat across the fire from the women and visited with them. They were sisters who had come to gather piñons. There were no White Eyes in that place, so they had nothing to fear.

"You are brave women; don't you fear strange Apaches?"

One of the women, the wife of Big Mouth, smiled and shook her head. "Now that my brother is close, we feel very safe."

Nor was there reason for them to fear Apaches, even strange Apaches; for they did not molest women. Other bad things they sometimes did, but they did not molest women. Not even white women.

When Massai rose to leave, they gave him all the coffee they had brought. He thanked them and left. As he went back to his cave, he thought of the women and of his lonely life and tried to put the thought out of his mind. He knew, too, that they would not betray him to the White Eyes.

He did not come again to their camp, nor did he visit any of the others who

254

came to harvest the piñon nuts. Nor did he hunt while they were there. But when he thought that all had left the Rinconada, he took his rifle and concealed himself at the pool where the deer came to drink. He concealed himself and waited.

Massai may have slept, for a splash in the pool suddenly alerted him. Three young women were bathing in it. He did not move, for according to age-old tribal law spying upon women was punishable by death. Yet he watched fascinated as the girls bathed; they got out of the water, dressed, and took down their long hair and braided it. An idea possessed Massai. Already he had forfeited his life; he would take one of these young women. He jumped from his place of concealment and reached the startled girls.

"Come!" he ordered the first.

"Do not take me; my baby would die," she pleaded.

He turned to the next. She stood transfixed like a frightened deer, slender and beautiful, poised for flight. Her long braids swept the ground. Massai caught the end of one and motioned her to walk in front of him.

The others followed, pleading with him not to take her. He motioned them to leave. "Do not take her," one begged.

"Shall I take *you* instead?" he asked grimly.

They turned and fled.

With his rifle Massai motioned his captive on. They climbed to the mouth of the cave. He took the knife from her belt and tied her in the cave. Then he took food and water and placed them within reach of her.

"Here you will sleep tonight," he told her. "There are blankets to keep you warm."

He slept lying across the cave entrance that night. Awaking at sunrise, he lay for some time watching the sun brighten the east with its fiery glow and thinking out his future plans. Finally he arose, his mind made up.

Working quickly, Massai packed his supplies on a wild horse he had tamed, then returned to the cave, freed the girl, and motioned for her to make ready for travel.

Both walked beside the laden packhorse, heading up the trail and crossing the ridge between the Rinconada and Three Rivers. All that day they walked. Massai wanted to get beyond reach of pursuit that he knew would come. He took the winding trail between the White Sands and the Malpais, walking on the rock as much as he could. He knew that trail and where to find water. Late that night he tied up the girl and hobbled the horse, and they slept for a few hours.

Before daylight they took the trail again. In the foothills of the San Andreas was water; there they camped and rested. Massai tied the girl to a tree while he hunted, telling her that if she escaped he would follow and kill her.

During the journey she spoke only in answer to questions and then in monosyllables. After a week's traveling, Massai asked, "Have I mistreated you?"

She shook her head.

"Why, then, will you not talk to me?"

She raised her head to look him straight in the eyes. "You brought me by force. An Apache does not do that."

"Would you have come otherwise?"

"No!"

"Listen to me, then! It is true that I took you, but I have respected you.

255

Now, unless you continue the journey to my people willingly, I will give you the horse and food. You will be free to return to your home. If you go to my people, my mother will make the wedding feast for us. It is for you to decide."

She lowered her head.

"Which is it to be?" Massai's voice was stern, but she looked up into his eyes and saw what was in his heart.

"I will go with you," she murmured.

For the rest of the journey she rode the horse. She was happy, for, despite all, she now knew that Massai was a good man.

Massai's mother made the feast he had promised, so that all the people of Mescal Mountain knew that this was a marriage. There were no vows to be broken, as White Eyes do. To Apaches, marriage is a sacred thing—not to be lightly undertaken nor ended. And though Massai had a wife, though he might never see her again, there was no obstacle to his marriage. Such was the custom of my people.

And so they were married.

The years passed and my father and mother were very happy together— happier still when we children came. But still my father had to dodge the White Eyes, for the danger of discovery always threatened him. One dark day we fled Mescal Mountain to seek safety in the back country. Food was scarce on the trail; I remember clearly my father coming back to camp one day empty-handed. He carefully placed his bow and arrows beside the rifle he had left with my mother; then he seated himself with his back against a pine. I ran to him and nestled against his chest. He cuddled me in his strong arms and bent his head over mine.

"My little daughter, I brought no food. The deer have gone to the high mountains."

"You brought yourself; that is better."

"She speaks true, Massai," said Zan-a-go-li-che, my mother. "When you are with us we can endure hunger."

My father smiled tenderly at her. "You are a good wife, and my children are good. I am sorry that you must share my danger."

My mother's face was beautiful to see. "Danger, like happiness, is to be shared, my husband."

As she spoke, she slipped the *tsach* from her back and took the baby from it. My little brother was old enough to walk and he liked to be free of his cradle. Zan-a-go-li-che reached for the buckskin food bag and gave each of us one handful of pulverized dried venison and mesquite bean meal. We dared not build a fire, but this is a good food raw and is very nourishing. Though the portion did not satisfy our hunger, nobody asked for more. Each knew that when food was available there was no need to ask, for our mother fed us when she could.

My older brother, who was later named Albert, had brought a wicker jug of water from the spring. After we had drunk and lain on the ground, my father spoke.

"I should have left Mescal Mountain when the warnings first came. When Ussen speaks, the Apache should obey. He warned me first by the twitching of the eyelid that always means one is in danger. But I knew that old Santos [a

Mexican friend of the family] could not live long, and I would not leave him."

He was silent, staring into the darkness.

"Now the White Eyes are on our trail," he went on. "Two mornings past, when I went to the place where I had hidden the horses, a man tried to ambush me. Not till he raised his rifle was I sure that he had seen me. Then I had no choice—I had to kill him. You heard the shots and asked why I wasted bullets on a deer. It was not a deer; it was a man."

My mother spoke, "His horse?"

"It got away."

"It will go home and there will be soldiers on our trail from his place."

"Yes; sheriffs too, perhaps. Cowboys maybe—and those I dread more than any soldiers."

There was silence again for a long moment. "They cannot know who fired the shot," ventured my mother.

My father's laugh was short and bitter. "When has there been a White Eye killed west of the Río Bravo whose death has not been charged to Massai? When have I not been hunted like an animal?"

"But soldiers and Chiricahua scouts, too, came into our *ranchería* and did not find you, even though you were present when they inquired."

"They were looking for a tall man—one like Naiche—not for a short thin one like me."

"Why?"

"My friends, who were left on the train after my escape, must have told them that I was very large to protect me from being caught."

My mother said no more. After a time my father spoke again. "I must tell you that Ussen has again warned me. This time He has spoken clearly so that there can be no mistake.

"I am not to reach Mescalero; I may not reach the Río Bravo with you. But we are only one day's journey from the village of which I have told you."

He turned to Albert.

"My son, you are young to become the protector of your mother and the younger children. But you are well trained. Always I have foreseen the need and have made a brave of you, boy though you are. You are skillful with both bow and rifle. Bullets are swift and far-reaching, but arrows are silent and sure. Remember to use the rifle only when attacked by White Eyes. For game—the bow. It will obtain food for you."

"My father, I hear," replied Albert.

"I may not return in the morning. If I do not, take your mother and children to the Mexican village on the Río. Stay hidden in the brush until dark, for there may be White Eyes at that town. Watch for a house where there is no man, no big boy. Then, after dark, tap on the door and in the language of Santos ask for help.

"I have talked with those who know the place. The railroad crosses the river there on a trail built of logs. You too can cross that trail, no matter if the river is high. Hide by day and travel by night toward the Rising Sun till you reach the spring at the foot of the mountains. Your mother knows that place. Stay by the water until you can kill game. Then head for the White Mountain and skirt it to the south. There you will find a trail into the Rinconada. Your mother knows that place also."

I saw my mother's sad face light in a smile.

"From there she will guide you to her family. Stay on the Mescalero Reservation. It is my order."

"It will be obeyed, my father. But the horses?"

"You may not have the horses. The White Eyes cannot trail us, but they may be able to follow horses. I am telling you what to do if that happens."

My mother pulled the blanket over her face. My father went on, speaking quietly. "In the early morning I will go to the place where we hid the horses. You are to remain here. It is my order."

My brother bowed his head.

"If I do not return, my son, you are not to wait—you are to leave at once. It is safe to travel by day because of the dense undergrowth. Now we must sleep. I have spoken."

When I awoke it was still dark, but my mother was sitting up, listening.

"My brother," I whispered.

She laid her finger on my lips. "He followed your father. Hush."

I huddled close to her in fear and she drew me under her blanket. The others slept. Just as the first gray light stole into the east I heard a shot, then another, crashing loud in the stillness. My mother hugged me to her. She made no noise but her body shook.

It was daylight when I heard the light patter of moccasins. I touched my mother in the darkness. Soon my brother crept through the dense brush and joined us.

"They killed him?"

"I think so. The White Eyes had trailed the horses and were waiting for us. As he reached to untie his bay, there was a shot and he fell. Even as he did so he called to me to run. I did. I crossed the little hill and slid down the high steep bluff. Then I circled widely, walking on the rock ledge so that they might not be able to follow. Let us start now, as he commanded."

My mother shook her head. "He may not be dead. I cannot go until I know."

"They will be hunting for us. We must go!"

"Not even to save you children can I leave now. Take them and I will stay. Go to my people, as he told you. I do not fear death."

"But the baby! My sisters!"

"We will all stay. What does death mean, now that Massai is gone? I hope that he is dead. Death is better than being a captive of the White Eyes."

We lay in the thick brush at the edge of the mesa and watched. There was a camp in the canyon with many men and horses. Scouts left the camp, fanning out in all directions, some on horseback and some walking. Toward evening they came straggling back.

My mother again gave each of us a handful of our emergency rations. We drank from the jug; and with the remaining water mother bathed the baby, warming the water in her mouth and letting it trickle over his little body. Then she wiped him dry with soft, clean grass and packed him again in the *tsach*. He wore no clothing, but she covered him with the soft skin of a lynx before lacing the buckskin straps across him.

The White Eyes were building a big fire—a much bigger fire than was needed for cooking. It burned far into the night and must have been frequently replenished. Not even the White Eyes kept a big fire going all night. I wondered why these were so foolish. Twice I awakened to find my mother still sitting, still watching.

Next morning we could see nothing, for the canyon was filled with fog. When it lifted there were no White Eyes, no horses, and only a little smoke.

My mother spoke. "I will go down and see if I can find his body. It must have burial. No Apache would leave a relative or even a friend to the coyotes and vultures."

"But they may be waiting to ambush us," my brother objected.

"True. We must wait and keep careful watch all day. If we see nothing, we will risk going tomorrow."

"We are almost out of food," said my brother.

"Keep watch. I will try to find something."

"Let me try to kill a rabbit, mother."

"Are we animals, to eat raw meat? You know that we cannot cook it. No Apache would eat raw meat. There is still enough food for each to have a small bit. I will try to find some roots."

"Do not leave us, mother. On the way tomorrow we may find some cactus food."

She sat down beside us and covered her head.

That night we went to bed without eating; the food must be saved for morning so that we would have strength for the walk. We had water—and with that alone an Apache can endure much hunger.

My brother spoke again before we slept. "My father was a good man. Why did the White Eyes hate him, hunt him like a mad wolf, and finally kill him?"

"It is a hard thing to understand, my son. We cannot know why they want to kill all Apaches. Already they have robbed us of everything we had—our game, our land, our freedom. It was not enough. They want our lives also. That is all I can tell you."

"May I go with you to the camp, mother?"

"Yes, my son. Very early in the morning. Try to sleep now."

I think that my oldest sister was about twelve. (We kept no records, of course.) She kept the baby and us three younger girls while my mother and brother were gone. We did not ask to go. We did not cry. Apache children do not disobey, and they do not argue.

We huddled under the blankets until they returned. My mother carried a sack of meal and she gave each of us some of the food before she spoke. We ate it very slowly and when we had finished she gave us more.

"There is some for morning," she said.

We wanted to know about our father, but she did not tell us until later. They had approached the camp cautiously, even after they felt sure that there was no one there. They crept to the still-smoldering fire.

My mother took a long stick and stirred the ashes. There were partially burned sticks among them—and something else. Bones—charred bones. She raked them out of the ashes, laying them aside in a little heap. She tried to get every fragment. With them she found a small, blackened object—the buckle of an ammunition belt. She recognized the buckle by a dent made by a deflected bullet. She held it in her hands and talked to it.

"This is all I have left of you, my husband. All these years you took care of me and the children, and you were kind to us. Now you are nothing but bones and ashes.

"The White Eyes thought you a bad man, and they hunted you like an animal. They shot you down like a wild beast. They burned you so that in Ussen's land you would have no body. But Ussen knows all things and He can make you another body. To Apaches, the man who bravely defends his family, his home, and his people is a good man. He will not walk in darkness. To Ussen you are a good man. To me you are a good man, for I am an Apache. And I call to Ussen to avenge your death.

"I have nothing but this buckle and your memory. That is a good memory—one for your children to cherish. I have nothing to give your children but that memory, but it is enough. It will always give them courage. It will give them respect for the memory of their father.

"Right now your spirit may be here, listening. I cannot go with it on its journey, but always we will be with your memory."

She fastened the buckle to her belt with her knife and firesticks. Then she wrapped the bones carefully in her shawl, and she and Albert scooped out a hole with their hands and a sharp stone and buried what was left of my father there. They heaped stones upon the grave and left him to make The Journey. He had no horse, no weapons, not even a body. But Ussen would know that an Apache and a brave warrior came. Ussen would understand.[2]

We started toward the Río. My mother carried the baby on her back and the rifle in her hands. Albert went ahead with his bow and spear. My oldest sister had one blanket; the rest we had to leave, for we had no way to transport it. Cora had the water jug and the third girl the food bag. I walked till I was exhausted, and then they took turns carrying me for short distances. We kept on the ridge as long as we could, and then we stole from one clump of vegetation to another until we got near the village. We hid in a big clump of underbrush near San Marcial while my brother crept close and scouted the place.

He was gone about an hour; it was dark when he returned.

"There is one White Eye family at the tepee where the train stops," he reported. "The rest are Mexican. There are men at every house but one—that of an old woman at this edge of the *ranchería*."

"We go to that tepee," said my mother, "and ask for help."

When we tapped on the door a voice asked, "*¿Quién es?*"

---

2. The buckle was given to me for safekeeping by Alberta Begay. In a letter to this author dated April 2, 1957, Mrs. Evelyn Dahl, who carried out years of research on the Apache Kid, stated in part:

> The men of the posse who killed Massai were Harry James, Bill Keene, Mike Sullivan, Walter Hearn, and Burt Slinkard. Ed James, Harry's younger brother, caught up with the party but would never admit who actually did the decapitating. Ed James died in '51 or '52. His last letter to me was in March '49. The height and weight he gives were a guess as the man was dead by the time he joined the party but James himself was 36 at the time. Bob Lewis, a sergeant in the first company of the Mounted Police, told me in 1950 before he died that fall, that he rode into the yard at Chloride one day shortly after the killing and found Bill Keene boiling the head in an iron vat. Both of them were sick at the stomach. When I asked Bob if the men had buried the body he said, "Hell no."

For other accounts of the Massai story see Miles, *Personal Recollections,* p. 529; Paul Wellman, *Death in the Desert* (New York: Macmillan Co., 1935), p. 454; and Betzinez, *Geronimo,* pp. 144–45.

In Spanish, mother replied: "A woman and children, cold and hungry."
The door opened.
"*Pasen,*" said the old woman.

Z an-a-go-li-che and her children were welcome in the Mexican woman's home, but there was no food but shelled corn and very little of that. Zan-a-go-li-che knew that the family, as big as it was, could neither stay at the woman's home nor attempt the long journey to Mescalero. Therefore, with the Mexican woman's help homes for three of the girls were found with other Mexican families. The fourth, Alberta, was placed with the white agent and his wife who lived in the second story of the railway station. Alberta was approximately four years old at the time.

Zan-a-go-li-che, with the baby boy in a cradle on her back and the oldest boy, crossed the river on the railroad track and set out on foot for Mescalero.

About thirty miles east they found a spring of which the mother had known and there they camped, hoping that animals might come there to drink. The older son had a rawhide lariat, and when the wild horses came for water he dropped a loop around the neck of one. It dragged him a long distance before choking down. He partially hobbled it and led it back to the waterhole. They tied a rawhide thong around its lower jaw and alternately walked and rode the rest of the distance to Mescalero.

The three went directly to the home of Marion Simms, Zan-a-go-li-che's brother, but he did not recognize her until she related incidents of their childhood. Then he took her and the two children to the agency and told Mr. Carroll the whereabouts of the four little girls.

Because Marion spoke English well, Mr. Carroll took him to Tularosa and bought a round-trip ticket to San Marcial by way of El Paso. When he arrived there the Mexican woman who had first taken them in told where to find the missing children. Each of the Mexican families courteously returned its charge to him. But when he went to the railway station, the agent, the only white man in town, refused to let him have Alberta. He said that they had no children and had become greatly attached to the little girl. Moreover, they had incurred considerable expense for her in the way of food and clothing. The child begged to go to her mother and they finally decided that if Simms would pay her expenses he could take her. He had less than ten dollars—money given him by Carroll for food. Having no alternative, he gave every penny to the couple and boarded the train with Alberta.

Zan-a-go-li-che, now reunited with her children, took all to the Mescalero agency to be enrolled. Mrs. Jefferis, wife of the clerk, happened to be in the office. The mother and children seated themselves on the floor in a circle and, while Simms was interpreting information as to approximate age and name of each, Mrs. Jefferis noticed that one by one they were, as surreptitiously as they could, taking and eating bits of food from a buckskin emergency bag. She walked around the circle and found that the starved children were eating dried grasshoppers.

CHAPTER 11

RETURN OF THE MESCALERO EXILES

Owing to nationwide publicity regarding the arbitrary imprisonment of nonhostile Apaches, particularly those who were not Chiricahua, perhaps as a token gesture a few were allowed to go home in 1889. Principal among them were those Mescalero Apaches who had been kidnapped in a Chiricahua raid under Geronimo prior to his surrender in 1886.

One of them was Ih-tedda, the girl Geronimo had selected from those kidnapped and taken as his wife. When the offer to free the Mescaleros was learned by Geronimo, he ordered Ih-tedda and their two-year-old daughter, Lenna, to return to her parents at the Mescalero Reservation in New Mexico. She begged to remain with her husband, but he stated, "Any minute we may all be shot. There is no reason why you and our daughter should lose your lives. You must return to Mescalero." Ih-tedda and Lenna, along with the others freed, left for New Mexico by train, accompanied by a soldier and his wife.

When an Apache wife returned to the home of her mother, she was automatically divorced and free to remarry. A few days later her parents, against her wishes, married her to Old Cross Eyes, a retired scout with a pension of eight dollars a month. From that time she was called Katie Cross Eyes; her husband became Old Boy.

Katie gave birth to a son soon after and registered his name at the agency as Robert Cross Eyes. Fifteen years later Robert was sent to the Indian school at Chilocco, Oklahoma, still with the name of Cross Eyes. Later, however, Katie requested that his name be changed to Robert Geronimo. When Chilocco students from Fort Sill came home for the Christmas holidays, they reported that there was a boy at Chilocco who claimed to be the son of Geronimo. Daklugie wrote to the agency at Mescalero for the dates of Katie's return, of her marriage to Cross Eyes, and of Robert's birth. When Geronimo received the information he said, "Well, he *could be* my son."

During the following summer Robert went to Geronimo's home at Fort Sill, but it was not long until Daklugie was asked to take the boy and care for him. Ramona consented and there was a pleasant relationship for a time. That relationship came to an end when, in Daklugie's absence, Robert took out his host's fine racing horse and rode it to death. Daklugie went to Eugene Chihuahua to secure a home for the boy. His reply was, "Ask the lady of the house." Viola assented, and Robert lived with them until Eugene sent him to Carlisle.

Robert lived with the Chihuahuas again when he returned from Carlisle and after the Fort Sill Apaches had moved to Mescalero. With them he remained until he married.[1]

Another Apache family imprisoned with the Chiricahuas was released in 1887. The father was Charlie Smith, a scout imprisoned with the Fort Apache group. Charlie, born a Chiricahua, married a Mescalero and, according to custom, joined the Mescalero tribe. The mother and son, Cumpah and young Charlie Smith, were those who had been kidnapped with Ih-tedda by Geronimo's warriors before their surrender in 1886. The family was reunited when the families in the prisoner group with Geronimo at Fort Pickens were combined with the prisoners from Fort Marion.

Charlie Smith and his family returned to their home at White Tail. Charlie, now called Alabama Charlie, died there. Charlie Smith, Jr., after his father's death, became the hunter for his mother and the younger children. Ammunition was expensive and had to be used sparingly. When asked if it was true that he took only one bullet when he went hunting he replied, "I need only one deer." Charlie killed mountain lions, and the still more dangerous lobos, also with one shot.

He attended the Indian school at Albuquerque and was a very apt pupil. During a summer vacation he met and married the beautiful daughter of Muchacho Negro. His father-in-law was considered the most formidable man on the reservation. Many Apaches feared him, and the fact that Charlie had his friendship is indicative of his tact and forbearance.

During the Pershing campaign in Mexico Charlie served as a scout until he was captured by Mexican cavalry. It was over a year before an exchange of prisoners enabled him to return to his regiment. Considering the tradition of hatred between Apaches and the Mexicans, he was lucky to be alive.

In the army he was famous for his marksmanship. In one shooting match the contestants were to fire five shots each. They drew numbers to determine the order of competing. After two soldiers had fired five shots each, Charlie took his place. Each of his bullets hit the bull's eye. The fourth contestant, Captain Bradley, shook his head and declined to compete. It was impossible, he said, to beat a perfect score.

Fifty years later when General Omar Bradley visited Fort Bliss, he learned that Charlie, his former scout, was still living and made a trip to Mescalero to see him. "That" said Charlie, "was the proudest day of my life."

Charlie served on the Mescalero police force and shortly became chief. He was small, quiet, unassuming, and very intelligent, and he was a very efficient

1. When I came to Ruidoso in 1949 I learned that, after the death of Cross Eyes, Katie had been cared for in the hospital because there were no homes available for the elderly at that time. Through the courtesy of a nurse (Apache) who interpreted for me, I got Katie's brief but concise account of her abduction, of her marriages to Geronimo and Cross Eyes, and of Robert.

Top, *Ih-tedda;* bottom left, *Lenna;* bottom right, *Robert Geronimo.*

Lenna Geronimo.

officer. When asked if in the line of duty he had ever been forced to kill any-one he replied, "If I had to shoot I aimed at the arm, and I never even broke a bone."

When questioned as to the laws by which he judged the accused—those of the federal government or the unwritten ones of the Apaches—he said, "You know that in some cases the two conflict. If an Apache wife is unfaithful her husband must kill her or cut the tip of her nose off. White Eye law punishes a man who does either; Apache law ostracizes the one who does neither. Some cases, such as murder, are not subject to the jurisdiction of the tribal court but are tried by a federal judge in Santa Fe. In minor offenses I used our own laws. And I never had much trouble."

Charlie retired from police duty to become judge of the tribal court and served in that capacity for several years before asking to be relieved.

After the death of his first wife Charlie married Aggie, daughter of Tiss-nolthos, one of Geronimo's bravest warriors. They lived at White Tail until all but one other family had moved their houses to the village. At eight thousand feet winters are cold and at times snow is very deep. Charlie was pressured to permit his house to be moved to a site on Highway 70 about three miles from Mescalero. There, despite their protests, he and Aggie were provided with propane heat and electricity. Though they soon adjusted to the latter, they preferred to burn wood.[2] But they were not as happy as when living in their old home. Both loved the seclusion and type of living almost as free as it had been before they had been taken to Florida.

There Charlie hunted and took others after game. There he roamed through the forest and explored the caves. Near Pajarit Spring he found the fallen stones of a crudely constructed wall obviously built for defense. Obviously too, as numerous cartridges indicated, there had been a skirmish with U.S. troops. In a cave nearby, Charlie found an old Spanish sword. "That was the best knife I ever saw," he said. "It would bend double without breaking." When asked if Spanish soldiers could have been there he responded, "Don't know. It might have been put there by an Apache who killed one."[3]

Charlie Smith had worked with Dan Nicholas in collecting and translating the coyote stories and many other Apache legends into English. These were used in Henry Hoijer's *The Apache Lists*. Nicholas mastered the International Code so that the texts might appear on one column of the page in the Apache language, with English on the other.

"For all that work," said Charlie, "we were paid twenty-five cents an hour and got one sentence in the book."

When asked if he was the primary source used by Morris E. Opler in his *An Apache Life-way*, Charlie responded affirmatively but stated that other individuals had also been consulted. He also responded that he was "Chris" in Opler's biographical and anthropological study *An Apache Odyssey*. "But I did not tell

---

2. Once when I took some students of history to meet Aggie and Charlie we found him seated on top of his small, potbellied wood stove in the living room. When suffering from arthritis he placed a cushion on the warm stove and sat on it, and the warmth considerably relieved the aching. When given an electric heating pad he was at first afraid to use it because he thought it might set the bed on fire.

3. Daklugie said of Charlie's account: "It could have been a Toledo blade. I had one that I got in a cave out of Casa Grande. The Mexicans said that it was from Toledo."

him nor anybody else the things that are in that book. Apaches do not discuss their private lives with anybody." He was obviously annoyed but explained, "There were several people working here at that time—scientists, I believe they called themselves. It is possible that some White Eye down at the village told them that stuff. But one thing is sure: I did not."[4]

---

4. Morris E. Opler, *An Apache Life-way . . .* (Chicago: University of Chicago Press, 1941); and *Apache Odyssey, A Journey Between Two Worlds* (New York: Holt, Rinehart and Winston, 1969).

CHAPTER 12

LAST OF THE LIPANS

PHILEMON VENEGO

Though I live on the Mescalero Apache Reservation, I am a Lipan. We were that branch of the Apaches who roamed, for the greater part of the time, east of the Río Pecos and claimed all of that land to the Gulf of Mexico. Our rights were disputed by other tribes, especially the Comanches, Kiowas, and Wichitas, and also by many living in what is now Texas.*

You knew Chief Magoosh's son, Willie, and his grandchildren, Richard and Willie, Jr.? But the chief was dead before you came. He was a great and good leader—and the only bald Apache I ever saw. There were people who thought that he had been scalped, but that wasn't true. Why no hair grew on his head I don't know. He was like White Eyes in that respect—some White Eyes. When my people first saw them they thought them queer and repulsive because instead of having hair where it should grow they had it on their faces and bodies, just like animals. But what impressed them most, of course, was the whites in their eyes. We don't have that; our eyes are coffee-colored where yours are white. That is how you got your name White Eyes.

Magoosh was a great chief. He could go for days without food and people said that when he returned from the warpath he could eat a whole "ship" [sheep]. I never saw him do that; and, anyway, they might have been smaller than the "ship" we have now.

As a boy, Magoosh witnessed the fall of the Alamo. The Lipans were in sympathy with the White Eyes in that fight and would have helped the besieged men if they had been able.

---

*Philemon Venego, a Lipan Apache approximately seventy-five or seventy-six years of age, from whom much of this information was obtained from a series of interviews over a period of over twenty years, both at White Tail on the Mescalero Apache Reservation and at my home in Ruidoso, New Mexico. Prior to hearing this story from Philemon Venego, I had learned of it from May Second, daughter of the last Mescalero chief, Peso. It had been told her by Rose Tee (Tahnito), a Lipan who had married a Chiricahua, John Tahnito, the tribal judge for several years. Numerous others also provided information, among them Willie Magoosh, Dan Nicholas, James Kaywaykla, Daklugie, Eugene Chihuahua, Bessie Ibarra (daughter of Antone Apache), Mrs. James A. Carroll, Mrs. Ted J. Sutherland, Clarence Enjady, and Jennie Carillo.

Magoosh, Chief of the Lipans.   (Eve Ball Collection)

Willie Magoosh, son of Magoosh.   (Eve Ball Collection)

Some years after the Alamo the Lipans suffered an epidemic of smallpox. It was in a very virulent form, and few who took it survived. Philemon said that it was almost the only form of illness the Apaches knew. How they got it his people did not know, but they were sure that it was from the Mexicans. When they killed an enemy they used none of the victim's clothing except the ammunition belt (for which they sometimes killed) and the shirt. They suspected that the illness might have been occasioned by their wearing these shirts.

Their Medicine Men could do little or nothing for the victim of smallpox. But they realized that if the groups remained together there probably would be more deaths than if they separated. Magoosh held a council and it was decided that the Lipans should divide into small bands, each to be under the command of a leader or headman and composed of relatives. "Venego, my father," said Philemon, "was to be in charge of ours. Arrangements were made that, when and if the sickness ceased, we were to reassemble when and where the chief should select a time and place."

Venego's band went south to the Rio Grande, crossed it, and settled in the mountains near Zaragosa, a small Mexican village down the river from El Paso. There they lived on relatively friendly terms with the natives. Though there was not much contact, there was no enmity. The Mexicans hunted in the mountains but lived in small villages near water. During the years of their stay in Mexico, the Lipans acquired some of the habits and beliefs of their neighbors, especially in the field of witchcraft. All Apaches believed in it, but perhaps not to the same extent as the Mexicans among whom the Lipans lived.

Then came an occurrence that materially added to the already firm superstition regarding bears. Belief that the spirit of the wicked is sometimes reincarnated in the body of a bear was a part of the primitive religion of the Apache, and they killed the animal ordinarily only as they might a human being, in self-defense.

A Mexican woman started up the mountain to gather healing herbs. She failed to return to her village, and her family and neighbors went to look for her. They made an extensive search for several days before finding her. Except for being weary and frightened, she had suffered no harm. She told them that she had been captured by a bear. When it charged from a thicket she had run, but she was overtaken and caught by the animal. She fully expected to be killed, but instead the bear pushed and shoved her up the mountain trail to a cave. The entrance was very low and the animal forced her to wriggle through it on hands and knees. Inside, it was so dark that she could see very little. The bear did not follow her but began pushing heavy stones against the opening so that she could not get out. She feared that it might leave her there to starve, but it left and brought fruit of the cacti to her. The rich juice satisfied her thirst and the pulp her hunger. Part of her barricade had been removed when the animal gave her food, and she thought that she might be able to push aside another stone and escape. Cautiously she wriggled through the passage only to find the bear on guard outside.

Each morning the animal checked the barricade before leaving and each evening it brought fresh food to her. After having been a prisoner for about a week, one morning after the bear's departure she heard voices—Mexican voices. She crept as near the exit as she could and called loudly. The voices came closer and at each call she answered. After an agonizing wait, a man she recognized came into her view. He ran toward her with others following him, and they released her. It was almost sundown when they reached her village. At the outskirts they discovered that the bear was following them. In spite of their taboos, they killed the bear.

Through Antone Apache, a bachelor, and the Villas (a Lipan family), the Lipans learned of this episode, and it was a means of drawing them into a friendship with the Mexican people of the village. It was possibly through these Mexicans, some of whom had men in the army, that Antone Apache learned that many years ago, before the War between the States waged by the White Eyes, Magoosh had taken the few remaining members of his band to join the Mescaleros. There was a vague rumor to the effect that they were living in southern New Mexico on a reservation—nobody knew exactly where. Antone Apache felt that he, the only unmarried man, was the one who should attempt to locate their chief and his people and, if possible, take those in Mexico to join their brothers.

In order to avoid a second trip, it was agreed that if he did not return within two moons those in the group with him were to attempt to follow. But what if he should be killed en route? He would not, he assured them. They were to come northwest, a long distance. When they reached the Pecos they would recognize it by the taste and effect of its waters. Once across the Pecos they should look in the mountains for their people. Had not the Apache always sought refuge in the mountains?

Antone Apache had been gone less than a month when Mexican cavalry swooped down upon the camp of the Lipans for the purpose of impressing them into military service. They were especially eager to secure Venego, but he eluded them. To their surprise they did not conscript any of the others but threatened the Lipans with severe punishment if their leader did not surrender.

Meanwhile, Antone Apache, who had never seen a map and who had not left Mexico since the band had gone there, unaided and traveling by night, found the Pecos; and a little later he arrived at the Mescalero Apache Reservation. There he remained in hiding, watching eagerly for a glimpse of someone he might recognize. The first positive identification he made was of Chief Magoosh. Because they wore nothing except headbands, moccasins, and breechclouts, he had no difficulty in identifying the chief: surely there could not be two bald Apaches. Nevertheless, Antone Apache did not make his presence known to Magoosh until he had an opportunity to approach him when he was alone. Then another difficulty arose: the chief did not recognize him! That he overcame by giving the Apache distress signal, which no Apache dares ignore. Magoosh took the man to his camp and learned of the location and problems of his people. They were, Antone Apache said, barely surviving and were in constant danger of conscription by the Mexican army. Could they be brought to join their chief and their brothers at Mescalero?

Magoosh was hopeful that they could. Their agent, James A. Carroll, he said, though an Indah, was a good and honest one. The Mescaleros considered him to be the best they had ever had. Magoosh had hopes that Carroll would understand the desire of the Lipans to be united with their friends and relatives in New Mexico and make arrangements for their being admitted as members of the reservation.

The confidence of the Lipan chief was rewarded by the agent's writing to Washington for permission to bring the missing band of Lipans to the reservation. But a decision was so long in coming that Carroll, weary of the delay, took matters into his own hands. It was charged that he ruled the Mescalero Apache Reservation as though it had been his own principality, but his worst attackers conceded that he ruled it to the advantage of the Indians.

Carroll consulted Father Migeon, parish priest at Tularosa, who sometimes came to the reservation and said mass in the Carroll home. Father Migeon was fluent in Spanish. He wrote to the governor of Chihuahua and asked that the band of Lipans be permitted to leave Chihuahua and come to the Mescalero Apache Reservation. Terrazas replied that not only would he be glad to be rid of them but that he would furnish the transportation. He added that the Lipans had been removed from Zaragosa to Chihuahua.

Carroll hastily provided the young priest with funds for rail fare, food, and clothing for the band and sent him to Chihuahua City. Upon his arrival, Father Migeon found the wretched prisoners, thirty-seven in number, in a corral at the outskirts of the city. They were being treated like cattle under guard in filthiness with no shelter and little in the way of clothing or covering. They were fed ears of corn, thrown to them as to animals, which they ate raw because there was no wood.

Among the prisoners was Venego, father of Philemon, under pressure to join the Mexican cavalry as scout. This he absolutely refused to do, even though he was promised that his people would go free if he did so.

Father Migeon secured an audience with the governor and he was successful in getting this condition removed. He was also promised that transportation to the border would be provided for all the following day. With the money thus saved the priest spent the day securing more food and clothing for the band. He also bought blankets for all. What his emotions were when the Lipans were herded into a cattle car is not a matter of record, but he decided to accompany them. The train crew insisted upon his occupying the caboose with them, and he accepted their offer gratefully.

Upon their arrival in Juarez, he presented the *conducta* of the governor and was allowed to cross the International Bridge unimpeded and enter El Paso. There he purchased passenger-car tickets for the train bound for Tularosa.

PHILEMON VENEGO

I remember the trip well. I was about nine or ten years old, I think, and understood that we were to see our relatives and friends and have a home on the reservation. When we got off the train, there were Apaches with wagons at the station to meet us. We did not recognize our relatives but they made themselves known to us. How glad our people were to see each other! Men embraced with tears streaming down their faces.

When we got to Mescalero, the Nantan, Mr. Carroll, through his interpreter José Carillo, made a talk to us. He told us that if we would keep the peace and be good Indians we were to have the privileges of the other Apaches already there and to share equally with our brothers, the Mescaleros, who were giving us the rights they enjoyed. We were to be safe and happy. If we had grievances we were to report them first to Chief Magoosh and then to him.

And now, how many of us are left? You know that it is the mother who determines the membership in the tribe. Husband and children belong to her band. Among our people there were few girl children. Rose Tee had none; and there were no girls among the Mendez family. There were boys, yes; but their children are not Lipans. Now there are my mother and me; I do not think of a dozen others.

We are the last of the Lipans.

CHAPTER 13

ARRIVAL OF THE
CHIRICAHUA EXILES

DAKLUGIE

A t last it had come—the hope for a permanent home, a home among our brothers, a home where we could be free, a home where we could go to mountains and pray to Ussen as our ancestors had done and as our mothers had taught us to do.

We were too well acquainted with the broken promises of the federal government to believe anything its executives told us. In addition to the characteristic hypocrisy of the White Eyes they had the queer custom of changing chiefs every four years. It takes that long or longer for a man to learn how to be a chief. Perhaps they were still trying to find one they could respect and trust. Perhaps they never will. That's the way it looked to me.

But we could trust the Mescaleros. We were not the first homeless band to which they had given refuge. When the Lipans sought a home they took Magoosh and his people and gave them equal rights with themselves. They did the same for Natzili and his people when the buffalo herds were exterminated. And though the Jicarillas far outnumbered them, they welcomed and kept them until they were moved to northern New Mexico.

We looked forward to this move as did the Hebrews to the Promised Land. And though we thought that the one-fifth of our people who chose to accept land for themselves in Oklahoma and become independent of the federal government were making a great mistake, we recognized their right to make that decision.

Hardest of all was forsaking our beloved dead. Quietly we visited the resting places of our people for a last farewell. We knew that they were in the Happy Place, awaiting our coming. We knew that they understood and that they approved of our leaving.

We were informed that the train that was to take us to Tularosa, New Mexico, was a combination one. That meant that it had freight as well as passenger cars. It also had facilities for cooking.

Nearly every family had a team and wagon. Some had agricultural imple-

273

ments and all had some household equipment. Those with more than could be hauled at one load could store their possessions in freight cars while they returned to their deserted houses for the rest. The teams, cow ponies, and wagons were loaded last.

We were en route only one night.[1] And true to their promise, Mr. Jefferis, the Agent at Mescalero, and Ted Sutherland, first superintendent of livestock, met us at the station.

We had been forbidden to take dogs; but when the doors were opened, they simply poured off those cars. Perhaps the train crew, too, loved them.[2]

Thankful though I had been at our liberation, I had misgivings on some subjects: though we hated White Eyes and their life-way in general, we had been in contact with them for twenty-seven years and had learned to like and adopt some of their customs. We had found houses comfortable and convenient. And we had gladly conformed to their standards of cleanliness.

On my visit to Mescalero four years previous, I had found the people living as primitively as we had before being forced into captivity. They still used tepees. There were few who attempted to conform to our standards of cleanliness. They still ran sheep, and we exceedingly disliked sheep.

We camped at the village not far from the agency. For a few days, being reunited with our brothers and visiting with them kept our people occupied. But soon they came to Eugene and me and asked that our band have a place of its own, apart from the Mescaleros, where we could have houses and run cattle. True, we brought none; but we could buy them. We did not want to herd sheep, but for a while we did.[3]

Mr. Jefferis was reasonable and understanding. He had been chief clerk under James A. Carroll, and he wisely followed Mr. Carroll's practices. He told us to ride over the reservation (nearly a half-million acres) and select a place for our village. With all who wished to participate, Naiche, Eugene, and I did so; and we chose to make our homes at White Tail, about twenty-three miles from Mescalero and about eight thousand feet high.

Every man of our band except Chato went. Greatly to our relief, he stopped at Apache Summit, about ten miles east of Mescalero. He knew that he was unwelcome with us and equally so with the Mescaleros. How they knew that we regarded him as a traitor I do not know, but they did.

Accustomed as I had been to the damp, penetrating wind at Fort Sill, I did not know that the still, dry cold of the mountains would be less serene than I anticipated.

What with every family except that of Chato provided with a tent of heavy canvas, we began gathering and piling wood. We banked the tents with the good earth and left only the opening without it. Our doors, as had those of our

---

1. The train arrived at the Tularosa station on April 4, 1913.

2. This is a favorite story of many of those interviewed.

3. Ted Sutherland, in an interview, stated: "The Chiricahua had brought their horses but were strictly forbidden to transport cattle and dogs. The prevalence of 'Texas fever,' transmitted by ticks, had been so devastating that transporting cattle across state lines had been prohibited by legislation. The Apaches sold their herd before leaving Oklahoma. He went on to tell of the dogs, which "simply 'boiled out' of the cars."

tepees, faced the east. Every morning, as the tip of the sun rose above Mother Earth I stood before my door with arms and eyes uplifted in deep thanks to Ussen. After twenty-seven years as a prisoner of war, I was at last a free man with new hope for the future of my children and my people.

"Enjuh!"

The tent village was located on a level plain near the agency where there was good grass, wood, and a little stream of clear cold mountain water falling from the mesa on which St. Joseph's Mission was later erected.

After a week Chief Naiche, Daklugie, and Eugene Chihuahua requested their own village site. Jefferis agreed and the Indian leaders, after a three-day reconnaissance, decided upon White Tail as their place of abode. It was situated near Pajarito [Little Bird] Mountain, upon a mesa with tall timber and meadows belly-deep to a horse in gramma grass, one of the most nutritious of foods for animals. There was an ample supply of pure water from melting snows and an abundance of white-tailed deer. It was from those that the area took its name. There was small game also; but what pleased the Chiricahua most was the large number of elk that fed on the mesa.

They began preparations; but the day before the move was to be made Haozinne, wife of Chief Naiche, climbed the steep hill to the mesa from which came the waterfall and did not return. They found her dead of a heart attack and postponed going on until after her burial.

Again the Mescaleros assisted with the move. There could not be said to have been a road, but there was a trail made and utilized for hauling logs to Blazer's Mill. Not until a substantial bridge had been constructed across a deep arroyo was it safe to cross it with a loaded wagon.

The tents were set up, as was the Apache custom, facing the east. The Chiricahua cut and stacked wood on the north side of the opening to each tent. They built long piles extending toward the east as a protection against snow drifting before the entrance, and they used the wood farthest from the tent first.

Many of them had iron stoves but all had fire holes in the center of their tents for heat. And around the outside they banked the tents with earth. It was a long, cold winter, the worst they had ever experienced. They were determined to secure houses before another. This they were unable to do; they lived under these conditions about four years.

"My father," said Maude Daklugie Geronimo, "and my uncle, Eugene [Chihuahua], just raised hell till we got them. Mr. Jefferis, too; he risked losing his job to help us. And the government *did not give us those houses!* They were paid for by sale of lumber from the reservation."[4]

DAKLUGIE

I knew that when we got houses the Mescaleros would demand them. They did. They got four-room buildings with porches, and barns and chicken houses just like ours. So far as I know nobody on the reservation ever raised a

---

4. Maude Daklugie Geronimo, interview.

chicken, but we made good use of the barns.

For a long time the Mescaleros lived in brush arbors in summer and tepees in winter. They used the houses for storerooms for food, hides, and sometimes wood; but they didn't live in them. Gradually they began to do so.

White people were afraid of the night air, but Indians loved it. Your race thought it caused sickness. Employees at the agency would hang blankets over windows to keep the night air out.

Meanwhile, Daklugie and others had learned from their experience with cattle that too close a relationship between people was apt to result in deterioration. Indeed, from their earliest time Apaches had a taboo against marriage of relatives; so it was with approval that they saw the young people from both tribes select wives and husbands from each other's tribe. A Chiricahua man was expected to live with his wife's tribe, but usually the young woman accepted the standards of her husband.

The Chiricahuas, of course, were dependent upon the trading post at Mescalero for supplies. Until the roads were improved years later they were accustomed to making the trips with pack horses. The distance necessitated spending the night, and when they did so it was usually in homes of men from White Tail. They took meat, hides, and any other product they had to the trading post and bartered it for ammunition, coffee, flour, and other commodities.

In spite of the numerous hardships it occasioned, the Chiricahuas still felt that they had chosen their location wisely. It afforded them the wild free life of which the years of imprisonment had deprived them.

PART THREE

THE APACHES OF
MESCALERO

CHAPTER 14

THE CHIRICAHUAS
RUN CATTLE

Before the coming of the Chiricahuas the Mescaleros had very few cattle. There had been at times thousands on the reservation, but they belonged to neighboring ranchers who paid no grazing fees until Carroll began charging a dollar a head per annum. The intruders protested, but Carroll collected most of the money due the Indians and they got what he collected.[1]

After the arrival of the Fort Sill exiles in 1913, Mescalero agent C. R. Jefferis was informed that the sale of seven thousand cattle and other assets in Oklahoma had brought $170,172.23. Purchases made before the departure of the Chiricahuas, left a credit of $162,000. A list of the sum due each owner was enclosed.[2] To Ted J. Sutherland fell the responsibility of assisting the Chiricahuas in reestablishing their herd in New Mexico.

Sutherland was young; he was the son of Jim Sutherland, part owner and manager of the famous Diamond A ranch between the reservation and the Pecos. He was a graduate of New Mexico Military Institute and an excellent judge of cattle. Most vitally important, he was honest. He could neither be bought nor be bullied into stealing from the Indians. With money belonging to the Indians, he bought two thousand grade heifers from various ranches in the area. He selected them very carefully. And from W. W. Cox of the Organs he selected registered bulls, four to each one hundred cows. He branded and turned them loose at Elk Canyon.[3]

Daklugie had not exaggerated the quality of the range on the reservation. In 1914 the first roundup was held and the first calf crop branded. Sutherland's friends on nearby ranches volunteered to help with the work without recompense. Included were Bernard Cleve from Elk; Ed Chandler, representing the Tanneyhills of the Spur; Carl Paxton (chief of police at Alamogordo); and Ed

---

1. Mrs. James A. Carroll, interview.

2. Major Goode to C. R. Jefferis, July 3, 1913, Records at the Mescalero Agency. See Lt. Purrington's report of August 22, 1909, pp. 190–93.

3. Ted Sutherland, interviews.

Ward, son of S. S. Ward, who owned the Flying H. Ed Morgan, Mescalero, drove the chuck wagon. Ted took also an Indian cook, Juanito.

Expert Mescalero cowboys accompanied the whites. They included Roman Chico (son of Chief Roman Grande), Clyde Blake, Andrew Mosquien, Miguel Little, John Big Rope and Everett Smith. Each had ten or twelve mounts which had been roped out of the wild herd and trained.

Before they started to Number One Camp (there were seven) they were joined by Daklugie. He had only one horse, and it was a poor one; but he had been in charge of the herd at Fort Sill and was expert with cattle. He asked no recompense.

As the chuck wagon pulled out from the Agency, a Model T Ford rattled up with a load of government inspectors. They held up the departure until a wagonload of goats could be procured and added to the train. They informed Sutherland that no beeves could be killed for food, that he and his men were to eat goat. Goat! To cowboys accustomed to butchering a beef every day—more if needed—this was a solar-plexis blow. In view of the fact that his friends were working without pay, except for food, it seemed to Sutherland that they should be well fed; but he offered no opposition.

TED SUTHERLAND

We camped in that flat at the Number One near Pajarito Spring. The old Ford gave up the race at White Tail but we didn't know it. Before daylight next morning, horses were pitching all over the place. Ace [Daklugie]'s mount stepped in a prairie dog hole and fell with him. I loaned him some of mine. We began roping and branding the calves and tallying the mother cows. We put USID (United States Indian Department) on them—and the bow and arrow of the reservation. We castrated the males, and we threw those we'd worked back of us so that we wouldn't be encumbered with them again.

I knew that no cowhand would work on goat meat, so we saved the mountain oysters. They're the choice part of the beef, anyway.

About ten o'clock, when we'd been at work six hours, the inspector showed up on the plain below. They couldn't drive the Ford through the brush and arroyos, and they couldn't ride the horses—I'd left some for them—so there they sat with the wagonload of goats.

At noon we feasted on fried oysters, ranch-style beans, sourdough biscuits, and coffee. What the inspectors ate I don't know—we didn't miss any goats when we got back five days later. We didn't have time to bother about them, and they never got in sight of us.

There had been plenty of rain and the grass was good. I never saw better calves. From those 2,000 heifers we got 1,984 calves! I never saw such a good calf crop before. It's possible that some of them were twins, though that is rare in cattle.

And there were really not 2,000 three-year old heifers, for we found the remains of two. One had been killed by lobos and the other hanged herself in the fork of an oak; stuck her head in and couldn't get it out. The skeleton was still hanging there.

I wondered why Daklugie came along, for we weren't paying him. He told me frankly that he had no faith in the honesty of white men and wanted to know how many of the cattle I'd stolen. From that time on I had no better friend.

This prodigious task was performed in five days, and ever since the Mescalero Reservation has had cattle. Each October and November, sales are held at Number One Camp.[4]

DAKLUGIE

As I anticipated, when the Mescaleros saw what cattle brought us they wanted them, too. They did get some, but not until two or three years later. The head of each family got cattle, but many of the Mescaleros—some of our people, too—sold or ate theirs, so that now there are many families who do not own any.

Now [1954] the council and agent are trying to take our cattle away from us and brand all in the arrow of the reservation. Nobody can run more than 80 mother cows now. I have 80 in my own brand (the A D Bar connected) and I average about five thousand dollars a year from the sale of yearlings. Nearly all of mine are registered, but I have a few good cows that are not. So mine sell for stock cattle. But if everybody's cattle are thrown into one brand, nobody will get much out of them. Why not? Well, it is too good a setup for graft. I won't be dead a year before that is done.

At that time there was much cattle theft from big ranches. Fences were laid on the ground, trucks driven over them, a ramp lowered, and the cattle driven into vehicles. Very seldom was a thief apprehended.

When I suggested to Ace that the reservation, too, probably lost cattle that way he was indignant. "It doesn't happen," he snorted. "We'd trail them and catch them."

Somewhat skeptical, I asked him how they could trail a truck once it had entered a paved and well-traveled highway.

"No white man could," he retorted. "No white man is smart enough. But every tire leaves a different impression, and some of our older men have been excellent trackers. They could read that sign." When next I talked to Eugene he assured me that this was possible.

I was fortunate to have found a rancher near Ruidoso who cut and froze for me high-quality, tender beef. One noon at the table Daklugie said, "I usually butcher my own beef but occasionally have to buy some. I never get good tender meat like this. Where do you buy it?"

"I didn't," I assured him. "This is A D Bar beef! I never eat any other!"

He snorted, laid his fork on his plate, and glared across the table at me. The others burst into loud laughter. And he, too, finally relented and grinned.

---

4. Ted Southerland, interviews.

CHAPTER 15

COMPLICATIONS

The Mescalero Apaches of New Mexico had a long record of generosity toward exile bands and tribes of Apaches. Perhaps their looking on the mountain fastness ranging southward from the sacred White Mountain as a haven from their own seasonal wanderings, along with their generally non-hostile outlook (since about 1850), motivated them to extend fellowship to others.[1]

The first Apaches to fall back to those mountains permanently were other Mescaleros [those who eat mescal] driven west out of Texas by the increasing power of the hated Comanches.

When Natzili and his band from the area about the present site of Amarillo asked for a refuge they had been welcomed, and the relationship had been amicable. So, too, had been the arrival of the Lipans under Magoosh.

But when the Jicarillas came, complications arose.

In the winter of 1883–84, under the administration of Major W. H. H. Llewelyn, the Jicarillas from northern New Mexico obtained permission to live on the Mescalero Reservation. The trip of over 500 miles was made by wagon and 47 days were required for it. While en route there were several deaths from smallpox, and there was much unhappiness and dissatisfaction among members of the displaced tribe.

At that time there were enrolled at Mescalero 462 people. The Jicarillas numbered 721. That alone was sufficient cause for problems. In order to somewhat simplify matters the newcomers were divided into three groups, and each was placed at a distance from the others. One was located on the Río Tularosa, another at Three Rivers, and a third on Carrizo Creek near the present site of Ruidoso.[2]

Andrew Mosquien said that there might have been a few cattle on the reservation before Llewelyn "issued" about a hundred to the Jicarillas. Later, to

---

1. This chapter has been compiled from interviews with Daklugie; Kanseah; Solon Sombrero, grandson of Natzili; Willie Magoosh; Andrew Mosquien; Ralph Shanta; Percy Big Mouth; Elizabeth McKinney; Hugh Coonie; Eugene Chihuahua; James Kaywaykla; Dan Nicholas; Margaret Pelman Robinson; Paul Blazer; Carisso Gallarito (Dan Nicholas interpreting); and Margaret Balache Big Mouth.

2. Sonnichsen, *Mescaleros,* pp. 214–15.

satisfy the Mescaleros, Llewelyn bought more cattle, some of which were distributed among the Mescaleros.

When asked about Llewelyn's status as an agent, Mosquien, as did several other of the older Apaches, had no hesitation in expressing their dislike of him. A descendant of Running Water said, "It was too bad Muchacho Negro didn't kill him when they had that ruckus at the corral!"

In general the Mescaleros felt the Jicarillas to be overbearing and arrogant. "They had almost twice as many people as we did," said Percy Big Mouth, "and they tried to run our reservation. One good thing: they didn't stay but a year or two."[3] They were moved once again to northern New Mexico with reservation headquarters at the time in Abiqui.

Daklugie, aware of tension that had developed with the Jicarillas, was desirous of maintaining good relationships between the hosts and his own people. He, Naiche, and Chihuahua did what they could to promote harmony. Despite their efforts, however, frictions developed. From the time of their arrival the "Fort Sills," as they were called by the Mescaleros, had themselves ostracized Chato as they had in Oklahoma. The Mescaleros had learned of his conduct as a scout, and he realized it. Not accepted by either, he established a home at Apache Summit, where he had to haul his water over ten miles. He lived there, apart from the others, for years.[4] Eugene Chihuahua explained that Chato feared Kaytennae and Daklugie, and especially the former. Still, he did have at least a few friends. "Coonie was his right-hand man," said Daklugie.

"The Fort Sills," said Margaret Pelman, "were uppity. And they wanted to run things. Some of them had gone to Carlisle to school. Some of us had, too. Eric Tortilla and Robert Geronimo went. So did Viola Massai. She married Eugene Chihuahua. I went to Carlisle, too. While I was there they put me in the hospital and operated for cataracts. After that I could see well, and I learned fast."

"I think that they were a bit unfair to Chato," said Dan Nicholas. "He had attended school at Carlisle and was a very fine penman. He wrote a beautiful Spencerian hand; so they made him tribal secretary. I think much of the dislike was caused by his having official letterheads entitled *The Chiricahua Apache Reservation.* Of course the Mescaleros did not like that!"

The Chiricahuas were represented on the tribal council along with the Mescaleros and Lipans. The council could make rulings, but for many years the white agent had absolute power, for he could veto any ruling made by the council. This amounted practically to dictatorship. Consequently there was great antagonism toward most of the agents. The Apaches knew that some of them were selling supplies furnished them by the government. However, instead of being stored they were transferred to wagons owned by the tribe and Indians were ordered to drive them to wholesalers in Las Cruces to be sold. Carisso Gallarito (Crook Neck) told of his having been ordered to deliver one such load, a delivery of food, to a wholesale house in La Cruces. He refused to take a second. Paul Blazer told of this incident and of another when, instead of sugar, *white sand* was delivered at Mescalero.

---

3. Ibid., p. 217. The Jicarillas left in 1877.

4. Dan Nicholas was one person who liked Chato.

Until the appointment of James A. Carroll, the agents had been retired military officers, accustomed to giving orders to inferiors who could not protest commands. Still, men like Carroll excepted, the Apaches considered many of the ex-army men preferable to the civilians who followed them.

"A dictator," said Daklugie, "can be the best of all leaders, provided that he is honest and puts the best interest of his people ahead of his own greed. If he is ambitious for money and power he can be the worst. And therein is the danger." When challenged with the question of whether or not Apache chiefs were by nature dictators, Daklugie retorted, "Certainly not. They submitted plans to a council for approval or rejection. They listened to their warriors. They were dependent upon the approval of their people to hold them. They were far from being dictators."

Although Daklugie, at the time he was interviewed, was no longer chairman of the council—he was not even a member—he often helped out. "When the papers get stacked so high that they can't see over them the chairman calls me to clear the desk. Somebody has to make decisions. It is not easy. There are sure to be requests that must be denied. That means hard feeling. I've had more than my share of it."

"But people say that when you speak the Apaches fall on their faces."

Daklugie shook his head. "Don't you believe a word of it," he said. "Apaches have minds of their own. I've seen stubborn White Eyes, but you don't know what stubbornness means till you deal with Apaches."

Daklugie was a powerful example of those of whom he spoke. Determined to gain the release of the prisoners of war, he made the trip to Washington at his own expense and was able to win the consent of the Secretary of War, the Commissioner of Indian Affairs, *and* the Senate. The motion before the Senate failed of unanimous passage by one vote—that of A. B. Fall of New Mexico, who objected due to *his* determination to have the Mescalero Reservation made a national park. (Fall owned a large ranch adjacent to the reservation.) In 1912, the year before the Chiricahua release, and again in 1916, Fall introduced bills for that purpose. The year after Fall's 1916 bill followed its predecessor to defeat, Daklugie "met Senator Fall at the trading post. When he spoke and offered his hand, I took it. After all, we'd won the reservation. He said, 'I have to hand it to you, Daklugie. I didn't think it could be done, but you've won.' If his ranch had been at stake the senator might have understood the reason for our stubbornness and why the Apaches had won."

CHAPTER 16

LAND CLAIMS

For decades both the Mescalero and Chiricahua Apaches attempted to reclaim title to, or compensation for, large sections of land taken from them in Arizona and New Mexico. Ultimately both tribes were successful in winning substantial money awards. The Mescaleros were first, by four years, in collecting their claim. It was agreed that the money would be shared jointly by all tribes at the Mescalero reservation, however, and that when other tribes won cases their awards would also be shared. Having so agreed, the tribes cooperated with and assisted each other, knowing that everyone stood to gain.

The Mescalero claim was essentially based upon the presidential Executive order of May 29, 1873, which established the first Mescalero Reservation and at the same time relinquished to the government all Mescalero tribal lands not included within the reservation boundaries. The course of events over the next forty years was complicated and discouraging. The Mescaleros were to be the prey of some of the most dishonest, ruthless, and corrupt ranchers, traders, and Indian agents in the western experience.[1] An eyewitness account of this period follows, the account emphasizing the efforts on the part of the Mescaleros to make good their reservation existence and to hold on to what little they had.

BIG MOUTH

After the Bosque Redondo we returned to the Bonito and camped upstream from the fort. The soldiers did not want us to live there. They did not want us to live anywhere. They had sent us to Fort Sumner to die, and they could not leave us alone in our own land. They killed many, mostly women and children. So again our people slipped away in the night. It was late in the fall and very cold. We left fires burning and took everything we could carry and went silently into the forest. When we camped, we scattered so that when the cavalry followed some might escape. We could not risk fires, so we ate what cold food we had and huddled together for warmth. One old woman who had a blanket took several orphaned children and covered them with it. She had only a very little food but gave each a mouthful; there was none left

---

1. For an interesting account of this hectic period, see Sonnichsen, *Mescaleros,* pp. 134–76.

for her. She got them to sleep and hovered over them as best she could. When the men came at dawn, the children were safe, but she was dead.

The men stayed in the rear to enable the women and children to escape. But they had no ammunition, and when the cavalry overtook them they could make no defense. Cadette talked with the officer and agreed to return to Fort Stanton.[2] Again there were many promises—promises of protection, food, blankets, and good treatment. Cadette told them that neither he nor his people would go again to Fort Sumner—that they preferred death at once.

"You will not be killed," the officer said. "You will be protected by the soldiers. You will have a White Eye to be your agent and see that you get food and that our promises to you are kept. You will be on a reservation, but it will be here in your own land."

"We are on our own land now," replied the chief.

"You cannot have all the land between the rivers. You must stay in the mountains."

Cadette knew why that was done; the White Eyes were coming into our country and settling along the rivers and in the canyons.

The officer said that every Mescalero must come to the fort, babies and all, to be counted and tagged and that once in seven days one member of the family was to come and get food for those of his group. We did as they said, but we got no food. "Come again on the seventh day and there will be cattle for you."

Seven days is a long time to be hungry, but we gathered what we could in the woods. There were no piñons that year, but mesquite beans and acorns could be found. Apaches had always lived largely on venison, and without meat we were weak. But most of our people had enough to enable them to live.

On issue day, Saturday, we went and we got some cattle; but they were poor and thin, and there was little meat on them. In two days we were without food again. Still we obeyed orders and made no trouble. Next time, a White Eye and his son were there to kill the cattle and divide the meat. Again we had enough for only two or three days.[3]

Then the soldiers told us to get out; they said that we were polluting the water supply of Fort Stanton.

"Where shall we go that you won't follow and kill us?"

"It doesn't matter. Just get out!"

"But where?"

"Anywhere but here. Isn't it all your country?"

Then the agent said, "If you leave, you don't get any more food."

How could we know what to do?

Some wanted to go to Mexico, but we had few horses and no ammunition. It was too far for the women and children to walk. We were not like the Chiricahuas, who could do without horses. We were accustomed to having them.

Then the three chiefs met with Cadette. Natzili, whose name means Buffalo, was chief of the band that came from where Amarillo is now. He said, "The Guadalupes and the Pecos—that's ours and it's good country; and the Penasco and Weed have plenty of water and wood."

2. Ibid., pp. 89–95.

3. Eve Ball, *Ma'am Jones of the Pecos* (Tucson: University of Arizona Press, 1967), pp. 37–44.

"Pecos water!" said Cadette.

Gregorio, a chief and Medicine Man, spoke next: "There's the Hondo and the Bonito with plenty of good water. We can raise corn and make little gardens like at the Bosque."

Ramón Grande spoke, "You pick a place for your people, you other chiefs. It's all our country; we can go anywhere we want."

"We must stay together," said Cadette. "The agent will go with us; he is as eager to leave the soldiers as we are. And if he goes we will get meat, flour, sugar, coffee, and blankets. He has said it."

"I have not finished," said Ramón Grande.

"Let my brother speak."

"On the west side of the mountain is the Río Tularosa. The water is good. There is wood; there is game. That is the place I choose. There are a few white men on the river, but the agent says that they will have to leave."

"Deer and elk too," said Cadette.

The others listened to Ramón Grande.

"What will you do, Natzili, and you, Gregorio, when you run out of wood on the Pecos? You two will already be dead but your children will have to build little fires and reach out for little twigs to burn. You make a mistake to go to the Pecos."

"That is right," said the others. "We never thought about timber and game—just water. We have never had to live in just one place, and we didn't think what it would mean. We will go to the Tularosa with you, Ramón Grande."

The agent wrote to Washington and got a paper with a place marked out for a reservation. He showed it to the chiefs and explained what it meant. They did not like to have all their land taken from them except that one little bit, and they sent it back. A second time they would not agree to accept what was outlined, but on a third occasion they took the boundaries offered.[4]

"This line takes in Fort Stanton," said the agent, "but the cavalry needs some pasture land for the horses and cattle. They want to use about seventy-eight thousand acres of your land; but if the federal government ever quits using it, it will go back to you, the rightful owners. And this promise will be put into writing and a copy of it given to you. A lawyer [Colonel A. J. Fountain] will make the writing, and you will have a copy of it. You must keep that copy and not lose it, for as long as you have it nobody can take your land from you."

The chiefs asked: "Our boundary reaches up to and will enclose the fort?"

"Yes," replied the agent, "but you are to live over on the Tularosa."

So it was agreed. The agent's office was moved to Blazer's Mill, where he rented a house until buildings could be put up at Mescalero. That was in 1873. This all white men should know: The government of the United States did not give any land to the Mescaleros; instead, it *took* nearly all they possessed. All they had left was a small area that at that time seemed worthless. This was set forth in a paper made by the president himself and signed by him.[5] This writing was put together like a little book.

"What good is the president's writing if his word is not good?" asked Natzili.

---

4. Paul Blazer, interview.

5. President Grant's Executive Order of May 29, 1873.

"The same man is not president very long," said the agent. "This little book binds those who come after him to keep his promises."

"Don't you let that book run wild," said Colonel Fountain, "it protects you in keeping your land. There is a copy of it in Washington, but you keep yours."

"I will keep it for you," said the agent.

"I will keep it myself," said Gregorio. He was the Medicine Man, and also a chief. So they let him take charge of the book. He had his wife make a buckskin bag in which to put it. And he carried it with him wherever he went. When a new agent came, Gregorio showed him the book, but he always took it back and fastened the bag to his belt.

One day Gregorio rode up on the mountains, and when he returned the bag was gone. He sent skillful trailers to follow his tracks up the mountain. They did that easily, but they did not find the bag. Perhaps it had caught on a limb and had been thrown off the trail. Perhaps it had been flipped into a tree. Nobody ever knew, for they could not find it.[6]

Now the federal government has ceased using Fort Stanton for any purpose. It was turned over to New Mexico for a tuberculosis hospital. The hospital needs the buildings and equipment for its operation, and about four thousand acres of grazing land for its herd. The Mescaleros expected their grazing land to be returned to them, in accordance with the executive order, but it has not been done. New Mexico returned it to the Department of the Interior. Our claim for it is pending. When did the government ever keep its promise to the Apache?

There are two other men on the Mescalero Reservation who know these things; Sam Chino and Carisso Gallarito. Both are very old; both have given their testimony as to the truth of this story.

When will the Mescaleros get justice?

That I would like to see. But I am old, very old—perhaps a century. I have served as a scout with the cavalry and have received a pension and a medal for my services.

Are the Indians not citizens?

Are they not entitled to justice?

I had not thought of attending the meeting at Fort Stanton, but when Daklugie and Maude Geronimo rang my doorbell I could hardly refuse. Ostensibly, they had already started out and the car had broken down. They had managed, however, to reach my driveway at eight o'clock in the morning and they asked me to take them in my car.

The roads were not paved and we did not reach the building where the hearing was to be held till nine o'clock. Daklugie hurried Maude and me through the door by the speaker's stand and to the center aisle, where he pushed Maude ahead of him to a seat—leaving me the chair on the aisle. Senator Dennis Chavez was behind the podium, and Representative Fernandez, Congressman from New Mexico, was at his left. They were there to conduct a hearing regarding the disposition of the Fort Stanton land the Mescalero Apaches had been promised.

---

6. Carisso Gallarito, interview.

The central part of the hall was filled with white people, some of whom represented organizations greedy for the land and ranchers who thought that, because it joined their ranges, the land should be divided among the thirteen who had been running cattle on it for years (without paying grazing fees). I recognized some of them. There were also representatives from the university who wanted it for testing crops.

The Apaches had previously agreed that they would concede, without compensation, the buildings, including a well-equipped hospital and land sufficient for maintaining a dairy herd. But they would not relinquish their ownership of the grazing land.

There was a commotion at the back door and two busloads of Apaches entered to occupy the remaining seats. Among them I recognized Percy Big Mouth, son of the only scout who had participated in the wars against the Apaches. He was 106 at that time and had told me the story of the contract obtained for the Mescaleros by Colonel A. J. Fountain.

"Just look at the White Eyes," said Daklugie. "They've flocked in like buzzards for the kill."

Senator Chavez, presiding, announced the first speaker of what turned out to be a long list of spokesmen—all white. When the last had finished, Chavez asked that they hear from anyone else in the audience who wished to present a claim. There was no response.

"Aren't you going to do anything for your people?" I asked Daklugie.

"They wouldn't let me talk," was his reply. "I know too much. *You're* going to do the talking. Nobody would suspect you of knowing anything."

"Last call," announced the senator. I was literally pushed from my chair and, as I stepped toward the table, Representative Fernandez met me and said, "Now, don't be afraid. Give me your name and tell me whom you represent so that I can introduce you."

I responded with my name and told him that I represented my interest as a writer. Then I found myself pouring forth the story of the injustices done to the Apaches—the broken promises, the indignities, and the story of the lost document. It, I told them, was not available, but a copy could be obtained from Washington.

Dennis Chavez demanded that I tell by whom I was employed, and I told him that I alone was responsible—that I deplored the treatment meted out to both the Spanish-Americans and Indians. I could feel keenly the disapproval of the white claimants in the room, and when I dropped into my chair I was seething at the way Daklugie had trapped me into sticking my neck out so far. Then, for the first and only time in my life, I heard the Apache war whoop. The Indians stood, threw their hats in the air, and raised the roof. Daklugie, for once, laughed.

Weeks later a decision came from Washington: the Apaches were to retain their land. I doubt that Daklugie's strategy greatly influenced the decision, but at least it aided greatly my securing interviews with the Apaches in the future. Eventually, claim to the Fort Stanton grazing lands was absorbed into the overall claim to lands lost as the result of the 1873 treaty.

The Mescaleros filed claim for a vast section of land—nearly a third of New Mexico, including the entire southeast quadrant. After a long hearing the U.S. Indian Claims Commission determined that most of that claim was legitimate (see map).

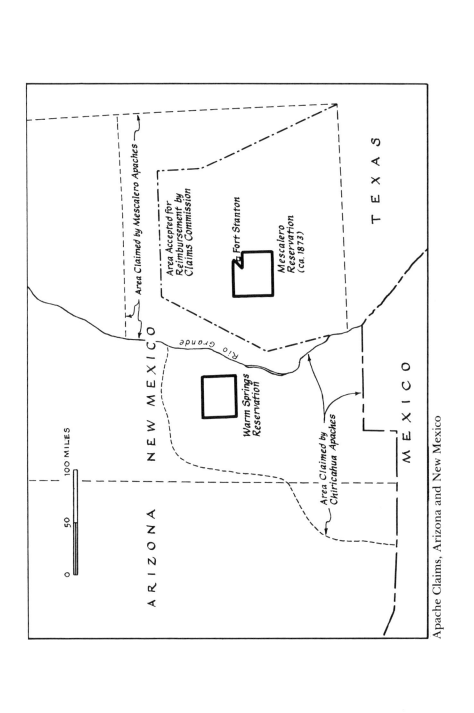

Apache Claims, Arizona and New Mexico

On April 27, 1967, the Commission "ordered, adjudged, and decreed that
. . . final judgment in Docket No. 22-B be and is hereby entered in favor of the
plaintiff, the Apache Tribes of the Mescalero Reservation in behalf of the Mescalero Apache Tribe, against defendant the sum of $8,500,000.00.[7]

The Chiricahua Apaches wanted above all else to return to their old reservations in Arizona. Even though life at San Carlos had been unendurable, the conditions at Turkey Creek met with their approval and they
wished to be permitted to make their permanent homes there. When convinced
that this would never be permitted they began to consider the possibilities of
making a claim for compensation for *all* the tribal land lost rather than just for
the loss of the reservations given to Cochise and Victorio—a promising strategy
being employed by numerous tribes.

It is interesting to note that Daklugie so disliked the white race and its laws
that he would not admit having gained anything from conditions forced upon
the Apaches. Nevertheless, he had accepted Geronimo's edict as to the necessity
of his learning what both considered to be the chicanery of the oppressors so
that he might be able to protect his people from trickery and deceit.

He and others who had been in school at Carlisle learned of the possibility
of obtaining some recompense for the loss of the two reservations taken from
them.

The return of these influential young men from Carlisle gave the tribe hopes
that their land, which no Indian had wished sold, might bring at least a small
part of its real value to the tribe. Outstanding in wishing to secure this by the
white man's means rather than by violence, in addition to the farsighted Daklugie, were James Kaywaykla, Rogers Toclanny, Chief Chihuahua, Victor
Beitie, Sam Haozous, and Eugene Chihuahua. At Carlisle they had learned
that disputes and sometimes injustices could be made right by legal minds.
They knew little of legal processes but they had learned that men made a pro-
fession of such tasks. They inquired for attorneys and, several years before
being freed from their status as prisoners of war, they secured the services of an
attorney to present their claim. But it was not until after four-fifths of them
came to Mescalero in 1913 that much was done along that line.

Those who stayed near Cache, Oklahoma, were the first to employ an attorney to represent their interests. Since that group had no tribal organization
or governmental aid, the one-fifth who remained did this by voluntary contri-
butions. James Kaywaykla kept records and gave information as to repeated
collections paid the attorneys.

The other four-fifths, now at Mescalero, were at first too busy starting
homes at White Tail and bringing cattle to the reservation to do much else.
But it had long been an objective, and they resumed the demand for restitu-
tion. In 1920 Rogers Toclanny, a Warm Springs Apache who had rendered
faithful service as a scout, received a letter from E. B. Marett, Assistant Commissioner of Indian Affairs, which in essence stated that the president had established the Warm Springs Reservation by executive order dated April 9,
1874—but on August 25, 1877, he had restored "the said lands . . . to the public
domain." Therefore, ". . . any rights the Indians had to said lands expired on the

---

7. *Decisions of the Indian Claims Commission* 18 (New York: Clearwater Press, 1973): 379.

date of the restoration, or on August 25, 1877."[8] The Apaches thereby learned a classic lesson on the viability of the executive order policy: What a president gave today he could take away tomorrow.

Still, though this was a discouraging start, at least the movement for which Daklugie, Kaywaykla, Chihuahua, and others had hoped for years was at last under way. There was a long and bitter series of legal battles involved, which at times seemed hopeless. Finally, solid claims were filed before the Indian Claims Court for damages regarding loss of 14,858,051 acres of "aboriginal lands within the Chiricahua Tract"; and on August 25, 1971, exactly ninety-four years after the Warm Springs Reservation was taken away, the Court handed down its final judgment.

It is hereby ordered, adjudged and decreed by the Commission that:

1. The plaintiffs shall have and recover from the defendant on their claims in Docket Nos. 30-A and 48-A, the sum of $15,967,300.00, subject to the terms set forth in the stipulation filed by interlocutory order entered this day.

2. The plaintiffs shall have and recover from defendant on their claims on Docket Nos. 30 and 48 the sum of $527,796.00, subject to the terms set forth in the stipulation filed herein on August 17, 1971, and adopted by the Commission by interlocutory order entered this day.

The Chiricahuas were therefore successful in gaining a judgment against the United States for a total of $16,489,096. (The stipulation in the decision allowed only $7,700 as a gratuitous offset.) Together the Apaches at Mescalero had won just under $25 million.[9]

---

8.   E. B. Marett to Rogers Toclanny, 1920, Records at the Mescalero Reservation.

9.   *Decisions*, 26: 197–98. Four months prior, the Commission had found in favor of the Jicarilla Apaches (Docket No. 22-A) in the sum of $9,150,000; and in 1972 a combined group of Apache tribes and groups living at the Fort Apache Reservation in Arizona (Docket No. 22-D) received $4,900,000. Ibid., 25: 248; 28: 421–22. Of the sixteen million dollars awarded to the Chiricahuas, one-fifth was forwarded to their fellow tribesmen who had remained in Oklahoma.

CHAPTER 17

THE FUGITIVE

Bihido was respected and liked by all who knew him. He was a mild, quiet man, and it was a shock to both the employees and the Indians when he was arrested for murder.[1]

Several families from Mescalero had gone in wagons to Carisso (Carizzo) Canyon to hunt deer. Unfortunately, a trader had seen their camp and had sold some of the men whiskey. They paid him with venison. While the women were cooking their evening meal, the drinking continued. Bihido's wife was preparing a bed of coals for broiling fresh venison by raking them into a heap with a stick. Though the limb she was using was green it was burning. When Bihido, who had drunk far too much bootleg whiskey, lurched toward her, instinctively she warded him off with the stick in her hand. The smouldering end struck him in the eye. Partially blinded and suffering with agony he grasped her by the shoulders and shook her. When he released her she fell. He and others bent over her and found that she was dead.

The somewhat sobered group hastily hitched up, placed the body in a wagon, and set out for the agency. They arrived at daybreak, and as soon as Mr. Carroll came they told him that Bihido's wife had been killed accidentally in a fall.

At first the report was not questioned; but when rumors to the contrary were circulated, an autopsy showed that the woman had been strangled and her neck broken.

Bihido was tried by the federal court in Santa Fe and convicted of murder. After he had been in the penitentiary about three years, Eugene Chihuahua was summoned to appear in Santa Fe as a witness in yet another murder case.

EUGENE CHIHUAHUA

While there I had several talks with the warden. When Joe Bihido walked through the warden asked if I knew him. I did, and in reply to his ques-

---

1. This account has been pieced together from information provided in numerous interviews with Eugene Chihuahua, Mrs. James A. Carroll, Eloise Carroll Sutherland, Newt Platta, Victor Randall, Robert Decherle, Eloise Shields, Gertrude Torres, and others to be mentioned in subsequent footnotes.

tions as to Bihido and his character I said that Joe was one of the best men I knew. I added that there was no doubt in my mind that his wife's death was unpremeditated and that her use of the burning stick was instinctive, as was her husband's shaking her.

"Then why," asked the warden, "didn't those who saw it tell it in court?"

"Because they are Mescaleros," I told him. "They distrust and fear the white man's courts."

"But you do not?"

"I am a Chiricahua. We have had twenty-seven years' experience with white people and understand these things better."

At that time I did not know of an attempt to secure a pardon for Joe Bihido. I don't know that my testimony helped get it. If so I am wondering if I did him a favor. It might have been better for Bihido if they had kept him in Santa Fe.

Bihido returned to the reservation but not to his tepee. For a while he lived under an overhanging ledge of rock in the canyon below Head Spring [source of the Río Tularosa]. He killed deer, cut wood, and prepared for winter. But before the snows came he moved into a cabin nearby with another lonely man.

At first it seemed to be a happy arrangement for both, but that was a terrible winter and the two men became snowed in. Still, they were beside a stream, they had wood, and they were adequately supplied with food.

Sometime in December the owner of the cabin reported to the agent that Bihido had borrowed his rifle to kill a deer. When he did not return, he went in search of him. He found Bihido dead. Either the gun had been accidentally discharged or Bihido had killed himself.

Again a first report about Bihido was initially accepted, and again people grew suspicious. Why was the wound in the back of his head? Could he have been killed in the cabin and his body dragged to the place where it was found? A coroner's jury was sworn in and went to the scene of the tragedy. They also inspected the cabin in which the two had lived. It was clean—too clean. The suspect admitted that the gun was his but said that he had loaned it to Bihido. He stoutly maintained that the man had killed himself.

An all-Indian jury returned a verdict of murder. The police took the accused to the little building where the frozen body of Bihido had been placed. When they threatened to lock the defendant up with the corpse for the night he promised that he would tell the truth if they would not force him to stay there.

He was taken to Alamogordo and put in jail. There he confessed to having killed Bihido.[2]

A few nights later he and four or five white prisoners escaped from jail. Two of them went with the fugitive to the barn of a rancher where the Apache knew that horses were kept at night. Having obtained saddled mounts, the three separated.

The fugitive was trailed up the Tularosa. At Bent he turned the horse loose

---

2. F. C. Slates, *The Indians of the Southwest—Today, Yesterday, and the Days Before That* (n.p., n.d.). Slates was coroner of Otero County at the time. He was called to the agency by Mr. Boggett to conduct a joint inquest and investigation.

and continued on foot. A man on foot is harder to trail than a horse. The pursuing police lost the trail. "I think that they may not have wanted to find him," said Newt Platta. "He may have waded." That night there came another snow that made expert trailing impossible. "So there he was, thinly dressed in the middle of winter. He had no blankets and no weapons. How he survived nobody knows; but he was an Apache, and he did."

He had a son living alone in Elk Canyon, and that place was watched day and night for a long time. Though he may have taken refuge there he was never apprehended.

Several years passed. An Apache who went to Mexico told of having seen a man whom he thought might have been the fugitive. When he tried to approach him in a crowded market the man faded and could not be found.

It was believed that he followed the primitive plan of life by migrating with the seasons.

Many thought that he spent the summers on the reservation and that he watched the Puberty Ceremonials in July from a hiding place on the mountain. The Indian police had orders to arrest him, but if they knew of his presence they might have ignored it.

When the Apaches left their homes one October to camp and harvest piñons there were rumors of a wild man having been seen on the reservation. One night, near the Cow Camp Number One on Pajarito Mountain, a strange man stealthily approached two women sitting beside their dying supper fire. "Do not be afraid, my sisters, I will not harm you. I am hungry for coffee. I have not asked anyone for years. Will you give me what is left?"

"That and food, too," was the reply. "We have cooked enough for tomorrow. We want you to have all the coffee we have brought; we can get more." They poured water on the coals, left food and coffee outside, and strolled slowly to the closest tent.[3]

The fugitive? Perhaps. The two women would not say. Neither was a relative of his, but he was an Apache and their brother.

At one time several families lived near the confluence of Elk and Silver canyons on the reservation and did some farming. Solon Sombrero, Eloise Wilson and her husband, Dave Balin, one of the Treas brothers, and one of the fugitive's sons had homes there.

At about midday Byron Treas rode by the home of the fugitive's son and stopped for coffee. The table was laid for two, and his host had poured two cups of coffee. He handed one to his caller and invited him to sit and share the meal. Without the slightest hesitation the host said that he got so lonely that he pretended to have a guest and had even prepared food for him. Byron Treas felt sure that at that moment the fugitive was in the house, but he gave no indication that he did. He left after eating and did not mention the incident. Under no circumstances would he have reported the occurrence to the police because he was definitely in sympathy with the unfortunate man.[4]

Even the officials were sympathetic. An effort was made to have the indictment dismissed. Because there was no evidence that he was living, this was not done.

---

3.   Nora Fatty and Maggie Lester, interviews.

4.   Byron Treas, with Eloise Shields, interviews.

For several years he may have visited one or both of his sons occasionally. But if he did, his presence was not known to anyone else. Eventually the Indians came to believe that the fugitive had died, perhaps in Mexico.

Apaches keep their secrets well.

CHAPTER 18

THE SHANTAS

S hanta Boy got his name according to Apache custom. Being an orphan reared by nonrelatives, he was given his father's name, followed by "Boy."*

As did nearly all Mescaleros at that time, Shanta Boy herded sheep and gradually acquired a small flock. During the summers he ran them in the lush range in the Rinconada. When winter came, he and his family drove them across the saddle and down the west slope of Sierra Blanca. In time they built several comfortable modern houses which the family still owns. They were comparatively close to the Mexicans at Tularosa, and as their herds increased they employed sheepherders from the village.

Phoebe Shanta Wilson, daughter of Shanta Boy, recalled accounts of attacks on stagecoaches en route from El Paso and Mesilla. These encounters occurred when her father was a young man, and he had participated in them; but she gave few details. She was more communicative regarding what Newt Platta termed "a ruckus at the Shanta place." It was reputedly a killing over an attempt to steal Shanta Boy's horses.

VICTOR RANDALL

T he way I heard it was that it was over somebody's trying to steal Shanta's sheep. But it might have been that some White Eye bootlegged bad liquor to the whole bunch and they just got drunk and fought. They were all good men and respected by the tribe. Not one of them would have killed anyone unless he'd been drinking.

A *tiswin* drunk? It wasn't *tiswin* that usually caused the trouble. We didn't have enough corn to make much *tiswin*. It is not distilled; it's just fermented and about as strong as beer. It takes a lot of drinking to get drunk on *tiswin*. When you read about these *tiswin* drunks, just remember that they were mostly whiskey or *tequila* drunks.

---

*Information for this chapter was provided by Phoebe Shanta Wilson, Newt Platta, Victor Randall, Father Albert Braun, Ralph Shanta, Sr., and Ralph Shanta, Jr., Paul Blazer, Bernard Second, and Amelia Naiche.

But anyway, there were some killings, and some trials. Shanta Boy was sent to the federal penitentiary at Leavenworth, Kansas—Roman Chiquito, too. He was the young chief and a good man like Shanta Boy. Maria Boy was in on it, and somebody else—I can't remember his name—and Choneska. Choneska was a Chiricahua from Cochise's band. He'd married Elmer Wilson's daughter, a Mescalero, so he was a member of our tribe. And he was a Medicine Man. He had the Power.

The federal penitentiary is in the broad, level valley of the Missouri River in northeastern Kansas. The road followed the heavily timbered stream. The fields, level and rich around the grim buildings, were planted to corn. In places the rows were more than a mile long. About the fields there was a barbed-wire fence, one that was considered impenetrable.

Prisoners on good behavior, called trusties, were allowed to work in the prison cornfields. The five Apache prisoners had become trusties soon after their arrival. After the corn grew so tall that the machinery used for cultivating broke the stalks, the trusties used very heavy hoes to cultivate it.

The penitentiary kept bloodhounds for trailing escaped prisoners. No inmates except the guard who fed them were permitted to go near the dogs. They were believed to be very strong and ferocious.

At five o'clock in the evening a whistle was blown to summon the field workers to the buildings. The trusties were given fifteen minutes to report after it had sounded. The Apaches were able to determine the approximate time by the sun, and they arranged to make their last trip to the distant fence just at quitting time. With the heavy hoes, they detached the wire from two posts and crawled through the opening. They crossed the dirt road and took refuge in the heavy undergrowth along the river, and there they shed all their clothing, except for their shoes. Then they started west.

Within a very short time they heard the dogs baying and they knew that armed guards would be following closely. As the fugitives had anticipated, the bloodhounds—two of them—overtook them. Then the baying ceased.

The guards, confident of two hours of daylight, felt sure that the escapees had been overtaken and treed; but they were puzzled by the silence of the dogs. Being unable either to find tracks or be guided by sound, they searched the area and called out for their dogs. The prisoners, and the dogs, had seemingly vanished! The guards finally gave up the search and returned to the penitentiary.

As the guards had surmised, the hounds had overtaken their prey and had gone silent. But where were they? The fugitives had annexed the bloodhounds and had taken them along! How was this possible? "Well," said Bernard Second, grandson of Choneska, "my grandfather had the Power over dogs, and he made medicine. How do I explain it? I don't. You either understand or you don't. If you understand, you need no explanation; if you don't—well, it's useless to try to explain."

The Apaches and their bloodhounds lay hidden during the day and traveled at night. Not one of them had ever seen a map, but they were expert at

Shanta Boy. (Eve Ball Collection)

reading the stars. Though they had been taken to Leavenworth by train, they had no difficulty in finding their way back home.

Food was the first and imperative need. With a knife an Apache can survive, but they had none. To their joy, the hounds supplied them with rabbits! Though they much preferred to cook meat, they dared not risk a fire. They had to make do with fire sticks that they made.

Clothing, too, was a requisite. Though the nights were warm, the Apache is modest and these men wanted some fabric from which to contrive breech-clouts. With the hounds to tell them whether or not a house was protected by dogs, they scouted for gunny sacks or other fabric material.

Though it was very warm, they saw a farmer butchering a calf one day and lay hidden, watching and waiting. That night they got the hide from the fence, then one of the fugitives slipped up to the stump upon which the meat had been cut and found, to their very great satisfaction, a knife. Their capability was now considerably improved, but they refrained from butchering any domestic animal, fearful that they still might be followed. They need not have worried about pursuit just then, as it had been decided to pick up the search at Mescalero, the fugitives' destination.

It was when they left the protection of timber along the river that they encountered their greatest problems. Wrapped in a gray or tan blanket, an

Apache could so closely imitate a boulder as to escape observation; without any, as they were, he must make use of sparse vegetation.

Guided by the Fixed Star, and possibly by an instinctive sense of direction, they made their nocturnal progress southwest. It was not until they struck the Pecos that they could positively identify their proximity to the reservation. There was no mistaking either the taste or the laxative effect of that water. Two nights' walk brought the Capitans into view. There now were convenient hiding places in the arroyos. And when the White Mountain floated in the blue ahead, they knew that Ussen had guided them to their home.

Once on the reservation they took refuge in Shanta Boy's retreat, the Rinconada. They had anticipated that the guards from Leavenworth had preceded them. They knew also that, though all were enrolled at the agency, no Apache would ever have heard of them.

Somebody had thoughtfully left bows, arrows, knives, dried venison, and clothing in a cave close to Shanta Boy's summer camp. Somebody, too, had used the Indian post office to warn them that the guards had searched the place. This had been done by placing rows of stones along the trail. By each was a small twig indicating that the passerby carried a gun. The Apaches could read these things and they could profit by the warning. Repeatedly, armed guards searched the Rinconada for them unsuccessfully. Finally, they gave up the search and left.

"And," said Phoebe, "they say that some of the best dogs on the reservation today are descended from that pair of bloodhounds."

Among other famous members of this family is Virginia Shanta Klinecole. When she was born her mother developed complications in labor and it was feared that she would die in delivery. They sent a boy on horseback to the Fall ranch to ask Father Albert to administer the last rites of the Church. When he saw the patient he declared that she would live; and, with the priest's assistance in the delivery, the mother pulled through.

From that time on, Virginia was a favorite of the priest. When she was only two years old he would tie her belt to his and, with the child sitting behind him, ride over the country. He watched with interest and pride Virginia's love for school and her great aptitude for learning. While serving as chaplain in World War II, Father Albert had served with a Kiowa-Apache, Bruce Klinekole, in the regiment from New Mexico. After the war ended both returned to Mescalero. It was there that Bruce met Virginia; Father Albert performed their marriage rites.

Virginia was elected to membership in the tribal council and, because of her outstanding abilities, she was further honored by being elected as the council chairman. She is the only woman in the United States ever to have held that position. During her administration she initiated and achieved many things beneficial to the tribe. She got modern, comfortable houses built, and she made excellent provisions for the elderly and infirm. She also achieved much better relations with neighboring communities.

Virginia Klinecole is still a valuable member of the council. She is also coordinator for the Apache children attending junior and senior high school at Tularosa. All emotional or disciplinary problems are handled by her. In addition to these duties Virginia and Bruce have reared a fine family and are beautiful and friendly people.

CHAPTER 19

PERICO AND GOLD

Among the warriors who came from Fort Sill to Mescalero were some who, at times, had been on the warpath with Nana.[1] Following the massacre of Tres Castillos, Kaytennae, Perico, and others had been with the Warm Springs chief when they ambushed a mule train on the Mexican border. Instead of the ammunition they needed so desperately, the large cowhide bags were laden with silver bars.

Nana, who had the Power over ammunition trains, was both chagrined and apprehensive. This white gold was not taboo as was gold, but he knew that it could cause trouble among Apaches as it did among White Eyes. He ordered his men to dig a hole in the bed of a dry stream and bury the stuff. One bar was placed in the fork of a tree to mark the site. When about two years later the band returned to salvage the silver, they could not find it. For Nana, who had a photographic memory for locales, this seemed strange. Had he intentionally misled them? That question still remains to be answered.

Contemptuous of money as the Apaches had been in their primitive life, they had become aware of the purchasing power of silver and gold. There was no taboo against the *possession* of gold. Nuggets in the sand of a dry stream bed might be picked up and used for barter, but digging in the earth for it was forbidden. In 1870 and 1871 Apaches brought small nuggets and even gold dust (in quills of turkey feathers) to trading posts. These they bartered at Dowlin's Mill for merchandise.[2]

The warriors, and occasionally a scout, talked of the wild, free days before they were dispossessed of all that they treasured except their religion. One of their favorite subjects was that of gold and silver that they had cached in a canyon in Mexico. It was, they said, "a three-day walk west from Casas Grandes." Their loot had not been buried; it had been concealed in a cave close to an overhanging ledge near the rim of a canyon. To reach it they had

---

1. Information for this chapter was provided by James Kaywaykla, Isabel Enjady Perico, Clarence Perico, Alberta Begay, Marion Cojo, Jasper Kanseah, Charlie Smith, Del Barton, Robert Barton, and Fred Peso.

2. Never have I known of an Apache's using anything made of gold, though it is possible that some of the younger ones do. They, as Bernice Peña has said, "don't know that they are Indians."

made Indian ladders (one pole with notches cut on either side for toe-holds). They had climbed from one ledge to the next higher, each laden with bars of silver and gold on his shoulders. After hiding the treasure they had descended and left their ladders on all but the lower ledge.

Perico attempted to recruit companions for retrieving the cache. Some suggested the grave probability of being detected by the Mexicans and killed. Perico readily admitted the danger. Marion Simms, brother to Alberta Begay, and three others decided to join him.

As a boy Perico had been befriended by a Mexican family near Casas Grandes. In an emergency he felt sure of their help. He knew the exact location of the canyon and acted as guide. They found it without difficulty. They identified it by blackened stones from cooking fires and smoke on overhanging ledges. When Perico climbed to the lower ledge, to his great delight there was a notched pole on it! The rest would be easy.

He slept little that night. Stealthy footsteps alerted him and aroused his fear that the party was being watched. He did not inform his companions until they were cooking their morning meal. It was unnecessary to tell them that an attempt to move the gold would be fatal. They had been discovered sooner than Perico had anticipated.

That night they quietly left the canyon, Perico heading for the home of his Mexican friends and the others heading for the border. When he reminded the elderly couple of their hospitality to an Apache boy, they welcomed him. He told them that he had no money to pay for train fare to El Paso, and they sent a telegram for fare addressed only to "Isabel, Mescalero." Strangely enough, it was delivered to his daughter. She sent money for her father's ticket.

Before it arrived the Mexican couple sold some of their calves and provided Perico with funds for a ticket to El Paso.

Long before the coming of the Chiricahuas, rumors of buried treasure and of gold deposits on the reservation were of common occurrence. It should be remembered that it was not so much the invasion of the rancher that angered the Indians as that of the miner. There was buried treasure on the reservation. There were gold deposits there. Mexicans herding sheep on the White Mountain knew of caves in which somebody had hidden quantities of treasure.

Even today there are people who believe these reports. A young Mescalero who has had two years in college told me recently that he knew where "a pickup load" of gold could easily be obtained. When asked why he did not do it he shook his head. "I'm not about to bother that gold," he said. "I've got trouble enough without that." But he would answer no more questions.

A trader who lived on the reservation for years says that he knows of five different deposits of gold there. He came to me to write articles or a book on the subject, but I had to decline. Why not write it himself? He wasn't a writer, he said, but he did know gold when he found it.

Charlie Smith, too, knew where there was "plenty of gold." He had found it on Pajarito Mountain. He carried a buckskin "poke" of nuggets which he wished to sell. Nearby in a cave he had picked up many Spanish coins, very old ones. "Just look at the dates." I did. They were very old, and I believed them to be genuine. About the gold I was doubtful. I sent some pieces to be analyzed; they were iron pyrites, but not to Charlie Smith. He believed them to be gold.

301

About ten days later, his wife, Aggie, and his son came. Charlie had boarded a bus and gone to El Paso where he had hoped to sell both the coins and the gold. He had been gone five days and should have returned. Why hadn't he come home? I thought I might learn. By telephone I called Del Barton, secretary to William Hooten, editor of the *El Paso Times*. Had she or Robert, her husband, seen Charlie? They had not, but because motel rooms and food were cheap in Juárez he might have gone to Mexico. Mr. Hooten knew the chief of police across the line. Sure enough, they were holding Charlie for identification as an American citizen. The Bartons drove to the jail. The chief met them there and released Charlie. The Native American returned to his own. As for the coins and gold—apparently Charlie had not found a buyer, at least not that trip.

After the U.S. Treasury, cattle and lumber are the primary sources of income on the reservation. If it has mineral resources, so far they are undeveloped. When and if other sources of income are depleted, even the Apaches may resort to the forbidden mining—but not until then.

CHAPTER 20

JASPER KANSEAH

I first met Jasper Kanseah when Evans Istee, grandson of Chief Victorio, went with me to White Tail to see his father, Charles. Charles and Jasper were walking down the road. When we arrived at the Istee home, Dora, Charlie's wife, shared a picnic lunch with us on the porch. There was little conversation while we ate, and what there was was in Apache. Evans explained that all his life his father had feared that he would be killed because of his relationship to Victorio. Charlie was an old man and had refused to be interviewed. Because of his apprehensions he very seldom went down to the village.

Jasper was less reticent. Though he volunteered little, he answered direct questions.[1] Encouraged by Evans, Jasper began the first of many accounts of his boyhood as a free Apache before his surrender with Geronimo in 1886.

When Jasper Kanseah first called at my home he brought his wife, Lucy, and their daughters Velma and Abbie. Before entering the house Jasper Kanseah inquired as to my marital status; upon being told that I am a widow, the four came in and were seated. Apache etiquette requires a social visit before the purpose of the call is discussed. After it, Jasper Kanseah, who allowed me to call him Jasper after we became acquainted, talked rather freely. The women, as is their custom, spoke only when asked a question.

Jasper told of his boyhood, of seeing Cochise, and of being taken into Geronimo's band. He told of his apprenticeship under Yahnosha and of being honored to be voted a full warrior at a younger age than was customary.[2]

After Jasper and the women left the house Velma returned to the door. "My father was a warrior with Geronimo," she informed me, "but he is a good man. He was just a little boy and had no choice as to going. He is a good man."

I assured her that I believed so.

"And," she continued, "Geronimo was a good man and a very brave one. So was Yahnosha. Even some Apaches blame them for the twenty-seven years that our people were prisoners of war. But they just had the courage to keep on fighting after the others gave up."

---

1. The Apaches I interviewed were always reticent to speak openly until I had gained their respect and trust.

2. For Kanseah's accounts see chapters 19 and 20, Book One.

The Kanseahs stopped frequently after that and we became good friends. Sometimes they brought me venison of very high quality. When I asked Jasper how he managed it, he answered, "Mrs. Lady, every evening the deer come down off the mountain to drink at the *tanque* [an artificial pond]. They have a path right in front of my porch. I just sit there till a nice young fat one comes along."

One day Jasper brought a box of papers and asked to leave them with me. They were "letters and pictures," Jasper said, "and my army discharges. I served nine years as scout for the Seventh Cavalry at Fort Sill and have three honorable discharges."

I suggested that they should be left in a vault at the bank.

"I don't trust banks," he said, "and I don't trust White Eyes. I want you to keep them."

"My house might burn."

"Mine could, too. I'll leave them with you."

When I reminded him that he might want a pension later he replied that he had one already. With misgivings I placed his papers in my files. Several times I asked if he would not take them, but he would not.

Lucy died suddenly, and Abbie brought Jasper to inform me. They told me that everything that was hers had been destroyed or would be buried with her. Jasper had moved to his daughter's home; his house perhaps would be vacant for years. Three days after his wife's funeral the Kanseahs returned, this time after dark. Jasper had come for his papers. It was with a sense of relief that I returned them to him.

"Mrs. Lady, Abbie may need these when I go to the Happy Place."

"You?"

"Lucy, she's gone. Now there is nothing to keep me here."

"But you have sons and daughters. You have many friends who love you."

"I have many more who have gone ahead of me."

I reminded him that he had good health and might be with us many years. He shook his head and started toward the door.

Within a week's time his daughters returned. Jasper had died in his sleep during the night.[3]

---

3. Illogical though it is, the old Apaches seem to have premonitions of impending death. I asked how they explain their seeming knowledge that death is close. The reply I received was to the effect that they cannot explain it, but that such premonitions are common.

CHAPTER 21

CHIHUAHUA

Eugene had a magnificent baritone voice that with training might have qualified for the Metropolitan, and he frequently sang solos in both the English and Apache languages. He was the head Medicine Man in charge of the Dance of the Mountain Spirits, which is performed at night. Eugene not only led the singing, but he also composed many of the songs.

A few days before the date set for the Ceremonials I started to Alamogordo and stopped at Mescalero to see the Chihuahuas. When I stopped at the foot of the steps leading to their porch Eugene was singing a prayer. I waited for him to finish before going to the door. He was obviously depressed and I asked if he was ill. He shook his head. Just then Jennie stepped out onto the porch and said, "He's worse than sick. He's lost his contact with Chief Chihuahua." Eugene explained that the chief, who had died years before, disapproved of his attending church. And Eugene needed his guidance.*

"It's clay for the Ceremonials," he explained. "As head Medicine Man I should get it. But the clay is seven miles away and I cannot walk that far."

"But you have horses," I said.

"There are three fences between here and the clay. Cutting them is forbidden."

"I'm on my way to Alamogordo. I'll bring you some powdered poster paint."

"I don't know whether or not Ussen would like that," said Eugene. "He told us that we must do exactly as he ordered."

I tried to make him understand that this commercial paint is a form of clay. And I asked what colors were needed.

"I paint the men's bodies black above the belt," he said, "with charcoal. But I need white, blue, and yellow for the symbols."

"Red?" I asked.

"Red is for war dances."

"I'll get the others."

Eugene shook his head and I suggested that this would not be his first devia-

---

*Eugene's father, Chief Chihuahua, who died at Fort Sill in 1901, was his *spirit control.* Apparently Apache spirit controls are similar to Christian guardian angels.

tion from ancient procedures. Instead of going to the forest to dress and be painted, the young men were using his barn for that purpose. When I took the paint to him he was still in doubt as to the advisability of using it.

It was an extremely hot and dry summer, and I did not attend the rites until late afternoon of the fourth day. When I ascended the steps at Eugene's, I found Daklugie and Carisso Gallarito on the porch with him. He opened the door for me and I went into the living room with Jennie.

A car stopped at the foot of the steps and two young white men climbed them and asked for Chihuahua. When Eugene had identified himself, one of them spoke to Daklugie. As was his custom, Daklugie ignored the white man's greeting. Carisso spoke no English, but he nodded. Without being asked the callers took chairs and one said, "You think you can make it rain?" Without awaiting Eugene's reply he went on, "We are anthropologists from the university. Trained scientists say that we will have no rain for months."

Eugene spoke, "I do not think that I can make it rain. You have been misinformed. I am a very old man and can remember things that happened when I was four years old. Since that time I have attended the Ceremonials, and not once has Ussen failed to keep his promise to the Apaches. He will not fail us this time."

"But science proves that it will not rain—"

Daklugie had had enough. Suddenly he broke in, "I bet you a hundred dollars that it rains."

"It hasn't rained for three months, and it won't for another three," said one of the white men.

"Bet you a hundred," repeated Ace.

The callers took inventory and came up with fifty dollars.

"You understand," said Daklugie, "that the Ceremonials do not end until sunrise. At midnight all White Eyes are asked to leave the feast ground. If I lose—or if you lose—there can be no payoff until morning."

"We need somebody to hold stakes," said one of the young men.

"The white lady in the house," replied Eugene. "She's white but honest."

I was so overwhelmed by his endorsement that I found myself putting two small rolls of bills into my purse. Why had I been so stupid? I certainly would not spend the night at the feast ground. But Daklugie had gone. I told Eugene that he must keep the bets. I had no intention of staying after midnight and being put in jail.

He grinned. "Who do you think makes the medicine here?" he asked.

"Daklugie."

He nodded. He knew very well that I was reminding him that, though he was head Medicine Man, he was dominated by Daklugie.

Then he asked, "Do you think we'd let the police put you in jail?"

"How could you prevent it?"

"By our medicine," was the reply.

I took Eugene and Jennie up the hill to the feast ground in my car. The two white men chose to leave their car at Eugene's and walk up. The dust was two inches deep, and the air was sultry. Ordinarily, at that altitude, even in July, one needs a coat. At eleven-thirty the white "scholars" came to me to collect their bet. I did not have the money. I had entrusted the stakes to the white man in charge of the bingo game for St. Joseph's Mission (I knew that he had official sanction to stay till morning). I explained to the bettors that I was leaving, pointed out the man who now had the stakes, and informed them that if it did not rain they could collect—at sunrise. As they walked away there was a little flicker of lightning in the southeast. They turned to make another appeal for their winnings.

"You can see that it won't rain," said one. "Won't you tell that man to pay us?"

Then came the announcement over the loudspeakers that all but Indians must leave immediately. Then, as people were moving toward parked cars, there came a terrific burst of lightning and thunder. Huge drops of rain splashed in the loose dust. Eugene, Jennie, and I hurried to get into my car.

The cloudburst lasted only a short time, but everything was soaked and water rushed down the steep slopes. I drove Eugene and Jennie home, said goodnight, and waited, with the motor running, until they got to the door. Suddenly an angry voice spoke. "We left our car here. Some thieving Indian has stolen it." There stood two white men—bedraggled, without money, without their car.

Eugene, obviously savoring the moment, calmly responded to their insinuation, "White man, maybe; not Indian."

"But what are we going to do?"

"There's a motel down the road about three miles," said Chihuahua as he went in and closed the door.

I lost no time driving away.

For a short time the Number One Cow Camp was minus a cook, and Eugene agreed to substitute until one could be employed. Ray Reed, the white man in charge of the cattle, asked Eugene to live in the house with him. The cowboys, all of whom were Apaches, slept in the bunkhouse.

Because of the dry hot summer, grazing was poor. To conserve grass for cattle, Ray had the cowboys round up about three hundred wild horses. They were kept in a big corral with the gate padlocked. They had been sold to a company that made dog food, and Reed was awaiting shipment.

One morning Reed found the gate open and the broncos gone. Again the whole force began the task of roping and returning them to the corral. The horses were now wary, and much more time and energy were required for a second capture. Ray Reed slept with his keys under his pillow; but in spite of his precaution he again found an unlocked gate and an empty corral. He went to Chihuahua.

"Eugene," he said, "You and I have been friends for years. But you are the only person who could have got my keys without waking me. Why did you turn those horses loose?"

Eugene didn't blink. He eyed his White Eye friend and said, "Horses are the only friends an Apache has. I didn't want to see them made into dog food."

Ray did some fast thinking. "Neither do I," he said, "I just hadn't thought about it that way."

He did not gather them again.

During the last year or two of his life, Eugene spent much time in the hospital. When I found him at home he informed me that he and Jennie

Eugene and Jennie Chihuahua, 1961. (U.S. Army photograph)

had decided that I was to have the contents of a trunk filled with photographs and papers.

"Next time you come," he said, "bring some boxes and take these things home with you." However, I felt that if I asked for them both would think that I did not expect him to live very long. So I did not mention getting the papers again.

When I went to the hospital I took Jennie with me. While she visited with Eugene, one of the nurses told me that if an infant cried at night he would try to get up and care for it. "But," she added, "when he is delirious he stands, brandishes an imaginary ax, and threatens death to the White Eyes." This was so contradictory to anything I knew of Eugene that I found it incredible. I had thought him one of the mildest and kindest people I knew.

The last time I saw Eugene in the hospital he said, "My daughter, there are two things I want you to do for me. I want you to make a writing for the paper because I have told you about my family and I know that you will get it right. And I want you to make a pumpkin pie for the journey. You know, it is a four-day trip and we need food." Then he smiled and said, "And I know that it won't be a storebought pie."

When I was informed by telephone of his death I went to Jennie immediately. A few minutes after she was told that he was gone she had, as was their custom, burned the contents of the trunk. The embers were still smouldering on the frozen ground.

She accepted my invitation to stay at my home until after the funeral service. (The mortuary was less than a quarter of a mile from my home.) She asked me to call Robert and Del Barton, their adopted children who lived in El Paso. They too came to Ruidoso as fast as they could get there. They took Jennie to see Eugene at the mortuary each of the four days prior to his burial.

I stood beside them while Jennie painted his face, adjusted his medicine hat and card, and said her last farewell. She requested that the pumpkin pie be placed in the casket with him. On the grave was placed the symbolic basket of fruit and nuts which the primitive Apaches felt was as necessary as white people feel flowers are.

It was a bitterly cold day when Eugene was buried. I tried to persuade Jennie to stay awhile with me, but she preferred to go to her own home.

That I could understand.

CHAPTER 22

DAKLUGIE

One April morning Daklugie came to the door carrying a large cardboard box full of papers. Maude and Evangeline followed with smaller ones.

"I've been intending for some time to bring these," he said. "I meant to sort them first but we can do some of that today. There are some clippings and pictures I want Maude to have."

As I began protesting the responsibility of the custody of his records he said, "You can't help yourself. I'm giving them to you!"

As he took letters from worn envelopes, he laid some aside for his daughter. He did the same with the photographs. Where he found duplicates, each of us got one. He handed a letter to me. It was from Father Albert Braun congratulating him and Ramona on the celebration of their fiftieth wedding anniversary and commending them for an observance of their long, happy marriage.

"I did some interpreting for him," Ace continued, "until he learned to give his sermons in Apache. After he did we went to his church sometimes. Ramona liked the dignity of the service and wanted to go."

He leaned back in the big chair that was his favorite and said, "You went to the cemetery at White Tail when Ramona was buried. You remember the road that leads up the hill from the highway? It is the only way to the cemetery. I saw Ramona last night. She stood at the junction of the roads. She called to me and asked why I didn't come. I told her that I could not until Ussen speaks but that it might be anytime. I said that she must be patient and wait for me. Then she faded into the night."

He did not seem depressed or unhappy. Though I had never seen him more affable and gracious, I was puzzled by his moodiness and his skipping from one subject to another. He spoke of Eugene, their boyhood experiences, and their close friendship for three-quarters of a century. There was no more loyal friend than Chihuahua.

I thought of my recent visit with Eugene. He had inquired, "How are you and my brother-in-law getting along on that book?"

"We're not," I had told him. "We're on the warpath."

"What's he been doing?"

"He never misses a chance to say harsh and unkind things about white people."

Eugene had eyed me quizzically. "Well, aren't they true?"

"Perhaps. Well, I know that some of them are, but they happened long before I was born."

"But not before Daklugie and I were. We saw these things. Our women and children have never wronged your people, but they were butchered just the same."

What could I say?

Eugene had gone on, "You are very fortunate to have had the chance to get what he knows. There is no one else who has the knowledge he possesses. There are no Apaches who would have written it for him; and I did not think that he would ever permit any White Eye to do it."

I had assured him of my gratitude to both him and Daklugie.

"And if you had seen women and children butchered as he did—he saw his mother killed, his youngest sister killed, and his older one wounded—you might feel just as he does."

I had come to a realization of that.

When Daklugie spoke of Eugene I replied that I knew what a kind and mild person he was. To my surprise he burst into laughter. "Mild? Chihuahua mild? He's about as mild as a grizzly. You should have seen him when those two men came out to the house during World War II. I was not at home, but Ramona and Jennie were there. When they told Eugene that they had come to enlist the Apaches' help *for* Germany he reached for my rifle and told them that he'd give them two minutes to get over the hill and stay put. They made it in less!"

Those fierce old warriors! Of course I should have known; but they were so soft-spoken, so courteous, and so generous with information that I had almost forgotten the military reports.

"The officers needed alibis," Ace said, "especially those who pitted their intelligence against Geronimo's. Toward the end [before the 1886 surrenders] their troops just outnumbered his five hundred to one. So they made Geronimo a monster." He stopped and laughed. "At times he was!"

Daklugie rambled on. On previous visits he was much better prepared to dictate whatever episode he had planned to discuss. When he spoke again he asked a strange question: "Do you believe in ghosts?"

"I'll give you the answer a famous Frenchwoman gave to that question: 'I don't believe in them but I'm afraid of them.' "

"Then she did believe in them?"

"I can't tell you that I would be unafraid if, alone at night, I chanced to see white-draped figures," I replied.

He was silent for awhile.

Again Ace spoke: "Eugene and I are largely responsible for bringing our people here. At the time we did it we did not have the wisdom to know that we were making a terrible mistake. We thought that we had made the right decision. We had no alternative except that of staying in Oklahoma and becoming farmers. No Apache really wanted to farm; but those who did it are better off than are the ones who came to this reservation. Why? Because those at Fort Sill became dependent on themselves by the farming experience, and they seem to have been strengthened. While it is true that we were in captivity in Oklahoma, it was an entirely different type of supervision. The Apaches will tell you that they did better under military control than under the civilian

Ramona.

administration. The officers at Fort Sill had wisely left both the management and decisions largely up to the chiefs or headmen, each of whom had a village. Their primary functions were to maintain order and standards. It is different here at Mescalero, even though it is perhaps the richest in natural resources of any in the United States.

"But, when we go to the Happy Place we will know what should be done. If I should come back to tell you would you be afraid of me?"

"I have never been," I told him, "and I don't know why I should be if such a thing should happen."

This was getting entirely too serious and it was foreign to my comprehension. I told him that I did not understand it and that if I did it would never happen to me. Their communication with the dead was beyond my understanding.

"Because you make it complicated. It is very simple."

"Why not go to some of your people who do have the ability to communicate with those who have gone?"

"Because they are just reservation Indians. They have been born and reared in captivity. They haven't the courage to do anything about it. In one way they are still in captivity of a worse kind than we were as prisoners of war. They have been deprived of all initiative since they became members of the tribe here. All decisions are made for them. They see nothing ahead for themselves or their children. They have never been free nor thrown upon their own

312

resources. They know that they can't own land [individually], though they can own houses. At times many go hungry, but they know that they won't starve. The government does see to that.

"How many people on this reservation do you think could leave it, get employment, and live on their own resources? Very few? You are right. There are three strikes against them before they start: they are Indians; they have been downgraded till they lack confidence; they are not treated as equals."

"But what could anyone do alone? Especially any person with no organization with votes?"

"Just what you are trying to do. Get our story published. Let people know the facts. In time Indians of other tribes will write the history of their people. And if these things have no effect, it will be Ussen who decides. We used to think his promise to restore this land to us would be done by means of some cataclysm—earthquake, volcanic eruption, flood perhaps. Now it may come about by the atomic bomb.

"When that comes all life will be destroyed except that of a few, but they won't know how to survive when they can't go to a store and buy food in tin cans or bread already sliced. When that time comes, go to my people. They will take care of you."

I had known of this expectation of the restoration of North America to the Indians from Eugene. He had told me that everyone would die but that after four days the Indians would be restored to life. The buffalo would return to the plains, the antelope to the hills, and the deer to the mountains.

Daklugie's mood changed. He chuckled with irony over attempts to get him drunk so that he might tell White Eyes of gold deposits and buried treasure on the reservation. He knew, he said, exactly what those plying him with liquor—good liquor—had in mind. He knew also exactly how much he could drink and remain sober. They'd learned nothing from him.

Then he surprised me by saying that even after he and Eugene went to the Happy Place they would protect me as they were doing at that time. That they did so was a new idea to me, but apparently not to Evangeline. She nodded and said, "And they will, Mrs. Ball. Don't you ever be afraid of anything. They have the Power."

I was too astonished to thank them.

Daklugie said, "There will be many times when Eugene or I will sit in this chair. You will be unable to see us, but we will be here.

"Before you got that television there were sounds and people in this room. You could not see or hear them, but they were here. This TV shows pictures to you. The Apaches don't need a mechanical device to show people or to communicate with those who have gone. That is the difference."

"They are to be envied," I told him. "They are very fortunate. I do not have this ability, but I envy those who do."

He nodded and arose.

It had been a strange day, so strange that not until Daklugie had collected his family and gone to the door did I remember that I had an appointment with the dentist the following Thursday. I asked them to come an hour later than usual the next time, and they agreed to do so.

When I returned to the house the following Thursday, I found a note on the door. It read as follows: "Please come out to Carisso. My grandfather died this morning of a heart attack. Evangeline."

BIBLIOGRAPHY

INTERVIEWS, INDIAN

Ahidley, Philip, Navajo
Allard, John, Chiricahua
Apache, Bessie Ybarra, Lipan
Balin, Dave, Chiricahua
Balachu, Margaret Big Mouth, wife
    of Mack Big Mouth, Warm
    Springs
Bearing, Nelson, Arapaho
Begay, Alberta, Mescalero
Betzinez, Jason, Chihenne
Big Mouth, Mescalero
Big Mouth, Percy, Mescalero
Big Mouth, Mack, Mescalero
Big Mouth, Margaret, Warm Springs
Big Rope, Darlene Enjady,
    Chiricahua
Big Rope, Bessie, Mescalero
Big Rope, Leroy, Mescalero
Chato, Helen, widow of Scout Chato,
    Chiricahua
Chee, Rachel (Mrs. Ralph, Sr.),
    Mescalero
Chee, Ralph, Sr., Chiricahua
Chee, Ralph, Jr., Mescalero
Chee, Clifford, Mescalero
Chico, Walter, Mescalero
Chihuahua, Eugene, Chiricahua
Chihuahua, Jennie, Mescalero
Chihuahua, Edna Comanche,
    Chiricahua
Chino, Sam, Chiricahua
Cleghorn, Mildred, Chiricahua
Cojo, Marion, Mescalero
Cojo, Katherine, Mescalero Medicine

Woman, Mescalero
Comanche, Freddie, Mescalero
Comanche, Lemuel, Mescalero
Comanche, Lizzie, Mescalero
Comanche, Willie, Mescalero
Coonie, Dah-tes-te (Tah-des-te), sister
    of Geronimo, Bedonkohe
Coonie, Hugh, Chiricahua
Coonie, Eliza, Chiricahua
Crow, John, agent
Dahteste (Ta-dos-tie), sister of
    Chihuahua's wife, Chiricahua
Daklugie, Ace, Nednhi
Daklugie, Ramona, Chiricahua
Daklugie, Maude Geronimo,
    Chiricahua
Daklugie, Lydia Shanta, Chiricahua
Darrow, Ruey, Chiricahua
Decherle, John, Mescalero
Decherle, Salvador, Mescalero
Enjady, Clarence, Mescalero
Enjady, Darlene Big Rope, daughter
    of Isabel and Clarence, Chiricahua
Enjady, Isabel Perico, Chiricahua
Enjady, Wallace, Chiricahua
Enjady, Wayne, Chiricahua
Enjady, Dolores, Mescalero
Enjady, (Mrs. Allard), Mescalero
Fatty, "Old" (Gordo in books), Warm
    Springs
Gaines, Aileen Second,
    granddaughter of George Martine,
    Nednhi
Gaines, Irene, Mescalero

Scott, Gladys (Mrs. Marion Cojo), Mescalero
Second, Bernard, Mescalero
Shanta, Lydia Daklugie, wife of Ralph Shanta, Jr., and daughter of Daklugie, Chiricahua
Shanta, Ralph, Sr., Mescalero
Shanta, Ralph, Jr., Mescalero
Shanta, Phoebe Wilson, Mescalero
Shanta, Virginia Klinecole, Mescalero
Shields, Eloise Wilson, Mescalero
Shields, Henry, Mescalero
Smith, Charlie, Mescalero
Smith, Aggie, Mescalero
Smoky, Maggie, Comanche
Sombrero, Solon, Mescalero
Stonecalf, Timothy, Cheyenne
Sundayman, Elias, Mescalero
Tahnito, John, Chiricahua
Tahnito, Rose, Lipan

Torres, Franklin, Mescalero
Torres, Gertrude, Mescalero
Torres, Herbert and Laverne, Mescalero
Treas, Henry, Mescalero
Treas, Byron, Mescalero
Treas, Rudolph, artist, Mescalero
Venego, Philemon, Lipan
Wilson, Elmer, Mescalero
Wilson, Hallie Magoosh, Mescalero
Wilson, Eloise Shields, Mescalero
Wilson, Woodrow, son of Elmer Wilson, and Medicine Man, Mescalero
Yahnosha, warrior with Geronimo, Chiricahua
Zuazua, Kate, Lipan
Zurego, Minnie, Warm Springs
Zhunni, Calvin, warrior with Geronimo, Chiricahua

INTERVIEWS, NON-INDIAN

Amonett, (Mrs. Ed)
Aranda, Daniel
Atchison, William
Baird, James
Barton, Mr. and Mrs. Robert
Blazer, Paul
Blazer, Mrs. Emma Thompson
Bonnell, Mr. and Mrs. Bert
Bonnell, Mrs. Faye Champion
Braun, Fr. Albert, O.F.M.
Burdett, Madeline
Burrows, Jack
Bragg, Tom
Browning, Clyde
Camillus, Fr., O.F.M.
Campbell, Mrs. Stella
Campbell, Jesse
Carabajal, Daniel
Carroll, Mrs. Eloise Sutherland
Carroll, (Mrs. James A.)
Chase, Mrs. C. C., daughter of A. B. Fall
Chase, Mrs. Emadair Jones
Chase, Mrs. Maryena Roberts
Chavez, Carlos, Attorney General of State of Chihuahua

Clark, (Mrs. E. Lindquist)
Clark, Mr. and Mrs. L. D.
Craig, Judge Carl
Craig, (Mrs. Carl)
Davidson, Mrs. Amelia Bolton
Debo, Angie
Davenport, Mrs. Nancy
Dunaway, Mrs. Nancy
Dow, Hiram
Evans, Mr. and Mrs. Sam
Fergusson, Erna
Fields, Ronnie, son of Wesley
Fulton, Maurice Garland
Gillilan, Dick, brother of Jim
Griffith, Fred
Gunter, Ab
Hall, Mrs. John
Hawkins, Mrs. Jessie Lee
Henn, Nora (Mrs. Walter)
Henn, Walter
Hepler, Elmer
Hiles, Mr. and Mrs. Jack
Hinton, Dr. Harwood P.
Hix, John
Humphries, Keith
Jackson, David

Jefferis, Mrs. C. R.
Johnson, William (Bill)
Jones, Mr. and Mrs. Elliott
Jones, Bill, Sam, Nebo (Nib), and Frank, sons of Heiskell Jones
Judia, Bert
Kelly, Frank, manager of Tribal Store
Lake, Mona Lee, daughter of Oliver Lee
Lee, Mrs. Minnie, grocer at Ruidoso
Lindamood, Mrs. Aileen
Lockwood, Frank
Mahill, Frank
Mahill, James
Mayer, (Mrs. Paul, Sr.)
Metz, Leon
Mes, Ramón and Theodora
Miller, (Mrs. Felix)
Montgomery, John
McGonagill, Mr. and Mrs. Ernest
McGonagill, Mr. and Mrs. Joe
McGuire, Marvin B.
McKnight, Joe
McNatt, Stanley
Mullin, (Mrs. Robert N.)
Murphy, Mr. and Mrs. Pat
Nelson, Rose
Nelson, Mr. and Mrs. Joe
Ogilvie, Mr. and Mrs. Kenneth
Otero, Joseph, Superintendent at Mescalero
Penfield, Edward
Peso, Mrs. Frederick
Phingston, Mr. and Mrs. Fred
Prather, Tom
Pryor, Mrs. Rafeleta
Pullens, Denese
Rainbolt, Al
Reed, Ray

Reddy, Mr. and Mrs. Herbert
Rigdon, "Skipper"
Rigsby, Mrs. Edith, daughter of Frank Coe
Runyon, Mrs. David
Sanchez, Lynda
Sanchez, Juanita
Sanchez, Ben
Sanchez, Max
Schend, Mr. and Mrs. Dick
Sedillo, Sixto
Shinkle, Mr. and Mrs. James
Slaughter, Fannie and Sally
Snow, Mrs. Clara
Spencer, Truman, Jr.
Storm, Dan
Sutherland, Eloise (Mrs. Ted)
Sutherland, Ted
Thomas, Mrs. John
Thompson, Col. Frank
Titsworth, Mrs. Anne, daughter of Frank Coe
Toodson, Dr. and Mrs.
Tully, James V.
Tully, (Mrs. James, Sr.)
Welch, (Mrs. Joe, Sr.)
Welch, Herbert
Welch, Joe, Jr.
Weisner, Herman
Wilson, Mrs. Belle
Woodward, Mr. and Mrs. Jimmy
Wratten, Albert, son of George Wratten
Wright, (Mrs. C.)
Yeager, Dorothy Emerson
Yoder, Martie (Mrs. Hal)

Books

Adams, Alexander B. *Geronimo*. Berkeley: Berkeley Publishing Corporation, 1971.

——————. *The Camp Grant Massacre*. New York: Simon and Schuster, 1976.

Armstrong, Virginia. *I Have Spoken*. Chicago: Swallow Press, 1972.

Arnold, Elliott. *Blood Brother*. New York: Duell, Sloan & Pearce, 1947.

Atkins, Daisy. *'Way Back Yonder: Old West Reminiscence of a Lady on Horseback*. El Paso, Tex.: Guynes Printing Company, 1958.

Ball, Eve. *In the Days of Victorio*. Tucson: University of Arizona Press, 1970.

——————. *Ma'am Jones of the Pecos*. Tucson: University of Arizona Press, 1969.

——————. *My Girlhood among Outlaws*. Tucson: University of Arizona Press, 1972.

Bancroft, Hubert Howe. *The Works of Hubert Howe Bancroft*. Vol. 17. San Francisco: History Company, 1889.

Barrett, S. M., ed. *Geronimo's Story of His Life*. New York: Duffield & Co., 1907.

Bartlett, John Russell. *Personal Narratives of Explorations and Incidents in Texas, New Mexico . . . 1853*. New York: D. Appleton & Co., 1854.

Basso, Keith, and Opler, Morris E., *Apachean Culture History and Ethnology*. Tucson: University of Arizona Press, 1971.

Basso, Keith H., ed. *Western Apache Raiding and Warfare, from the Notes of Grenville Goodwin*. Tucson: University of Arizona Press, 1971.

Bennett, James A. *Forts and Forays: The Diary of a Dragoon in New Mexico, 1850–1856*. Edited by Clinton Brooks and Frank Reeve. Albuquerque: University of New Mexico Press, 1948.

Betzinez, Jason, and Nye, Wilbur S. *I Fought with Geronimo*. Harrisburg, Pa.: Stackpole Co., 1959.

Bigelow, Lt. John, Jr. *On the Bloody Trail of Geronimo*. Edited by Arthur Woodward. New York: Tower Publishers, Inc., 1938.

Bourke, John G. *An Apache Campaign in the Sierra Madre*. New York: Charles Scribner's Sons, 1958.

——————. *Indian Wars*. Palo Alto, Calif.: Lewis Osborne, 1968.

——————. *On the Border with Crook*. Lincoln, Neb.: University of Nebraska Press, 1971.

——————. *With General Crook in the Indian Wars*. Palo Alto, Calif.: Lewis Osborne, 1968.

Brandes, Raymond S. *Frontier Military Posts of Arizona*. Globe, Ariz.: Dale Stuart King, 1960.

Browne, John Ross. *Adventure in the Apache Country: A Tour through Arizona and Sonora*. New York: Harper & Bros., 1869.

Burns, Walter Noble. *The Saga of Billy the Kid*. New York: Garden City Publishing Co., Inc., 1925.

Calvin, Ross. *Sky Determines: An Interpretation of the Southwest*. Albuquerque: University of New Mexico Press, 1968.

Clum, Woodworth. *Apache Agent*. New York: Houghton Mifflin Co., 1936.

Coan, Charles F. *A History of New Mexico*. 3 Vols. Chicago: American Historical Society, 1936.

Cooke, Philip St. George. *The Conquest of New Mexico and California* Albuquerque: Horn and Wallace, 1964).

——————. *Scenes and Adventures in the Army*. New York: Arno Press, 1973.

Comfort, Will Livingston. *Apache*. New York: E. P. Dutton & Co., 1913.

Conner, Daniel Ellis. *Joseph Reddeford Walker and the Arizona Adventure*. Edited by Donald J. Berthrong and Odessa Davenport. Norman: University of Oklahoma Press, 1956.

Corle, Edward. *Desert Country*. New York: Duell, Sloan & Pearce, 1941.

Cremony, John C. *Life among the Apaches*. Tucson: Arizona Silhouettes, 1951.

Cressinger, A. W. *Charles A. Poston, Sunland Seer*. Globe, Ariz.: Dale Stuart King, 1961.

Crocchiola, Stanley Francis Louis. *The Apaches of New Mexico, 1514–1940*. Pampa, Tex.: Pampa Print Shop, 1962.

—————. *Fort Stanton, New Mexico*. Pampa, Tex.: Pampa Print Shop, 1964.

Crook, General George. *General George Crook: His Autobiography*. Edited by Martin F. Schmitt. Norman: University of Oklahoma Press, 1946.

—————. *Resume of Operations against Apache Indians, 1881–1886*. Washington, D.C.: Government Printing Office, 1887.

Cruse, General Thomas. *Apache Days and After*. Edited by Eugene Cunningham. Caldwell, Idaho: Caxton Printers, Ltd., 1941.

Cummings, Byron. *Indians I Have Known*. Tucson: Arizona Silhouettes, 1952.

Dale, Edward Everett. *The Indians of the Southwest*. Norman: University of Oklahoma Press, 1949.

Davis, Lt. Britton. *The Truth about Geronimo*. Edited by M. E. Quaife. New Haven, Conn.: Yale University Press, 1929.

Debo, Angie. *A History of the Indians of the United States*. Norman: University of Oklahoma Press, 1970.

—————. *Geronimo: The Man, His Time, His Place*. Norman: University of Oklahoma Press, 1976.

DeVoto, Bernard. *A Year of Decision, 1846*. Boston: Little, Brown and Co., 1943.

Dobie, J. Frank. *Apache Gold and Yaqui Silver*. New York: Little, Brown and Co., 1939.

—————. *Tongues of the Monte*. Boston: Little, Brown and Co., 1935.

Dunn, Jacob Platt, Jr. *Massacres of the Mountains: A History of the Indian Wars of the Far West, 1815–1875*. New York: Harper & Bros., 1886.

Emerson, Dorothy. *Among the Mescalero Apaches: The Story of Father Albert Braun, O.F.M.* Tucson: University of Arizona Press, 1973.

Emory, Lt. William H. *Lieutenant Emory Reports*. Albuquerque: University of New Mexico Press, 1951.

Farish, Thomas Brown. *Arizona History*, Vol. 2. San Francisco: The Felines Bros. Electrotype Co., 1915.

Faulk, Odie B. *The Geronimo Campaign*. New York: Oxford University Press, 1969.

Forsyth, George A. *Thrilling Days in Army Life*. New York: Harper and Brothers, 1900.

Goodwin, Grenville. *Among the Western Apaches: Letters from the Field*. Edited by Morris E. Opler. Tucson: University of Arizona Press, 1973.

—————. *The Social Organization of the Western Apache*. Tucson: University of Arizona Press, 1969.

—————. *Western Apache Raiding and Warfare*. Edited by Keith Basso. Tucson: University of Arizona Press, 1971.

Gregg, Josiah. *Commerce of the Prairies*. Dallas: Southwest Press, 1933.

Guiteras, Eusebio, trans. *Rudo Ensayo, Arizona and Sonora, 1763*. Tucson: Arizona Silhouettes, 1951.

Gunnerson, Dolores A. *The Jicarilla Apaches: A Study in Survival*. De Kalb: Northern Illinois University Press, 1974.

Heitman, Francis B. *Historical Register and Dictionary of the United States Army, from Its Organization, September 29, 1789, to March 2, 1903.* 2 Vols. Washington, D.C.: Government Printing Office, 1902.

History of New Mexico: Its Resources and People. New York: Pacific States Publishing Co., 1907.

Hodge, Frederick W. *Handbook of American Indians North of Mexico.* 2 Vols. Washington, D.C.: Government Printing Office, 1912.

Hoijer, Harry. *Chiricahua and Mescalero Apache Texts.* Chicago: University of Chicago Press, 1938.

Horgan, Paul. *A Distant Trumpet.* New York, 1900.

Horn, Calvin. *New Mexico's Troubled Years: The Story of the Early Territorial Governors.* Albuquerque: Horn & Wallace Publishers, 1963.

Horn, Tom. *Life of Tom Horn: A Vindication.* Denver: The Louthan Company, 1904.

James, George Wharton. *Indians of the Painted Desert.* New York: Little, Brown & Co., 1902.

James, Will. *Lone Cowboy: My Life Story.* New York: Charles Scribner's Sons, 1930.

Keleher, William A. *Turmoil in New Mexico, 1846-1868.* Santa Fe, N.Mex.: Rydal Press, 1952.

Leckie, William H. *The Buffalo Soldiers: A Narrative of Negro Cavalry in the West.* Norman: Oklahoma University Press, 1967.

Lister, Florence C. and Robert H. *Chihuahua: Storehouse of Storms.* Albuquerque: New Mexico University Press, 1966.

Lockwood, Frank C. *The Apache Indians.* New York: Macmillan Co., 1938.

——————. *Arizona Characters.* Los Angeles: The Times Mirror Press, 1928.

Longstreet, Stephen. *War Cries on Horseback: The Story of the Indian Wars of the Great Plains.* New York: Doubleday & Co., Inc., 1970.

Lummis, Charles F. *General Crook and the Apache Wars.* Flagstaff, Ariz.: Northland Press, 1958.

——————. *The Land of Poco Tiempo.* New York: Charles Scribner's Sons, 1893.

McKenna, James A. *Black Range Tales.* New York: Wilson-Erickson, Inc., 1936.

McLuhan, T. C. *Touch the Earth: A Self-Portrait of Indian Existence.* New York: Promontory Press, 1971.

McMaster, Richard K. *Musket, Saber and Missile: A History of Fort Bliss.* El Paso, Tex.: Complete Printing & Letter Service, 1962.

Massonovich, Anton. *Trailing Geronimo.* Edited by E. A. Brininstool. Los Angeles: Gem Publishing Co., 1926.

Melton, A. B. *Seventy Years in the Saddle and Then Some.* Kansas City, Mo.: Cole Printing Service, 1950.

Miles, Gen. Nelson A. *Personal Recollections and Observations.* Chicago: Werner Co., 1896.

Montgomery, Ruth. *A World Beyond.* Greenwich, Conn.: Fawcett, 1971.

Neihart, John G. *Black Elk Speaks.* Lincoln: University of Nebraska Press, 1961.

Ogle, Ralph H. *Federal Control of the Western Apaches, 1846-1886.* Albuquerque: University of New Mexico Press, 1940.

Opler, Morris E. *An Apache Life-Way: The Economic, Social and Religious Institutions of the Chiricahua Indians.* Chicago: University of Chicago Press, 1941.

——————. *An Apache Odyssey: A Journey between Two Worlds.* New York: Holt, Rinehart and Winston, 1969.

Parker, William Thornton, M.D. *Annals of Old Fort Cummings, New Mexico, 1867–68.* Fort Davis, Tex.: Frontier Book Company, 1968.

Patton, J. Harris. *A History of the United States of America from the Discovery of the Continent to the Close of the Thirty-sixth Congress.* New York: D. Appleton and Company, 1865.

Pearce, T. M., ed. *New Mexico Place Names: A Geographical Dictionary.* Albuquerque: University of New Mexico Press, 1965.

Proctor, Gil. *The Trails of Pete Kitchen.* Tucson, Ariz.: Dale Stuart King, 1964.

Prucha, Francis Paul. *American Indian Policy in the Formative Years: The Indian Trade and Intercourse Acts, 1790–1834.* Lincoln: University of Nebraska Press, 1970.

Ringgold, Jennie Parks. *Frontier Days in the Southwest.* San Antonio, Tex.: Naylor Company, 1952.

Romney, Thomas Cottam. *Mormon Colonies in Mexico.* Salt Lake City, Utah: The Deseret Book Company, 1938.

Ryus, William A. *The Second William Penn: Treating with Indians On the Sante Fe Trail, 1860–1866.* Kansas City, Kans.: Frank T. Riley Publishing Co., 1913.

Sabin, Edwin L. *Kit Carson Days, 1809–1868.* Chicago: A. G. McClure & Co., 1914.

Santee, Ross. *Apache Land.* Lincoln: University of Nebraska Press, 1972.

Schmitt, Norton F., ed. *General George Crook: His Autobiography.* Norman: University of Oklahoma Press, 1960.

Scott, Hugh Lenox. *Some Memories of a Soldier.* New York: Century Company, 1928.

Sedelmayr, Jacobo. *Jacobo Sedelmayr: Missionary, Frontiersman, Explorer in Arizona and New Mexico.* Four original manuscript narratives, 1744–51. Translated by Peter Masten Dunn. Tucson: Arizona Historical Society, 1955.

Shinkle, James D. *Fort Sumner and the Bosque Redondo Indian Reservation.* Roswell, N.Mex.: Hall-Poorbaugh Press, 1965.

Smith, Cornelius C., Jr. *William Saunders Oury: History-Maker of the Southwest.* Tucson: University of Arizona Press, 1967.

Sonnichsen, C. L. *The Mescalero Apaches.* Norman: University of Oklahoma Press, 1958.

——————. *Pass of the North.* El Paso, Tex.: Western Press, 1968.

Spicer, Edward H. *Cycles of Conquest: The Impact of Spain, Mexico and the United States on the Indians of the Southwest, 1533–1960.* Tucson: The University of Arizona Press, 1962.

Stanley, Fr. See Crocchiola

Terrell, John Upton. *Apache Chronology.* New York: World Publishing Co., 1874. (Courtesy Mrs. Clara Woody)

Thrapp, Dan L. *The Conquest of Apacheria.* Norman: University of Oklahoma Press, 1967.

——————. *Juh, an Incredible Indian.* Southwestern Studies Monograph No. 39. El Paso: Texas Western Press, 1973.

——————. *Al Siebert, Chief of Scouts.* Norman: University of Oklahoma Press, 1964.

Twitchell, Ralph E. *The Leading Facts of New Mexico History.* 2 Vols. Cedar Rapids, Iowa: Torch Press, 1911–1912.

Utley, Robert M. *Frontiersmen in Blue: The United States Army and the Indians, 1848–1865.* New York: The Macmillan Co., 1967.

Walker, Henry Pickering. *The Wagonmasters.* Norman: University of Oklahoma Press, 1967.

Warfield, Col. H. B. *Apache Indian Scouts.* El Cajon, Calif.: Privately printed, 1964.

Webb, Walter Prescott. *The Great Plains.* Boston: Ginn & Co., 1911.

Wellman, Paul. *Bronco Apache.* New York: Doubleday & Co., Inc., 1964.

——————. *Death in the Desert.* New York: Macmillan Co., 1935.

Welsh, Herbert. *The Apache Prisoners in Fort Marion, St. Augustine, Florida.* Philadelphia: Office of the Indian Rights Association, 1887.

Whipple, Lt. Amiel W. *Report upon the Indian Tribes.* Vol. 3. Washington, D.C.: Government Printing Office, 1855.

Williams, Oscar Waldo. *The Personal Narrative of O. W. Williams, Pioneer Surveyor, Frontier Lawyer.* Edited by S. D. Myers. El Paso, Tex.: Western College Press, 1966.

Wissler, Clark. *Indians of the United States, Four Centuries of their History.* New York: Doubleday, Doran & Co., 1940.

——————. *Red Man Reservations.* New York: Collier-McMillan, Ltd., 1938.

Worcester, Donald E. *The Apaches: Eagles of the Southwest.* Norman: University of Oklahoma Press, 1979.

ARTICLES

Aranda, Daniel D. "Josannie, Apache Warrior," *True West* 23 (June 1976).

Ball, Eve. "On the Warpath with Geronimo," *The West* 15 (August 1971).

——————. "The Apache Scouts: A Chiricahua Appraisal," *Arizona and the West* 7 (Winter 1965).

Basso, Keith. "In Pursuit of the Apaches," *Arizona Highways* 53 (July 1977).

——————. "Western Apache Witchcraft," [University of Arizona] *Anthropological Papers* (1969).

Begay, Alberta, as told to Eve Ball. "Massai, Bronco Apache," *True West* 6 (July–August 1959).

Blazer, Almer N. "Beginnings of an Indian War," *New Mexico* 16 (February 1938).

Bourke, John G. "Medicine Men of the Apaches," [Bureau of American Ethnology] *Ninth Annual Report.* Washington, D.C.: Government Printing Office, 1890.

Brandes, Raymond. "Don Santiago Kirker, King of the Scalp Hunters," *The Smoke Signal* 1 (Fall 1965).

Clum, John P. "Apache Misrule," *New Mexico Historical Review* 5 (April 1928).

Clum, Woodworth. "The Apaches," *New Mexico Historical Review* 4 (1929).

Corle, Edwin. "Shoot 'em If They Run." *Arizona Highways* (October 1951).

Dorr, L. L. "The Fight at Chiricahua Pass in 1869." Edited by Marian E. Valpulse and Harold H. Longfellow. *Arizona and the West* 13 (Winter 1971).

Ellis, A. N. "Recollections of an Interview with Cochise, Chief of the Apaches." *Kansas State Historical Collections* 13 (1915).

Ellis, Richard N. "Copper Skinned Soldiers: The Apache Scouts." *Great Plains Journal* (1966).

Folk, Paul J. "The Martyrs of the Southwest." *Illinois Catholic Historical Review* 11 (July 1923).

Gregg, Andy. "The Forts of New Mexico." *Drums of Yesterday,* Series of Western Americana No. 17. Santa Fe: The Press of the Territorian, 1968.

Humphries, Keith. "Tale of the Pioneers." *New Mexico Magazine* (April 1939).

_____. "They Watered at Fort Cummings." *New Mexico Magazine* (August 1939).

_____. "Trail of the Pioneers." *New Mexico Magazine* 17 (1939).

Kanseah, Jasper, and Ball, Eve. "The Last of Geronimo's Warriors." *New Mexico Magazine* 33 (June 1952).

McCann, Frank D., Jr. "Ghost Dance: Last Hope of Western Tribes." *Montana Western History* (January 1966).

McCormick, Wilford. "Apache Neighbors." *New Mexico Magazine* 16 (July 1938).

Mooney, James. "The Ghost Dance Religion and the Sioux Outbreak of 1890." [U.S. Bureau of American Ethnology] *Fourteenth Annual Report, 1892–1893.* Washington, D.C.: Government Printing Office, 1898.

Myers, Lee. "Military Establishments in Southwestern New Mexico: Stepping Stones to Settlement." *New Mexico Historical Review* (January 1968).

Nicholas, Dan. "Mescalero Apache Girls' Puberty Ceremonials." *El Palacio* 6 (October 1945).

Oaks, George, as told to C. V. Rinehart. "I Fought at Beecher's Island." *True West* (September–October 1956).

Opler, Morris E. "A Chiricahua Apache's Account of the Geronimo Campaign of 1886." *New Mexico Historical Review* 13 (1938).

_____. "A Mescalero Apache's Account of the Origin of the Puberty Ceremony." *El Palacio* 52 (October 1945).

Reed, Walter. "Geronimo and His Warriors in Captivity." *The Illustrated American* 3 (August 1890).

Reeves, Frank D. "The Federal Indian Policy in New Mexico, 1858–1880." *New Mexico Historical Review* 13 (1938).

Rope, John, as told to Grenville Goodwin. "Experience of an Apache Scout." *Arizona Historical Review* 13, nos. 1 and 2 (January *and* April 1936).

Smith, Cornelius C. "Old Military Forts of the Southwest." *Frontier Times* (August 1930).

Tomkins, Walter Allison. "Old Fort Bowie, Guardian of Apache Pass." *Arizona Highways* (March 1959).

Turcheneski, John Anthony, Jr. "The United States Congress and the Release of the Apache Prisoners of War at Fort Sill." *Chronicles of Oklahoma* 54 (Summer 1976).

Waltman, Henry G. "Circumstantial Reformer: President Grant & Indian Problems." *Arizona and the West* 13 (Winter 1971).

Worcester, Donald E. "The Apaches in the History of the Southwest." *New Mexico Historical Review* (1975).

Unpublished and Government Documents

Goodman, David Michael. "Apaches as Prisoners of War: 1886–1894." Ph.D. diss., Texas Christian University, 1968.

U.S. National Park Service. *History of the Old Spanish Forts.* Washington, D.C.: Government Printing Office, n.d.

U.S. Dept. of Interior. *Report of the Joint Special Committee,* "Condition of the Indian Tribes." Washington, D.C.: Government Printing Office, 1967.

U.S. Congress, Senate. *Correspondence between Lieut. Gen. P. H. Sheridan and Brig. Gen. George Crook regarding the Apache Indians.* Sen. Ex. Doc. 88, 51st Cong., 1st sess. (Vol. 2682).

_____. *Apache Indians.* Sen. Ex. Doc. 35, 51st Cong., 1st sess. (Vol. 2682).

_____. *Education of the Apaches in Florida.* Sen. Ex. Doc. 73, 49th Cong., 2nd sess. (Vol. 2448).

_____. *Surrender of Geronimo.* Sen. Ex. Doc. 117, 49th Cong., 2nd sess. (Vol. 2449).

_____. *The Apache Prisoners of War at Fort Sill.* Sen. Doc. 432, 62nd Cong., 2nd sess. (Vol. 6175).

Letters (A Selection)

Note: Where no recipient is indicated, the letters are to Eve Ball. Originals and copies of all letters are located in the author's personal file.

Anderson, Allie, to Paul Blazer (copy).

Apache Agents to Commissioner of Indian Affairs (copies), courtesy of John Crow.

Apache Agents James A. Carroll and C. R. Jefferis to Hugh L. Scott (copies).

Barrett, S. M., to Ace Daklugie, September 23, 1931; September 30, 1937 (copies).

Barton, Del (Mrs. Robert); numerous letters over a period of several years.

Barton, Robert; numerous letters concerning Indians.

Braun, Father Albert, O.F.M., January 7, 1960; March 24, 1963; July 17, 1973; February 17, 1974; December 22, 1976.

Bret Harte, John; information regarding George Wratten obtained during research on the San Carlos Reservation for his dissertation.

Burrows, Jack, San Jose City College; numerous letters pertaining to Apache history.

Cleghorn, Mildred, granddaughter of George Wratten, July 18, 1972; December 10, 1972; information regarding her grandparents.

Capps, Benjamin; letter regarding probability of genocide.

Clum, John, to John Wasson, April 31, 1877, *Tucson Arizona Citizen.*

Darrow, Ruey, daughter of Sam Haozous and granddaughter of George Wratten; letters regarding her grandparents.

Debo, Angie; letters in which she most generously gave information from her great knowledge of the Apaches.

Fulton, Maurice Garlond; numerous letters. At one time he considered writing of the Apaches and had a collection of documents and information which he gave me.

Gibbs, Mrs. George, of St. Augustine (copy). She tells of George Wratten and of work done by women of her family in behalf of Apaches.

Haozous, Blossom, daughter of George Wratten; married Sam Haozous; information concerning her father.

Hinton, Harwood P.; numerous letters in response to requests for information as to sources for obscure and difficult-to-find material.

Jozhe, Benedict, prominent member of the Apaches who remained in Oklahoma when the majority came to Mescalero in 1913. I am indebted to him for a chronological chart of the descendants of Chief Mahco, of whom he is a great grandson.

Kaywaykla, James; numerous letters in reply to request for information on the Warm Springs Apaches.

Lentz, Arthur J.; letter to Durrett Wagner (copy), regarding the record made by Lewis Tewanema in the Olympic Games; letter courtesy of Mr. Wagner.

Loco, Moses, grandson of Chief Loco; letters regarding the history of his grandfather and other ancestors; also, a drawing made by him of Chief Loco.

Mehrens, Lawrence, August 24, 1968; letter concerning information obtained while working on his dissertation.

Metz, Leon; numerous letters; information as to the early history of Fort Bliss.

Morgan, Ronald Joseph, Special Consultant, American Indian Affairs; numerous letters. He wrote to Joe Samall of Western Publications for my address and has been very generous in giving both information and photographs from his collection. Mr. Morgan is working on a biography of Geronimo.

Myers, Lee, December 31, 1972; information on Fort Cummings.

Roberts, Charles D. (copy, courtesy of Ronald J. Morgan), March 12, 1960. He was present at the famous conference between Crook and Geronimo and had vivid recollections of the occasion.

Rosenthal, H. C., M.D., Jan. 29, 1966. Dr. Rosenthal had attended Ace Daklugie while he (Daklugie) was in the Veteran's Hospital in Albuquerque, and he offered some very interesting information.

Shepard, John A. (Bud) Jr., July 11, 1966; several other occasions; information on Apaches who chose to stay in Oklahoma rather than go to the Mescalero Apache Reservation.

Sonnichsen, C. L., numerous letters containing information on Apaches.

Thompson, James B., civilian stenographer at Fort Sill; January 25, 1961; March 3, 1961; September 1967; June 1968.

Thrapp, Dan L.; numerous letters. He has been very generous with his very extensive knowledge of the Apaches.

Wagner, Durrett; information obtained by him while in Washington and New York.

Whitehill, Olive, December 6, 1965; information relative to Cook's Pass and Cook's Peak.

Woody, Mrs. Clara T.; in defense of John Clum. She says "that he was basically right."

Wratten, Albert, son of George Wratten. He is working on a biography of his father and has been most generous with his information.

INDEX

V

Venego, 271
Venego, Philemon, 267–72
Victorio, xi, xx, 11, 19, 28, 34, 38–40, 47n, 52–54, 62, 70, 79, 83, 86n, 91, 103, 110, 111, 154, 181, 184, 185n, 200, 214, 250, 290, 303; at Tres Calientes, 50, 245n; death of, 83

W

Wade, James F., 112, 113
Wagner, Mrs. Pat, xx
Warm Springs Apaches. *See also* Chihenne Apaches, xi, xiv, xx, 34, 47n, 49, 50, 78, 79, 82, 84, 200, 245n, 250, 251, 290; in Florida, 127, 130, 131; at Mescalero, 184n; reservation, 291
Warrior training, 86, 87, 95–97, 103, 105
Washington, D.C., 28, 61, 112, 176, 214, 222, 225, 229, 249, 270, 283, 286–88
Welsh, Herbert, 138

White Cloud, 248, 249
White Mountain Apache Reservation, 29n
White Mountain Apaches. *See also* Coyoteros, 38
Wichitas, 267
Willcox, Orlando, 55
Witchcraft, xviii, 63, 64, 87
Wotherspoon, W. W., 155
Wovoka, 52
Wratten, George, 23, 106, 108, 110, 111, 126,131, 135, 150, 156; in Florida, 133–33; at Mount Vernon Barracks, 149, 151, 155, 158; at Fort sill, 160, 162, 163, 166, 185

Y

Yahnosha, xx, 26, 105, 110, 303

Z

Zan-a-go-li-che, 236n, 256, 261
Zele, 83